Demos Rising

the
LIFE
OF
IDEAS

SERIES EDITOR
Darrin McMahon, *Dartmouth College*

After a period of some eclipse, the study of intellectual history has enjoyed a broad resurgence in recent years. The Life of Ideas contributes to this revitalization through the study of ideas as they are produced, disseminated, received, and practiced in different historical contexts. The series aims to embed ideas—those that endured, and those once persuasive but now forgotten—in rich and readable cultural histories. Books in this series draw on the latest methods and theories of intellectual history while being written with elegance and élan for a broad audience of readers.

Demos Rising

Democracy and the Popular Construction
of Public Power in France, 1800–1850

STEPHEN W. SAWYER

The University of Chicago Press
Chicago and London

The University of Chicago Press, Chicago 60637
The University of Chicago Press, Ltd., London
© 2025 by The University of Chicago
All rights reserved. No part of this book may be used or reproduced in any manner whatsoever without written permission, except in the case of brief quotations in critical articles and reviews. For more information, contact the University of Chicago Press, 1427 E. 60th St., Chicago, IL 60637.
Published 2025

34 33 32 31 30 29 28 27 26 25   1 2 3 4 5

ISBN-13: 978-0-226-83757-4 (cloth)
ISBN-13: 978-0-226-83759-8 (paper)
ISBN-13: 978-0-226-83758-1 (e-book)
DOI: https://doi.org/10.7208/chicago/9780226837581.001.0001

Library of Congress Cataloging-in-Publication Data

Names: Sawyer, Stephen W., 1974– author.
Title: Demos rising : democracy and the popular construction of public power in France, 1800–1850 / Stephen W. Sawyer.
Other titles: Life of ideas.
Description: Chicago : The University of Chicago Press, 2025. | Series: Life of ideas | Includes bibliographical references and index.
Identifiers: LCCN 2024031915 | ISBN 9780226837574 (cloth) | ISBN 9780226837598 (paperback) | ISBN 9780226837581 (ebook)
Subjects: LCSH: Democracy—France—History—19th century. | Democratization—France—History—19th century. | Public administration—France—History—19th century. | Social structure—France—History—19th century. | Social contract—History—19th century. | State, The.
Classification: LCC JC201 .S389 2025 | DDC 321.80944/09034—dc23/eng/20240823
LC record available at https://lccn.loc.gov/2024031915

Contents

INTRODUCTION The Demos Revolution 1
1 Democratizing the Social Contract 16
2 Forest Democracy: A New Regulatory Landscape 38
3 Administrative Democracy: The Public City 71
4 Health Democracy: The Body Politic 103
5 Workplace Democracy: Equity and Popular Arbitration 130
6 Capital Democracy: A Very Social Contract 156
7 Substantive Democracy: The Nonsecular Foundations of a Democratic Social Science 184
8 Imperial Democracy: Colonial Empire and the Limits of the Demos 212
CONCLUSION The Mixed Social Constitution 238

Acknowledgments 245
Notes 249
Index 293

INTRODUCTION

The Demos Revolution

> The people, metamorphosed into monks, had taken refuge in the cloisters, and governed society through religious opinion; the people, metamorphosed into collectors and bankers, had taken refuge in finance, and governed society by money; the people, metamorphosed into magistrates, had taken refuge in the courts, and governed society by the law. This great kingdom of France, aristocratic in its parts and its provinces, became democratic as a whole.... There is an entirely new history of France to be told or rather the history of France has not yet been written.
> FRANÇOIS-RENÉ DE CHATEAUBRIAND, *Mémoires d'outre tombe*[1]

In 1822, the political philosopher and statesman Pierre-Paul Royer-Collard stood before the legislative assembly in Paris and boldly declared, "Democracy is everywhere." He then explained that one found democracy "in industry, in property, in laws, in memories, in things, in men." In short, he concluded, democracy "dominates our society."[2] Just a few years later, François-René de Chateaubriand announced in his memoirs that through religion, finance, and public law, France had become "democratic as a whole." No doubt, Alexis de Tocqueville's *Democracy in America* became the most widely read classic to employ this new understanding. Democracy, Tocqueville argued in the introduction, was best grasped as "a vast social movement." Mores, customs, practices, and attitudes, he argued, were no longer animated by a society of aristocratic privilege, but were subject to a new "equality of condition" that permeated all aspects of social life.

From where we stand today, there is certainly a strangeness to announcing the triumph of democracy in France in the 1820s and '30s. Brothers and then a cousin of Louis XVI reigned as kings; popular sovereignty was a distant thought; elections were restricted to only the wealthiest sliver of the population (fewer than two hundred fifty thousand men); and controls over the press, associations, and civil society were extreme. These constitutional monarchies of the first half of the nineteenth century remained politically rigid and conservative until their sudden demise in 1848. It is, then, precisely the oddness of the widely accepted idea in the period that France was a democracy that makes its investigation so potentially meaningful. Starting from a mystery, this book opens a new door into the history of democracy, and explores its consequences for modern governance.

Until the present, studies explicitly tracing the history of democracy have paid relatively scant attention to the first half of the nineteenth century, wedged as it was between two ostensibly far more important moments. First was the massive eruption in modern politics in the late eighteenth century that R. R. Palmer famously dubbed "the age of democratic revolution," in which the French Revolution played a starring role.[3] Histories of the Atlantic revolutions in recent decades have helped us come to terms with the centrality of slavery, empire, and commercial globalization, and have provided indispensable correctives to any straightforward assumptions about these revolutions' potential for democratic emancipation. But even as they demonstrate the tremendous imperfections and persistent modes of domination within democratic ideas and action during the period, they have also reinforced the basic fact that the late eighteenth century played an essential role, for better and for worse, in the history of something they referred to as democracy across the Atlantic world.[4] Then, leaping over the first half of the nineteenth century, our histories of democracy have focused on the gradual expansion toward universal male suffrage and the triumph of representative government in the nineteenth century. In France this period was marked by the transition from Napoleon III's Second Empire to the establishment of the first stable and durable republican regime, the Third Republic (1870–1940).[5]

Placed between these periods, the Bourbon Restoration (1814–30), the July Monarchy (1830–48) and the short-lived Second Republic (1848–52) have long been considered a time "when the old order based on authority and tradition was but a ghost, [and] the new synthesis of science and democracy was still unborn."[6] Historians have thus read the period as a struggle between the forces of antimodern reaction yearning for the old regime and a new brand of republicanism mobilized through class struggle, popular sovereignty, and revolution.[7]

Work in recent decades on the political thought and culture of the period has certainly nuanced this picture. Since the 1970s, we have become familiar with an impressive array of post-Revolutionary French liberals—including a deeply liberal reading of Tocqueville himself—that has shifted the liberal gaze from limiting old-regime despotism to preventing modern Terror.[8] In response, it has been shown, postrevolutionary liberals crafted a rich tradition of political thought that remained skeptical of a republican effacement of individualism while promoting new modes of liberty.[9] According to studies of French liberalism in this period, the most fanatical moments of the revolution were the result of unchecked democracy and its passion for equality. As a result, in this reading, democracy was to be tempered by an emphasis on individual freedom, pluralism, and social reason. We have also gained many insights into the contributions of republican theorists, activists, and workers in the first half of the nineteenth century.[10] In these accounts, the fight for expanded suffrage, women's rights, abolition of slavery, and the condition of the working class bound democracy to the achievement of the republic, and thus necessarily to the end of royalty. The idea that a Bourbon restoration or bourgeois monarchy could contribute to democracy's history as anything other than an impediment was anathema.

Grappling with these liberal and republican readings of postrevolutionary French politics was already at the core of my book *Demos Assembled*, in which I offered an alternative explanation for the consolidation of democracy in the second half of the nineteenth century. Though liberalism and republicanism played important roles in the story of democracy's establishment in France, I argued for tending to the specific problems posed by the latter. At the core of the book was the idea that democracy must be understood historically as both a mode of social organization and a political regime. The concept of political liberty elaborated in the middle decades of the nineteenth century, I argued, was grounded in a specific conception of the relationship between society and the individual in which a society of equals was guaranteed through self-governance. Postrevolutionary liberal fears of the state were democratized, providing a new impetus for modern government and administration to preserve the general welfare by means of provision, utility, antipauperism, and public regulation. Specifically, the democratic state "came to stand for a transformation in the relationship between the sources of power, modes of participation, and the institutions best able to channel them. It therefore marked the emergence of a social and political condition rooted in the self-government of an autonomous society."[11] Instead of problems of regime or constitution, I argued that the establishment of the French Third Republic was best understood within the larger democratization of liberalism and the impact of this process for the construction of a modern state.

Demos Rising, as its title and periodization suggest, offers a prequel to that story. It explores how democracy developed into a mode of social organization that required popular governance and administration in the first half of the nineteenth century. Beyond postrevolutionary liberal critiques of Jacobin statism and anti-individualism or debates on the birth, ambitions, and contradictions of republican universalism, this history of democracy shows the impact of a broader democratic transformation in Europe, the Americas, and the Mediterranean.[12] While *Demos Assembled* highlighted the international context within which this transformation of the democratic state took place by focusing on a dialogue principally between France and the United States and Britain, this book focuses on the French dialogue with German thought on cameralism, regulatory police, and administration, in particular with Hegel and the young left Hegelians who came to Paris in the 1830s and 1840s.

Democracy as Social Organization and Government

One reason historians of democracy have paid scant attention to the first half of the nineteenth century is the surprising ways democratic life was understood in contrast to our contemporary definitions. Since democracy has come to be overwhelmingly associated with popular sovereignty expressed in regular elections, the precise meaning of the word *démocratie* in the eighteenth and early nineteenth centuries has remained somewhat baggy. Even as he championed its importance, Robert Palmer suggested that any well-defined sense of the term in the eighteenth century was almost impossible to discern, settling on the old notion that "at the most, democracy was a principle, or element, which might profitably enter into a 'mixed constitution.'"[13] This idea remained little changed some sixty years later in the introduction to a volume on a conceptual history of democracy: "In the classical tradition of political thought, 'democracy' was evaluated positively as a useful element only in a mixed constitution."[14] Pierre Rosanvallon's genealogy of the term insisted on its "semantic variety," arguing that the word was used in the eighteenth century "only to designate an obsolete type of political system."[15] Other accomplished specialists of the history of democracy have similarly confirmed that prior to 1789, it "became common to characterize it [democracy] as a primitive form."[16] A more recent history of democracy has used the term's supposed imprecision as the basis of its analysis, arguing that "no unequivocal definition is possible,"[17] while one of the most ambitious histories of democracy has concisely stated: "Disagreements about democracy constitute its history."[18] What follows takes a different approach, targeting a more precise, positive, and widespread understanding of democracy.

As I have demonstrated elsewhere, there was, at least in France, a relatively clear definition of the term leading into and during the French Revolution.[19] One finds a consistent employment of the term *démocratie* in the old regime as one of the three traditional forms of government established in the Aristotelian tradition: monarchy, aristocracy, and democracy. As Richard Tuck has convincingly argued, in France, Bodin set the stage for this usage when he claimed that Aristotle had glossed over an essential distinction across this tripartite division between sovereignty and government.[20] In fact, Bodin argued, the division between monarchical, aristocratic, and popular or democratic power had to be applied to both sovereignty and government, such that it was possible to imagine, for example, a monarchical sovereign with a democratic government, the combination which he considered ideal.

By mid-eighteenth-century France, the word *démocratie* came most commonly to refer to the government or administration side of this division, as attested by the works of Marquis d'Argenson and Rousseau. D'Argenson argued, like Bodin, for a monarchical sovereign and a democratic government or administration. Rousseau, on the other hand, understood popular sovereignty to be a cornerstone of a republic, and reserved the term "democracy" for a government in which a majority of citizens could be magistrates.[21] This definition built on the Bodinian amendment to Aristotle by designating a state with popular sovereignty as a "republic" and reserving the term "democracy" specifically for popular government.

While "democracy" continued to refer to popular government well into the nineteenth century, during the Bourbon Restoration and the July Monarchy, democracy underwent a new revision of Bodinian proportion, this time with a division within the notion of *démocratie* itself. "Democracy" not only came to mean a type of government but took on a capacious second definition as a mode of social organization, grounded in a rejection of aristocracy and natural social hierarchy across all forms of social life. As Pellegrino Rossi argued in his *Cours d'économie politique* of 1836–37: "We form a democratic society; what is more, we live in an epoch of democracy. Whether we fear or celebrate it matters little. What is essential is to understand the time in which we live and not to misunderstand the society of which we are a part."[22] By the 1840s, this idea had also spread to German thinkers, as Friedrich Steger noted that democracy was "a form of society, frequently held as a model, [that] has suddenly become a truth among us. Theoretical discussions are faced today with a being in flesh and blood. Democracy has shifted from a bookish existence to real life."[23] Democracy thus not only came to refer to a form of popular government, as it had since Bodin, but took on a new sociological character as a mode of social organization specific to the modern age. As the above quotations by Chateaubriand, Royer Collard, Rossi, Steger, and Tocqueville suggest, this conception of democracy was so wide that it gripped thinkers of all persuasions, becoming the term through which the massive changes of postrevolutionary society were being apprehended.

The first and especially the second volume of Tocqueville's *Democracy in America* (published in 1835 and 1840) sat at the heart of this "democratic" moment, providing a particularly sophisticated account of the processes and consequences of the democratization of society. François Guizot had already placed democracy at the core of his historical arguments, which contained thinly veiled critiques of the restored Bourbon monarchy in the late 1810s and 1820s: "On the Continent the advance of civilization has been far less complex and more complete. The diverse elements of society, religious order, civil order, monarchy, aristocracy, and then democracy have developed not simultaneously but successively. Each principle, each system has developed in turn. To each century belongs a system, if not exclusively, predominantly."[24] By the Second Republic, Guizot recognized that "such is the dominion of the word democracy that no government and no party dare live or aspire to power without inscribing the word on its flag,"[25] while at the same time he remained convinced that in spite of its inevitable rise, "today's chaos is hidden behind one word: Democracy."[26] In contrast, while the term was less prevalent in the 1820s and in the 1830 revolution on the left, by the late 1830s and especially the 1840s the term was ubiquitous among such thinkers as Louis Blanc, Alexandre Ledru-Rollin, Eugénie Niboyet, Jeanne Deroin, and Désirée Gay.[27] "Ten years ago, the school of democracy was barely formed," Blanc stated in his best-selling *Organisation du travail* in 1839, pointing out that then, "it was only applicable to the liberal school, which is today in power and ... still lives on its old errors."[28] On the far left, Étienne Cabet echoed these ideas when he wrote: "The doctrine of equality and fraternity or of democracy is today the intellectual conquest of Humanity; the realization of this doctrine is the goal of all efforts, all struggles, and all combats on earth."[29] Their ambition, alongside a wide range of thinkers of the period, was to unite France behind an understanding of the consequences of a democratic society.

Recovering the postrevolutionary conception of democracy allows us to restore a world of meaning through which actors of the period understood the great social transformation that was taking place around them, as well as its consequences for collective self-government. Through this broadly accepted understanding, we see that figures as varied as Royer-Collard, Guizot, Adolphe Thiers, Tocqueville, Barrot, Hortense Allart, and Honoré de Balzac on the one side, and Blanc, George Sand, Cabet, Deroin, Ledru-Rollin, and François-Vincent Raspail on the other, all concurred that the ineluctable consequence of the French Revolution was a democratization of society.

To understand where they disagreed and what animated the debates treated in the chapters of this book, it is necessary to grasp how the broadly shared idea of democratic society intersected with the previous definition of democracy as popular government. The broad agreement that France was experiencing an inexorable democratization of social relations displaced, but did not settle, the age-old Aristotelian question of the best form of government. Rather, the emergence of a democratic society both revived and reinvented the long-standing question in very different terms. The dominant question became: Was a democratic society best served by a democratic government or by some other form of institutional organization? In other words, it was argued on different political sides that a democratic society could choose to govern itself democratically or not. Debates over the type of government that should serve a democratic society formed the backdrop for the vast reflection on governmental and administrative power during the first half of the nineteenth century.

As Tocqueville revealed, the stakes of democratic government were especially high under these new conditions. First, a democratic society that did not self-govern was open to an unprecedented and even more brutal form of tyranny than old regime absolutism, because isolated "equal" individuals lacked the social resources necessary to ward off a new more pernicious kind of despotism. As a result, the question of how to govern a democratic society generated some of the most original political philosophy and history of the period. Hortense Allart offered one of the clearest definitions of the problem in *La femme et la démocratie de nos temps* in 1836, tracing how France offered a new model for polities in the modern age through its daring democratization of society. As profound and important as this new movement was, the danger, she argued, was in how to govern the new democratic society. Unlike in Britain, which maintained a hereditary aristocratic society, it was necessary to govern France, a democratic society, with a new meritocratic aristocracy of talent. She therefore offered the solution of aligning "two principles, born of nature and strengthened one through the other, aristocracy and democracy."[30] For Allart, "while the great majority stagnates, an aristocracy is forming: such is the democracy of our time."[31] Women, she argued, were to play an essential role in cultivating the new aristocratic values required to govern a democratic society. "Hence, within this new cultural age, women will lead this society of justice and equality to great lengths."[32] Allart's ostensibly contradictory assessment that "the society of equality is the true aristocracy"[33] is only comprehensible from within a widely shared perspective on democracy that dominated the first half of the nineteenth century: the profound democratization of the social left entirely open to the question of the best form of government.[34] It was from a similar perspective that Guizot redefined how to govern a democratic society by arguing for the representation of public reason instead of individual will,[35] and Thiers mobilized a radically new pragmatic approach to politics always in the making.[36]

On the other side of the political spectrum, Flora Tristan insisted that it was one of the essential characteristics of her movement "not only to surveille the Government, but to govern itself; not only to control power, but to exercise it."[37] The journal *Voice of Women*, launched in March of 1848, presented the case of women in the new republic as a denial of the aristocratic government in democracy that only male suffrage implied: "We cannot accept the idea of privilege and democracy at the same time, and yet while the least intelligent male citizen is able to vote, the most intelligent female citizen is denied suffrage."[38] Blanc similarly argued for the democratization of administration in a republic as well as the distribution of decision-making into associations of workers within the workplace. Likewise, Raspail sought to democratize health services and prisons, and still others, as we shall see, sought the democratization of all modes of administrative decision-making from religion to capitalist enterprise and municipal administration.

While the terrain upon which the question of whether or not—and if so, how—a democratic society could self-govern will primarily be studied in France, its intellectual origins were not hermetically sealed within the nation's boundaries. Innovations in government drew on German administrative and political thought of the early nineteenth century, most clearly manifest in G. W. F. Hegel's *Philosophy of Right*, and especially his treatment of the police and corporations of the ethical life that constitute the transition from civil society to the state as an immanently historical process. Hegel's critique, however, remained steeped in the language of civil society and avoided democracy per se as an ideal. It was in the same years in France that the radical social and political changes diagnosed by Hegel were interpreted in specifically "democratic" terms. These two currents—Hegel's radical immanentization of social regulation on the one hand, and the sociological-historical reinvention of democracy as a mode of social organization on the other—came together in a transformative movement in the 1820s, 1830s, and 1840s. Geographically, this potent mixture was elaborated in Paris; intellectually, the synthesis was formulated among young left Hegelians who fled Germany for the French capital, such as the very young Karl Marx and Lorenz von Stein as well as French démoc-socs like Alexandre Ledru Rollin, Louis Blanc, and Raspail. Their pragmatic program in turn contributed to social and political movements across Europe and, in some cases, the world.

It was through these social movements, this book argues, that a new relationship between the democratization of society and democratic government took lasting shape. Though the popular movements of 1830 and 1848 were the most visible and emblematic in the period under study here, uprisings and new modes of public engagement erupted on a monthly and sometimes weekly basis for decades in Paris, in provincial cities, across the countryside, and in the deep forests of France and Europe. "Crowds gathered so often that the newspapers didn't even speak of them anymore," Flaubert recounted of the period in *L'Éducation sentimentale*.[39] No doubt these social and political movements crystallized in particular sites and toward specific reforms and reactions, but the enduring consequences of public action extended far beyond the ephemeral utopianism and white heat of popular outrage. They participated in what is better understood to be a prolonged, three-decade *revolutionary moment*, which only came to a close with the military reaction of Napoleon III. These social and political movements contributed to a transformation in governance that became constitutive of a new definition of state/society relations, provoking "frequent and dense encounters between the state's administrative institutions and the population."[40] What follows argues that the legacy of this dilated revolutionary experience is best understood as the historical fashioning of a wholly modern political subject: the creation of a self-governing democratic society, a demos.

From Civil Society to Demos

Critical and liberal theorists of the late and post–Cold War era adopted civil society as the indispensable social form required for the birth and sustainability of modern democracy. By the turn of the third millennium, civil society acquired its contemporary definition as a site of critique and social practice located between the family and the state, necessary for the historical construction of a liberal democratic modernity. We learned that "the concept of civil society indicates a terrain in the West that is endangered by the logic of administrative and economic mechanisms but is also the primary locus for the potential expansion of democracy under 'really existing' liberal-democratic regimes."[41] Developed outside the arms of the state, protected from arbitrary administrative intervention by law and constitution, civil society has provided a foundation for understanding the origins of modern liberty and ensuring the practice of associative collaboration necessary for public critique and private flourishing. Bolstered by historical, critical, and theoretical conceptualizations, various accounts of the civil society thesis have continued to play a central role in our understanding of the rise and consolidation of democracy. In the specific field of nineteenth-century French history, civil society has been studied as the realm where "battles for autonomy are won," when "the state is driven out of a reawakening civil society, a new sphere of activity, a public sphere begins to form."[42]

And yet, as normatively important as the turn to civil society has been, historians of modern France have continued to debate exactly how useful such a notion was for the actual development of French politics.[43] Though the term *société civile* certainly existed historically in France,[44] it was still obscure enough that the national newspaper *Libération* could headline its front page on July 20, 1988, with the question: "Tell me? What is Civil Society?"[45] The question of whether or not, or which sort of, civil society actually existed in France in the postrevolutionary age has been an important historiographical question since the 2000s.[46] Claude Lefort had already noted the impossibility of asserting any clear distinction between civil society and the state in the emergence of the modern political in the wake of the French Revolution when he wrote: "Civil society (if we are to retain the term) is itself inscribed within a political constitution, and it is bound up with the system of democratic power."[47] Instead of positing a nautral separation between civil society and the state, Lefort presented the democratic political as a historical condition in which it was possible to make such distinctions. Pierre Rosanvallon built on this approach in his ambitious history of civil society in modern France when he traced the discourses grounded in the Jacobin "myth" or "imaginary"—what he preferred to call a "culture of generality"—that erupted in 1789 and which solidified into a dominant story the French have told themselves since. Marked by unshakable Jacobin rejection of liberal civil society within political discourse, however, associative modes of organization nonetheless emerged unwittingly, informally, and out of pragmatic necessity in the French political model.[48]

Rosanvallon himself recognized an essential challenge in using the civil society paradigm to structure an investigation of modern French democracy when he openly admitted that the term "civil society" was "equivocal [*équivoque*],"[49] since it had been so attractive in the last decades of the twentieth century precisely because it appealed both to those on the left who were searching for a democratic renewal by turning away from a state-centered society, and to those on the right with an openly conservative critique of the state. In 2004 he could still optimistically suggest that such "equivocation" was "positive" since it had seemingly—if inadvertently—brought lasting positive change to modern democratic regimes during the antitotalitarian moment of the last decades of the Cold War and its immediate aftermath.

But the times have certainly changed, and changed quickly. One is struck by how far and how fast the political and analytical potential of the civil society paradigm has been shaken, finding itself victim of the claim, perhaps best articulated by David Harvey, that it was complicit with a pervasive depoliticization and a new dominance of private over public interest, "giving rise to the illusion that . . . some separate entity called 'civil society' is the powerhouse of oppositional politics."[50] The result has been that while the term "civil society" continues to be used in everyday language, it has slowly become less convincing as the sole explanation for the social origins of robust modern democracy. Despite the undeniable normative potential of civil society, its rapid success in the latter part of the twentieth century should therefore not blind us to the fact that it may not have been the central—nor even the most common—mode of social organization to be historically associated with the birth and success of modern democracy. One may therefore ask the question: Did French democracy (and perhaps other democracies around the world) not develop through a different set of social practices, which were in fact quite distinct from the civil society model?

This study—and the larger project of which it is a part—responds to this question by recovering the terms that actors of the period used to understand the social transformation they witnessed following the French Revolution. They argued that they were living in a new age, which was defined by the emergence of a vexingly capacious notion of "democratic society." They further argued that the new mode of social organization had been rooted historically in the egalitarian thrust of the Reformation, consolidated by the absolutist monarchy's war on the aristocracy, and imposed by the French Revolution's inauguration of a new civil equality. In their view, and in terms very different from arguments that eighteenth-century commercial society had produced the possibility of a new realm of civil equality, it was administrative centralization and the process of leveling by social and political institutions that was responsible. Moreover, while social leveling had played a central role in the slow dismantling of the feudal aristocratic order, the positive construction of a democratic society in all realms of social organization was understood to be culminating before their eyes. A democratic social life was being built on the foundation of the radical politics of the revolution and the modern administrative state that had so deeply transformed French society. In Richard Rorty's terms, democratic society was becoming a social condition to be made rather than found.

In the nineteenth century, Tocqueville and many of his contemporaries of the Restoration and the July Monarchy referred to this "democratic society" or "democratic social state" as being grounded in an "equality of condition" in contrast to "aristocratic society." This equality of condition was neither economic nor political, to the extent that a democratic society was not necessarily defined by an equal distribution of goods or by universal suffrage, or even, for example, by a republican form of state. This equality was instead understood to be a general sociohistorical situation, or what Tocqueville famously referred to as a "primary fact," which shaped "the march of society; gives a certain direction to the public mind, a certain turn to the laws; to those governing, new maxims, and particular habits to the governed."[51]

Throughout this period in France, the term "democratic society" was used far more prevalently and with much greater precision than "civil society." One of Tocqueville's essential ambitions in his *Democracy in America* and his *Old Regime and the French Revolution* was to determine which institutions and processes had made modern society democratic, how that society might in turn govern itself democratically, and the dangerous consequences of its not doing so.[52] While Tocqueville's intervention remains one of the most well-known, formulating the possibilities and challenges of democratically governing a democratic society was common throughout the period discussed in this book. Hortense Allart interpreted this democratic ideal in a new direction, toward the equality of women, in *La femme et la démocratie de nos temps*. She argued for two definitions of the people: "The word *people* has been understood in two distinct ways: some have understood by the term people the fecund source of so many talents, where the mass of men, are rich with their own future and emotions," while others, she argued, "understand by people those who will forever remain a sort of limited, vulgar group." The name she gave to this second notion of the people was "the crowd [*la foule*]," and what defined the "crowd" in democracy was their "inability to create anything other than to sing the praises of their chiefs."[53] The social ambition of the new, modern democracy, she insisted, had to be the accession of women to the first group through education. Only then, by including women and men "of talent," would the new democracy find the necessary resources for government in all of society.

In his masterful rendering of the first half of the nineteenth century, *Les Misérables*, Victor Hugo explicitly referred to a self-governing democratic society as a "demos." During the book's extraordinary climax on the Parisian barricades, Hugo offers a historical and conceptual treatment of the worker's revolt against the Second Republic in June 1848. Posing an enduring question in the history of nineteenth-century French politics, Hugo asked: How does one explain that a portion of the people revolted against a republican regime based on universal suffrage? He responded by arguing that two social forces potentially animated democracy. On the one hand, he argued, there were the "downtrodden," the "scoundrels," "the crowd," the "populace," and the "ochlocracy." Theirs was a misery not to be disdained. Their desolation had a noble past: "Athens was an ochlocracy," "scoundrels made Holland," and "the populace saved Rome," Hugo insisted. But despite these past achievements, "their violence contradicts the very principles through which they are nourished," he argued, concluding that "the path they choose contradicts right." Hugo therefore characterized June 1848 as "the ochlocracy insurgent against the demos." The "demos," he argued, was synonymous with "common right," and, most of all, with "the government of all by all."[54] In other words, the demos, argued Hugo, was the legitimate subject of a constituted self-governing order.

But it was no doubt Marx who provided the most sophisticated characterization of the central subject of modern democracy in his *Critique of Hegel's "Philosophy of Right"* in 1843, when he wrote: "In democracy none of the moments obtains a significance other than what befits it. Each is really only a moment of the whole Demos."[55] In this passage, Marx introduced the "demos" as a form of social organization that was fully immanent to itself—that is, grounded in modern democratic society's ability to shape itself toward its own ends. For Marx, the modern demos had little to do with suffrage, and even less to do with parliamentary representation. He presented the "demos" as "a constitution of the people," which was opposed to a "form of the state," in which "political man has his particular and separate existence beside the unpolitical, private man." It was in this context that he imagined an ideal where "society regulates the general production and thus makes it possible for me to do one thing today and another tomorrow."[56] To be sure, Marx's ideal was never realized in precisely the terms in which he imagined it. Nonetheless, he did give voice to a widespread concern of his day that made public regulation essential for shaping modern society, and the term he used to describe this ideal was "demos."

What follows pursues a history of the "demos" not only for the term's rhetorical authority and legacy, but also because these historically specific characterizations by Victor Hugo and Karl Marx of a modern "demos" explicitly refer to a process in which the central subject of a modern democracy is not a people in revolt, nor a distended constituent moment, nor an assemblage of private persons who occasionally voice their opinion through suffrage. Instead, the demos signifies a politically constituted self-governing society of equals. Historically, this political subject rose primarily in the context of two constitutional monarchies that drastically limited suffrage and became increasingly conservative in their apprehension and treatment of social and political problems. Hence, in this critical period for the ascendancy of a modern demos, the vote remained more aspirational than a practical force. The legacy of the demos revolution was therefore not only the expansion of suffrage—though in 1848 it did achieve that as well—but also the push to promote a society of equals through self-government across the full range of social activity. *The modern demos was grounded in its own historical development and practice as a collective self-governing body.*

A Pragmatic History of the Political

The structure of this book illustrates an approach to the history of democracy as both a set of practices and a world of ideas. The methodology, which draws from intellectual history and the history of political action and governance, may best be described as a *pragmatic history of the political*.[57] Chapter 1 therefore outlines the historical conceptualization of modern democracy that animated social and political thought in the period. By recovering this interpretive framework, I explore the intellectual history of democracy and seek to contribute to contemporary democratic theory by offering a world of meaning that has become hidden to us, but which framed practices of democracy and public power during this formative period for political modernity. I have chosen to characterize the conceptual backdrop as the process of democratizing the social contract.

Recovering this hermeneutical frame is essential to explaining how and why democracy took the particular historical form it did in nineteenth-century France. Thus the stage is set for the concrete history of specific democratic experiences in the first half of the nineteenth century, explored in the subsequent chapters. By extension, it is a basic claim of this pragmatic history of the political that a critical conception of democracy must be grounded in historical experience, including past theories of democracy and actions that were understood as democratic even if they would no longer be considered as such today. The remainder of the book therefore explores how specific practices of administration and regulation in the realms of the environment, municipal governance, public health, the workplace, large capitalist enterprise, religion, and empire were transformed against the backdrop of the democratized social contract. To be clear, the solutions provided were imperfect at best, and in many cases remained profoundly unjust and unacceptable by any contemporary measure of democratic equality. This does not change the fact—indeed it makes it even more imperative to understand—that these practices formed a crucial moment in democracy's past. To borrow the words of Chateaubriand: "The practice of democracy may be observed even as we mock the laws that same democracy passed as theory."[58]

In tracing one targeted, if singularly significant, set of processes on the European continent in the first half of the nineteenth century to illustrate the ascension of a modern demos, this book is not intended to tell the history of democracy as prescriptively synonymous with the past precincts of one nation, or to afford the French case a degree of universality that would be as historically inaccurate as it would be normatively problematic. This account is committed to pursuing a critical history of democracy.[59] Nonetheless, France did explicitly invest the terrain of the "democratic" and "democracy" with particular precocity and intensity. And following the Enlightenment and the French Revolution of 1789, political actors, social and political theorists, and writers of all sorts from around the world did consider France to have a peculiarly strong relationship to this mode of social organization and government. As a result, the fortunate confluence of a particularly rich democratic experience, a deep commitment to reflecting on its consequences, and the tremendous historiographical production on France over time and across continents provides a robust legacy for a novel theorization of democracy drawn from empirical study. It goes without saying that similar studies in other times and places will be required to explore how influential the French experience may have been, as well as the temporal and normative multiplicities of the political constitution of the social in the modern age.

1

Democratizing the Social Contract

> The problem of democracy was seen to be not solved, hardly more than externally touched, by the establishment of universal suffrage and representative government.... The problem of democracy was the problem of that form of social organization, extending to all areas and ways of living in which the powers of individuals shall not be merely released from mechanical external constraint but shall be fed, sustained and directed.
>
> JOHN DEWEY, *Liberalism and Social Action*[1]

To follow the construction of a modern administration in the first half of the nineteenth century, it is necessary to reconstitute a set of ideas and debates that treated regulatory power as a democratic problem. Such contextualization requires an examination of some of the most influential and lesser-known texts of the postrevolutionary period. Only by placing their ascendancy and varied reception alongside the rapidly shifting meanings of the idea and practice of democracy, may the origins of a rich and largely forgotten tradition of social self-government be uncovered.

In the opening pages of his *Nouveaux principes d'économie politique*, published in 1819, J.-C.-L. Simonde de Sismondi recast a fundamental distinction of modern politics when he argued that "the science of government" must "be divided into two major branches." On the one hand, there were "high politics" that "gave nations a constitution" and guaranteed "liberty," and according to which "all men were subject to its laws." This essential aspect of political life had been the privileged focus of eighteenth-century political thought, he argued. However, according to Sismondi, the fundamental realm of constitutionalism could only be properly grasped in conjunction with a second mode of government: the management of social life focused on "the physical well-being of man," ensured by a "true system of administration." Administration "offered work, the purchasing of care and procurement," and "preserved health, maintained life, ensured necessities for children and the elderly, [and] provided food, clothing and lodging for every man."[2] In sum, Sismondi argued, "through high politics, government must ensure the advantages of liberty for all citizens." But it must also "care for all," he insisted.[3] By asserting the dual—constitutional and administrative—ambition within his new principles of political economy, Sismondi seized on the two sides of a new contract underpinning the transformation of public power.

By the 1840s, the distinction formed the cornerstone of histories and theories of public law. In 1843, Émile-Victor Foucart, dean of the University of Poitiers Faculty of Law, organized his foundational encyclopedic project on public law around this distinction.[4] The first volume, he explained, focused on political right and questions of "constitution," and "the natural and political rights to be enjoyed by citizens." The second volume concentrated on "that part of public law that is principally concerned with the management of collective interests toward social welfare."[5] The *Dictionary of Political Economy* (1854) placed this new equilibrium at the core of its article on "police": Responsibilities of police included "the care necessary for providing citizens with certain advantages that facilitate their relations, contributions to the enjoyment of life and prevention of the obstacles that impede well-being," at the same time that such expansive powers were to be constantly checked by "the sole true principle of human society, liberty." "It is to ensure the triumph of liberty and not to destroy it that governments are instituted," the entry concluded.[6] Ensuring liberty by increasing social obligation—or by what the Second Empire jurist M. F. Boeuf referred to as preserving individual "rights" *from* and "obligations" *to* the collective good,[7]—formed the foundation of a new contract between public agents and the public.

This new social bond developed through a redefinition of the relationship between political right and administrative action. These bookends of public law had already enjoyed a long history by the nineteenth century, captured in the foundational distinction in European public law between *potestas* (political right) and *potentia* (capacity to rule).[8] Guizot explicitly highlighted this dual capacity of modern governance when he explained the difference between "*puissance, potentia* in Latin" and "*pouvoir* . . . which correspondes to the Latin *potestas*." He furthered his demonstration arguing that "with authority and the appropriate title, you have a just and legitimate power [*pouvoir*], the path of right; with *puissance*, or force, you have the physical or executive power, the path of doing." He then concluded: "A power [*potestas*] orders by virtue of authority, and executes by virtue of its *puissance* [*potentia*]."[9] Thus, what captivated the imagination of jurists and political theorists in that period was certainly not the novelty of *potentia*, that is, the ability to execute or administer toward social welfare per se. Rather, what Sismondi and his colleagues sought to justify was its vastly increased scale and the range of public responsibilities that would be required to ensure individual liberty in this new age of social obligation.

And yet, building the modern administrative state necessary for a new social contract confronted real difficulties. Most importantly, increasingly vast demands on government ran headlong into the suspicions of underlying tyranny that had fanned the flames of eighteenth-century liberalism. Persistent fears of absolutist abuses of ministerial power, the legacy of the Terror, and Napoleonic despotism remained forceful in the aftermath of Waterloo.[10] As a result, the question of how to oversee and hold administrative institutions accountable took on new importance, with a relevance that has continued to this day.[11] In response, the period under study witnessed two checks against the supposed dangers of administrative tyranny: what the legal historian Martin Loughlin has referred to as "the competing claims of *Rechstaat* and *Polizeistaat*"[12]—that is, the control of administrative power through judicial and legislative oversight on the one hand, and bureaucratic expertise on the other.

As important as these approaches were and remain, a third, democratic approach existed which, though it has since been forgotten, was central to the construction of a modern administrative state. To understand such an approach, it is necessary to return to the idea of democracy presented in the introduction to this book as a mode of social organization. Public actors, theorists, and activists in France understood administration to be tightly bound to the construction and maintenance of a "democratic society." Indeed, as Tocqueville argued in his *Old Regime and the French Revolution*, democratic society had been primarily achieved through the absolutist administration's war on the nobility, and was consolidated by the Revolution. But if democratic society had been crafted, it also had to be preserved. And as history had revealed, this could only be achieved through constant public intervention. The problem then, as Tocqueville and his contemporaries described it, was not administrative power per se, nor its achievements, but the way in which it had achieved its ends. In short, the means through which social leveling was achieved under absolutism and the revolution were condemned, not its outcome. Upholding a democratic society therefore required tackling administrative tyranny first. And this, they argued, was to be achieved by at once expanding administrative power to ensure a society of equals, and making it more porous to the people to prevent any arbitrary means of doing so.[13] Democracy became the cornerstone of the new social contract in which the powers of public administration could legitimately expand to ensure liberty and social equality.[14]

This chapter traces the intellectual lineaments of a democratic administration in France in the first half of the nineteenth century. It is structured around the dual revision of two major figures in France, Hegel and Rousseau. For the first, historians of political thought have noted the tremendous influence of Hegelian thought on radical democratic politics in the period,[15] just as legal historians have highlighted its importance for the democratization of administration in the late nineteenth and early twentieth centuries.[16] This chapter shows Hegel's precocious influence on public law in France, where his ideas percolated through the dense reflection on democratic society and government. An account of how Hegel's ideas on the regulatory state were democratized provides only half the story, however. Also necessary was a revision of one of the towering monuments of early modern political thought: Rousseau's social contract, in specifically historical and sociological terms. This dual revision placed history, the social individual, and a reflexive approach to governance at the heart of the modern administrative state. Using the language of the nineteenth century, I refer to this dual revision as a process of democratizing the social contract.

Reinventing Regulatory Police

Sismondi's "new" political economy claimed to be taking direct aim at the school of Adam Smith. Indeed, for Sismondi, increasing the wealth of nations through the "abstract" notion of laissez-faire was not only foolish but dangerous. Necessary instead, he argued in the opening lines of his *New Principles of Political Economy*, was attention to the well-being of individuals in society, which could only be achieved through a reconceptualization of regulatory powers.[17] Historians have noted Sismondi's influence on Hegel's thoughts on regulation. As Gareth Stedman Jones notes in his analysis of Hegel: "What appears to have impressed Hegel most powerfully were Sismondi's strictures against laissez-faire, and his emphasis upon the need for some form of protective and corporate framework to replace feudal protections in the countryside and guild regulations in the towns."[18]

Important traces of Sismondi's influence can be found throughout Hegel's work, but in particular in his chapter "Police and Corporations" in the *Philosophy of Right*. Here, Hegel proposed that rather than serving as a solution to limited resources, distribution, and production, market relations within civil society also generated negative side effects which required a renewed attention to regulation. Only by introducing new governmental powers to direct the market could civil society ensure the essential contribution of private individuals to the modern state by reducing the deleterious effects of industrialization, and in particular the development of massive inequalities and impoverished masses.[19]

Hegel's chapter has already been highlighted by social theorists and historians for two reasons. First, it is where he introduces the theme of how the antinomies of capital produce a "rabble," which would contribute to Marx's theory of the proletariat.[20] Second, it is in this short chapter that Hegel sketches a theory of how capitalism contributes to overseas imperial expansion, which would prove so important for future Marxist theories of imperialism.[21] Alongside these foundational arguments, there is another equally important theme running through this chapter of the *Philosophy of Right*, but which has been the object of less attention:[22] Hegel's novel weaving together of individual liberty and regulatory police as essential to the transition from two major sections of his "ethical life"—that is from the section of "civil society" to that of the "state." Building on his reading of Sismondi and his critique of Adam Smith, Hegel fully endorsed the ideal of private freedom in civil society for the pursuit of individual satisfactions.[23] But even as it facilitated personal fulfillment, he argued, private interest could not exist primarily outside the arms of an administrative state, as Smith had suggested. "Because [Hegel] refuses to consider civil society an independent world," Jean-François Kervegan argues on Hegel's notion of police, "administrative authorities must actively intervene in civil society to prevent dangerous consequences both for individuals and for society itself that arise from market production."[24] As a result, the satisfaction of private needs and desires required the collective development of a public authority. In Hegel's account, ensuring a productive relationship between the realization of an individual's particular talents and ambitions in civil society and the collective obligations of the state depended upon a reinvention of the role of police—that is, the domain of administration that cultivated the technologies and mechanisms necessary for civil society to remain a sphere of liberty where individuals could shape social relations and contribute to the public good.[25]

The influence of France hangs over Hegel's treatment of the police.[26] Hegel understands the question of police and corporations to have been radically transformed by the world inaugurated in 1789.[27] In the section on the police, for example, when discussing "Society's right . . . over the arbitrary and contingent preferences of parents, particularly in cases where education is to be completed not by the parents but by others," Hegel suggests that this question rose to greatest prominence in France. That country had gone furthest in highlighting the role that society, as opposed to the family, must play in a child's education. He similarly draws on the Revolution in his discussion of corporations when he argues: "The consideration behind the abolition of Corporations in recent times is that the individual should fend for himself. But we may grant this and still hold that corporation membership does not alter a man's obligation to earn his living. Under modern political conditions, the citizens have only a restricted share in the public business of the state, yet it is essential to provide men—ethical entities—with work of a public character over and above their private business."²⁸ Central to Hegel's problematic is how police powers and regulatory bodies calibrate the relationship between the sphere of individual liberty and collective organization.²⁹

Hegel's account provides an important perspective on the radical transformation of regulatory and administrative power in the first half of the nineteenth century.³⁰ As Hegel understood it, the collapse of old-regime corporate structures opened new opportunities for the pursuit of individual and private interest. And yet it was the very expansion of this realm of personal liberty that contributed to the ravages brought on by industrialization, massive urbanization, epidemics, and deforestation. For Hegel, the response could be found in a reinvention of regulatory power that was hardly limited to censorship, repression of popular movements, and discipline. To be sure, the police emerged as a fierce and sometimes even deadly means for maintaining order in modern society. But, as Hegel observed, regulatory police also became a necessary force for reconceiving and ensuring the very idea of how individuals could contribute to a "good society," how it should be organized, what individuals and groups could expect from government, and how that relationship was to be negotiated and maintained. This tension between arbitrary and regulatory police shaped the birth of a modern democratic administration, and modern democracy itself.

Democracy and Administrative Regulation

For all Hegel's importance in describing the new ideals of modern regulatory practice in the construction of a modern state, the process of its realization did not precisely follow a Hegelian script in France. Hegel had rethought how the regulatory theories of *polizei* inherited from eighteenth-century cameralism were central to the state-building project. And he had done so by building partially on Sismondi's critique of laissez-faire economic policy, establishing the groundwork for an immanent conception of regulatory power; society acted upon itself to police the particular and contingent situations of individuals with undefined powers in order to ensure their liberty. Hegel nonetheless employed a revised language of liberalism through the term "civil society"³¹ alongside some republican idioms,³² and he avoided the language of democracy:³³ "The democratic principle was not a constitutive element in Hegel's theory of the state in 1820." Indeed, his *Philosophy of Right* marked a "historical-philosophical devaluation of democracy."³⁴ While the ambitions were shared, a different discourse and set of practices emerged around similar questions in France, framed in specifically democratic terms.³⁵ The focus on democracy emerged out of the new ideas on "democratic society." The maintenance of this new mode of social organization required a redefined regulatory power, administration, and government. Following the Revolution of 1830, Paris, "the spiritual home of all European progressives,"[36] beacon of democratic thought, and foyer of revolution, witnessed an elaboration of Hegelian thought toward a democratization of regulatory power.[37]

The first Hegelian moment in France was particularly precocious.[38] Starting as early as the 1820s and continuing steadily into the early 1850s, Hegel's work enjoyed a wide reception in France.[39] This first "Hegelian moment" was manifest across literature as well as in the political and legal thought of the period. In 1833, the *Revue de Paris* highlighted his influence on the philosophy of Cousin as well as on that of Lerminier.[40] But Hegel's reception spread far beyond the influence on Cousin. The opening volume of the *Revue du progrès social* spoke unflinchingly in 1834 of the "grandeur of his doctrine," that would "mark a new era in the history of philosophy."[41] Balzac dedicated the 1840 edition of his novel *Gobseck* to his friend Barchou de Penhoën and his "beautiful work on German philosophy" titled *Histoire de la philosophie allemande depuis Leibnitz jusqu'à Hegel*.[42] In 1843, *La revue des deux mondes* published an article titled "The Contemporary Crisis of German Philosophy," opening with the "Hegelian School."[43] "Hegel has his place," the article stated, "not only among those brilliant geniuses, those poets of intelligence such as Plato, Malebranche, or Leibniz, but also among that smaller and more austere group of legislators among whom we may place Aristotle, Bacon, and Kant." And, the author went on to argue, it was necessary to continue to develop Hegel's thought, "since it is a question of the universal ideas of reason. It is the stroke of a pen to help advise a prince; he has decided the outcome of states. Hegel's logic will revolutionize thought."

Hegel's reception was sufficiently widespread that the jurist A. Ott stated unabashedly in 1844 that "from Kant and Fichte, only general principles remain," while "Hegel," he concluded, "is the only one who remains standing today. He is the only one whose school today remains vital and who exerts a direct influence on the current development of philosophy."[44] In 1844, Louis Prévost defended a thesis in Toulouse on Hegel,[45] while in that same year Karl Rosenkranz's first biography on Hegel was translated into French.[46] In 1847, Joseph William published the first volume of his *Histoire de la philosophie allemande depuis Kant jusqu'à Hegel*. Alfred Darimon summarized in 1848 that "in philosophy... we understand fairly well Hegel and his school" (ix–x); and indeed, Hegel was so ubiquitous that in his first manuscript of *L'Éducation sentimentale*, written in the mid-1840s, Flaubert recounted the life of a young provincial student who discovered life in Paris by reading "Hegel, oui, oui, ...

such a fashionable thing [*des choses à la mode*]."[47] In the heart of the demos revolution, Hegel was indeed "in fashion."

While Hegel's influence can be found broadly in French thought of the period, it had an especial impact on a corpus of thinkers gathered in Paris who were interested in the democratic question in the 1830s and 1840s. Among the Germans living in Paris, the democratic movement was spearheaded in the early 1840s by Arnold Ruge and Karl Marx, who sought to gather "the talented democrats they knew: Moses Hess, H. Heine, Herwegh, F. Engels, Karl Grün on the German side, and Lamartine, Louis Blanc, Pierre-Joseph Proudhon, Victor Considerant, Pierre Leroux, Lamennais, Étienne Cabet, and two other great women thinkers: George Sand and Flora Tristan."[48] But the influence of German and specifically Hegelian thought in these years quickly spread beyond this initial cast of characters. As Warren Breckman has argued, many of the most significant left-wing German intellectuals sought the convergence of German philosophy and the French tradition of revolutionary egalitarianism.[49]

Amid the tremendous variety of ideas that circulated within these circles, democracy was consistently presented as an essential mode of modern social organization *and* governance. Heinrich Heine captured the spirit of this movement, just after his arrival in Paris in 1831, when he wrote his "On the Democratic Principle" in 1832.[50] "Democracy," he argued, "needed to be precisely and rigorously defined" as " 'the principle according to which all men on this earth are born equal and noble; no one is privileged in the state by birth.' "[51] Heine insisted that it was the Americans and the French who had best captured this ideal. But while the Americans had achieved this mode of social organization in a distant land, the French had achieved it in the heart of Europe. France therefore offered a model for pursuing the democratic ideal in his German homeland.[52] Another German residing in Paris, Moses Hess, cited Tocqueville's *Democracy in America* in epigraph before arguing: "Germany and France are the two extremities of East and West. . . . Out of France, the country of the political struggles, true politics will one day come forth, just as out of Germany, true religion will emerge. Out of a union of these two, the New Jerusalem will be established."[53] In this new society, distinctions between poor and rich would disappear, women would be equal to men, and children would be educated by the state instead of the family, while health and welfare would be the responsibility of public authorities, leading to a "new society similar to the classical polis."[54] The novel social ideal would in turn be governed by "three powers": "the people as a mass—or the body of the people; the people as the executor of laws—or the will of the people; and finally, the people as legislator—or the spirit of the people."[55] For Hess, the new democratic society would self-govern at every level.

A disciple of Hegel and Parisian resident of the 1840s, Lorenz von Stein, captured the centrality of history in the democratic construction of a modern administrative state. Well integrated into the circles of French socialism in Paris,[56] Stein set about to write the first "social history" of the state—making himself not only one of the first social historians, but also one of the first self-declared "social scientists" through his history of popular uprisings in France since the French Revolution. Out of this history, he offered a conception of the state which could be located between Hegelian idealism, Marx's later radical economic materialism, and Louis Blanc's attention to the role of the state in establishing social justice in a democracy.[57] Stein's account argued, first of all, that the constitutional ideals of the liberal social contract inherited from the early modern period played an essential role in the construction of the modern polity with its ideal of individual rights: "The principle which governs the state, therefore, presupposes for the realization of this principle first of all a constitution which addresses itself to every citizen and guarantees liberty to the individual."[58] While essential, however, the rights revolution of the eighteenth century only comprised half of the state's mission in modern times. For Stein agreed with Hegel and Marx that rights were essential, but that if left alone, they would be unable to combat one of their essential side effects: the unfettered right to pursue individual prosperity would necessarily generate massive social inequalities. He therefore argued that there were two essential forces at play: the society and the state.

Stein argued that since the French Revolution, social movements had taken on a second character, with a new ambition to alleviate social inequality. The branch of state power to emerge from these social movements was the sphere of the regulatory state. Hence, alongside the constitutional organization designed to ensure rights, there emerged another essential pillar of the modern state, what he referred to as the "organs constituting the external life of the state, [what] is called the administration of the state." Every state had an administration, he argued, which "must aim to promote by legitimate means the highest development of all citizens."[59] A modern state therefore ensured rights through formal positive legal protections and through equality ensured by the administration, or what he called "its two contents, constitution and administration"[60]—or, as he also called it elsewhere, a "contract between the real and the merely legal society."[61] The constitution provided a legal foundation for a political ideal, while the administration ensured the real substantive improvement and highest development of all citizens.

It was precisely the history of this relationship or "contract" between the two that became "the point of departure of the social movement toward liberty."[62] The diachronic movement toward liberty achieved its full impact "whenever the government, overwhelmed by internal or external pressures, yields to the demands of the hitherto dependent class and introduces the necessary changes in the constitution and the administration."[63] Internal and external pressures, in particular social movements, he argued, forced the twin pillars of the modern state toward transformation. And out of this transformation emerged a new contract in which "a natural and inevitable alliance of these two elements develops."[64] In Stein's conception. social movements emerged out of the new regime of rights in order to challenge the inequalities that an overemphasis on rights would produce. In other words, popular uprisings were an exercise of constitutional guarantees—not against government, but toward the expansion of the real ends of government in the interest of the public good. Hence, "the republican or democratic element," Stein argued, "considers it its main task to provide a clear formula for a constitution and to define the legal framework of a democratic government, while the social movement is concerned with the administration and administrative tasks, i.e. the social use of the means available to a democratic government."[65] With this term, "the social use of the means available to a democratic government," Stein captured the substance—or what he called the "meaning-content"[66]—of social democracy. Stein, therefore, seized an essential contribution of the vast social movements of this period: social movements were a means of building administrative capacity to ensure a more just society.

A figure much like Flaubert's protagonist in *L'Éducation sentimentale*, and later a presidential candidate during the Second Republic, Alexandre Ledru-Rollin, captured another element of the democratic reception in France of German and Hegelian thought in these same years.[67] What Ledru-Rollin took from Hegel was his critique of the sovereign individual. Kant, Ledru-Rollin argued, had negated the profoundly social nature of the individual. "Hegel," on the other hand, he insisted, had "sought to fill the gap by tracing a complete system of social philosophy."[68] This new "Hegelian" school had learned from the lessons of the eighteenth century, which had gone too far in its fascination for the sovereign individual: "The individual was nothing; he had to be something; they wanted him to be everything. Freedom was not being respected; so to give it back its luster, they despised all forms of authority."[69] As a result, the eighteenth century overstated the importance of individual liberty. It was precisely in bringing the individual back into his or her social context, Ledru-Rollin argued, that Hegel had opened a pathbreaking innovation for a new science of politics.

As groundbreaking as Hegel's reconsideration of Kantian liberty was, however, in Ledru-Rollin's reading Hegel did not entirely solve the problem. Remarking on Hegel's approach to the problem of how to reintegrate individual liberty back into the collective enterprise of the state, Ledru-Rollin argued: "Indeed, when one recognizes the legitimacy of all individual tyrannies, there is no other way to tame them than to hand them over helplessly to the tyranny of the head of state."[70] For Ledru-Rollin, the problem was precisely the power Hegel handed over to the head of state in order to ensure that individuals could pursue their particular interests as they wished while continuing to contribute to the collective enterprise of the state. According to Ledru-Rollin, the overwhelming power of the state in Hegel's philosophy emerged out of his profound idealism; that is, his emphasis on ideas over social action. Thus, even as he elaborated a "social philosophy," Hegel was still necessarily confronted with "the immobility, the impotence of any social application."[71]

It was precisely in this realm that the "French school," Ledru-Rollin argued, "would hardly be satisfied with pure thought, without relation." Building on the essential insights of Hegel's social philosophy that inserted individual reason back into the social, Ledru-Rollin sought a third essential step that grounded the relationship between the individual and society in practice, "because social life is relationships; what the individual conceives, he wants to realize."[72] For Ledru-Rollin, the great contribution of the French school was to "to recognize all the elements of social life, to take into account the absolute and the relative, the general and the particular."[73] The name Ledru-Rollin gave to this social understanding of the individual in which "social life" balanced the particular and the general interest was democracy.

> Let it be known that it is not by chance that democratic opinion expresses itself; it is not by a fantasy of opposition that raises its voice. No. It reasons its doctrines, and finds a solid base as much in the maxims of abstract science as in the teaching of facts, in the magnificent lessons of our forefathers as in the brilliant acts of our contemporaries. A political idea is nothing if it is not based on a scientific idea; but a scientific idea may only be judged if it produces a disastrous policy.[74]

For Ledru-Rollin, democracy had a deeply pragmatic dimension: though born out of ideas, it was tested in application and policy. Through democratic practice, he argued, the expansion of suffrage was an absolute necessity, but could only partially solve the problem. Alongside "increasing access to elections," the achievement of democracy also required such concrete measures as "raising wages." Ledru-Rollin conceived of this application of democracy to all forms of social life as spreading "from the overthrow of a throne to the establishment of the industrial tribunal."[75] For him, democracy as a social practice spread far beyond the electoral ballot.

This current gained steam in the 1840s. In 1843 and 1844, *La revue indépendante* gave special attention to the relationship between French and German philosophy, suggesting that this alliance would be the key to forging a more just social and political future. The first article by Louis Blanc on that subject—"Alliance intellectuelle: Allemagne et France," published in 1843—presented the fruits to be harvested from such an international exchange.[76] For Blanc, "an intellectual alliance between the two peoples is eminently desirable."[77] To achieve this alliance, the first necessity was the unification of Germany. However, this unification should not come at the expense of administrative decentralization. By achieving political centralization and administrative decentralization, Germany could begin the proper march toward freedom. Once unification was achieved, the next goal was to find an immanent principle that could guarantee a properly political relationship between all social activity and the state. Blanc explicitly criticized Hegel, arguing in response that it was "by granting to the State the ability to initiate vast and profound reforms, by placing it at the head of industry, by bringing under its control all that is of general interest and by crushing intellectual anarchy" that "political centralization creates force and harmony."[78] Furthermore, Blanc argued, It is clear that Germany can only arrive at democracy through unity." In his argument, political centralization was the means to achieving liberty on a national scale, and administration was the means through which society acted upon itself as society. As we shall see in chapter 3, expanding suffrage in this view was not solely a process of granting basic political rights. It was also a necessary means for preventing regulatory administrative power from becoming driven by distant, arbitrary, or despotic experts.

Carving out a space for a democratic politics from within a nascent socialism, the work of "democ-socs" like Ledru-Rollin and Blanc participated in a broad attempt to democratize Hegel's ideas on government. Arnold Ruge wrote a preface to the German edition of Blanc's *Histoire de dix ans* in 1843 as the exchange between Hegel and French democrats reached new heights. Ruge and Blanc's intellectual exchange provided one of the essential sources for Ruge's project for a new and short-lived review, *Deutsch-Französische Jahrbücher* (German-French Annals), which he opened with an article titled "Toward an Entente between the Germans and the French."[79] The project fell under the twin spirit of the democratic legacy of the French Revolution and of left Hegelianism, and was captured in Ruge's *The Origins of the Franco-German Couple: Critique of Nationalism and Democratic Revolution before 1848*.[80]

An article then published in the *Revue independante* in 1844 titled "L'École de Hegel à Paris" captured the spirit of this movement.[81] The article opened by citing Louis Blanc's previous contribution, and suggested that the new French-German alliance could be achieved as Ruge and Marx further developed Hegelian thought in Paris.[82] This Hegelian school had "demonstrated that Germany was locked in the past," while "France, which is so prone to action, too often forgets the philosophical principles necessary to calm the ardors of its temperament."[83] It was necessary that "Germany lend to France the discipline of its philosophy. And France lend to Germany its practical spirit and revolutionary instincts." Thanks to this exchange, "Hegel would preside over a great new international contract,"[84] in which "the idea of liberty leads and governs itself."[85] Ruge had said little less himself when he wrote to Marx in August 1843: "We are going to establish, here in Paris, an organization where we will judge ourselves and all of Germany with an absolute liberty."[86] To which Marx responded, just before arriving in Paris in October: "So you are in Paris, the old superior school of philosophy and capital of the new world."[87]

It was in this context of development of a democratic thought through Franco- German exchange in 1843 that Marx began preparing his devastating critique of Hegel's constitutional monarchism, and began an outline of what a democratic alternative would look like in his critique of Hegel's philosophy of right.[88] Marx's early critique of Hegel's principal work on politics was written within this context of a dialogue between German neo-Hegelians and a specifically democratic thought in France. His early, democratic reflections on Hegel were to be published in the first edition of the *German–French Annals* he was developing with Ruge, who was already planning their move to Paris.[89] Though not yet in Paris, Marx was clearly drawing on his understanding of French democratic thought. "The modern French have conceived it thus," he argued; "in true democracy the political state disappears. This is correct inasmuch as qua political state, qua constitution it is no longer equivalent to the whole." One idea Marx gathered from his reading of the French was the changing place of what he called the "political state" in a democracy. In his view, this state in democracy would not disappear in the sense that there would no longer be a state. Rather, it would disappear as a particular mode of political organization that was distinct from other forms of social activity. In other words, what would disappear was the very distinction between a political state as the site of the political and a civil society as the site of private action.

As a result, Marx's understanding of democracy could only very partially be reduced to suffrage, or to "a mere set of procedures and practices" or "legal forms."[90] Though he did not deny the importance of universal suffrage in democracy, the core of Marx's democratic theory formed out of the peculiarity of democracy as opposed to monarchical or aristocratic regimes. Reminiscent of French democratic thought—also captured by Tocqueville, though in very different terms[91]—Marx's democracy was characterized by a fundamental reconfiguration of a society of equals in relation to itself as its own agent of self-government. In this context, Hegel's distinction between a civil society consisting of an apolitical "property, contract, and marriage" realm on the one hand, and a political realm of government on the other, disappeared. In a democracy, Marx argued, all affairs were recognized as constituted by the society itself. Drawing on the French model, he therefore shed Hegel's mobilization of the term "civil society," preferring the term "demos," which he defined as the "constitution of the people," opposed to a "form of the state," in which "political man has his particular and separate existence beside the unpolitical, private man."[92] Importantly, Marx's conception lies squarely within a longer tradition of invoking the "demos" as a social form in which a society of equals necessarily self-governs. Within this social form, the state is not opposed to a private sphere, but rather constantly asserts its status as demos by self-governing:[93] "The abstraction of the state as such belongs only to modern times because the abstraction of private life belongs only to modern times." However, "in a democracy, the abstract state has ceased to be the governing moment." In a democratic state, Marx continued, "the constitution itself has been formed into a particular actuality alongside the real life of the people, the political state has become the constitution of the rest of the state." In other words, unlike in constitutional monarchy in a civil society where a portion of private activity remains outside the state—that is, where only the state is political while private actions remain outside politics—in a demos, the entire state and every aspect of people's lives is politically constituted and therefore requires self-government.

So a demos—that is, a self-governing society of equals—ends not in the disappearance of the state, but in the elimination of an autonomous bureaucracy as the objective end of a political state distinct from a civil society of private wills. Indeed, Marx argued that Hegel had "not developed the executive," since he had maintained "particular interests of civil society as such, as interests which lie outside the absolutely universal interest of the state." As a result, "the executive [was] a particular, separate power" distinct from the administrative powers, such as corporations, that regulated civil society. In such a theory, the substantive administration of social problems by the police and corporations remained within civil society, while the bureaucracy served the political state under the control of a constitutional monarch. "As Hegel has already claimed the powers of the 'police' and the 'judiciary' for the sphere of civil society," Marx argued, "nothing remains for the executive but their administration, which he treats in terms of bureaucracy." So the result of Hegel's faulty logic, Marx argued, was that even though he placed regulatory police within the realm of civil society, their mission was granted and overseen by an autonomous bureaucracy that in turn shaped society: "The police, the judiciary, and the administration are not deputies of civil society itself, which manages its own general interest in and through them. Rather, they are officeholders of the state whose purpose is to manage the state in opposition to civil society." For Marx, this distinction, which he argued put the civil society and the state in a constant relationship of war, was anathema in a democratic age. He thus concluded his discussion of administrative power in a democracy by arguing: "The executive power is the one most difficult to develop; it, much more than the legislature, belongs to the entire people." In short, for Marx, democracy was even more the domain of the executive than of the legislative. In a democracy, administration and regulatory power had to be in the hands of all members of society. Democracy was first and foremost the realm of self-government. "Democracy was thus conceived by Marx as the political self-realization of man."[94]

Marx's democratic administrative critique of Hegel has been cited not only as a key moment in his intellectual development, but as a resource for elaborating a robust political critique of later Marxism.[95] His analysis clearly provides important theoretical insights into the transformations of Hegelian thought on administration in the nineteenth century, just as it sheds light on his own intellectual trajectory.[96] However, his precise treatment of democracy as such must also be placed within a fine-grained understanding of the reigning conception of the relationship between democratic administration and a democratic society shaped by Franco-German exchange in the 1830s and 1840s. Indeed, though chock full of the rhetorical power and theoretical sophistication that would become his hallmark, Marx's conception of democracy also mobilized the key themes that framed democratic thought in France in the period. Through a critique of Hegel, Marx argued that a "demos" was a democratic society that chose to govern, and thus constitute, itself democratically. Democracy was the mode of social organization in which all members of society were defined as agents of their own government and administration.

Together, this broad cast of French and German intellectuals sought to democratize what they presented as Hegel's fundamental contribution to the construction of the modern administrative state. At the core of this democratizing project, highlighted by Lorenz von Stein, Alexandre Ledru-Rollin, Louis Blanc. and Karl Marx, was a special emphasis on the role of history, a socialized individual, and an ideal of realizing social transformation through reflexive action back on society. This democratized state, grounded in a historical, sociological, and pragmatic approach to modern government, would in turn provide the groundwork for a vast revision of one of the central legacies of the Enlightenment, Rousseau's social contract.

Toward a New Social Contract

As Stein suggested, what emerged out of these conceptions of regulatory practice, resistances to them, and responses to that resistance was a gradual, aggregative, and informal transformation of society through administrative action. The result was more than a mere inflation of governmental interventions; it was, rather, a profound difference in kind. Ledru-Rollin, Marx, and Stein all specifically cited Hegel as one of the sources of their new conception of a self-governing society on the backdrop of Parisian revolution. And just as Hegel had rethought the role of police and corporations in regulating individual freedom toward the public good, Parisian political activists and theoreticians who engaged with his work considered that actual regulatory practices, resistances to them, and responses to that resistance amounted to much more than squabbling over interminable lists of duties and interdictions. To borrow the terms used by Stein, the unprecedented process of regulating, resisting, and re-regulating expanded into a new *contract*.

Contract theory in political thought has been broadly presented as giving way in the nineteenth century to utilitarianism and then finding a resurgence in the second half of the twentieth century.[97] While recent work has productively challenged the opposition between utilitarianism and contract theory,[98] important revisions, and thus self-conscious continuities, in social contract theory on the European continent have received very little attention. In fact, a vast revisionism of contract theory blanketed political and administrative thought in nineteenth-century France. There should be little surprise that the country that enshrined Rousseau as an ideological founding father of the Revolution consistently celebrated the towering legacy of his *Social Contract* while relentlessly attempting to amend it. Balzac's notorious Jacques Collin—alias Vautrin—spoke for a postrevolutionary generation when he cried out at the climax of *Le Père Goriot*: "I protest against the profound deceptions of the Social Contract, as stated by Jean-Jacques, who I proudly claim to be my teacher."[99] As Balzac's great antagonist suggested, to be a student of "Jean-Jacques" in the nineteenth century was in fact to revise the social contract.

This revision developed principally in three directions. First, political thinkers, historians, sociologists, and politicians of the period refused what they considered an overly formalistic rights-based notion of the contract formed by independent sovereign wills at a given moment.[100] Any real social contract, it was argued, necessarily changed and adapted over time, and attention to that historical development was necessary to regulate and manage increasingly complex social relations. Second, they rejected what they considered an overly narrow notion of the social composed of abstract, discrete, and atomized individuals. As Vautrin clamoured: "Does anyone here have, as I do, ten thousand brothers ready to do anything to help you?"[101] This postrevolutionary conception of the social contract turned instead on social obligation. Finally, precisely because it was social, this obligation was collectively organized and managed toward specific social aims. Hence, the political thinkers drew new attention to everyday government and administration for ensuring the well-being of the social individual.

Here too, Hegel had opened a wide door to social and historical revision in his *Philosophy of Right*.[102] Hegel had famously critiqued Rousseau's *Social Contract*, which he argued "reduces the union of individuals in the state to a contract and therefore to something based on their arbitrary wills, their opinion, and their capriciously given express consent."[103] He noted that since the individuals of early modern contract theory only joined together through individual will, the social contract they supposedly created "contains only a negative phase, that of limitation." Such a focus missed in turn the positive contributions the individual made as a member of a state. Nonetheless, by critiquing Rousseauian contract theory, Hegel was hardly refusing the idea of contracting as a whole. Rather, in his view, the social contract had two parts, which he referred to as covenant *and* performance, or common *and* particular will. That is, any initial commitment was inscribed in time through performance, and while an individual particular will joined in a contract, such a decision could never be disassociated from the common will that surrounded it.

Revising the social contract became a mainstay of democratic political thought in France. It was certainly no accident that Victor Hugo staged the first shot fired past Marius in the climax of *Les Misérables* on the *rue du Contrat Social*. In her historical fiction *Mauprat*, George Sand insisted on the "rustic philosopher" Patience, who "acquired a copy of the *Social Contract* and had it tirelessly read it out."[104] In another novel, *Indiana*, she highlighted the limits of an individualist conception of contract theory when she blamed the despotism and suspiciousness of the heroine's husband on the fact that he "had only ever studied the social contract of *to each his own*."[105] Tocqueville provided his deeply original rendering of Rousseau's work when he recounted the founding of the New England colonies in the second chapter of the first volume of *Democracy in America*.[106] Outlining the earliest moments of Puritan settlement in the seventeenth century, Tocqueville argued in the original manuscript: "You must not believe that the piety of the Puritans was only speculative, or that it proved to be unfamiliar with the course of human concerns." Rather, he argued, "they immediately enacted an agreement" which was "the social contract in proper form that Rousseau dreamed of in the following century."[107] Even more striking was the result of this historical social contract, which Tocqueville referred to as a "fervor for regulations"[108]—that is, the most extraordinary expansion of regulatory power a European people could have imagined: "Mere flirtation between unmarried people is severely suppressed"; "Laziness and drunkenness are severely punished"; "Innkeepers cannot provide more than a certain quantity of wine to each consumer"; "A law prohibits the use of tobacco"; and "In the year 1649, a solemn association was formed in Boston whose purpose was to prevent the worldly luxury of long hair."[109] In his explicitly *democratic* revision of Rousseau's social contract, Tocqueville posited concrete historical examples of regulation toward social welfare as the foundation of a modern polity.

Hortense Allart, whose *La femme et la démocratie de nos temps* offered a woman's perspective on the ideas of the *doctrinaires*, similarly insisted that Rousseau was the father of modern democracy, having "claimed in the Social Contract that all voices in the state were of equal value."[110] In her view, however, his egalitarian ideals had been misapplied during the revolution, which had marginalized the "genius" of Mirabeau in favor of Robespierre's "mediocrity." To overcome such errors, she argued, it was necessary to transform this legacy through a new study of society. "Organize science for this nation, make of it something worthy of the inspiration it has received!"[111] she announced, insisting that "a new political science is necessary." "Any social state has its science," she added, convinced that "man attains beauty through science."[112] For Allart, this science would reveal not only the true genius inherent in a new French democracy; it would also pave the way for those women with talent to shape the public good.

Pierre-Joseph Proudhon provided one of the most ambitious revisions of contract theory as a self-declared disciple of Hegel: "I have had three true masters," he wrote to his editor; "first the Bible, then Adam Smith, and finally Hegel."[113] As the Second Republic came to a close in 1851, Proudhon captured the spirit of a revised contract when he suggested that the problem with Rousseau's social contract was that there was nothing "social" about it. As a result, Rousseau "had understood nothing of social contracts," he argued.[114] In Rousseau's account, Proudhon continued, "the social contract was not a commutative act nor even an act of society," but a mere "act of arbiters, chosen by citizens, outside any preestablished convention." In his view, a "real, positive contract" was rooted in the questions "What do I owe my fellow citizens? What have they promised to myself?"[115] These questions provided the foundation for a social pact that went far beyond guaranteeing individual liberty. It was a question of recognizing the mutual contraction of obligations between social individuals. If one did not have a clear sense of the social responsibility of specific individuals toward specific ends, Proudhon argued, then "the thousand infractions regulated by the police of cities, countryside, rivers, forests were nothing but punishments." Under such conditions, "your police, your judgments, your enforcement was no more than a series of abusive acts."[116] Protecting individual liberty was profoundly unjust without a clear sense of social duty. "The social contract must increase welfare and freedom for every citizen."[117] The new social contract, Proudhon argued, required the protection of public welfare *and* liberty. To do so, it had to push into all those areas that Rousseau had entirely ignored: how to organize work, education, property relations, industrial power, economic rights, transfer of goods, exchange, prices—in other words, "that mass of relations that for better or worse, constitute man in perpetual society with his fellow man,"[118] and which animate the subsequent chapters of this book. Elaborating this revisionism, Jules Simon stated that "some free thinkers suppose that society is a social contract, by which they mean an association which is purely of human origin established by will." Such a conception was misguided, Simon insisted, since "society is not created by man, whatever Rousseau might argue. It is not a contract between each one of us. We are born in a society and in a society that is already organized."[119]

In the years that followed, revising the social contract along the lines proposed by Simon became central to founding the discipline of sociology. Auguste Comte had prepared the terrain for the sociological critique of Rousseau's social contract, referring to it as "the savage negation of society itself."[120] In his *Introduction à la sociologie*, a founder of modern discipline of sociology Guillaume De Greef (1842–1924) argued that Comte's positivist ambitions had shattered contractualist notions of individualism and liberty. "The equally absolute theses of 'the individual against the State' and 'the State against the individual' represent only transient stages of social evolution: the solution of their antinomy is in the development of the social contract, no longer placed with Rousseau, at the beginning of societies, but at their apogee."[121] De Greef captured a core contribution of this contractual revisionism; by turning the social contract on its head, he reversed its origin. For De Greef, the social contract did not found society, but rather emerged as a product of increasingly dense and complex social relations that emerged sui generis.[122] As a result, in his view, the social contract was gradual, accretive, and reciprocal; that is, it emerged to regulate, harmonize, and improve the social relations that always existed between social individuals. "There is no society, in the true sense of the word, except where physiological unity and collective social strength are equally respected. This mutual guarantee can only be approximated by the development and perfection of the social contract."[123]

This reversal of early modern social contract theory found its way into the heart of Émile Durkheim's early sociological writings. Challenging Hobbes and Rousseau,[124] he attempted to align social contract theory with a new, more sociological conception of the social: "If we put all metaphysics aside, a contract is nothing more than a spontaneous adaptation of two or more individuals to each other, under conditions determined by the social and physical environment in which they are placed."[125] The new social contract did not found society out of abstract rights-bearing individuals, Durkheim argued. Rather, it regulated a social organism that always and already existed at various levels of complexity. In short, Tocqueville, Proudhon, De Greef, and Durkheim's historical and sociological conception of the social contract emerged out of socially situated relations between individuals. These concrete relationships were then regulated over time to monitor social obligation, ensure individual well-being, and care for collective social development. Such regulation could only be achieved, these authors argued, by developing a strong grasp of the society in which one was living. Hence the structural role of history and sociology in ensuring a social contract in a democratic society.

The thinker who elaborated this idea most fully in the nineteenth century was Alfred Fouillée, in his *La science sociale contemporaine* (1880). Here Fouillée summarized the core of his revisionist "social scientific" vision of the social contract by arguing that two opposing conceptions of the social had shaped the state/society relationship since the old regime: an abstract, metaphysical view he situated in the Enlightenment, and which had given rise to Rousseau's social contract on the one hand, and the organic, romantic, and in many cases conservative vision of the social on the other, in which individuals were joined not by their individual wills, but through communities based on natural and unshakeable social bonds. The dichotomy, he argued, was ultimately false. In the modern age, Fouillée argued, the two were combined into a new contractualism that integrated individual liberty or will on the one hand and an organic or collective vision of society on the other. He referred to this new contract as "contractual organicism." "Those who believe that free contract or free agreement means arbitrary agreement are left with the old notion of freedom of indifference or absolute free will," Fouillée suggested of early modern contractualism. He opposed this conception to a "self-reflexive will" which "implies the simultaneous consciousness of several inclinations striving to be actualized, that is, multiple ideas which tend to be realized."[126] In this case, he continued, the contract is not a product of individual "caprice, nor does it exclude the regularity of effects nor the possibility of foreseeing the future."[127] "In a free nation, that self-governs," Fouillée continued—capturing the essential notion of the demos as a self-governing democratic society—"you will soon recognize that organization is strengthened by freedom itself; that the more contractual an organization is, the more organized it really is."[128] For Fouillée, the new contractualism was grounded in the ability to regulate and govern *for* liberty.

As these thinkers demonstrated, the effects of this revised contract were profound. First, while a number of terms were used to encapsulate this new contract that consistently, indeed endlessly, negotiated over time the mutual and often conflicting responsibilities of public service, social obligation, and individual liberty, from Allart to Fouillée there was an overarching scaffold for this larger transition based on its "democratic" nature. "Formerly an object of pure curiosity and a luxury reserved for a few thinkers," Fouillée observed, "the study of society and its laws will eventually become for all, in our democratic nations, a study of primary necessity."[129] As Bruno Karsenti has pointed out, the birth of the social sciences in the nineteenth century did not just serve democracy. The social sciences were democratic in the very way they generated a reflexive and immanent understanding of the social that fashioned self-government.[130] The incremental regulation of complex social relations forced a reconfiguration of the political legacy of liberal individualism and rights toward a democratized social contract.

Most importantly, this democratized social contract was understood to emerge out of existing social relations that could be shaped and guided over time instead of serving as the founding act of a political society. Charles Comte highlighted this idea when he argued in 1817 that constitutions, no matter how well designed, were incapable of solving concrete social ills. What was necessary, he argued, was to gather a sense of social problems first and then adapt government to society.[131] Guizot similarly highlighted the importance of studying society first and building government second when he argued: "It is through the study of political institutions that most writers, scholars, historians, or publicists have sought to know the state of society, the degree or kind of its civilization. It would have been wiser to study the society itself to know and understand its political institutions. Before becoming a cause, institutions are an effect."[132] On the other side of the political spectrum, George Sand stated the frank impossibility of "reconciling the happiness and dignity of those oppressed by society without changing society itself."[133] Victor Considerant similarly argued that if "the work of the revolution has been completed, the work of democracy has yet to begin." In terms reminiscent of

Hegel, he stated that "the Revolution in 89 and 1830 have only realized right through its negative, abstract form."[134] What remained was the social organization of democracy not just "in theory" but "in fact [*dans les faits*]."[135] Giving priority to understanding society in order to properly govern in nineteenth-century political thought contributed to overcoming what Céline Spector has referred to as a "major defect of political philosophy from the perspective of the social sciences," namely their tendency to systematically deduce political systems "from human nature rather than the state of a given society."[136] In a social-scientific understanding of society, sound governance could not be limited to protecting individual liberty from a potentially tyrannical state by merely mixing forms of government. It also required grasping the fundamentally complex relationships and conflictual nature of socially and historically embedded individuals. Fashioning a democratic social contract depended on knowing the kind of society and social relations that had to be regulated and transformed. So, while nineteenth-century French social and political theorists embraced the idea of a social contract, they rejected what they presented as the social contract's classic, pre-Revolutionary Rousseauian formulation built on free-willing, sovereign individuals gathering of their own accord to form a political society. Together, the priority of the socially embedded individual and the imperative of a historical and social-scientific understanding of a "democratic society" for legitimate governmental action democratized contract theory in France.

As we have seen, the conceptual challenge of a democratized social contract occupied many of the brightest minds of the first half of the nineteenth century regardless of where they sat on the political spectrum. It was, however, hardly the remove of a rarified theoretical project. Indeed, the elaboration of a democratic social contract took place through administrative and regulatory practices, texts, laws, and codes produced in the continual confrontation between government and the governed around public problems. It is to these concrete modes of public action, participation, and resistance, where the actual process of building a democratic social contract took place, that we now turn.

2

Forest Democracy

A New Regulatory Landscape

> Is not the state linked with each of its citizens by a thousand vital nerves, and has it the right to sever all these nerves because this citizen has himself arbitrarily severed *one* of them? Therefore the state will regard even an infringer of forest regulations as a human being, a living member of the state, one in whom its heart's blood flows.
>
> KARL MARX[1]

The chamber maid, Noun, asked Indiana why her husband was prowling through the woods of their estate with a rifle. Someone was apparently roaming the property. Unsettled by the potential disaster of an innocent man being shot, the two women glanced at each other, for they both knew what Indiana's despotic husband was capable of. "It is frightening to imagine they may kill someone?" pronounced Noun. For a moment, they reassured themselves with the idea that it was a typical situation: "Oh, it is probably just some thieves! Some poor peasant who has come to steal a handful of wood for his family. . . ." The two women sought comfort in the thought that even Indiana's husband surely wouldn't kill a man for such ordinary activity. Then the reality of the situation struck them: It was unlikely that someone was stealing wood on their property "so near to the entrance of the Fontainebleau forest where wood could be stolen so easily. It would make no sense in that case to wander in a walled estate and expose oneself to such danger."[2] And then the shot rang out.

The opening scene of George Sand's *Indiana* treats the theft of wood by peasants and the war with property owners as a banal and almost everyday occurrence. The trespassing of a peasant to provide wood for his family is the first thing that comes to the minds of Indiana and Noun. And the idea that Indiana's husband might shoot a man for such simple needs revealed just how authoritarian and suspicious of Indiana he was: he who claimed to be the unchecked master of his house and domain. Discussions of the fruits of the forest, their ownership, and their uses were so common they could provide the starting point for Sand to set the stage for the first novel written under her masculine pseudonym.

The epigraph to this chapter, from Marx's article on the theft of wood and George Sand's *Indiana*, suggest how the widespread and wide-ranging debates over forests raised questions about how they should serve the public good and who had the right to regulate their usage. Confrontations in the forests throughout France broke out as urban intellectual and political elites created massive new regulations to combat what they perceived to be the devastating effects of deforestation brought on by the vast sale of aristocratic domains and the liberalization of forest usage during the French Revolution. For scientists, experts, politicians, and policymakers of the period, the accelerated destruction of forests since the late eighteenth century had unleashed a change in average temperatures, new fluctuations in annual rainfall, flash floods, and devastating washouts, and were having a deep impact on overall atmospheric conditions. Even if their understanding of the how and why was limited, there was a startlingly prescient awareness that humans could be a major force in shaping the climate.

Faced with the urgency of this devastating deforestation, public authorities initially employed a largely despotic regulatory response. The protests and revolts throughout the forests from the late 1820s through the late 1840s broke out then, in response as much to the means through which these regulations were established as to their potential consequences. The result of this confrontation between a precocious scientific awareness on the part of scientific and political elites, a despotic imposition of new regulations, and their impact on the daily lives and needs of forest dwellers was a radical politicization along a continuum between the human and the natural. In this confrontation, the high stakes of environmental politics played out around attempts to find new modes of non-despotic regulatory power that at once protected forests, fought off fears of climate change, and respected the quotidian habits of those living in France's woodlands. In the first half of the nineteenth century, a radical new relationship between humans and their environment was forged not only through industrial capitalism's insatiable appetite for natural resources, but through the politicization of environmental regulation.

Shifting our revolutionary gaze away from industrial capitalism, urban workers, and the shop floor, and toward the relationship between humans and their forests, pushes us first to shift our temporal scales of revolt and revolution. Environmental historians have increasingly been drawn to the political metaphor of an "old regime" to describe the relationship between humans and nature through the notion of the "biological old regime." Fernand Braudel famously argued that "even at the end of the eighteenth century, vast areas of the earth were still a garden of Eden for animal life." He further suggested that "what was shattered in both China and Europe with the eighteenth century was a biological ancien régime, a set of restrictions, obstacles, structures, proportions, and numerical relationships that had hitherto been the norm."[3]

As Pritchard and Zeller have similarly argued, the end of this biological old regime took place between 1750 and 1850 as coal freed industry and entrepreneurs from the limits imposed by annual solar-energy flows.[4] While accounts of the end of the biological old regime have provided an important framework for rethinking the natural foundations of industrialization, we know less about the actual revolutionary politics that brought the regime to an end. In fact, the biological old regime was ended not simply by industrialists or by urban and capitalist elites, but also by a political and social revolution on the part of actual people, especially those of the countryside who helped shape new modes of environmental regulation.

These revolutions took place on a different time scale than the one favored by traditional accounts of nineteenth-century revolution. The idea that a political-ecological revolution could take place in three days in late July in Paris in 1830, or in a few days in Paris in late February 1848, or that it can be measured by whether or not the country changed dynasties, is almost risible. Instead, this revolution took place over multiple decades—still a flash in environmental time—through confrontations between those living in the forests and those trying to regulate them. We are therefore pushed to see that the biological old regime also came to an end through revolutionary action, and that the period stretching from the 1820s through the early 1850s consisted not so much of a series of successful short revolutions and failed revolts as of one distended revolutionary moment. The period witnessed a revolution in the relationship between human beings and their forests in this tip of the massive Eurasian landmass, which included France and some of its neighbors.

Second, against the idea that revolutionary moments were punctuated outbursts in periods of state breakdown followed by state oppression, taking the political and intellectual elites' claims on anthropogenic climate change seriously suggests a different story of popular revolt and public power. Regulatory control certainly offered new opportunities for capture by elites to serve their dominant economic and political interests. But our recent discovery of the Anthropocene forces us to recognize the extent to which these regulatory ambitions were not solely an ideological manifestation of the elites' own interests. Indeed, scientists have largely corroborated their claims that anthropogenic climate change was in full swing by the early nineteenth century, and that deforestation was at least partially responsible. In this context, what appears is a complex relationship between a prolonged set of protestations on the part of local populations and consistent attempts on the part of public authorities to regulate and intervene in what they considered the dangerous uses and abuses of forest environments. This back-and-forth began in the 1820s, first taking policy form with the revised forest code of 1827, and later intensified in the 1830s and 1840s as a new awareness of the environmental impact of deforestation confronted the practices and needs of rural populations. By the 1850s, a new awareness of the relationship between humans and their environment had taken root: one in which public authorities had a key role to play in managing the environment in the name of the public interest to challenge the ecological devastation brought on by humans. The creation of a modern regulatory power was thus subject to pressures from social and cultural elites, scientific communities, and popular movements. This revolutionary moment was hardly a short-lived uprising against the state. But it was nonetheless a revolution of tectonic proportions. It is thus better understood as a prolonged negotiation that transformed key ideas about the continuity between humans, the public good, and the environment.

The Problem of Deforestation in the Early Nineteenth Century

In the wake of the First Empire, a series of urgent administrative problems came rushing in on the new monarchy. Among them was the alarming state of France's forests. Between 1750 and 1850, the world suffered nothing short of the most drastic phase of deforestation and "certainly the most destructive age yet seen for the earth's primeval forests."[5] From 1650 to 1750, between 54,000 and 216,000 square kilometers of European forests were cleared, while between 1750 and 1850 those numbers increased between three and ten times, growing to 186,000 square kilometers by the most conservative assessments and to 596,000 for the highest.[6] Over the next century, that number decreased back down to approximately 81,000 square kilometers as European powers turned toward new reforestation projects, depleted the resources of their imperial peripheries, and supplemented the use of wood with other materials. Because of the massive shift in landed estates during the French Revolution, France was particularly affected by deforestation. Andrée Corvol notes that between 1791 and 1840, for example, the department of the Var in France lost 44 percent of its forest cover, while the lower Alps lost 71 percent![7]

As important as wood remains today, in the late eighteenth century and first half of the nineteenth century, forests were still one of the most versatile and important natural resources for energy consumption, and hence for economic growth. While forests of the old regime and early industrialization conjure up images of traditionalism, stasis, and immobility, they were in fact one of the areas most deeply touched by shifts in industrial production, and by agricultural pressures due to rising demographic growth, transportation, and urbanization.[8] Indeed, from the early eighteenth century to the mid-nineteenth century, the woodlands of Western Europe, and of France in particular, were transformed as profoundly as the continent's great cities.[9] Wood had of course long provided the basic source of fire for heating and cooking. Similarly, the forests provided essential resources for daily life, especially among peasants, to meet a wide variety of needs: from grazing for animals, including goats and sheep, to soap making, food gathering, and basic wood-related necessities (furniture, torches, etc.), as well as the supplementing of income with cut and gathered wood.[10] Many of these basic needs remained into the nineteenth century, since urbanization did not lead to declining demographics of peasant forest communities until the second half of the century. At the same time, however, starting in the seventeenth and especially into the eighteenth and nineteenth centuries, France's forests also provided many of the materials necessary for meeting French military needs, and most importantly warships. Likewise, while much urban construction was done with stone, wood also provided lumber for construction needs in some of France's cities and specifically in its ports.[11] In 1851 Adolphe Thiers noted, "Brittany must give all its wood to Brest, Lorient, and Nantes; and Brittany can barely meet these needs. As a result, during certain periods it has been necessary to abandon the idea that Brest would be a port for construction, since there wasn't enough wood."[12] At the same time, pressures for more arable land made the destruction of forests for agricultural production, especially in the wake of bad harvests, increasingly acceptable. Finally, by the 1840s wood was also increasingly necessary for the construction of the rapidly growing railroad lines and for the growing industrial needs of ironworks, which required wood transformed into charcoal. These needs generated unprecedented markets for industrial cutting.[13] Massive deforestation therefore threatened almost every aspect of life from everyday subsistence and livelihood to the military, urban development, and transportation networks. No nation, especially one with imperial and world commercial ambitions, could afford to ignore the state of its forests.

The immense devastation of French woods certainly did not go unnoticed. As early as the last years of the eighteenth century, awareness grew that France was at risk of losing its forest cover, especially in mountainous regions. In 1797, Jean-Antoine Fabre, a chief engineer from the Ponts et Chaussées stationed in the Var, insisted on the dangers of deforestation in his *Essai sur la théorie des torrens et des rivières*, arguing that "the destruction of the woods that cover our mountains is the primary cause of the development of washouts."[14] Just a few years later, Jean-Baptiste Rougier de La Bergerie, agronomist and prefect under Napoleon, published his *Mémoires et observations sur les abus des défrichements et la destruction des bois et forêts*, declaring, "Here we see cleared, sterile earth after years of productivity: now all we see are rocks in what were the best pastures.... Elsewhere we observe changes in the direction of winds, temperatures, and precipitation."[15] Not only did these authors denounce the disappearance of French forests; they concluded that their destruction was wreaking environmental havoc.

These critiques only gained steam in the nineteenth century. As central as the forests had been in the Revolution and in the First Empire, the political stakes of woodlands increased with the Bourbon Restoration. The forests became a key political issue even in the "first" Restoration before Napoleon's one hundred days, when the Chamber voted to return all the *biens nationaux* that had not yet been sold, many of which were forested lands. On September 13, 1814, the Chamber voted that the lands without new property owners would be returned. Soon after, in 1816, forests once again brought the complex legacy of the French Revolution into bold relief when the minister of finance proposed to pay off the debts left behind after the Empire by selling off more than four hundred thousand hectares of forests that had been the property of the Catholic Church prior to the Revolution. The project was abandoned, but arguments for selling off forests to pay state debts were regularly renewed through the Restoration and the July Monarchy. These debates gave policy on woods more salience, primarily around two sets of issues: the legacy of the French Revolution and the tensions between public and private uses of forests. As Adolphe Thiers suggested in his refusal to sell forest lands in 1832: "Certainly a forest of a few thousand hectares would not be administered as well by a private individual as it would be under [public] control."[16] What emerged in the Restoration, then, was at once a highly politicized conception of forest ownership and a wide set of questions about its role as a public good.

When combined with the growing awareness of environmental devastation wrought by deforestation, the political context of forest ownership generated a growing sense of urgency. An archetypal model of the high civil servant that emerged out of the Napoleonic era, Pierre-Henri Dugied, sounded the alarm. Born under the old regime, he rose to become prefect in multiple departments in the rural regions of southeastern France. Tending to his administrative duties with a scientific gaze on the region of the lower Alps, in 1819 Dugied echoed the work of Rougier de La Bergerie and Fabre to launch an administrative salvo on the disastrous situation of the forests: "Currently 430,613 hectares are lying fallow in the department of the Basses Alps; this is more than half of its territory. In the past, the majority of these 430,613 hectares were covered in forest." He then concluded, sparking one of the most ambitious regulatory projects of the postrevolutionary period: "It is time to remedy this state of affairs; it is time to recreate the past."[17]

Like his administrative predecessors, Dugied did not simply regret the destruction of forests out of old-regime nostalgia or because of the potential loss of resources for industrial and public power. It was also the very real environmental consequences that he vehemently deplored. While Dugied penned an important and influential essay, his work built on a growing awareness of the role of forests in protecting against erosion and atmospheric conditions. By the time of the Revolution, it was widely accepted that forests played a key role in soil enrichment and cleaning the atmosphere, marking the birth of a new age of "arboreal necessity," as Andrée Corvol calls it.[18] This necessity manifested itself through an awareness of the positive relationship between humans, human communities, and woods. In cities, one witnessed the growing obsession with planting trees as well as a new awareness of their role in improving conditions for human life. Dugied's book marked an attempt to rethink administrative regulation in light of growing pressures and attentiveness to the role of trees in preserving the health of the nation. He was not alone. By the 1820s, administrators, politicians, scientists, and others progressively recognized that deforestation was a major public concern. They acknowledged that the destruction of forests created desertlike mountain valleys covered in nothing but rocks from one end to the other. A lack of trees led to massive washouts, mudslides, and floods, leaving entire communes without fertile soil and natural protections from extreme weather.

The growing attention to forests was manifest in a journal titled *Annales forestières* (*Forest Annals*). The monthly review insisted that "it is incontestable that the question of forests in France is one of the most vital questions of the age."[19] The first article published in the 1842 issue, "Reforesting the Mountains: The Alps and the Pyrenees," opened with an alarming assessment: "We were terrified by the deforestation and the nakedness. Everywhere we looked, the sides of the mountains were bare and crisscrossed with ravines."[20] This publication put steady pressure on public opinion and the government in favor of new forms of protection and increased resources for forest management.

Annales forestières was just one voice among many. Works from a wide range of authors contributed to public awareness. Charles Lardy recounted the extraordinary devastation wreaked by storms on the other side of the Alps, in the Swiss cantons of Grisons, Tessin, and the Valais. On August 27, 1834, Lardy recounted how unusual heat had melted all the mountain snow from that year and previous years, and even portions of the glaciers. When a terrible storm ripped through these cantons on the night of 26–27 August, unprecedented volumes of water rushed down the mountain. Without the forest trees to slow the racing waters, entire villages were submerged. Some of these villages were still recovering when the disasters repeated themselves with equal force on September 15 and 16, and then again on October 5 and 6, 1839. Over the course of his inquiry, Lardy realized that one of the essential problems with combating these disasters was that, in his terms, there was almost no forest regulation in many of these cantons. "Measures of regulatory police must be taken in the forests in order to stop the destruction," he demanded.[21]

Perhaps the most important and influential work on this question was Alexandre Surell's *Étude sur les torrents des Hautes-Alpes*.[22] An engineer of the Ponts et Chaussées like Fabre, Surell spent two years observing the impact of deforestation in the Alps in the mid-1830s. Signaling the book's importance, the minister of the interior, Jules Armand Stanislas Dufaure, ordered that the book be published with the support of the ministry in 1841. The book's ambition was to uncover the cause of the torrents and washouts that plagued wide portions of the French Alps and to raise public awareness. "Is it not high-time that public opinion be alarmed?" Surell exclaimed. The problem, he insisted, was to understand why the destructive force of floods had radically increased since the late eighteenth century. "Why should there be new torrents?" he asked, arguing that this problem could only be satisfactorily understood by reckoning with the human impact on the environment. In his view, the acceleration of floods in these regions was clearly not a natural evolution of the landscape. "Could the terrain have changed its form or nature on its own?" he queried. No, he responded: "It is obvious that some foreign circumstances have intervened, modifying the primitive conditions." He then drew the obvious conclusion: "Everywhere one sees new torrents, there are no forests, and everywhere one sees recently deforested areas, new torrents have formed." He continued, "Wherever the woods have been cleared, the soil has been carried off by waters." Surell further insisted that "this great department is rushing toward its ruin," condemning the fact that "the administration, which has the duty to oversee the conservation of its territory, has done nothing to prevent this disastrous fate." So the cause of such dangerous processes of deforestation was as evident for Surell as it had been for Lardy; it was the "cuts made within regulatory police that have opened clearings across the forests."[23]

These lapses in regulatory execution also had other, even more pernicious effects. As horrible and destructive as mudslides, washouts, and torrents were, for many they were secondary to a deeper more fundamental and dangerous consequence of deforestation: climate change. Many had noted that the weather seemed susceptible to increasingly radical swings since the Revolution: the winters of 1789, 1792, and 1822; the drought of 1800; the infamous year without a summer in 1816; and the horrible winter of 1821.[24] Emmanuel

Le Roy Ladurie has noted multiple meteorological crises in the first half of the nineteenth century which led to grain crises in 1811, 1816–17, 1830, and 1846–48.[25] Such drastic shifts in weather were not only psychologically unsettling but had a direct impact on the availability of food supply, causing panic and political unrest. While the variability of harvests due to difficult weather was as old as agriculture itself, a new awareness and concern developed during this period on long-term climatic trends and anthropogenic change. Such erratic weather was increasingly seen to be part of a larger trend in changing climate patterns resulting from human action: "Climate was no longer understood as a site, as a given, but as a range of dynamic processes that join together to produce the character of a place."[26] This novel conception of the climate therefore also opened the possibility that humans could play a role in its transformation, in this case through relentless deforestation. Scientists and politicians began focusing on this theme as unsettled weather patterns confirmed the sense that something profound was happening meteorologically. Already in 1802, one of the founding fathers of modern ecology, François-Antoine Rauch, had decried the impact of deforestation on climate deregulation.[27] But by the 1820s the question had become a sufficiently mainstream preoccupation so that in 1825, the Royal Academy of Brussels sponsored an essay contest on the question, asking: "What are the changes that massive deforestation on neighboring lands and communes may have on the temperature, the cleanliness of the air, the direction and violence of winds, the abundance and location of rain which provides running water, and in general everything that constitutes our current physical state?"[28]

The winner of the competition was Alexandre Moreau de Jonnès.[29] By the Restoration, Jonnès already had his own colorful history as a former revolutionary (close to Jean-Lambert Tallien), military man, and high-seas adventurer during the empire, and finally as a statistician and polymath during the Restoration and July Monarchy.[30] As he settled into his new role as a state-sponsored scientist in the Restoration, Jonnès noted that from 1792 to 1815 the forests had been reduced by more than 1,124 leagues, from 3,337 to 2,213, or by almost a third. At this rate, he argued, "it will take little more than a half-century for all of the forests of the kingdom to disappear."[31] While he recognized that numerous studies already highlighted this decline as well as the importance of forests for the wealth of the country, he lamented that "we have not attempted to establish in precise terms its impact on atmospheric conditions." In particular, Jonnès was interested in the impact of deforestation on "the temperature of place; the frequency and quantity of rain; atmospheric humidity; the origins of river water; winds and the clarity of the air; the fertility of the soil; and the social state of peoples."[32] Jonnès then concluded that deforestation had a profound effect on all these elements of the climate. He observed, for example, the radical difference in temperatures at similar latitudes in regions with forests and those without. From this he drew conclusions about the change of climate over time: "It is possible to assert, through numerous testimonies, that the lands which today are entirely deforested were once filled with trees, and that the destruction has changed their climate."[33] Convinced that climate change did not happen in just one lifetime, he looked to examples from ancient, medieval and Renaissance literature. He noted that Ovid's accounts suggested that temperatures must have been more than eight degrees lower than they were at the time he was writing.[34] Jonnès's conclusions were unambiguous: the unprecedented destruction of forests was radically transforming almost every aspect of the climate, including annual temperatures, humidity, rainfall, air quality, winds, and soils.

Jonnès was certainly not alone in his assessment. The early utopian socialist Charles Fourier took great pains to sound the alarm of environmental destruction and climate change at the hands of greedy capitalists and a corrupting "civilization" responsible for "the material deterioration of our Planet that is leading to its obvious decline."[35] Fourier argued that the destruction should have been of primary interest to the French, and to Europeans more generally, since "the temperature has been changing rapidly, the excesses have become common, and the agriculture has been subjected to regular losses."[36] The problem, he insisted, was the refusal to recognize the role of human beings and what he referred to as the ravages of "civilization" in this destruction.[37] "Skeptics ask: How could a pygmy such as man influence a colossus like the Earth? My response is that the assumption that we are pygmies is inexact, that the egg shell is larger than the egg, and that the humankind that surrounds it and exploits the globe is truly greater than the planet itself."[38] The "harmony" that was so dear to Fourier's social vision had been unsettled not only economically and socially but environmentally as well by the same greed and barbarism. Even if it were decided that an eighth of the land should be left to the forests, he asserted, half would be destroyed anyway "as had been done in France where the majority of the woods now cover only 1/18 of the territory." For Fourier, this exploitation and "climatic disorder was a vice inherent in civilized culture," which was subject "to the struggles of individual interest against the collective interest."[39] Indeed, the destruction of the woods and its climatic impact were signs that civilization was incapable of self-regulating without his principles.

The republican scientist, savant, and politician François Arago similarly insisted on the climatic impact of forests. "The forests necessarily have a noticeable influence on the temperature of surrounding areas," he asserted, concluding that "the destruction of forests necessarily leads to a modification of the climate."[40] The medical doctor from Montpellier, Joseph Fuster, concurred in his *Des changements dans le climat de la France: Histoire de ses revolutions météorologiques* (1845) that climate change was taking place.[41] He maintained that the climate had been deteriorating in the north and the south of France since the seventeenth century. This change, he recognized, was no doubt part of a natural process, but "nature and man have worked relentlessly together to speed up these changes."[42] One observer in the Finistère similarly lamented that "in recent years, significant alterations in old climatological conditions have been noted: the winters, though not colder, are less humid; the heat begins earlier and has been more and more constant." The Breton observer concluded that "among the causes that have an influence on the temperature, one must cite the deforestation of Brittany."[43] By 1848, there was wide ranging consensus within the scientific community that deforestation had impacted the environment. As one botanist, Émile Mouchon, confirmed in his dictionary on exotic vegetation: "Such has been the impact of progress in agriculture that France itself should bitterly deplore the unfortunate deforestation across a large share of its territory, which has rightly awakened the interest of savants and of the government."[44]

As Mouchon noted, amid this generalized concern about human agency in climate change, scholars and increasingly government stood in broad agreement that not only forests but deforestation were an urgent *public* problem. While forests had been essential to questions of the public interest since the old regime, a growing awareness of the consequences of deforestation changed the very terms in which the problem was framed. It was no longer a question of simply managing a resource effectively for the good of the prince and the state. It was now a question of managing the complex interplay of private property, state prosperity, and the long-term effects of environmental devastation. This new attention required a shift from simply enforcing laws and regulations to a new, more historical and sociological understanding of the relationship between human communities and forests. Dugied had insisted in his early work of 1819 that deforestation required a new relationship between private and public power. "This is a public *interest* of the first order," he contended. "If you agree with me that what I am describing is a reality, then I ask if it is not sufficiently important that we force property owners ... to bend their particular interests to greater considerations."[45] Jonnès similarly insisted that addressing the problem of deforestation and climate change should play a central role in what he referred to as a "public economy" bound to the improvement of "society." "The conservation and expansion of the mountain and planted forests that are essential to prevent this destruction are indispensable measures of public economy for modern society," he argued.[46] And Surell stated in no uncertain terms that "while we grant that these measures may temporarily impose sacrifices on a few private individuals or communes, should such annoyances which weigh upon a few private interests, and will only be momentary, outweigh the general interest?" He then concluded: "It is to the state that [property owners] look to solve long-term problems; it is for the state to nobly carry through its mission; it is up to the state to be alarmed and look for solutions in those areas where the present generation is absorbed in its daily tasks and neither plans nor has any concern for the future."[47]

The government certainly was not deaf to these cries in the name of the public interest. Not only did the Ministry of the Interior republish Surell's book, but it also commissioned a group of scientists, administrators, and political economists to investigate the problem of deforestation in French mountains.[48] In response to Minister of Finance Jean Lacave-Laplagne's request for a commission to inquire into the state of French forests, the political economist Adolphe-Jerome Blanqui delivered the committee's report, which opened: "Finally the cry of the distress by our fellow citizens in the Alps has been heard.... This cry, in keeping with the devastation, has not been without its own echo across the state, and the state has responded that the time of reparations has finally come." Blanqui declared the urgent nature of the situation: "We have no time to waste, or in fifty years from now, France will be isolated from Piedmont by a desert just as Egypt is separated from Syria."[49] His report is filled with arguments and language about the public interest and the necessity of state intervention: "It is in the interest of the state"; "No private individual is wealthy enough to defend such property"; "We are always brought back to the intervention of the state"; "Only the state is powerful enough to look over the future and ensure the advances necessary for our posterity"; "Only the lasting state is in a position to create durable things."[50] The answer, in Blanqui's words, was to be found in the public power's ability to regulate and protect the general human and environmental interest, even if it meant overstepping into the private sphere. If the changing nature of the climate and the massive damage to the environment was indeed the work of man, then only the state "was capable of matching the enemy, with the hope of conquering it."[51]

So while there was nothing radically new in the idea of the public interest, it was the object and degree of the public intervention that had changed. Deforestation and its environmental and climatic consequences became a crucial public concern because they stretched beyond regulation for the creation of a more well-ordered and prosperous state. Deforestation threatened the livelihoods of individuals and potentially the national economy, but more importantly, it also threatened French "society." From agricultural production to the provision of wood for the construction of ships and, later, railroad lines, the fabric of the modern nation seemed to be running up against the greed and avarice of private individuals, a growing industrial demand for wood and its by-products, and the environmental destruction arising from the inability to properly regulate in favor of public needs. It was precisely in this supposed high moment of European liberalism and capitalist expansion that calls for new modes of regulation in the name of the public interest over private property were formulated, raising a whole range of important questions about the responsibilities of government. The result of this call for regulatory action against ecological disaster was a comprehensive attempt to update a wide set of legal technologies that had existed for centuries. The forests of France and Europe had hardly been ignored by the tentacular and far-reaching regulatory powers of the old regime state. Indeed, there was a long tradition, reaching back in some cases to the Middle Ages, of forest regulations and use-rights. The question in this age of environmental emergency, however, concerned how these old regulations would be rewritten in the service of a public power that would be up to the pressing task of dealing with environmental disaster.

A New Forest Regulation

In this postrevolutionary context, the new mix of scientific understanding of anthropogenic climate change, conceptions of public and private power, and regulatory capacity shifted the ground on which forest administration was being elaborated. So if in one sense the age-old problem of maintaining order in the forests, which had been present since the Middle Ages and had been codified by Colbert in 1669, continued to provide an important foundation for future regulatory thinking, there was a whole range of new problems that forced a reconceptualization of these traditional forms of regulatory police.

First, if forest police powers were no longer merely a question of maintaining order and ensuring the wealth of the prince—and therefore an old-regime "pastoral" conception of the public good bound to the princes' ability to ensure the health and safety of his flock—but were instead a question of preserving the environment and preventing climatic change for a public that actively made demands on itself and therefore the government, then merely updating the old system of the police powers for maintaining order was clearly inadequate. Moreover, the very relationship between the public and the private had been transformed since the final decades of the old regime. The back-and-forth between regulation and deregulation between Louis XV and Louis XVIII had politicized the question of what private individuals had a right to do with private and communal forested lands. In such a context, a simple renewal of the old-regime-style regulatory system for the forests, even under the brothers of Louis XVI, was impossible. In short, the growing scientific and political awareness of these administrative questions made them pressing just as the administrative legacy of the old regime, the Revolution, and the empire remained overlapping and conflictual.

We now have an extensive literature on the early modern history of the police powers. Growing out of the late medieval construction of the state, and then largely codified under the old regime, the police ensured the power to "govern man and do him good."[52] Reaching into almost every range of social life from weights and measures to the sale of grain, urban reform, and the press, the regulatory police powers became a central feature of early modern governance. As Paolo Napoli has highlighted, the police powers were a deeply pragmatic conception of governance, focusing on the ends of governance above all.[53] "From the perspective of law, the state is the institutional manifestation of a political community of free and equal persons," Markus Dubber has argued. But from the perspective of police, the state "seeks to maximize the welfare of his—or rather its—household."[54] Martin Loughlin has similarly highlighted this distinction suggesting that the "relationship between police power and law would eventually become a critical issue in the framing of modern governmental powers."[55] Similarly, works by Steven Kaplan, Philippe Minard, Vincent Milliot, Vincent Denis, Catherine Denys, Paolo Napoli and many others have revealed how the extraordinary regulatory powers of the police underwent a massive transformation in the decades leading up to and during the Revolution.[56] Indeed, the history of the police in these last years of the old regime and the Revolution was hardly unidirectional. As Kaplan has shown in the realm of grain and bread, for example, the last half of the eighteenth century witnessed a series of attempts at liberalization followed by new attempts to return to police regulation, all before the Revolution, challenging any supposed distinction between "free markets" and "regulatory police" for most of the actors, either in theory or in practice.[57] This fluidity raised the ideological, political, and cultural stakes of regulation, feeding court politics, urban dissatisfaction, and peasant revolts.

Forests sat at the center of these debates on regulatory police. When Colbert called for the elaboration of a forest code, completed in 1669, he built on years of administrative investigation into France's forest cover. He noted in 1663 that he "knew of no other matter in which there was greater disorder than in the royal forests."[58] Typical of the police powers of the old regime, the code reached into almost every conceivable aspect of forest activity from gathering to planting to cutting, regulating five key areas: jurisdiction and competence, the police and rights of different tribunals and authorities within the administration of the waters and forests, details of the police regulation necessary for their conservation and improvement, the portions currently owned by the king, and the punishments and fines to be applied.[59] The code became a central pillar in the great set of ordinances of the old regime, contributing to what was considered by many in the nineteenth century to have established the foundations of the French administrative state.[60] Forests even had their own "exceptional courts," the *eaux et forêts*, where infractions were judged and new decisions made.[61] Michelle Vovelle thus concluded that, "at least since Colbert, the Forest was a problem of State."[62]

Like other aspects of old regime police, the forest code confronted the deregulating ambitions of the late eighteenth century. In his *De l'ordre social*, for example, Guillaume-François Le Trosne leveled an ideal-typical physiocratic critique when he wrote: "We had plenty of wood for construction and far more than we have today, and the forests were better planted before they were regulated and governed by tribunals created to police them."[63] Le Trosne was just one among many voices against the forest code. In the last decades of the old regime, one heard regular critiques of the exceptional legal powers held by forest guards. In many cases, these complaints came from rural inhabitants themselves. "At the end of the eighteenth century and the beginning of the nineteenth," Martine Chalvet argues in her history of French forests, "this legislative arsenal was all the more difficult to enforce in that it was highly contested by all the nation's subjects: from the nobleman to the peasant, from the seigniorial officials to the parliamentarians, from the master of the forge to the physiocratic property owner."[64] It is no surprise, then, that the Constituent Assembly attacked the supposed abuses in the beginning of the Revolution. The law of December 25, 1790, removed the special jurisdiction of the forests and put them under the authority of regular courts. This was followed by the radical liberalization of the forest regulations with the law of September 29, 1791, and especially article 6: "The woods belonging to private individuals will no longer be subject [to these laws], and each property owner will be free to administer and dispose of them as he wishes."[65]

Creating what the legislators of the Restoration exaggeratedly referred to as an "unlimited liberty," the early years of the Revolution did reduce administrative intervention into privately owned forests. First, the regulations were no longer enforced by special jurisdictions or exceptional courts under the control of the forest guards and the administration. Moreover, in 1791 the legislative assembly had acquired a large share of the executive authority that had previously fallen under the authority of the king and his administration.

As a result, in the area of forest regulations the legislative assembly not only offered new liberties and fairer trials but also offered a glimpse of what a new, more popularly grounded administrative power might look like, since it was precisely the Constituent Assembly that had been delegated an important share of the administrative responsibilities necessary for managing the forests. Though this prototype of a less despotic administrative system was relatively short-lived, it did leave two important legacies. First, as Tocqueville would later note, the Constituent Assembly of 1791 offered the first example of taking administrative functions out of the hands of the executive and putting them into bodies of the state that were subject to greater popular pressures, like the legislature.[66] Second, it provided new opportunities for forest owners and private citizens to use their own property as they wished, largely outside the controls of regulatory police.

As with so many other realms of regulatory power, Napoleon attempted to reintroduce stricter administrative controls on the private use of forests. With the law of 9 floréal, year XI (April 29, 1803), he brought an end to the liberties introduced by article 6 of the law of September 1791. From this moment forward, it was necessary to ask for prefectural permission to cut trees in forests. But, as one commentator noted, this law extended restrictions on cutting down trees without administrative permission, but did not reinstate the prior penalties. As a result, the law remained without sanction.[67] Consequently, the impact of the imperial legislation on forests was relatively small. When the Restoration began to study the question, "the essential elements of the law of September 1791 and the decree that accompanied it had survived."[68] This left the new postrevolutionary Bourbon regime with both a legacy conflicted between revolutionary and imperial intentions, and a tremendous lack of clarity about how forest regulations were to be enforced and who was to enforce them. In his work on judicial authority of 1818, Henrion de Pansey asserted that "police regulations are those which are directly related to things which can be considered as common to all," adding that "the common things by their nature are air, fire, and water"[69]: all elements directly related to forests. In his *Dictionary of Modern Police*, published in 1823, P.-Julien Alletz made regular reference to the imperial regulations, even as few of them specified the actual mode of enforcement. For example, the opinion of the Conseil d'état of August 5, 1809, stipulated that "the forest administration is limited to overseeing that the holder of a 'majorat' acts as a paternal caretaker without destroying his property." At the same time, Alletz noted that "punishments of the ordinance of waters and forests of 1669 have been maintained."[70] The contradiction was patent: on the one hand, the liberal push toward deregulation had made each property owner a paternal caretaker to be protected from overzealous regulation or outside coercion. On the other hand, remnants of the seventeenth-century code existed, but were either unenforceable or outdated.

Across the second half of the eighteenth century and the first half of the nineteenth, this complex regulatory legacy mixed with another important tradition of regulatory police coming out of German states: cameral sciences. Built on the *Polizeiwissenschaft* tradition that had thrived in German states from the early modern period through the mid-nineteenth century, the cameral sciences had contributed an elaborate administrative science on forests.[71] As the cameralist Günther von Berg argued in 1802: "*Policey* is like a well-intentioned genius who carefully levels the way for those committed to his care, cleans the air that they breathe, secures the villages and holdings in which they dwell and the streets along which they walk, protects the fields that they cultivate, secures their homes against fire and flood, and they themselves against illness, poverty, ignorance, superstition, and immorality." He then concluded, "Its helping hand is ever-ready, and we are invisibly surrounded by its unceasing care."[72] Forests thus fell squarely within these preoccupations of "care" for populations. Moreover, the cameralist tradition contributed to a more "scientific" approach to forestry. In his history of the transformations of early modern police, Mark Raeff notes, "In the eighteenth century we have a more or less 'scientific' approach as the ordinances prescribed methods of building up the future lumber and forest reserves of the territory. The role of the foresters underwent a shift as well; it became more positive. No longer would the foresters merely guard and protect: they also had to initiate and supervise the methodical and rational building up of future fuel and lumber resources."[73] This shift from mere guarding and protecting to a positive caretaking role ensured a privileged place for the cameral tradition of regulating forests.

The German administrative scientific approach to forests found an audience in France during the Revolution, thanks to a host of Germans who either came to France during the Revolution or worked for France in regions conquered by Napoleon.[74] This importation contributed to a rethinking of regulatory power and the public interest in forests. The *Annales forestières*, discussed earlier, for example, was patterned on similar German publications and designed to "develop an original conception that aimed to adapt lessons of German forestry to the natural and political conditions of French forests."[75] Because forest science brought with it a sophisticated understanding of the nature of forest management—as opposed to the rule-and-order model of Colbert's forest code—the German tradition helped reshape the administrative state, combining the "natural" and the "political" as part of a modern regulatory power.

Signs of a new, more elaborate understanding of forest environments could be seen across forest science in France.[76] The first texts used to teach forestry were by German authors, in particular Georg-Ludwig Hartig.[77] As the translator of Hartig's works, Jacques-Joseph Baudrillart, argued in his own treatise on forests: "We hope to penetrate into the physical and natural sciences on which they depend, and apply to their exploitation the three branches of public economy [*économie publique*] with which they are concerned: the principles of jurisprudence, police, and administration."[78] The innovation was a combination of jurisprudence, policing, and administration and a new scientific approach to forestry. This new interest in forest science led to the creation of the first school of forestry in France, the school of Nancy, created in 1824 by Bernard Lorentz. With an early student, Adolphe Parade, Lorentz wrote one of the first books of forestry in France under the heavy influence of the German forest science tradition. Of course, Lorentz and Parade remained convinced of the importance of that tradition, recognizing in the preface to their first edition in 1837 that "without a doubt, it would be impossible to write on the culture of forests without drawing from the works of German authors." At the same time, they insisted on the specificities of the French case: "A German work always has the double inconvenience of not taking into consideration the current state of our forests, because of how they have been treated up to present, and of being inapplicable, in a number of ways, to the French soil and climate, as well as the needs of its inhabitants and its government."[79] Founders of French forestry during this period, Lorentz and Parade broke new ground by seamlessly combining an attention to soil and climate with an attention to inhabitants and problems of government. Perhaps most important was their emphasis on politics; in France, forest regulation was also a political issue.

With these innovations, the idea of regulation as an administrative practice and the new understanding of the forests themselves had shifted dramatically: from Absolutist administrative intervention to liberalization, and finally to scattered attempts to reestablish regulatory effectiveness through an international scientific movement. Hence, by 1823, preliminary studies were being launched for a new forest code. When the bill came to the floor for discussion in the French legislative body, the Chamber of Deputies, in 1827, it was explicitly presented as an attempt to overcome the excessive liberalization of the revolution while updating older forms of regulatory police. "The conservation of the forests is one of the first interests of society, and as a result, one of the great duties of government," explained the Vicomte de Martignac, who presented the bill to the Chamber. "All necessities of life are bound to its conservation."[80] While the language had an antiquarian old-regime ring to it, the ambitions would prove to be unquestionably modern.

In his defense of the bill, Martignac first needed to explain how regulating the forests under a postrevolutionary Bourbon monarchy combined the great administrative tradition of monarchy with a new respect for private property inherited from the early years of the Revolution. A new, more effective regulatory system was to operate under administrative principles established by the Empire, while also providing the guarantees of a constitutional monarchy. In this regime, Martignac argued, "the limit has been clearly drawn between the different powers and institutions" of the state.[81] "Today, royal authority has been established on more positive foundations." He therefore began by consciously recognizing that the radical changes in the history of forest regulation since the seventeenth century posed a specific set of problems in a postrevolutionary context. In particular, the Code of 1669 had "tied together administration and jurisdictional power. . . . These powers of the police, repression and conservation were grounded in their control over legal courts and the administrative instruments" necessary to manage them.[82] In other words, regulations, enforcement, and penalties were all covered under one common administrative system. While some statutes and many of the punishments—such as bodily torture!—were clearly outdated, many key regulations, especially over private lands, and all special jurisdictional powers of the forest administration had been removed during the Revolution. Martignac showed how the law of September 29, 1791, therefore subtracted many of the most elaborate regulatory powers through the establishment of a more general set of laws, while also removing any special enforcement that had characterized the use of forests under the old regime. The result, explained Martignac in terms that could be applied to much of the regulatory organization of France in the Restoration, was that "we find ourselves today between incoherent remains of an old legislation which has been turned on its head, and the beginnings of a new legislation that is little more than a sketch."[83]

One of the great contributions of the new regulatory regime was a clearer division between legislative and administrative powers. The new system was to allow for generalized legislative rule setting through an elected Chamber of Deputies on all issues of public and private property, procedure, punishment, and prohibitions. At the same time, however, the administrative agents were to be able to act independently, "leaving to the government the ability to modify and improve the internal administration of the forests and benefit from the useful lessons of everyday experience."[84] The new forest code left ample room for both the parliamentary elaboration of just laws and administrative action and intervention. Martignac concluded that one of the key ambitions of the new regulatory authorities was their ability to operate under the legal guarantees established by a constitutional regime, which were the legacy of 1791, while granting the authority and flexibility necessary for regulating the public domain.

Beyond a new balance between administration and rule of law, the Revolution had also left another important legacy within the forests: deregulation and the new relationship it introduced between public authority and private individual rights. It was broadly believed in the Restoration and the July Monarchy that the forest policies of the Revolution had been too "liberal." In his *Treatise on Rural and Forest Legislation* of 1824, for example, Louis Cappeau regretted "the unlimited liberty granted by article 6 of the law of 29 September 1791, which leaves people subject to the whims of those who preceded them, while also binding future generations."[85] In 1827, Martignac decried "the inconvenience of unlimited liberty" left as a legacy by the Revolution.[86] It was perhaps Michelet who best captured the (overstated) consequences of Revolutionary forest legislation when he wrote:

> During the Revolution, all barriers fell: the poor joined together in the destruction. They climbed, with fire and spades in hand, up to the eagle's nest; they cultivated the abyss, hanging by a rope. The trees were sacrificed to most banal uses; two pines were felled to make a pair of clogs. At the same time, the little livestock, multiplied infinitely throughout the forest, hurting the trees, the small trees, the young sprouts, and devouring hope. The goats above all, the animal of those who possess nothing, the adventurous animal who lives on the commons, became the instrument of demagogical invasion.[87]

Hence, re-regulating while balancing private and public interests was a fundamental ambition of the postrevolutionary code.

This new balance required a redefinition of the "public interest." Achieving it was the principal question that occupied the representatives throughout the legislative debates. First, a redefinition of public power pushed them to redefine the foundations of administrative powers necessary to enforce a new code. Most importantly, it forced them to elaborate what should fall under the realm of the public: "Unfortunately, private interests, that is, those whose direct immediate action is felt with the greatest power and empire, are frequently in opposition to the great interests of the country, and the laws that protect it are all too often powerless."[88] The idea of a public power was necessary even as it was changing. If regulatory police had long been associated with the public good over private interest, what changed in this period was an emphasis on public problems which needed also to consider private rights. As M. Avoine de Chantereine argued, "This code must establish what is most useful, and prevent anything that does harm to public order and the rights of a third party, as well as defend against anything which is unjust or harmful.

It must remain within common law anytime that special legislation does not require it to stray, and modify the general organization of laws necessary due to the imperious exception necessary for the prosperity and conservation of the forests."[89] For Chantereine, the obligation to maintain public order required a host of new capacities. Most importantly, it necessitated a defense of law while authorizing exceptional interventions on behalf of the public good. Integrating the legacy of the old regime and the revolution therefore required a more variable and complex notion of public authority based on principles of administrative intervention. In the service of the public, the forest code had to walk the fine line between avoiding despotic administrative intervention and maintaining room for exceptional actions in the name of the public interest. The result was an increasingly robust, ends-oriented conception of the public good grounded in the tension between regulatory police and legal justice. "The forests were presented as a social and ecological necessity, that is, as a good of public utility that only a general and long-term authority could protect, since it remained, in theory, independent of private interests and short-term market fluctuations. In this moment of floods and natural catastrophes, the state was the sole guarantor of security and the public good, with an obligation to intervene."[90]

Notably, the expansion of regulatory police in the name of the public interest necessarily required a more elastic and contextual understanding of how administrative intervention related to the law. The code, argued the representatives, had to grant sufficient freedom to administrators so that they could respond to particular circumstances in the name of the public interest. The deputies therefore provided a battery of arguments designed to grant greater administrative authority in the name of pragmatically serving the public interest: "It is impossible to determine any general statutes on this point"; "In all things there are necessities that create a course of events to which we must submit in practice"; "We cannot determine within a law the specific periods [for certain activities] as was the case with the ordinance of 1669. This is an administrative affair."[91] If the administrative officials were to serve the public interest, their actions could not all be determined in advance, but had to be grounded in a robust notion of social obligation. "This is the price for a society that guarantees its members safety and property. This is the sacrifice of the interests of each individual for the interests of all. . . . The question of a general interest, the question of public utility is, in reality, the only thing to be considered. This principle may not be contested."[92]

At least one representative had a name for this kind of system, in which legally protected private rights had to be balanced with the public interest.

Defending the balance between public intervention and respect for private property, he argued that there were two ways of understanding private forest rights. On the one hand, there was the "English"—or what he also called the "aristocratic"—system, in which one had certain rights, such as estover, based on private property. If one did not have land, in such a system one had no such rights. France, however, functioned under a different system, inherited from the Revolution, one that he referred to as "democratic." In this system, one had rights as an individual member of a community instead of as a property owner. In the French or "democratic" system, every individual had a right, but such a right was granted because one was a member of society. Unlike the "aristocratic" rights grounded in the singularity of one's possession, democratic rights were guaranteed to people as members of the state. In his work on the history of private property (1839), the jurist Édouard Laboulaye similarly argued that in "aristocratic" societies, where "the family is the political unit of the state," no particular individual in the family has property rights. Instead, the rights are passed from one generation to the next in the name of the family, along with the rights that the property guarantees them. The French system, however, was fundamentally different, he argued: "In relation to property, it is not difficult to ascertain, complete liberty for the person . . . in a word, and to summarize, individual democratic legislation."[93] This conception of democracy established the groundwork for a new mode of administrative intervention. In the words of one historian of the forests and the state in the eighteenth century, Gérard Buttoud: "If the Revolution marked an important date in the juridical and spatial definition of the modern forest, it is because for the first time it elaborated the forests in terms of property. The forests, which had up to that point belonged to a social body as a whole and were practically the space for the exercise of overlapping usages where one use dominated, could now be understood as a private space."[94] However, if the rights were vested not in the property itself but in the individual who owned it, then public authority had a different responsibility in ensuring the conservation both of the land itself and of those individuals who might own it in the future. Public power needed to defend the property of private individuals and to protect the very land they owned in the name of a larger social interest.[95] What Laboulaye referred to as a democratic system therefore pushed this question of forest administration onto a suppler and more variable conception of individual rights grounded in the public interest. In the realm of forests, the primary ambition of such a democratic system was to establish a new forest administration that would oversee usage of the forests with renewed vigor by balancing administrative prerogative with the demands of public rights.

Weapons of the Weak: Law and Administration

As we have seen, if forests had been the object of regulatory police for centuries, the emergence of a new awareness of anthropogenic climate change and the deregulating ambitions of the Revolution fundamentally altered the terms upon which any potential new regulation could take place. In at least one fundamental sense, the discovery of human-driven environmental change ushered in a new framework for thinking about regulatory power. It was now necessary to protect an imperiled environment to guarantee the well-being of those who benefited from its abuse. Legislators and scientists understood that giving in to the short-term demands of absolute individual rights or customary community usage in the present meant the destruction of the environment and thus any ability to ensure the communities' welfare in the future. Paradoxically, protecting the lands that individuals and communities owned—that is, the foundation of their liberty—suddenly also required restricting their free use of private and communal property. This was largely a problem of temporality: protecting the environment required making decisions that would over the long term serve the individuals who lived there *and* guarantee their livelihood. In the short term, however, it threatened their livelihoods by restricting and regulating their access to some of the essential resources of their community. Such protection required a public authority that stepped far deeper into the realm of the private at the same time as it needed to respect some of the fundamental legal foundations of the postrevolutionary polity grounded in individual liberty.

The cries for action against deforestation continued alongside more rigorous processes of controlling forests in the public interest. These calls, as we have seen, came largely from Paris, gaining steam in the 1830s and 1840s. Inspired by the works of Dugied, Surell, Blanqui, and others, the *Annales forestières* continued to support the new efforts of the administration to regulate the forests and the cause of forestry in France. As the first issue of 1842 explained: "We now recognize that theory can only emerge out of practice, and that an appreciation of effects is the only way to discover causes. It is experience, observation of facts—in a word, practice—that will lead the forest economy to make progress."[96] The *Annales forestières* insisted on the importance of practice for the development of forest administration and its primary goal of preventing the ravages of deforestation. In turn, it assigned blame for the difficulty of improving the forest lands to "the flaws in surveillance, the infidelity, and often the collaboration of those who are charged with preventing the abuses" and "the greed of property owners of the flocks. . . . Their desire to increase their numbers is responsible for the excesses we see today.

It is speculation alone that destroys the mountains."[97] The more effective the administration was, the more guards there were, the better they were trained, the better they were paid, and the more they would be able to prevent the immoderations of forest dwellers.

Unsurprisingly, the path toward preservation and reforestation was hardly smooth. Indeed, there was resistance on the ground due to stricter enforcement of regulations as early as 1827. The task of enforcement, which challenged the immediate livelihood of many of the poorest populations of rural France, raised a new and very difficult issue: how to bring the populations themselves into the process of redefining administrative power to prevent abuses by new regulatory agencies.

The new regulations were designed to give proper authority to forest guards to prevent a whole range of practices—from the cutting of trees to create more arable land to "jardinage" (a process of cutting the largest low branches on trees in a forest) and the use of forests for pasturing. For example, the code established that, barring some special dispensation, stricter controls were necessary on the grazing of goats or sheep in communal forests, since they not only ate forest cover but also decimated tree bark and weakened especially young trees. The challenge, of course, was that such restrictions directly undermined the livelihoods of these communities without offering any clear alternative. Within months of the establishment of the new code, resistance, protest, and violent opposition broke out across the nation's mountain woods among populations who depended on these lands for their livelihood. Between 1828 and 1850, the new forest administration and its forest code were confronted by peasants and local populations who acted locally—oftentimes against forest guards—but whose impact was ultimately national. The populations of the Pyrenees in the south, the Massif Central in the center, the Alps and the Vosges in the east, and Britany in the west, among others, rose up in various modes of everyday resistance. In some cases these actions outnumbered the more famous urban uprisings of these years. For example, in 1848 forest movements in the east and in the Pyrenees involved more people than the urban revolts in the spring of 1848, requiring the mobilization of sixty thousand soldiers to restore order.[98]

The War of the Demoiselles (Maidens) in the Pyrenees, which hit its peak between 1829 and 1831 and continued into the middle of the nineteenth century, was no doubt one of the most famous of these legendary revolts, in which men dressed as women to challenge the forest guard's authority and assert their traditional claims to forest rights. As Peter Sahlins notes, essential elements of these revolts were claims to maintain traditional practices and modes of forest administration: "The peasant communities claimed the right to take firewood and pasture in the forests within their boundaries, and some outside them. More importantly, they claimed their right to exploit these forests according to their own practices of production, not those of the forest administration; and finally, they claimed the authority to exercise sovereignty over the forests, to police, in the Old Regime sense of the word as 'administer,' the forests by themselves."[99] They were also revolting against the increasing abuses of the "ironworks," which were devastating the forests through the need for wood coal.

But the enigmatic Demoiselles were not alone. Resistance against the guards and implementation of new forest regulations increased at a steady pace from 1827 onward. In 1841 alone, at least four "affairs" made their way into the press. A forest guard named Schwarz, in the county of Haslach near Strasbourg, was fired at on July 25, 1841, by a game poacher who then disappeared. Schwarz, a forest guard of more than twenty years, supposedly fell into the arms of his wife, who was walking with him. He died, leaving the woman with their ten children. The shooter, discovered to be a man named Rodong, was soon declared guilty and sentenced to death.[100] In the Pyrenees, on March 7, 1841, a similar crime took place; a forest guard named Cabos in the canton of Tarbes was assassinated. Dominique Clarens Pegeot and Bertrand Clarens Menjoulet were accused of the murder. In the trial that followed, only Dominique was accused, and the jury provided a lenient sentence in his favor, claiming attenuating circumstances.[101] In the upper Alps in the commune of Nibles, a forest inspector named Ailhaud disappeared on November 24, 1841. The body was discovered in a ravine, covered over with leaves in what appeared to be murder. A full investigation of the site and numerous clues indicated that Ailhaud had been hit in the head with a hatchet when he surprised his aggressors. It appeared that he had put one knee on the ground to write their names. Two local men named Burle and Blanc were suspected, arrested, and confessed. Their trial in the lower Alps condemned Burle to a life of hard labor, and Blanc, as an accomplice, was given ten years of hard labor.[102] A similar struggle between a forest guard and local populations in the Alps, near Saint-Pons, took place when four men gathering wood were approached by a guard named Robin. The guard insisted they leave the illegally cut branches, but when he reached out to pick up the cords they were to leave behind, he was hit on the head with a stone, and then the assailants allegedly jumped on him, hitting him with an ax. The guard was left for dead, but was able to walk with a fractured skull to the hospital of Saint-Pons, where his life was saved.[103] In the Jura region in Mont-sous-Vaudrey, a guard named Bavilley came upon a local resident cutting branches of a thicket of three to four inches to make stakes. When asked to give his name and drop his billhook, the individual responded with threats. Soon the guard was surrounded, at which point he drew his gun and fired two shots at the men, grazing one of them. The men then attacked him with their billhooks. Bavilley drew his pistols; he killed one man, who had been holding him from behind, and injured another. The assailants then fled, and Bavilley fell to the ground, later making his way to the town hall of Mont-sous-Vaudrey.[104]

We are not without explanations for what motivated these revolts and acts of resistance. They were revolts by traditional peasant communities against new forms of capitalist modes of agricultural production backed by a predatory state,[105] and reactions to the destruction of a traditional moral economy that had existed outside state regulation, which was now being undermined by a new legal logic of capitalism.[106] Bringing the problem of climate change into the mix, however, challenges such readings of these "customary" practices. It seems reasonable to assume that there was genuine concern for the climatic changes and disastrous environmental impact of deforestation that had led to the new code of 1827. The challenge is that from an environmental historical perspective, the question of what was at stake in these peasant revolts looks somewhat different. There was undoubtedly, and simply, a process of criminalizing poverty in the widespread enforcement of these new regulations and denial of access to the fruits of the forest. But this was not the whole story.

During the first decades of the nineteenth century—no doubt due to the massive deregulation following the Revolution, the new demographic pressures (since peasants did not begin fleeing the mountains until after midcentury), and the growing demand for wood coal by industrialization and for modes of transportation like railroads—any possible ecological equilibrium for these forest dwellers was entirely shaken. Their traditional practices and claims to the forest had to change for these mountainous regions to be preserved and be able to preserve human communities over the long term. And yet these peasants depended on their previous practices for their livelihood. They therefore found themselves in a position that has unfortunately become all too familiar. It was the poor who were going to pay the price for the enforcement of new environmental regulations and controls. And yet, without such regulatory frameworks, the mountain terrains would continue to suffer, and, as many argued already at the time, the very environment on which people depended would be destroyed, and the climate along with it.

What came out of this conflict between the livelihoods of some of the poorest families in France and the need to reinforce the public good was a profoundly political debate on the very nature of the modern state and its regulatory powers that continued far beyond the mid-nineteenth century. At stake was not whether the peasants were part of an industrial capitalist system, which was still foreign to many of them. The question was how their communities would operate, how they would provide for themselves and their families in a system driven by industrial capitalism, *and* how the exigencies of the public good, which was also ultimately but not immediately their own, would be addressed. They were, in essence, encountering administration as a political problem.

The difficulties posed by this resistance were certainly not lost on the elites, even as they debated the question of deforestation behind the high walls of elite Parisian institutions. Blanqui, for example, argued for the administrative necessity of preventing deforestation by emphasizing long-term public interests, against the immediate demands of private owners and users, industrialists, and peasants alike. "Only the state is sufficiently powerful to care for the future and ensure posterity," he argued. "What can private individuals do with their small amounts of capital and their immediate needs to benefit within their short lives? The state, which lasts, is the only power able to create durable things. In the Alps, more than anywhere else, only the state is capable of confronting the enemy with the hope of taming it."[107] Blanqui's report before the Académie des sciences morales et politiques faced rigorous questioning by his colleagues who claimed to speak on behalf of the peasant communities. The political economist, politician, and Academy colleague Hyppolite Passy responded to Blanqui's argument:

> In order to restore and replenish the woods, to improve and consolidate the forests, it is necessary to immediately reduce the space granted to herds, which have become the only resource of these populations. And yet, is it possible that the communes will perform this act in an effective way? Will the local councils give their consent? This is highly doubtful. There would be immediate damage, and how to make them responsible for that which will make them suffer, and for which they will only be repaid in a distant future?[108]

The jurist and politician André Dupin offered a similar assessment:

> You think it will be easy to bring the local councils around and convince them to consent to your arrangements. Well! You do not know them; there are enormous difficulties in protecting their communal goods against their uses or bringing them toward sharing or a better mode of use. The government, thanks to the forest legislation, is authorized to buy pastures within the woods. Well! They often hesitate to exercise this right because one does not easily change the condition of populations, and in those places where you have a population of livestock farmers you do not easily turn them into a population of workers.... It would be a new principle of legislation to expropriate

people not according to public utility but in their interests, and to teach them to more effectively draw from their goods.... It will take a long time to change the habits of these populations.[109]

Joseph Portalis, son of the famous contributor to the Civil Code, defended with Blanqui against the opinions of Dupin and Passy. In his view, the populations were not as opposed to the restorative measures to prevent further deforestation and floods as his colleagues suggested. Moreover, he argued, the local councils were ready to support and execute these measures. "No doubt, reforestations will face some difficulties in the poorer communes, but it is necessary to enlighten them as to their true interests."[110]

This exchange was but a small piece of a much more elaborate debate and set of legal decisions on the forest code, in which the reactions of local communities were brought to bear on administrative regulation of the forests. Reactions to the enforcement of the forest code led to numerous trials in which the exact nature of this public power and how it could serve the public good were constantly discussed. André Dupin argued multiple cases as attorney general (*procureur général*) under Portalis's presidency in the Cour de Cassation. One of the most important cases he argued, which he referred to as "one of the most notable questions that can be posed within the context of civil law," was brought to the appeals court by eleven communes in Alsace on March 22 and 23 against the city of Hagenau and the prefect of the lower Rhine on use rights.[111] This case highlighted all the complexity of attempting to modernize forest police regulations in the postrevolutionary age. The communes that brought the case had enjoyed use rights over the forests of Haguenau since the thirteenth century. The forests were owned undivided by the city of Haguenau and the German emperor, who had given his rights to the Count of Hanau. The city and the count collected an annual payment in exchange for *forestage*, or use rights in the forests, by the eleven communes. The conquest of Alsace by Louis XIV in the seventeenth century, however, complicated this situation. Following the conquest, the Count of Hanau was reluctant to pay hommage to the French king. It was therefore also forbidden to pay the forest rights to a foreign king as long as there was some question of the count's allegiance. The problem was finally decided in 1773, when it was determined that the city and the French state (instead of the Count of Hanau) would no longer pay an annual sum, and that at the same time the use rights of the local inhabitants would be eliminated. While in theory this decision brought an end to centuries of use rights for the local peasants of the eleven communes, in actual practice the peasants continued to use the forests as pastures and for watering their animals. The case remained undecided during the Revolution, even as the eleven communes attempted to challenge the 1773 decision. With the code of 1827 and its enforcement, the problem came to a head. The city of Hanau attempted to restrict the peasants' usage, claiming that they had no formal proof of their use rights. The peasants responded that their continual use gave them the equivalent of a property right for pasturing and watering. In 1833 and 1834 the case was heard in Colmar, where the court decided in favor of the city against the peasants. It was appealed in Besançon in 1836, and then again, reaching the Cour de Cassation in 1842.

This was a case, Dupin argued, in which the regulation of forests touched on fundamental questions relating to the "three orders: the state, the communes, and private persons." Dupin regretted that he felt compelled to argue against the previous jurisprudence; but, he argued, "one must admit that for the most difficult questions, no one is beyond error." He began his argument by decrying the expropriation of peasant property and rights by communes through feudal power under the old regime. "If we study the documents of the period," he argued, "we see that following concessions made to peasants, principally to laborers in order to attract and help them settle on lands by giving them woods to build with and repair their homes, and pastures for their animals, as the population increased and the land acquired value, the lords then sought to take back the rights they had previously granted." Dupin regretted what he referred to as a "war" that took place between forest guards and these peasants as the powerful sought any and all means to unjustly "remove these users from the forests."[112]

At the heart of Dupin's argument was his observation that peasant use rights were in fact a form of property. Moreover, since the state had replaced the Count of Hanau as owner of the lands, it was actually acting not as a holder of public interest, but as a private property owner that had allowed for use rights up to the present. In this case, Dupin argued, "the state no longer acted as an administrator or a public power enforcing punishments against infractions; it was reduced to the role of property owner, and its adversary became its equal."[113] So while he recognized the necessity of regulatory police in the forests, in this case the state was not defending the public interest by taking use rights away from peasants. It was merely a private actor that had to respect the rights of those who had used the land for centuries. Dupin effectively reversed the relationship between the state, public order, and peasant use rights. "It is, in my opinion, a question of public order to protect; and when this property is not just that of a private individual, not just one commune, but eleven communes at a time, and twelve thousand people whose rights are called into question, it is also an issue of public order not to sacrifice these rights lightly."[114] Dupin then concluded his argument: "Is it not recommended to have some moderation in one's acts to avoid irritating the population... and is it not, in any case, more just to place the burden on [the forest guards] than to shift the burden onto the unfortunate users?"[115] Dupin's arguments were accepted, and the previous rulings were overturned. Moreover, he made regular arguments in favor of greater leniency on behalf of the peasants. In the cases he heard between 1836 and 1842, he systematically asked for a looser interpretation of the code in favor of the peasants. Dupin's claims reflected a fundamental concern about how forest regulations could be enforced in the midcentury amid the new environmental pressures. It may have been important to prevent deforestation, but one had to take care in removing potential use rights from peasants even if it was, in principle, for the public good.

There are signs that the leniency that Dupin argued for made its way into other administrators' understanding of their role. The district attorney of Prades in the eastern Pyrenees, for example, sent a message to the district attorney of Montpellier following the arrest of local individuals on July 26, 1848. The official from Prades opened his letter with a specific reference to the motivations behind the increasingly tight restrictions on uses of the forests: "I do not know if the national and communal forests of this arrondissement are sufficient to provide for everyone in the future all the wood necessary for heating and construction," he wrote, admitting that he did not think the administration had sufficiently studied the question. The problem, however, was that since stricter controls had been imposed, especially over the previous decade, the inhabitants no longer had the access to the woods necessary for their daily needs. An ordinance of 1846 prohibited them from allowing their animals to enter the zones to which they had previously had access. The local official insisted that with three months of winter left, they simply could not abide by these rules. He therefore argued that the fines of 107,000 francs leveled against the populations were unreasonable. Furthermore, he reminded his superior that the agents were hardly above reproach. Some of them abused their powers, taking out revenge on those they did not like. He concluded: "Whatever the context, citizen Procureur general, the aversion that our mountain inhabitants have always felt for the forest guards has increased in recent years, and has developed into full-fledged hate. The administrative agents have been considered tyrants in the country; when the revolution broke out, they were treated as such and chased out of their homes.... In general, a large crowd formed and walked to the home of the mayor. The mayor was then summoned to ask the guard to leave the commune."[116] A similar request on behalf of local populations was made by a representative from the lower Rhine to the minister of justice in 1849:

> It is hardly surprising that last year, in the midst of the Revolution, the populations who were caught up in misery and were looking to improve their sad situation allowed themselves some excesses in the forests by cutting some of the dead wood. For it is an established fact that the inhabitants of the lower Rhine were for a long time the absolute masters of the forests, and only cut down a very small number of green trees.... I believe that we would be performing a great act of justice and high politics if you accorded a full and total amnesty for all the forest infractions committed in this department.[117]

It would seem that those who revolted were often able to achieve concessions either through legal appeals or through the local, regional, or national administrations. As in the appeals court cases argued by Dupin, those who wanted to defend their use rights did have supporters within the administrative and the legal system. There was not, then, so much a traditional and latent antistatism in these forest communities as much as a deep politicization and an attempt to participate in shaping the regulations that impacted their daily lives.

The ability of the peasants to do this should hardly be overstated. Many more suffered the consequences than were able to shape the process. Nonetheless, the lineaments of a new kind of relationship were forming between an administration that defended a public interest and those people who were subject to it. These people wanted to have a say in shaping the public authority on which they increasingly depended to protect them even from themselves. They also wanted to shape how and when it could act on them. So for all that they learned to hate the forest guards, these were hardly grassroots antistatists. Peter Sahlins has pointed out, for example, that in the areas where the Demoiselles were most active, army recruitment was also most widely accepted.[118] Similarly, the idea that all forms of administration should be thrown out was anathema to peasants' conception of the forests. This is not to say that these mountain dwellers were ever enthusiastic about rules and regulations that prevented them from doing what they needed and wanted to do and in some cases had been doing for decades and even centuries. There are indicators that they recognized the ecological limits of traditional practices even as they continued some of them. But the question is to what extent, in certain key moments, the administration understood its task to regulate according to public needs and the well-being of individuals. In such a context, the challenge was hardly that of destroying the state to return to customary law. It was instead a question of finding a means of increasing administrative intervention in the name of the public interest while avoiding the "tyranny" of local forest guards described by the district attorney of Prades. It was also a question of subjecting the administration and regulations to popular pressures in a way that would preserve the very foundations of collective existence.

Histories of the state have had some trouble recognizing the popular foundations of this growing administrative authority. There were, however, some keen observers in the early 1840s who provided important insights into what this new state might look like and how it *should* function. It was perhaps Karl Marx who provided one of the most elaborate and sophisticated accounts of the administrative and legal complexities of these new forest regulations and their impact on the everyday lives of the poor peasants of the woods. Among Marx's earliest texts were his articles published in 1842 in the German newspaper *Rheinische Zeitung*, which was read by those just across the Rhine from the Haguenau peasants Dupin defended against the city of Hanau.

Marx observed a similar set of debates on forest regulations that were taking place in the Assembly of the Province of the Rhine. In a series of six newspaper articles critiquing the new legislation on the supposed "theft of wood" in the Rhine region, he presented his own conception of the relationship between the peasant and the state. In his view, breaking the regulations of the forest code was hardly a question of peasant antistatism or a popular uprising against the administrative power.[119] It was in many ways the contrary. Marx argued that the peasants were an integral part of the state; that they shared common concerns, and hence that their actions had to be taken into consideration in the enforcement and evolution of the forest regulations. To grasp this shift, he argued, it was necessary to have a far more complex conception of what the state actually was, and of its relationship to law. For Marx, the peasants who broke the forest codes in the Rhineland were bound to the state "by a thousand vital nerves." Consequently, cutting one of them through one infraction could hardly sever the profound connection between the state and the peasant. The peasant was a living member of the state, Marx argued, whether or not they respected every law at all times—especially those laws that challenged their vital interests in a time of need. As a subject of the state, if the peasant did break the law, it was because of the contingent circumstances of their existence. In short, the peasant had been pushed to do so by a lack of resources—a situation that was no fault of the peasant's. In such a context, it was unjust and ultimately inhumane to punish an individual for the arbitrary circumstance. "It is at least the legislator's absolute duty not to convert into a crime what circumstances alone have caused to be an offense," Marx argued. It was necessary instead to "exercise the utmost leniency in correcting as a social irregularity what it would be the height of injustice for him to punish as an antisocial crime."

Such actions in the forests, Marx argued, could simply not be punished as a crime. The state had to consider the person as a whole, "even an infringer of forest regulations as a human being, a living member of the state, one in whom its heart's blood flows, a soldier who has to defend his Fatherland, a witness whose voice must be heard by the court, a member of the community with public duties to perform, the father of a family, whose existence is sacred, and, above all, a citizen of the state." Marx then concluded, "Wood remains wood in Siberia as in France," warning against "this *abject materialism* that in connection with the law concerning wood, he should think only of wood and forest, and should solve each material problem *in a non-political way*, i.e., without any connection with the whole of the reason and morality of the state."[120] Politics, he insisted, was fundamental to understanding the basic material conditions that brought people to challenge the administration and regulatory laws. It was only by politicizing the administration, then, that the people's true relationship to the state could be understood.

After moving to Paris the following year, Marx in his critique of Hegel's doctrine of the state gave a name to this form of state which was connected to the people by a thousand vital nerves. He wrote: "Democracy relates to all other forms of the state as their Old Testament. Man does not exist because of the law but rather the law exists for the good of man. Democracy is *human existence*, while in the other political forms man has only *legal* existence. That is the fundamental difference of democracy."[121] The democratic state, Marx argued, was an immanent form of human organization which necessarily placed human need above abstract law. And as far as the forests were concerned, it was the kind of state that did not strip the peasants of their long-term rights on the basis of arbitrary possession by another. Seen from the perspective Marx outlines, this was a political struggle, in the deepest sense of the term, about what kind of state these individuals wanted to be a part of and how they wanted to be governed. By contesting and in some cases refusing the new administrative regulations, these peasants were in effect politicizing the administrative state and the public interest it was supposed to serve. In other words, they were democratizing the foundations of their collective lives.

3

Administrative Democracy

The Public City

Paris is Athens.
VICTOR HUGO, *Les Misérables*

Forest regulation played an important role in subordinating private rights and customary practices for the protection of the public good in the first half of the nineteenth century. Popular revolt, combined with the support of local magistrates and judges, helped curb the despotic expansion of administration in this vital realm of social life. The result was greater administrative reach into the deepest reaches of France's territory, and a redefined public interest. But as extensive as peasant rebellion was, and as urgent as the environmental crisis wrought by deforestation came to be, the condition of French cities and especially its capital was equally dire. Confronting the massive challenges facing one of Europe's most populous and certainly most rebellious cities required nothing short of a reinvention of city administration in the capital.

Here too, as in France's forests, the revolution left a conflicted legacy. Old-regime Paris had been administered by an extraordinary diversity of royal prerogatives, religious authorities, aristocratic privileges, corporate bodies, and communal offices inherited from the Middle Ages and the old regime.[1] Toppling this institutional patchwork ranked among the most extraordinary achievements of 1789. The Revolution destroyed the labyrinth of local venal offices, overlapping jurisdictions, and competing powers, replacing them with new municipal officers and assemblies. But as transformative as these changes were, the underlying assumptions about how much, how far, when, and to what purpose a city administration could and should intervene were not to be entirely transformed in a few short years of institutional reorganization. Despite the local revolutionary upheaval of the late eighteenth century and Napoleon's Empire,[2] a "municipal old regime" remained in the first decades of the nineteenth century.[3]

The contrast between this municipal old regime and the Parisian administration a few decades later in the Second Republic could not have been sharper. Conceptions of local public authority, what its responsibilities were, who it should serve, and on what scale it should intervene shifted profoundly from 1815 to 1852. The motor for this change was a democratization of the Paris administration. And essential to crafting an administrative democracy in the capital was the introduction of local administrative elections in Paris from 1834 to 1848.

Historians have emphasized the transformative impact of municipal and departmental elections during the July Monarchy, which brought almost five million men to the ballot boxes, while eligibility for national parliamentary elections remained under 250,000. Voting on a massive scale, it has been argued, prepared the groundwork for universal suffrage following 1848.[4] As important as this work has been, however, it has not taken measure of the impact of these elections in the capital city.[5] Historians' emphasis on provincial townships and cities has been justified by the fact that elections in the capital were restricted to less than 20,000 voters—in a city of between 600,000 and one million people. But if their impact was indirect for most Parisians, the mobilization around the elections spread far beyond those who voted. The creative energies unleashed by new forms of public engagement wrenched open old notions of municipal power, cultivating novel expectations, expanding the range of actors, regenerating the municipal mandate, and ultimately redefining the powers and scale of a modern administrative power in one of the largest and wealthiest cities in Europe.

Imperial Centralization

The Paris Commune and the Hotel de Ville's outsized roles in the French Revolution left a paradoxical legacy for constructing a modern municipal power in the nineteenth-century French capital. On the one hand, the feverish engagement of these local institutions in the revolutionary period had upset and contributed to reorganizing the overlapping old-regime municipal offices and practices.[6] On the other hand, the Paris Commune's profound politicization and the role it assumed as the executor and protector of the sovereign nation in key revolutionary episodes produced a persistent suspicion of popular municipal power in the capital.[7] The Consulate and the Empire attempted a radical depoliticization and de-democratization of the Parisian administration while at the same time building on the new municipal institutional foundation established in 1789-94.[8] The Directory's decision to replace the Parisian sections with twelve arrondissements was meant to destroy the scale at which the most radical local Parisian activity had taken place in 1792–93 while continuing the modernizing thrust of rescaling administrative power into larger equal administrative units. However, the First Consul reduced local autonomy and decision-making power in the municipality by placing local administration further under the direct control of the central state.[9] The Constitution of Year VIII established two prefects appointed by the national government, who served as the executives of the Department of the Seine and Paris. The first prefect was responsible for "general administration," while the second handled all issues of regulatory police—that is, maintaining order and regulating for the public welfare. The rest of the municipal body included appointed mayors for each arrondissement and appointed municipal officers who formed a municipal council and served as General Council of the Seine. The initial plan for the administration had left the Municipal and General Councils some autonomy against the powers of the prefects. But decision-making power was quickly transferred from the Municipal Council to the *conseils d'administration* led by the emperor himself.[10]

The Paris municipal council's influence consistently declined in the realm of budgeting. During the Empire, the city's budget was divided into three parts: the "ordinary budget," the "budget for the Canal de l'Ourq," and the "extraordinary budget." The city officials of the municipal council were only granted the right to discuss the ordinary budget; and even there, especially after 1806, it was frequently presented with a fait accompli. After 1806, Napoleon decided how the city's massive resources were to be used, especially those received from the tax wall around the city, the *octroi*. He also decided how the city of Paris would spend its revenues without awaiting the opinion of the local councils. In a tone that became familiar to local administrators during the Empire, Napoleon wrote on the projects for the city of Paris: "The *conseillers d'État* present during the council will examine the propositions for payment at the city's expense by allotting 400,000 francs to come from the goods taxed at the entry to the city."[11] On another occasion he wrote: "The budget of 1806 will include a sum of 500,000 francs to pave the areas which most desperately need them such as the rue de Castiglione."[12] This concentration of power for even the most local issues, such as paving roads, also allowed the emperor to prioritize usage of the city's tax money.

In 1810, Napoleon went so far as to announce that the prefect of the Seine "was a kind of minister" (*une espèce de ministre*), and saw that he was remunerated accordingly.[13] At the same time, the municipal council's capacity to represent the city was weakened by rivalries with other local administrative institutions. For example, on August 15, 1806, General Junot was appointed *gouverneur de Paris*. During the ceremony in honor of his new appointment, the city's mayors were listed ahead of the members of the General Council.[14] As mentioned above, the General Council and the Municipal Council consisted of the same members, convoked at different times to manage administrative affairs for one or the other of their mandates. The members of the General and Municipal Council therefore took issue with the hierarchy established during the ceremony, insisting that the General Council of the department was hierarchically above the mayors who served the arrondissements. The mayors responded, however, that since this was a ceremony for the *gouverneur de Paris*, it was a municipal celebration, and so, at the scale of the city, the General Council was simply the Municipal Council. Thus, in their view, the council was rightly subordinated to the mayors. The General Council refused to accept its subordination, and a few months later, in its session of 1810, it argued: "The General Council is always the General Council, when it is deliberating on communal affairs, and even though its attributions are not the same, its title and its primary character are not lost or modified. Its title indicates what it is necessarily: General Council at all times even when it is fulfilling other functions." The General Council concluded by insisting that "even if it is convened in the name of its municipal functions, it is the General Council that exercises power, is convoked, and thus which appears."[15] These concerns of municipal hierarchy were minor, but telling: actual attributions, administrative hierarchies, and responsibilities remained extraordinarily vague.

The result of these institutional ambiguities and the central state control over municipal government was an incapacity to recognize a local administration that was sufficiently independent to manage effectively Parisian interests on the scale of the entire city. Napoleon himself highlighted the limitations of a modern conception of Parisian administrative power when he argued in the heart of the Empire, on February 17, 1806, that "it would seem that [Paris] can only be truly represented by different corporations."[16] Napoleon's insistence on corporations as the foundation of municipal power demonstrated at once the persistence of old-regime conceptions of municipal power and the incapacity to imagine an independent, citywide public power. Indeed, the absorption of essential functions of local administrative power into the central government did little to challenge old-regime ideas of corporate administration and, as a result, traditional ideas on *how* local agents should actually manage municipal affairs.

Administrative finance remained particularly in line with old-regime notions. The prefect of Paris, Gaspard de Chabrol, opened discussions of the budget in 1818 by insisting that the city could not accumulate any public debt:

"You have witnessed the difficulty of maintaining balanced budgets and the extent to which these difficulties will continue," he argued.[17] There was indeed a profound resistance to taking out city loans for public projects.[18] Instead, in a continuation of the old-regime system of granting royal charters, the municipality of the Restoration continued to see private powers as its ally in solving many of the city's most pressing local problems. While the city did have a portion of its budget reserved for ameliorating the streets of the city, Chabrol insisted that any large-scale efforts had to be paid with private funds. "Private interest must be called in to aid general efforts. For example, the administration should grant a subsidy to the property owners of a street when they gather to enlarge it. Other means might also be discovered during the construction to lessen the expense for the administration."[19]

As a result, the ambition of urban projects remained modest at best. "If one considers that such a plan is too vast and unreasonable," Chabrol insisted, "then we must reduce it and only keep what is of the greatest necessity, like improving connections to isolated neighborhoods or enlarging commercial thoroughfares."[20] The city's minimalist approach to urban transformation increased its dependence on private initiative in the city's construction. The bankers Laffitte and Hagerman, for example, who were responsible for the new residential constructions in the northwest of Paris in the 1820s, focused primarily on the neighborhoods of Francois-Ier, Beaujon, Europe, Saint-Georges, and La Poissonière, where land was still available. However, allowing private enterprise to build in lieu of public investment resulted in the construction of new areas of the city while the old city infrastructures continued to deteriorate.

One of the largest challenges facing the city was water supply. The most thorough attempt to solve the problems of water supply in postrevolutionary France was the construction of the Ourq Canal. Napoleon had made it his personal ambition to transform the capital into a city worthy of his new empire, and part of that ambition was to have fountains running twenty-four hours a day, fed by a new canal. While the city participated in its construction by contracting a ten-million-franc loan from the national government, the construction of the canal fell under the indirect control of the emperor; as noted earlier, this was one of the special budgets that the municipality had no control over, since it fell outside the ordinary budget. Unfortunately for the municipal administration under the Restoration, the massive costs of the project and the financial difficulties facing the nation in 1815 left an unfinished canal and a lack of resources and municipal authority for its completion. While the problems of water supply continued to menace the capital city, the municipality was unwilling to provide financing for such a project.

> The most natural means of completing plans that are no longer commensurate with the city's resources is the help of private corporations. The most important of these vast enterprises is the completion of the Ourcq Canal. I have detailed in previous speeches my efforts to find corporations to finish this great work in exchange for financial control of the product upon completion.[21]

By the beginning of the July Monarchy, the canal had been completed by a private company. However, the result was that the municipality had to pay for access to water from the canal. Furthermore, beyond the high cost to the municipality, the service was restricted to those portions of the city where the distribution of water was immediately profitable. This left most of the old neighborhoods throughout the Left Bank with a poor water supply.

The dependence on private and corporate actors impacted other parts of the city as well. Waiting for assemblies of property owners to widen their streets was an increasingly inappropriate means of planning a city with such massive and rapid population growth. Moreover, the new requirements of wider streets, not only for demonstrations of state order and power, as in the case of the Rue de Rivoli, but for the movement of goods in and out of the central market and circulating through the city, demanded an investment that far outstripped what private interests were willing to advance. As a result, this municipal policy resulted in a haphazard and uneven advance of urban infrastructure. Paris's needs increased while the city lacked the administrative capacity to implement an effective municipal policy. As the 1820s wore on, the problems, which Chabrol had observed but remained unable to solve, mushroomed into a veritable urban crisis.

The Kind of Problem Administrative Decentralization Was

While the municipal structure created by Napoleon in year VIII crossed over from the Empire into the Restoration without alteration, a slow undercurrent of institutional change started undermining the rigid hierarchies of imperial administration and the old-regime conceptions of municipal authority. Two forces challenged this traditional municipal system in Paris, bringing with them the question of how to give greater autonomy to local administration and increase municipal administrative efficiency and effectiveness. First, while the local council and mayors remained appointees of the central government, the return of national legislative elections, even if they were limited to a small number of voters, brought the game of politics back onto the Parisian scene. The impact of these new electoral opportunities on the Parisian administration was obviously indirect, but the municipality was impacted since it held the responsibility to maintain the voter rolls. Moreover, the introduction of electoral politics and the growing opposition in the 1820s created a climate of increased debate and contestation. This could be seen in the council's resistance to some of the prefect's efforts, and its renewed participation in discussions of the budget.[22] The municipal administration was thus drawn into the increasingly tense political climate of the 1820s in the capital city. Critiques directed toward the Parisian municipality gained steam as the "lack of credit in the general opinion associated [the administration's] action with that of the [central] government."[23] Similarly, the centralized control over Parisian affairs came under fire as opposition political associations like *Aide-toi, le ciel t'aidera* called for the prefect of Paris to correct its voter rolls by adding more than three thousand voters in Paris. While the Parisian administration was not itself elected, these electoral issues raised the stakes of the local body's authority. As a result, the Restoration confronted growing pressure to allow Parisians more influence in the administration of their city.[24]

The terms under which the problems of municipal administration were posed in the Restoration increasingly took on a democratic language. The relationship between democracy and local administrative power had deep roots in eighteenth-century France. When the Marquis d'Argenson wrote his groundbreaking text on democracy in 1737, *Jusqu'où la démocratie peut être admise dans le gouvernement monarchique*, he was interested neither in limiting the king's power to make law nor in introducing the principle of popular sovereignty into the old regime.[25] Democracy, he argued, pertained to regulating and administering local and provincial affairs. Speaking of "popular administration" and "police attributed to popular magistrates" to describe the kind of democracy he had in mind, d'Argenson argued that it was up to the people, assembled locally and in provincial bodies, to administrate and ensure the regulations of general police. He captured the essence of his democracy when he wrote that his ambition was "that the public be admitted as far as possible into public governance."[26] While d'Argenson's book was only published posthumously, its wide reception would have an outsized impact on conceptions of administration and municipal reform in the century that followed.

D'Argenson was notably among the most cited authors in Rousseau's *Social Contract*, where he defined democracy as a form of government (or administration) for the execution of the law produced by the general will. Rousseau presented the clearest illustrations of the democracy he imagined in his discussion of the government of Geneva in his *Letters from the Mountain*. Explaining to his critics that "the democratic constitution has so far been poorly examined," Rousseau attempted to clarify this democratic constitution by describing how democracy in the city of Geneva functioned. "This is precisely what is prevented by the right of Representation stipulated in your Edicts. . . . This right gives you inspection, no longer over Legislation as before, but over the administration," he argued, adding: "In a State such as yours, where sovereignty is in the hands of the People . . . they are only gathered & speak authentically in the General Council; but outside the General Council . . . they can always watch over the administration of the Laws."[27] The term "democracy," as Rousseau's *Social Contract* and analysis of the city administration of Geneva demonstrated, referred to a means of locally administering and executing the law.

This administrative conception of democracy continued into the Revolution, fueling revolutionary ideas from 1789 through Thermidor.[28] The d'Argensonian idea that democracy would be a mode of popular administration that remained relatively agnostic about the site of sovereignty found a new, fertile soil in the Restoration. When Pierre-Paul Royer-Collard delivered his speech on the freedom of the press in the Chamber of Deputies on January 22, 1822,[29] announcing, "Democracy is everywhere," he was particularly interested in municipal public life. "Delegates of sovereign power clean our streets and light our streetlamps," he complained, suggesting that if "sovereign" (i.e., royal) power were occupied with such local issues, then "democracy has disappeared."[30] For Royer-Collard, democratic society should self-administer through locally elected magistrates.

The term that came to be used to describe democratizing administrative responsibility in the Restoration was "decentralization." Invented in the 1820s,[31] the word did not have the same connotations it does today. Those who, like Royer-Collard, pushed for democratic reforms in local administration from the 1820s through the early years of the July Monarchy were not arguing that local governments should conserve some share of local sovereign power against a central government.[32] The work of absolutism and then the Revolution and the Empire had definitively removed the idea that local communes contained original rights that were prior to those of the national administrative state and could be used to force concessions on the central government. Since Napoleon, as one specialist of French centralization has argued, "the communes had become mere administrative districts created by the state itself."[33] Subnational administrative units therefore had primary responsibility for executing laws made at the national level.

Décentralisation thus meant ensuring the effective execution of legislation through bodies that understood the local conditions and needs of a given population. It was therefore a means of increasing the administrative capacity of the state such that decisions made at the national level could be executed more effectively and smoothly. In the terms of contemporary social science coined by Michael Mann, decentralization was much closer to building state "infrastructural power"—that is, the capacity to achieve the state's ends *through* society instead of despotically ruling *over* it.[34] Allowing cities to choose their own magistrates was a means of helping grease the wheels of administrative action from the national down to the departmental and municipal level.

It was common during the July Monarchy to argue that France had become a great nation thanks to political centralization. The role of the French kings of the old regime in overcoming the tendency of feudal aristocracy to fracture the kingdom into smaller parts and prevent the construction of a great nation was celebrated. It was argued that one of the reasons why France had risen to such heights in Europe and the world was precisely that it had achieved strong political centralization. What was decried, however, was "administrative" centralization. While creating a common will, impulse, culture, language, and movement at the level of a country of thirty million people was a great accomplishment, making administrative decisions at the top of the state for an entire country was plainly considered despotic—or as Royer-Collard put it, using "sovereign power" to decide on streetlamps was both inefficient and tyrannical. To observers of the period, there were then two types of centralization: political and administrative. And political centralization was to be as celebrated as administrative centralization was to be decried. Tocqueville insisted on this point in his discussion of Algeria, as we shall see in the final chapter of this book. Louis Blanc captured the core of the distinction between political centralization and administrative decentralization when he penned his essay on municipal power, *L'État et la commune*, in 1841.[35] The problem with the municipal elections as they stood under the July Monarchy, he argued, emerged from a misunderstanding of centralization. Napoleon's greatest error had been to pursue administrative centralization at the expense of political centralization.

> The excess in ADMINISTRATIVE CENTRALIZATION is as disastrous as the excess of POLITICAL CENTRALIZATION is fecund. In our view, democracy can only generate a contented and strong people as a whole through the combination of two principles: political centralization, that is, the concentration in one place and in the same hands of the power to guide the common interests of all the parts of the nation, and administrative decentralization, that is, the liberty of purely special interests to develop according to their own morals [*mœurs*], habits, and local contrivances.[36]

Continuing in the French tradition of democracy as a form of popular magistrature, Blanc argued that politics should be solely reserved for the national legislative sphere in France. Administration, however, was to be democratized by introducing local popular participation in the execution of a general legislation. Like his contemporaries, Blanc was able to conceive of and promote a popular and "democratic" administrative power that effectively executed legislation and regulation in any given locality. "True centralization should spread Paris across the surface of France instead of amassing all of France in Paris,"[37] he concluded. So from Royer-Collard on the dynastic left to the democratic socialist Louis Blanc, there was broad agreement that the democratization of society required a more decentralized, and thus popular and democratic, administration. Where they disagreed was how far suffrage should be expanded on the "political" level of national legislative power as well as the place of monarchy. Considering the broad consensus across the political spectrum on the importance of a more democratic administration, there should be little surprise that departmental and municipal elections would become the cornerstones of state reform in the July Monarchy. These reforms would have profound consequences for the Parisian municipality.

"Administrative Elections"

Calls for local elections sounded throughout the 1820s. When an initial bill was brought to the floor in the legislative session of 1829–30 it was quickly interrupted by the Revolution of 1830. The overthrow of the Bourbons and the creation of a new constitutional monarchy only raised the stakes of administrative reorganization, prompting a quick return of the subject to the Chamber's floor. Elections for departmental councils were passed in 1831, followed by a bill on municipal elections in 1833 and finally a law on Parisian municipal elections that passed through separate legislation in 1834. In all, these reforms marked one of the most expansive injections of popular participation into public decision making ever seen in Europe, introducing almost five million new eligible voters into the administration of France's territories.

The language used to refer to these reforms—in terms that would strike most readers, especially in the Anglophone world today, as almost oxymoronic—was that of "administrative elections," as opposed to "political elections" reserved for the national legislative body. As a legislative deputy had argued in the discussion of the bill for departmental elections in 1831: "The councils of the department differ from the Chamber of Deputies in that their power is less expansive, less varied, less energetic; it is only applied to *local* interests; it is exhausted in the sphere of *administration*, and does not touch upon the sphere of the *political*."[38] The *Journal des débats* further described this distinction in 1833 during the debates on municipal elections: "How does one avoid the dissemination of politics into the [local] elective assemblies we are creating throughout France? There is only one way to do so, establish their origin and their members as distinct from *political* passions. They must occupy themselves solely with *local* interests."[39] The deputy and author of one of the most important works on local administration in the July Monarchy, Prefect Alexandre Vivien, later summarized this position in 1837 when he stated that "*political* attributions of the central government must be understood as being clearly distinct from any *local administration*."[40] As Rudolf Von Thadden has argued in his work on administrative reform during this period, these laws on local public authority may be better understood as laws to enhance participation and ensure the wise use of public financial resources while leaving the administrative unity of the country intact.[41]

As widespread as acceptance of administrative elections was across the political spectrum of the July Monarchy, democratization of the Parisian administration also raised concern since it conjured up not-so-distant memories of the most turbulent days of the Revolution. The representative Eusèbe Salverte openly asked the assembly: "Are we gathered today to create a Paris Commune like that of 1792 which was elected by all the citizens? No."[42] Indeed, the bill on Parisian municipal elections was conceived largely as a compromise between demands for a more participatory local administration and fears of the revolutionary legacy of the Paris Commune. As part of this compromise, there was a drastic reduction in the municipal franchise in the capital compared to the rest of France, hovering around twenty thousand eligible voters for a city that was galloping toward a population of one million. By limiting suffrage, it was argued, the revolutionary dangers of an empowered city hall would be reduced.

Further debate centered around the question of how the municipal councillors should be elected: should the council include three members per arrondissement for a total of thirty-six councillors, or four per arrondissement, which de facto meant one per *quartier*, for a total of forty-eight members.[43] The Orleanists and supporters of the majority argued against one councillor per quarter. Parisian notable Ganneron, later to be elected president of the General Council, argued in favor of the majority's position that "if the number of councillors is too great, the council may stray from its fundamental character; it may become an Assembly where one offers one's opinion instead of discussing business; one would talk instead of taking care of *Administration*."[44] The Orleanists feared that increasing the proportion between voters and councillors might create a miniature Chamber of Deputies in which opinions—that is *political* opinions—would drive the assembly's discussions.

As the Orleanist majority argued, having forty-eight members, or one councillor per *quartier*, had two further negative consequences. First, it meant that each *quartier* within the arrondissement would be "represented." Thus, instead of emphasizing the need to delegate administrative authority, the elections could become an attempt to best represent each *quartier*'s interests. This was already problematic enough, since the elected administrators were not supposed to "represent" anyone, but were instead supposed to manage the city's administrative affairs. But it was even more dangerous, they argued, since it shared a striking resemblance to the forty-eight sections of the revolutionary commune of 1792.

The left opposition disagreed. The mere similarity in number could not conjure up the tremendous upheaval of 1792. "The objections that have been put forth have all been taken from a past that has nothing in common with the present and which cannot return,"[45] one representative argued. Eusèbe Salverte similarly claimed that legislation based on preventing the revolutionary sections were grossly overstated: "Let us take an honest look at the question. Obviously if it were possible to relive the Paris Commune of 1794, no reasonable man would want to reestablish a municipal council. [But] you have confused two very different periods, the first is that of 1789. . . . Afterwards came a different Assembly which *took* the name of the Commune."[46] Assuaging fears of revolution, the opposition further argued that forty-eight councillors would necessarily be better than thirty-six simply because of the capital's tremendous population. "It is hardly too much to ask that 48 members be part of a commune as vast as that of Paris," a deputy argued.[47] The size of the Parisian population simply required a greater number of councillors: "Gentlemen, the principle in municipal matters is that the greatest possible number of citizens work together to name a given number of representatives in proportion with the number of voters."[48] Furthermore, forty-eight councillors were necessary to grasp the vast number of local interests in such a large city. As one deputy argued:

> The Commission fears the influence of local spirit [*esprit de localité*] and the *quartier*. I would like to make note of this fear, which has been at the heart of a municipal illness ravaging Paris for the last 30 years. It has attacked, undermined, and sapped the municipal power of Paris. . . . For three decades the city of Paris has not been administrated on the municipal level . . . it has become a sort of superior oligarchic power distant from its local interests and details as well as its general interests, assimilating the private affairs of the city to the administration of a great kingdom.[49]

Debates on administrative elections and the size of the municipal body raised new issues on the nature of their mandate and the ambitions of a local administration, prompting new ideas on the local body's administrative duties and how it could best serve the public interest.

While the debates brought these issues to the floor, in the end the bill itself remained silent on them. Surprisingly, nowhere in the law on the Parisian municipality were the actual responsibilities of the administration clearly defined. The law only set out the "local" nature of the administration's work by establishing the mode by which its members were to be elected, and their number. In other words, the actual responsibilities were not decided. Instead, the municipal administration's "local" nature was to somehow magically emerge from the process of designating local administrators. The legislative deputy Hector d'Aunay pointed out the limitations of such an approach during the debates on the bill on local Parisian elections: "Municipal franchise is the result of the responsibilities granted to the power, not the mode of nomination of those who must exercise this power."[50] Of course, Paris was not alone in this black box of local administration. It was a general tendency of the laws on municipal and departmental elections during the Restoration and the July Monarchy to focus on democratizing the mode of selection through election at the expense of outlining actual duties. As the historian Charles Pouthas noted long ago: "Little by little, for the Doctrinaires and the Liberals, decentralization and administrative reform were quite simply a question of establishing elections for local councils."[51]

Alexandre de Laborde's *Paris Municipe*, one of the most important works on the Parisian municipality in the first half of the nineteenth century, stated this problem unambiguously. Following a very brief tenure as prefect of the Seine in the immediate wake of the Revolution of 1830, he wrote *Paris Municipe* in 1833 during the debates on administrative elections in Paris. The title itself captured the problem at the heart of democratizing the local Parisian administration: *municipe* was the Roman term for a city that enjoyed "civil" rights and not "political" rights. Laborde highlighted the surprising (and telling) fact that, despite Paris's place in France and Europe, there was not yet one work dedicated to local administration and the city's right to manage itself:

> There are a number of histories of the city of Paris and an even greater number of descriptions of its principal buildings, but there is no work dedicated solely to an inquiry of its administration, employment, revenues, the management of its public buildings, everything that forms its *édilité*. And this in spite of the fact that its revenues surpass those of many small kingdoms, and the interests of this city are of great interest to all of its citizens.[52]

The reason for such stunted interest, according to Laborde, was once again the memory of the Revolution, which had prevented local participation in the city and evacuated any sustained interest in the municipal administration more generally. The first step was, therefore, to ground the new municipal administration in 1789, as opposed to the period of the revolutionary commune from 1792 to 1793:

> This municipal structure [from 1790 to 1792] was truly municipal and it was the product of elections. During the two years that it served, the city of Paris was managed with order, justice, and economy; the most respectable and enlightened of men were not ashamed to be a part of it. If ever we returned to this municipal organization, it is to these laws and this order of things that we must return. This organization lasted until August 10, 1792, a period of sad and devastating innovations that destroyed the constitutional monarchy, in the same way that July 14 destroyed the Old Regime. This new organization destroyed, in fact, the municipal power as a few violent men in each section imposed terror on the mass of peaceful and industrious citizens.[53]

The first period of the Revolution, Laborde argued, provided for popular participation within the administration while guaranteeing order.

Building on this model, Laborde emphasized how more popular participation in administrative bodies would improve their effectiveness:

> Is it not strange that at the very moment when we are discussing the most minute expenses within the chamber of deputies, on the other side of the city, we spend 40 to 50 million francs without any other controls than the honest and respectable men appointed by the authorities who have little influence upon them? And this in spite of the fact that since time immemorial, these same magistrates, head of the merchants, *echevins*, councillors were chosen through election. Are we surprised then by the great number of salutary reforms, useful projects, important improvements which have not been done or were stopped for petty considerations?[54]

For Laborde, local participation ensured a stronger administration: "Parisians will make good choices for their administrative offices. They will offer the positions to those who are well known within the neighborhoods in order to focus on useful issues and offer a wider perspective for wise improvements. They will not be hindered by petty considerations or ignorance."[55] The Parisian *municipe* was, in his words, to be governed justly through a participatory and delegated administration.

While in 1833 Laborde's remained the only work dedicated to the Parisian municipal administration, by 1850 there were three books and three periodical journals devoted to the subject. This alone indicates the impact of administrative elections and popular mobilization in transforming the capital. Following Laborde's *Paris Municipe* in 1843, a new journal on the management of the capital city, the *Gazette municipale de la ville de Paris et du département de la Seine* adopted the distinction between political and administrative affairs in organizing its content. In its first issue, the journal stated that it was designed to serve as an intermediary between the municipal administration, property owners, and commercial enterprises of the capital city. The publication was in fact the first such periodical on the municipal affairs of Paris. It fit within the context of a growing awareness of the specificities of administration in the capital city Laborde had called for. In so doing, it attempted to further cement the distinction between a productive popular engagement in administrative affairs and potentially explosive politics on the Parisian stage:

> The city of Paris, center of so many interests, is the only city in France which does not have an organization designed especially for the interests of those whom it is called to administer within the department.... This strange lacuna can only be *explained by the invasion of politics*, which, in the press, absorbs the ideas of the journalists and the economists. There are, however, other interests, which are no less real, but more direct, no less important, but more immediate. These are the **material interests**.[56]

Their aim was to specify the administrative interests, which were particularly Parisian, in the face of those "political" interests that had undermined the delegation of authority to an autonomous local administration.

The legislative representative Hector d'Aunay observed during the debates on the Parisian municipal elections that the law remained surprisingly silent on the actual attributions of the local administrative bodies, focusing instead on their mode of appointment:

> I think it would be wise to make a distinction between the responsibilities of the head of the Parisian municipality, that which belongs to the realm of governmental action, and that which is truly in the interest of the locality....
> I believe that it is impossible to organize a municipal power in Paris without having defined it, without having established a precise distinction between that which pertains to the government in the administration of the capital and that which is in the interest of the city.[57]

These questions were finally solved for the municipalities throughout France with the organic law of 1837, followed by a law in 1838 for the departments, which determined the exact responsibilities of the locally elected bodies. However, such a law was never passed for Paris. So it was not through formal legal decree that the actual administrative responsibilities would be articulated. Instead, the redefinition of local administrative power in the capital would take place far more pragmatically, through specific policy issues, the accumulation of publications, public engagement around municipal elections, and public responses to a rapidly expanding capital.

Democratizing Administration

The legislation on administrative elections in the capital did not at first glance seem dangerous for the political stability of the July regime. The government intended for no more than approximately fifteen to seventeen thousand voters for the municipal council—less than a fifth of the number of voters in elections for the National Guard, for example—and the mayors were to be chosen by the prefect of the Seine, who was appointed by the king, from the ten candidates who had received the most votes. Moreover, the appointed prefects remained the head executives of the city. Similarly, in 1834 and 1835 the government introduced harsh laws against liberty of the press and of associations. The government's strategy for controlling the Parisian population was to allow for popular participation in local administration while eliminating other potentially revolutionary activities.

Because political associations and the press were restricted while local elections were created, the local administration became a highly contested set of institutions. It was on the streets, in meetings, and in the back alleys around the Paris Hotel de Ville that local administrative power was expanded and transformed. This democratization of the Parisian administration took place in two phases. In the 1830s the opposition continued to expand its support among workers and the disenfranchised with a strategy of popular revolt and revolution. In the 1840s, however, its revolutionary ambitions were slowly combined with new attention to local Parisian elections. As a result, municipal administration became a centerpiece of popular politics in the capital.

Immediately following the Revolution of 1830, the republican press and associations mobilized for a renewed revolutionary thrust, rushing to the streets and building barricades. Amid this emphasis on popular revolt, a leading opposition newspaper, *Le national*, expressed its limited enthusiasm for the first Parisian municipal elections, arguing on January 15, 1834: "The Parisian public amounts to nothing in this whole affair. Its plazas will remain filled with junk; its streets will remain in an awful state; and its taxes forever raised. None of these issues have been given the slightest interest in this discussion. What will the population gain from it? Nothing."[58] The massive restriction of the vote made the local elections meaningless for the bulk of Parisians, the paper argued; the municipal oligarchy would merely perpetuate bad local administration. The opposition remained convinced that the constitution established in 1830 was just one stop on the long revolutionary process toward a democratic republic. As a result, the opposition denied that local elections reserved for less than twenty thousand inhabitants could provide sound governance and social justice. "The right to vote is so limited," they argued, "that outside of this limited circle, the efforts made by the candidates to attract votes is hardly noticed."[59] The opposition therefore limited its opinions on municipal candidates to a blanket condemnation of all the municipal councillors who had been chosen by the king during the previous four years of the July Monarchy.[60]

Le constitutionnel, a centrist newspaper, took a different approach, urging Parisians to vote. In keeping with its vision that the Revolution of 1830 had marked the end of *the* Revolution and that progress could only be achieved "when the calm in the streets and the safety of industry will allow for their free expression,"[61] it saw the Parisian municipal elections as an opportunity to participate in the management of the city's affairs, and not as a "political" opportunity to change the current policies of the government: "We have stated it incessantly: the voters are not called upon to grant a *political* mandate. In these grave circumstances, all *political* passions must be quieted."[62] The municipal elections, the newspaper argued, might have an influence on the national political scene, but such influence should only be indirect. "We must create a municipal culture and strengthen the political life which has been so debilitated and ill. As men of the city, you will become men of the nation. The political apathy of Parisian voters is perhaps due to the absence of municipal institutions, that indispensable complement to the representative regime."[63] The claim that Parisian municipal elections were an apolitical "complement" to national political life was a recurrent theme throughout the July Monarchy. The Orleanist *Journal des débats*, on the other hand, presented the official government vision of the municipal elections, reserving its praise for those candidates purely interested in particular administrative affairs: "The candidates for the municipal elections in Paris are of a remarkable quality; no *political* statements or utterances, simply the facts and the services they intend to render to the city. It is quite simply a question of demonstrating one's utility."[64]

The prefect of the Seine, the Count of Rambuteau, anxiously awaited the results of the first Parisian elections. In November 1834, he sent a letter to the twelve mayors in Paris, asking them to keep him well informed of the elections. "A great number of candidates will be present for these elections. I invite you to inform me of exactly what is happening in your arrondissement and to inform me of any present and future candidates as well as their chances of winning the election."[65] The results for the government were mixed. Out of the seventeen candidates who sought reelection following their royal appointment from 1830 to 1834, only eleven were successful.[66] While this was hardly a smashing victory for the government, each side claimed victory. The *Journal des débats* insisted that political considerations had played little part in the vote. The center left was also convinced that, "removed from any *political* preoccupations, they witnessed a certain merit and an *administrative* capacity."[67] The radical opposition, however, in keeping with its revolutionary ambitions, stated clearly in support of two of its most well-known candidates: "We will refrain from excessively celebrating the election of Laffitte and Arago. One would think that these honorable citizens are already the founders of the future Paris Commune.... In any case, we may at least suggest that Laffitte and Arago will not abandon their positions in a moment of danger."[68] For the radical opposition, the reference to 1792 was only lightly coated with irony.

The elections of 1837 drew similarly little interest from opposition newspapers. The prefect Rambuteau once again sent a letter to the mayors asking for further information on the preparation of the elections: "When you deliver the [voter registration] cards to each individual as is common practice, please inform them that an absolute majority is necessary for the candidate's election."[69] *Le constitutionnel* was also concerned, publishing just before the elections: "In spite of the repeated calls of the administration and the announcements printed in numerous newspapers over the last few days, the voters from the Seine, convened for tomorrow's election for the members of the 3, 5, 6, 7, 8, arrondissements, have shown little interest in collecting their cards at the Mayor's office."[70] The opposition newspaper, *Le national*, printed almost nothing on the election results and the affairs of the municipal council, except to argue: "The Chamber of Deputies has adopted a law on the municipality of Paris. However, the Parisian population remains as disinterested as if they had decided the administration of one of our puniest colonies."[71] As a local population, Parisians in this view were still ruled by a distant central government.

In 1837, the opposition attempted a campaign for electoral and parliamentary reform which resulted in the creation of a *comité central de la réforme* with Arago and Laffitte at its head.[72] The major ambition of this movement was to argue that all members of the National Guard should have the right to vote. In spite of the tremendous number of petitions it sent to the Chamber, the movement had little impact and resulted in suspensions of oppositional members within the National Guard in 1841.[73] Nonetheless, it revealed the terrain upon which the political battles of the second half of the July Monarchy would take place. The opposition increasingly looked toward the institutional opportunities provided by the regime to achieve its ends.[74] By the mid-1840s, the *Comité central* was transformed into the *Comité central de l'opposition de la Seine*. Making allies on all sides of the political opposition to weaken the Guizot government and expand suffrage, the Central Committee became a powerful political organization ushering in novel techniques in grassroots political organization and, above all, transformation of the Parisian municipal authority.[75]

Alongside popular revolt, participation in local administration found itself increasingly at the center of the opposition's strategy. By November 25, 1840, in an article titled "Elections of the General Council," *Le national* argued: "The elections of the General Council of the Seine, like those of all elected bodies, must take on an outright political character." Similarly, in preparation for the mayoral elections of Paris, which were held two weeks later, the Central Committee placed an article in *Le national*, emphasizing the importance of local elections:

> They [the government] will undoubtedly claim that in Paris the functions of the mayor and his assistant have nothing to do with politics; that their attributions are enclosed in narrow limits. . . . . But they are wrong, gentlemen. Here, as elsewhere, the opposition runs into the false claims and maneuverings of the government: here as elsewhere, they must fight.

By 1846 and 1847 the local administration was moving to the heart of oppositional politics.

The session of the General Council of the Seine in 1846 attested to this politicization. While the General Council ardently defended its budget and its particular interests, designating funds for sidewalks on public roads, widening important thoroughfares, and extending avenues to improve circulation throughout the department, the democratic debates on the popular role of public authority also expanded the municipal mandate. The municipal assembly sent a series of declarations to the government including the following: "In the interest of the country, and in the name of humanity, we recommend the immediate and total abolition of slavery in all French colonies." A democratized Parisian administration offered a stage from which to make demands on the national government and claims for universal justice.

The opposition's control of the local Parisian authority came to a head in the winter of 1847 during the famous banquet campaigns. The banquets must be placed in the wider context of the opposition's administrative ambitions. Organized by the Central Committee, the first banquets received a lukewarm reception in 1847. However, they slowly gained steam as the Central Committee combined its involvement in municipal elections with its banquet campaign. One of the best examples of their new strategy was the elections within the General Council of Seine for council president. Most of the members of the municipal administration were members of other administrative or political institutions in the capital. In her work on the Paris Chamber of Commerce in the nineteenth century, Claire Lemercier highlights what she refers to as the cursus honorum of Parisian notables in the Chamber of Deputies.[76] Those who wanted to make a career out of working within the administrative and commercial institutions of the capital often passed through the other local institutions and, principally among them, the Parisian administration. The General Council of the Seine voted for its president, and between 1834 and 1842 the presidency passed between the hands of three men: Guillaume Aubé, Auguste Ganneron, and Louis Besson. All three men were typical of the Paris cursus honorum. Lemercier suggests, for example, that Aubé "was a pure product of the local Parisian commercial institutions." A stalwart member of the Chamber of Commerce and appointed to the Conseil d'état, he presided over the General Council in 1835, 1837, and 1838, and almost in 1846. Besson was a member of the Conseil d'état, and Ganneron was a member of the Chamber of Commerce and matched all the criteria of a Parisian notable involved in local Parisian affairs. He was négociant, banker, president of the Commercial Courts (*Tribunal de commerce*), and member of the General Council of Trade (*Conseil général du commerce*), as well as a legislative deputy.

In 1842, however, the council presidency began changing more regularly. Finally, in 1846, Arago, one of the leaders of the Central Committee of the Opposition of the Seine, was elected president. In the 1846 election he defeated Aubé twenty votes to seventeen, and in 1847 he defeated Besson twenty-two votes to fourteen. Considering that tighter victories suggested increasing ideological conflict within the assemblies, and the fact that the average margin of victory since 1834 had been fifteen votes, these much tighter elections suggest that the General Council was increasingly ideologically divided. Moreover, considering their relationship to other Parisian institutions and Lemercier's analysis of the cursus honorum, the election of Arago also had other implications. Arago was not a member of the Chamber of Commerce, for example. In fact, he was part of a very different network of notables and savants who could be found within the council but who had not previously been a majority. Moreover, Arago was deeply dedicated to the democratic cause. In this sense, what was being rejected in Aubé, Besson, and Ganneron was not only their ability to preside over the council, but an institutional background and idea of commercial interests that had defined the traditional conception of municipal affairs.

In his first act as president, and against standard protocol, Arago addressed the local assembly. No doubt the speech was meant to heal the ideological conflict opened by the elections for president of the general council:

In giving me the honor of your votes, you have quieted those who see in us a smaller replica of the Chamber of Deputies. It is clear that each of you left your flag at the door; that here, we are merely handling the affairs of the department; that even the most conflicting opinions, when they are considered conscientiously and in a disinterested fashion, do not create discord among us.

In the presence of his fellow councillors, Arago refused the idea that the General Council could serve as a miniature Chamber of Deputies. But the full relevance of his speech was only revealed a few weeks later in the midst of the local Parisian elections. In a voter meeting in the 6th arrondissement to prepare for the coming elections, Arago contradicted his "official" speech:

Gentlemen, *Le constitutionnel* obtained the speech I presented after my nomination as president of the general council. They claimed to see in this speech my political sentiments.... They obtained this speech ... in order to say that there must not be a political aspect to the nominations of the members of the council. But I am going to demonstrate that you must, on the contrary, see a political message in them.... It is true that it is often difficult to place politics in the building of a sidewalk or in the construction of streets: ... but there are occasions when it interferes deeply. I have seen some cases in which politics have influenced our deliberations in an unfortunate way.... I return to the issue of leaving one's flag at the door. I regret that it was badly interpreted. How could I claim that it is necessary to hide our flag just at the moment when it is most necessary to carry it? If we hide our flag, we will not have the power to resist.

Arago's direct contradiction of his presidential address further highlights the extent to which the municipal administration was becoming a key political battleground for the opposition.

Hence, when the General Council of the Seine convened in November 1847, the conditions were propitious for oppositional control, and Arago was once again elected president of the council. The opposition newspaper announced these results as a sign of victory: "The session of the General Council of the Seine began today at the Hôtel de Ville. The conservative members supported Mr. Besson, from the House of Peers ... but over the last three years the majority of the Council has belonged to the opposition. The honorable Mr. Arago, already named president last year, was reelected by a large majority." With a firm majority in the General Council, a declaration in favor of national reforms was assured.

The declaration printed in the newspapers on November 13, 1847, was indicative of the increasing rivalry between the local assembly and the national government: "Considering that 16 years of experience have revealed grave imperfections in the electoral law of April 19, 1831 and demonstrated the necessity and immediate urgency of its modification, the General Council recommends that the government and the Chamber of Deputies carefully revise this law in the next legislative session."[77] As moderate as the wording of the assembly's declaration was, the local Parisian assembly had been turned into a force for change. The opposition commented upon this event the following day in the newspapers:

> The same choice in favor of the opposition is made each time that the Parisian voters are called to the ballots. In the elections of the National Guard as well as those of the Municipal Council, the opposition is triumphant. Arago, member of the left, presides over the General Council and all the government's power of seduction was insufficient to prevent the council from expressing a wish for electoral reform. Lastly, it is among the voters of the Seine that the Central Committee recruits and from whom the impulse of the banquet campaign is sent. The haste with which so many cities responded to the committee's call is an astonishing proof that public opinion has been awakened not only in Paris, but in all of France.[78]

In December 1847, the 2nd arrondissement was called once again to elect its mayor. The second arrondissement had been one of the most highly contested elections of the last ten years. In the preparatory meetings of the Central Committee of the Opposition in the 2nd arrondissement, it was decided that Jean-Jacques Berger would be the candidate. But by 1947 the political climate had radically changed. The opposition was no longer the only organization to promote its list of candidates. The government provided its official list of candidates as well:

> The voters have created a new list of candidates. The opposition acted frankly and precisely and published the names of its candidates. For his part, the Minister used all of his resources and composed a list that was published in the newspaper. Mr. Duchatel supports Mr. Dailly and the newspaper announced this morning that if this candidate is voted onto the final list, he will be chosen as Mayor. The two camps are thus in the presence of clearly distinguished colors. It is now a question of finding out who will win, the Minister or the voters.[79]

Local politics had officially entered a new phase in 1847 as the municipal elections pitted two camps against each other. The victory, however, left little doubt as to which camp had the most momentum in the capital city. Dailly, the government's candidate, received only 1,025 votes—134 votes short of being accepted on the list of ten candidates from which the government needed to choose—and once again, Berger was first on the list. The government was forced to recognize its defeat and to appoint Berger mayor of the 2nd arrondissement. On December 9, 1847, a front-page article in *Le siècle* tellingly associated Berger's victory with the increasing distance between the people of France and the national government: "Is it in vain that the Parisian population has given the government so many demonstrations of its courageous dedication by reminding it time and again?"[80]

Toward a Modern Municipal Mandate

The impact of the democratization of the Parisian administration went deep. In a traditional vision of municipal administration inherited from the old regime, councillors were chosen for their place within a social hierarchy, generally due to their financial position or their institutional attachments. In this context, administrative expertise or individual views on specific issues facing the city were of little importance. As Christine Guionnet has argued in her work on local elections in the July Monarchy, the traditional municipal mandate represented immediate social categories such as profession, because candidates were elected not for their administrative expertise but according to their status as town notables.[81] While such an old-regime conception of municipal power continued well into the Restoration and even the early years of the July Monarchy, the debates and political conflicts that arose around administrative elections ultimately transformed the municipal mandate. Most importantly, local magistrates shifted from notables who expected to be elected based on social status or profession to administrators who needed to solicit votes and public support based on their opinions and their ability to best do the work of municipal councillor.

As late as 1843, an Orleanist candidate named Michelot stated in his campaign announcement: "You have supported my candidacy for mayor three times without my making the slightest effort to seek a nomination. This time, I have come to claim your votes."[82] His pride that he had never previously solicited votes was ostensibly a means of demonstrating his appropriateness for the municipal mandate. In keeping with traditional notions of the mandate, he emphasized his role as a local notable rather than his expertise in municipal affairs, reminding the voters that he was a "lieutenant in the National Guard, chairman of the Loire railroad company, founder of a university institution in the 10th arrondissement."[83] He further argued in favor of his "holdings as a property owner which are entirely within Paris and are concentrated on the Left Bank."[84] At the same time, his decision to "call upon" the votes "this time" suggested a recognition that the electoral game was shifting and forcing him to change his approach. Hence, he also emphasized the importance of private and commercial interests in the capital, arguing for an "increase in the property values and the commercial activities of the 10th arrondissement,"[85] and suggesting ways to improve connections within the arrondissement to the center of the city and to the faubourgs.

The opposition, however, considered its mandate to be not a reflection of preestablished social distinctions, but rather an opportunity to transform the city through administration. The campaign bulletin of Victor Considerant presented a more resolutely modern conception of the municipal mandate. Opening with a statement on his political positions, he then turned to his views on what municipal councillors should do. "I believe that the legal importance of the general councils and the municipal councils will increase dramatically within the country's changing administrative system," he argued.[86] He then presented his ideas on why he should be elected. and the approach that the municipal administration should take in governing the city. He had elaborated these points in a set of studies published in 1843 titled "On the Administrative Unity of the Department of the Seine [*De l'unité administrative du département de la Seine*]," in the Fourierist newspaper *La démocratie pacifique*. Considerant argued that the municipal administration should have the power to rebuild the capital city as part of a larger project of social transformation. Voting for Considerant was hardly a choice for a local notable. Indeed, he made no mention of his past accomplishments or of his social position. Instead, his election materials discussed his positions on national politics and his vision of the responsibilities of the municipal administration, and concluded with a detailed discussion of the precise administrative needs and questions of his arrondissement and about Paris as a whole.

While the elaborate ideas of Considerant may have been exceptional, members of the opposition, in general, rarely mentioned that they would make efforts to serve property interests and rarely emphasized their social position. Instead, they sought election based on a very specific electoral agenda. The candidate Favrel of the 5th arrondissement stated that he would seek a series of specific reforms: he would reduce the taxes of the octroi and reform the taxes on windows and doors as well as the tax on salt and meat.[87] Similarly, candidate Monin-Japy stated that he was to be elected based on his political ideas, and that if elected he would put them into practice. "In proposing a few general ideas, my intention is to place you in the position of judging the views which I hold dear. If you approve of them, I promise you in advance that I will put all of my efforts into implementing these ideas."[88] M. Ségalas went so far as to make a series of campaign promises: "In the hopes of achieving the elimination of this tax [the *octroi*] and making it compatible with other local taxes, I would create a luxury tax such as exists already in England. This would be among my first recommendations [*vœu*] sent to the government as a member of the General Council."[89] So by the final years of the July Monarchy, administrative elections had become an opportunity to present new policies and to argue for one's ability to implement them.

The politicization of the Parisian administration similarly transformed the reasons why the candidates were chosen. Instead of looking for representatives from the dominant professions within the city, the voters began to demonstrate a real concern for conflicts of interest between profession and municipal mandate. In a preparatory meeting of the 11th arrondissement in 1843, for example, a voter from the audience asked the candidate Buchère how he hoped to reconcile his profession with is electoral mandate.

A VOTER: How will Mr. Bucher [*sic*] reconcile his duties as councillor with those of his position as property owner?
M. BUCHÈRE: My response is that I intend to keep my enterprise. I believe that it will even help me to understand better the needs of the arrondissement.
A VOTER: How will M. Bucher reconcile the interests of his clients when they are at odds with those of the city of Paris?
M. BUCHÈRE: If the interests of the arrondissement suffered from my status as a businessman, then I would give up my enterprise.
[Applause][90]

Buchère could hardly claim that his administrative legitimacy was a natural result of his profession or his position as property owner, nor did his wealth simply guarantee his being fit for office. Rather, voters were concerned with his ability to perform the functions of municipal councillor honestly *in spite of* his profession. The candidates, and increasingly the voters, expected individuals who would be dedicated to their mandate and who had a specific electoral program. Increasingly, the municipal councillors were chosen not simply to mirror elites of Parisian society, but to transform the city itself.

This transformation extended into a redefinition of the relationship between elected officials and the Parisian population. While a politics of notables, to use the historian André-Jean Tudesq's phrase, suggested that elected officials on the local and even national level were solicited due to their social status, electoral competition for administrative positions made voting a question of choosing the right person. The difference between *finding* and *choosing* the best candidate was made apparent in new arguments for accountability and transparency.

Le constitutionnel wrote in preparation for the municipal elections of 1843: "It is of the utmost importance that the candidates be convened for explanations so that the voters may be better informed and the qualities of the candidates be better appreciated."[91] During the same elections, in a preparatory meeting in the 10th arrondissement, a mayoral candidate, M. Tourin, declined an invitation to defend his tenure in office, sending a letter in his place, which announced that he planned to run for office, but that because he was well known by his fellow citizens, it would be useless to visit them and offer explanations. When the letter was read aloud, the audience was outraged.

A VOICE: Mr. Tourin lacks respect for his voters . . . (exclamations)
M. PAGNERRE: It should be noted that Mr. Tourin is not simply a candidate. He was an administrator and we deserve an account of his acts. (Yes, yes, indeed.)
A VOTER: Mr. Tourin's refusal to attend should mean that he forfeits his candidacy. . . . (yes, that's true!)[92]

Pagnerre, who in turn insisted that Tourin should step down in the face of his refusal to defend his decisions, was the secretary of the Central Committee of the Opposition of the Seine. His argument that voters should be ensured an account of the local administrator's acts became a keystone of the opposition's critique of conservative candidates. By introducing a rhetoric of accountability, they hoped to demonstrate that Orleanist candidates were part of a municipal oligarchy. In an article presented by the Central Committee, which prepared the electoral platform for the opposition candidates, they made the publication of the municipal councillors' deliberations central to their reforms. "Before you vote for a candidate," they explained, "be sure to obtain the formal promise that he will give you a full account, every six months or at least every year, of all the works in which he has participated either as a committee member or individually."[93] Martelet, candidate in the 7th arrondissement, argued along similar lines:

> Gentlemen, I will ask for publication of our proceedings. I do not mean the simple account of our works published in pamphlets that reach such a reduced audience! I mean the publication of our sessions like those of the legislative assembly. I suggest that during our discussion the room be open to all those who have advice or who might be impacted by the council's debates.[94]

The opposition candidate Favrel, for the 5th arrondissement, went even further, stating: "I will ask for the publication of our sessions as the strongest guarantee that the voters may have of their officials' acts. . . . I would like to remain in constant contact with you and enlighten myself with your wisdom and ideas."[95] These calls for electoral accountability were entirely new, and captured the ideals of a democratic administration. These new administrators sought to serve the public interest faithfully.

On November 27, 1846, just a day before the municipal elections for general and municipal councillors in Paris, the Central Committee published an extended article on the campaign platform for the elections in *Le national*. Summarizing the ideals of a democratic administration, the committee explained: "Representative government is not simply one or two platforms or the columns of a few newspapers. It is the habitual and permanent action of the nation on itself. It is the active participation of the country, the department, and the commune in all public affairs, in all national and local issues."[96] For the opposition, a vibrant democratic life was not only expressed in legislation and public opinion. The public also needed to be engaged in the execution and administration of its affairs on the local and departmental level.

A Parisian Administrative Interest

No doubt one of the most important outcomes of this transformation was a new substance and scale of municipal action that extended the sphere of administrative intervention and redrafted the nature of administrative responsibility. The legitimate scale of local administrative intervention in the capital throughout the first decades of the nineteenth century was sublocal. In his *Memoirs of the Hôtel de Ville during the Second Republic*, Charles Merruau described the Parisian administration during the July Monarchy: "It consisted of a distribution of small sums between the various arrondissements. One might suggest that all of this took place among the jealous rivalries of Municipal Councillors."[97] It is important to nuance Merruau's argument, for as a member of the administration during the Second Republic and under Haussmann, he was always looking for an opportunity to confirm Haussmann's claim that before him little had been done. His claims do, however, seem to bear some truth about the early part of the century. For example, the earliest statistical works of Louis-René Villermé from the 1820s took the arrondissement as the natural unit of analysis. Villermé wrote, "I considered each district of Paris as if it formed a distinct city."[98] Villermé's interest, then, in determining the relationship between mortality rates and social status mapped social and territorial divisions on to one another. As Joshua Cole remarks, "The populations of Parisian districts were not simply random composites produced by the principle of equality in membership and the accident of being neighbors. On the contrary, they were real collective bodies, whose common characteristics allowed one to make assumption about the lives of individual members."[99] Jeanne Gaillard has similarly argued that this approach can be seen in the urban planning proposals of the July Monarchy.[100]

She suggests that the municipal councillors held a "centralized" vision of the municipality, in which the core of the city was marked by a diversity of commercial activities. Municipal urban planning, then, was focused on establishing links between each of these arrondissements and the center.

In this context, it was each councillor's responsibility to ensure that his arrondissement was well served by thoroughfares leading to the center. Some municipal candidates in the early July Monarchy shared this vision. Michelot presented an electoral agenda that concentrated almost solely on improving the 10th arrondissement by "extending and building new roads perpendicular to the Seine in order to improve our relations with the right bank and with the railroad stations which correspond with the west and south."[101] Importantly, emphasis was placed on improving the relationship between his arrondissement and the city in general. He would hardly have proposed a general plan for Paris. Similarly, the candidate Chevalier, for the 7th arrondissement, insisted on the transformations of his district: "The speaker then examined the material improvements which currently face the General Council with a special emphasis on the enlargement of thoroughfares, notably, in the 7th arrondissement."[102] But this approach to urban planning did not withstand an increasingly democratized municipal policy.

Victor Considerant attached to his campaign bulletin his article "A Few Considerations on Traffic in Paris and a Note on That of the 10th Arrondissement." This article, published in the *Revue générale de l'architecture et des travaux publics* in 1844, was among the first extended studies of a vision of Paris as an urban whole. The value of this article for the creation of an early vision of urban planning has already been noted by Nicholas Papayanis, who has suggested that Considerant "understood perfectly well that city planning had to be comprehensive planning. Only when a 'comprehensive plan' was adopted by municipal authorities should work begin on any individual projects."[103] But what is of even greater significance is that Considerant included his vision for the rebuilding of Paris with the campaign materials sent to voters.

In a series of articles published in the newspaper *Le siècle* in 1843, the opposition directly attacked the piecemeal approach to "traditional" administration in the capital. The first article, dedicated to electoral reform, argued against the current system, which, it insisted, favored representation based on individual arrondissements at the expense of the city as a whole.

> The Municipal Council of Paris consists of 36 members. Each of the 12 arrondissements chooses 3 councillors. These electoral divisions produce results which must be felt everywhere to some extent, but which are particularly

damaging in this great and powerful city, the capital of arts and of civilization. I am speaking of the indecision that grows out of narrow and rival interests. These struggles from street to street and within each quarter attempt to transform each arrondissement into a commune within the commune and generate a majority for one bank over the other within the Municipal Council itself. The end result is that absence of unity, which is indispensable for realizing great things, and the absence of a perspective on the whole [*vue d'ensemble*] and for the future.[104]

The electoral geography of municipal representation, the opposition claimed, threatened the new needs of a growing capital city by creating cities within the city. The article proposed a solution to the fragmentation of urban interests by reorganizing municipal elections. As elections within each arrondissement tended to promote representation of sublocal interests, it was proposed that complementary councillors with a mandate to represent the entire city should also be elected by all the city's voters.

While the solution proposed by the article in *Le siècle* was not officially applied, it did demonstrate a new awareness of the importance of municipal intervention on a citywide scale, especially in a context where the problems facing the capital—rapid population growth, water and food supply, and the necessity of rebuilding old neighborhoods in the center of the city—were increasingly impacting the entire city. The arrival of twenty to twenty-five thousand workers each year in the capital was quickly revealing the limits of an administrative policy that could only intervene in individual arrondissements with the help of private individuals or corporations. The opposition members of the municipal assembly saw that the working populations were the hardest hit by these transformations, and turned their attention toward their interests, claiming that they represented the working and laboring classes. In his 1846 electoral speech, Horace Say stated his position in the following terms: "As voters, you are not only here in your own name. Because the law restricts the vote to such a small number of individuals, it imposes the duty, the mission, upon you to represent all those who cannot vote. I am speaking of those great numbers of workers [*travailleurs*] who have produced the riches and the glory of our glorious nation."[105] Say adapted the language of limited suffrage to suggest that the voters in municipal elections were themselves delegates who served on behalf of the workers who had been deprived of the right to vote. *Le national* seconded this notion of voters as delegates of the nonvoting working classes: "We hope that we will also inspire preliminary meetings where these questions will be debated and where the citizens . . . will have the ambition of permanent and useful improvement for the most populous and working classes."[106] The municipal campaigns of the opposition were replete with such references to representing the workers' interests, injecting the needs of new populations into the ambitions of administrative power.

The call to represent the interests of workers sharpened amid the increasing cost of bread in Paris during the winter of 1846. The economic crisis and the poor harvests of the mid-1840s pushed bread prices to new heights, and the municipality quickly realized that it would need to distribute coupons to workers and the poor. The question arose in the administration as to whether coupons could only be distributed upon proof of need. *Le national* immediately responded that such a method of distribution was humiliating for the working classes. "What is the meaning of words like 'needy workers'? Must one justify one's misery? In such conditions, charity becomes an insult. Will you not provide tickets on the grounds of a simple request on the part of workers? . . . The Municipal Administration must determine, on its own, its ideas on this question such that there will be no doubt."[107] This shift to a representation of working-class interests was essential for crafting a new relationship between the municipal officers and their city.

In effect, the increasing popular pressures on the Parisian administration were dismantling the piecemeal vision of public intervention. If the municipal councillors of the opposition no longer represented their arrondissement, but rather worked on behalf of the laboring classes, then it was the city as a whole that needed to be transformed. There was never a claim for bettering the condition of the workers in the 9th arrondissement, for example. Calls in the service of the working classes made reference to the city and its suburbs. In preparation for the municipal elections of 1846, the *Le national* presented its new municipal platform for the candidates of the opposition: "A general plan for all of Paris . . . an increase in the amount of potable water for the city . . . lighting throughout the city . . . the end of the octroi."[108] Indeed, the electoral bulletins and campaign announcements consistently proclaimed that the octroi unfairly burdened the workers of the city. The city needed a fairer distribution of local taxes based on differences in wealth. "What do we see in this great city where so many citizens push to improve our general prosperity?" Martelet began in the electoral meeting of the 7th arrondissement. "We see that today, as in the days of serfdom, the working classes sustain the majority of the tax burden in the form of a tax which is as damaging as it is inhumane."[109] Another candidate announced: "This question is of the utmost importance for Paris. Is it the general interest which is invoked in favor of the octroi? The general interest is not exclusively the interest of the most wealthy."[110] Favrel, in his campaign bulletin for municipal councillor, argued: "I will support all measures designed to diminish the tax of the octroi until it is completely suppressed and replaced by a more just tax. This burden weighs too heavily on the poor classes."[111] Similarly, Martelet, candidate for the opposition, expressed his ambition that "all of my efforts will be dedicated to a reduction, if not a suppression, of the tax which weighs heavily on indispensable commodities.... I will point out that this tax hits the hardest those products which are of the utmost necessity for all classes, products like meat and wine that the poor worker cannot access without a great deal of trouble."[112] Since the octroi tax wall surrounded the entire city and affected everyone within the city walls, especially workers, the demands to limit the tax's impact necessarily undermined the formerly piecemeal approach to local administrative action.

A second project highlighted by the opposition was the end of toll bridges, which became an essential element in the opposition's critique of the prefect of the Seine's policies: "The General Council of the Seine has asked, on many occasions and without any response, that the tax paid to the Company of Three Bridges, which expired in 1827, be abolished. The Prefect, however, instead of according our recommendation, announced in the session of 1845 that the tax be increased and legalized."[113] While one of the most common means of building bridges across the Seine was to license the construction of toll bridges to private companies, the radical opposition pushed for a democratization of public infrastructure.[114] "For far too long," it argued, "we have manifested against the toll bridges in the capital which burden above all the working and poorer classes."[115]

Similarly, the opposition made the transformation of the water system central to its municipal campaigns. Water should be pumped to poorer areas, and efforts should be made to balance access on the Right and Left Banks. In his speech at a campaign meeting in 1846, Arago argued: "At the Pont-Neuf, we have a hydraulic pressure of 6,000 horsepower [to distribute water throughout the city]. I thought that the city was wrong not to take advantage of this resource. I wanted to use this pressure to deliver water throughout the city.... Some say that there is already too much. I say that there is not enough."[116] Arago then explained the failed efforts to distribute water throughout the city to show how the conservative branch of the municipal council cared little for the poorer neighborhoods. In his *Études sur l'administration de la ville de Paris* (1846), yet another important work on the Parisian administration to appear in the 1840s, Horace Say began his discussion of the distribution of water by stating: "If there is a service which requires a master plan for the entire city, it is without a doubt that of the distribution of water in a large city."[117] He then insisted that "the poorer classes are only provided with sufficient amounts of water in cities where the administration accepts to manage its distribution."[118] An effective municipal governance in the eyes of the opposition needed to serve the public good through citywide policy.

The democratization of the Parisian administration transformed the very foundations of municipal power. Instead of distributing meager public resources and mobilizing private funds under the control of the central government in the service of individual neighborhoods, the increasing public pressures recalibrated the notion of the municipal mandate. Separating their electoral legitimacy from the representation of social status and profession, mandates were increasingly shaped by ideas, expertise, accountability, and transparency. Administrative officials were being elected to transform the city, not to reflect its social hierarchies. At the same time, the very notion of who should be served was transformed as voters themselves were considered delegates on behalf of the disenfranchised.

Following the 1848 Revolution, the newly elected president of the Second Republic, Louis Napoleon, recognized the importance of the democratic legacy that had emerged in the previous decades. Applying the political cunning for which he was so well known, he built on the essential contributions of this legacy while destroying its source. Indeed, by 1848 it was possible to imagine a citywide transformation from below the streets to the rooftops and the urban air. However, while towns and hamlets throughout France continued to elect their municipal councillors, the Second Republic removed local elections in the capital. Later, Napoleon III's coup d'état cleared the way for him to capture the democratic legacy of the 1830s and 1840s by introducing one of the most ambitious reconstructions of a city of the modern world. With little regard for the democratized administration, he appointed the "Baron" Haussmann to rebuild the capital. Napoleon III and Haussmann's project would have been unthinkable without the democratization of administrative power in the previous decades. And yet their reconstruction was accomplished without the participation of the people, and for an entirely different set of interests. A better example of administrative capture is difficult to imagine.

4

Health Democracy

The Body Politic

> Medicine is a social science and politics
> nothing but medicine on a grand scale.
> RUDOLF VIRCHOW[1]

> Votre salubrité est une invention révolutionnaire.
> VICTOR HUGO[2]

Paris had provided the stage for a vast new democratic experiment as municipal mandates, the scale of intervention, and the very idea of what a city government could and should achieve were radically transformed through administrative elections. Within the vast range of new public policy areas shaped by this democratization, public health was among the most important, for in the realm of health and sanitation, regulation was nothing less than a matter of life and death. Already an important part of Colbert's regulatory program under Louis XIV, in the following century a variety of prophylactic strategies, policies, techniques, and administrative measures formed the core of an increasingly elaborate doctrine of "medical police," which outlined the essential characteristics necessary for ensuring the safety and hygiene of the people in almost every circumstance from birth through death. In 1779 the German doctor and administrative theorist Johan Peter Frank presented his groundbreaking and almost exhaustive six-volume account of the role and responsibilities of medical police, providing a "landmark in the history of thought on the social relations of health and disease."[3] As Peter Baldwin has highlighted in his history of contagion and state construction in Europe, "since at least the era of absolutism, preventing and dealing with contagious and epidemic disease have together been one of the major tasks of states."[4] Hence, any account of the democratic construction of a modern administrative power must carefully consider the development of a public health movement.

At the heart of the transformation of public health in the nineteenth century was not the questions of whether public health and hygiene should be regulated, but rather that of how and by whom. Since at least the foundational work of Erwin Ackerknecht in the postwar period, historians have highlighted the fundamentally political character of medical regulation.[5] Within these accounts, and following Ackerknecht's original hypotheses, the history of how to regulate public health in European states has been subject to two diagnoses. On the one hand, there were the "liberal" doctrines, which downplayed or even denied the risk of contagion in the nineteenth century and thus emphasized the free movement of individuals to pursue individual interest despite the dangers. These liberals, it has been argued, tended to focus policy less on the control of populations than on sanitation, prevention, and hygiene. Britain provided the archetype for this "liberal" model.[6] Ackerknecht opposed to this model an authoritarian approach, which has also been referred to as a statist or "Continental" model. In this approach, reducing contagion took center stage and administrative regulations focused on establishing varying degrees of order, strict control of the movement of people and goods, and severe quarantine measures. Adapting this argument, Ann Elizabeth Fowler La Berge has argued that the development of a French public health movement in the first half of the nineteenth century is best understood as a "statist" process,[7] since above all, it was influenced and established by medical elites who sought the construction of an effective administrative authority to manage essential public sanitation issues. In Fowler's account, then, public health as a public good emerged from scientific and medical leaders who had little contact with the public themselves, and even less interest in offering a pedagogical foundation for a popular understanding of their own hygiene.

As useful as the liberal and statist histories of public health have been, however, some important questions remain. Perhaps most important is the essential coupling of health, social science, and politics offered by Rudolf Virchow, a German doctor and 1848 revolutionary, in the epigraph to this chapter. Social science was a central force in shaping democratic thought and practice on public health. But social science was not opposed to a democratic politics. Rather, it was in many ways constitutive of it. As a result, by understanding medicine as a social science, the democratic movement framed public health as a structural force shaping the well-being of individual lives, redefining the structural relationship between the individual and his or her social surround. The second part of this formula was equally important. The radical politicization of this sociological conception of medical treatment and prevention introduced a whole new set of "how-oriented" regulatory questions which pushed far beyond the opposition between statism and liberty; they were part of a common ambition to build state capacity against capture by distant elites and to increase the range of opportunities for people to understand, oversee, and participate in the solving of public health problems.

A Legacy for Public Health Reform

As with forests and municipal administration, the regulation and administration of public health during the Revolution built on reforms from the last decades of the old regime. A first series of reforms was proposed in the final decades of the old regime, within the Royal Society of Medicine in 1776. Placed under the authority of the famous doctor and biologist Félix Vicq d'Azyr, the creation of a centralized public health administration was designed to protect the population by preserving it from epidemics. In the same year, and just three years before the publication of the first volume of Johan Frank's magnum opus on medical police, the French doctor Le Brun published his treatise on how to manage epidemics and other public health crises. Here he argued for the essential connection between administrative police and medicine. "These means include as many objects relating to the police, as there are those which are properly of the resort of Medicine," he wrote.[8] While these treatises articulated themes common in the "liberal" model of public health—ensuring proper sanitary conditions to avoid encroachment on commercial activity and individual liberty—as well as the statist tendencies that would become a hallmark of French public hygiene, they also highlighted a more social dimension in public health. In particular, they insisted on the importance of a relative egalitarianism in access to public health services. Tracing the perspectives of the Encyclopedists, Montesquieu, l'Abbé de Saint Pierre, and Fleury, Charles Rosen has demonstrated the centrality of critiques of poverty in old-regime public health policy.[9] These key figures of the Enlightenment, he shows, considered that public health problems were exacerbated by poverty. Such an approach introduced a strong egalitarian dimension to questions of medical police and hygiene administration that would become a hallmark of the French approach to medicine during the Revolution and the first half of the nineteenth century.

The creation of the Comité de salubrité de la Constituante on September 12, 1790, built on these ideas,[10] and was enshrined in the drafting of the "Nouveau plan de constitution pour la médecine en France" of 1791. Its preamble announced that the "health of citizens is threatened on all sides."[11] Hence, this new "constitution" sought to guarantee "public instruction," since "one of the first foundations on which public liberty rests, and without delay, is the numerous changes required in [health] Administration." Under this new constitution, doctors, surgeons, and pharmacists were free to practice their professions outside any corporation, "each one having to exert its Art only under the tutelage of the laws."[12] And to avoid the abuses of the old regime, the constitution placed in its section on "medical police" the new requirement that a "*corps electoral*," consisting of "departmental electors and a certain number of doctors," be established to vote for the doctors within hospitals.[13]

Building on these ideas on September 30, 1791, Guillotin proposed on behalf of the Comité de salubrité a bill on "teaching and exercising the art of healing."[14] In maintaining a more open medical profession for doctors, surgeons, and pharmacists, the bill also attempted to introduce, albeit modestly, modes of popular access to and control of the practice of public medicine. Title IX of the bill established the creation of a "relief and health agency" consisting of nine individuals: four doctors, a pharmacist, and four "citizens." These individuals were to be appointed by the departmental administration. Article 5 offered clear guidelines for how this office was to function: "The agency will appoint, by an absolute majority of votes, a president, a vice president, and a secretary. The president and vice president will be renewed every six months. The secretary will be renewed every year. Both may be reelected."[15] Their meetings were to be held once a week, and their extensive responsibilities were enumerated in the bill: (1.) regulating all forms of food; (2.) managing epidemics; (3.) inspecting mineral waters and distributing drugs and medications; and (4.) overseeing cemeteries and funerals, and managing mines, prisons, and hospitals, as well as draining swamps, ditches, roads, and sewers. The bill then explained that in these key realms of public sanitation, the agency's essential responsibility was to ensure the proper "execution of the laws."[16]

The early years of the Revolution thus introduced an important set of themes that would remain central to the development of public health in France in the decades that followed: an emphasis on the social impact of medicine through the alleviation of poverty and a guarantee of medical treatment to the poor, an elaborate and ambitious range of areas to be covered by medical regulation, and a focus on *how* this treatment was to be offered by creating new procedures and controls that guaranteed legal protection and public participation in health administration.

Building a Public Health Movement

A lasting institutional transformation grounded in these principles only emerged in the first half of the nineteenth century. The Consulate and the Empire witnessed a new attention to public sanitation and hygiene. Against the backdrop of the industrial exigencies of early industrialization and then total war, the new Conseil de salubrité (Public Health Council) was founded in Paris in 1802, inaugurating what Gérard Jorland has since referred to as "the century of public hygiene."[17] With a jurisdiction focusing on the capital, it was charged with overseeing certain medications—under the rubric of liquids—as well as inspecting and regulating various types of industry and workshops. While the body's responsibilities and investigations remained limited in its early years, those responsibilities continued to grow throughout the period of the Empire, expanding gradually in 1804 and then in 1807 to include prisons and public bathhouses, open markets, cemeteries, slaughterhouses, and other potentially insalubrious sites of urban life.[18] In the years that followed, other cities in France—Nantes (1817), Marseille (1825), Lille (1828), and Strasbourg (1829)—created similar councils. Internationally, the Parisian conseil was certainly the most ambitious—with a wider range of responsibilities and expertise than those of similar commissions created in Leiden or in Manchester—but its responsibilities remained modest.[19] As in other realms of regulatory development, Napoleon succeeded in formalizing some key institutions of public power while the capacity to actually intervene in the daily lives of French citizens was reduced by the exigencies of war.

However, the steady growth of the Parisian population, a rapidly expanding industrial sector, and increases in the circulation of goods and peoples into and out of the city required new intervention on the part of public authorities. As discussed in the previous chapter, by the 1820s Paris was facing massive problems of housing and potable water, provoking the creation of a full-fledged public hygiene program. The Conseil de salubrité continued to assert its authority over medical and public hygiene questions at the national level while the Academy of Medicine was founded in 1820 to oversee "all matters relating to public health." The Conseil supérieur de santé was created soon afterward, in 1822.[20] Between these three bodies, a new level of administrative expertise was established for public health questions in France.[21] Alongside the institutional development of public hygiene was an authoritative perodical publication on these key questions that was to have an influential role, *Annales de l'hygiène publique et la médécine légale*, founded in 1829. The manifesto of the inaugural issue captured the new spirit of the public health movement:[22] "Medicine is not simply an object of study and a means of treating the ill; it has an intimate relationship with social organization; sometimes it helps the legislator in crafting laws, often it enlightens the magistrate in the law's execution, and it always oversees, with the administration, the maintenance of public health."[23] Highlighting how the French lagged behind the Germans in this realm, the *Annales de l'hygiène publique* clearly articulated the ambitions of the public hygiene movement: medical knowledge was to help weave a new social bond between legislation, courts, and the administration. The connection between doctors and administrators had already produced "impressive efforts, in the realms of preserving public health and advising the courts," the authors argued, "but [the effects] will become even more appreciable when the cooperation becomes more widely shared between doctors, judges, and administrators."[24]

One should certainly not overestimate the "public" nature of these administrative bodies or the overwhelming "social" conscience of the journal itself. The editorial board, many of the authors, and the audience remained elites and, in many cases, high-level administrators. Similarly, these administrative bodies understood their role to be that of encouraging industrial development while limiting only the most extreme or egregious modes of pollution and social damage. However, the creation of new institutional structures and the reputation of the *Annales d'hygiène publique* did open a new path toward the management and publicity of key medical questions. In the increasingly politicized environment of the 1820s, 1830s, and 1840s, discourses on just social organization, relatively equal access to medicine, and administrative reform opened the door to more popular influence on matters of public health.

By the 1840s, an interventionist ethos in the service of the public penetrated the Conseil de salubrité in Paris. The council published five years of painstaking work to show the coherence of its mission and accomplishments.[25] Between 1840 and 1845, this body alone drafted 428 reports on regulatory investigations. Even as it became increasingly vigilant in the heated political context of the second half of the July Monarchy, the council argued in its report that it had kept a sharp eye on favoring commercial development. Wary of being seen as hindering economic and industrial growth, it insisted: "It may be feared that the Conseil often yields to a tendency to close its eyes to the inconveniences inherent in the various systems used by the industry."[26] The Conseil published its results precisely to "dispel this fear" and to "demonstrate the attentiveness of the Administration, which watches with so much perseverance and success over the interests of all, as well as the effectiveness of the measures proposed by the Conseil, with its aim of preventing the more or less unpleasant consequences of various industrial processes."[27] It therefore insisted that of the sixty-four cases brought against industries in 1840, thirty-one were considered well-founded. This was less than 50 percent. And there is little doubt that these modest efforts did relatively little in the face of the industrial pollution exploding in Paris. But of equal importance in the heated political climate of the 1840s was the fact that the Conseil recognized the danger of "closing its eyes on the inconveniences of different procedures put in place by industry," and that its responsibility was to guarantee the "health, well-being, and interests of citizens." On the eve of the 1848 Revolution, this core philosophy had permeated conceptions of administrative action, even if the concrete actions remained insufficient.

Indeed, beneath the quantitative question of the number of investigations, a new qualitative understanding of the council's activity permeated its report. The cases were divided into six parts: (1) residual liquids from industrial establishments, (2) gaseous discharges, (3) dust and smoke, (4) causes of explosion and fires, (5) food and drink substances, and (6) illnesses and medical emergencies. The report added that "each one of these large sections was subdivided into as many divisions as was necessitated by the subject at hand."[28] The report then ended the introduction to the journal by explaining that "while all of the affairs on which the council is called to give its opinion are hardly of the same importance, it may be said that all of them, no matter how minimal, touch upon the health, well-being, and interest of our fellow citizens."[29] From the production of caramel to the examination of falsified yeasts, prison mattresses, and treatments against bedbugs, public authorities were called upon to examine and ameliorate the most detailed conditions of citizens' lives. In recounting the regulation of bathhouses, for example, the council explained its ambition: "To reconcile the means of supervision of the Administration and that of the owners of baths with the comfort sought by healthy bathers and the particular care required by sick bathers. Such is the difficult goal that must be attained; however, the public interest requires a prompt solution in the presence of the accidents that negligence can cause."[30]

This case and the more than four hundred others like it treated in the first five years of the 1840s by the Conseil de salubrité were driven by a wide range of urgent public problems ushered in by the disruptive forces of industrialization and urbanization. As disparate as this mass of cases may have been, what emerged from it was not only a composite list of unrelated regulatory decisions but a set of principles that permeated the new ambitions of public action. A new ethos of public service animated administrative intervention and regulation in the realm of public health.

At the core of this ethos were five elements, which could also be found in the development of other areas of administrative power across the first half of the nineteenth century. First, the introduction to the volume argued that the Conseil's investigations were "guided by the subject at hand." That is, the cases were to be investigated and solved according to the particularities of each situation, and would reveal very practical responses to specific public complaints. Second, the legitimacy of the commission was founded on its ability to find solutions to public problems according to the "demands of public interest." A language of public good, public welfare, and public interest permeated every one of the cases. Consequently, and third, there was a consistent interrogation about the right and even the necessity of intervening into private interests when the public interest demanded it. The members of the Conseil refused to erect the private sphere as a realm outside its regulatory reach. In turn, and fourth, measuring the appropriate degree of its reach was achieved by taking into consideration the social milieu within which individuals were acting. When discussing the regulation of "flour and bread," for example, the commission insisted that its oversight was justified because "in our social habits, bread forms the basis of our diet."[31] Finally, the commission stuffed its report with references to the past, inscribing its action in a historical development of public action. Explaining its motivation for writing these documents, it stated: "The jurisprudence of the Council will therefore appear, in a summary manner, as if to link the present with the past; this jurisprudence and the accomplished history of the Council will be completed by reproducing the salient features and the contingent points which characterize, so to speak, the specificity of the year 1845."[32] In sum, this new regulatory action was pragmatically driven to solve public problems in the service of the public interest through an attention to the social and historical conditions of modern life.

The legacy of public health as a means for combating poverty, improving social organization for access to health care, and fulfilling the fundamental role of legal, judicial, and administrative institutions pushed open the door to the democratization of public health. The democratic movement seized on this new philosophy of public action, using it to critique the administrators' efforts as insufficient. The increased attention to public hygiene, health, and sanitation was not solely due to the watchfulness of administrative and medical experts alone. To the contrary, it was precisely due to the public making ever more exacting demands on public health administrators.

Among those making new demands on the administration of health from a democratic point of view was Hortense Allart. Insisting on the limits of the official public health system, she argued that the management of health and hospitals was an essential problem that more democracy could more effectively manage. "All too often," she argued, "hospital administration, like public administration in general, is governed for its own benefit, losing site of the essential goal."[33] Doctor Ulysse Trélat similarly argued that improving public sanitation and hygiene required popular action and governance: "If our medical institutions are not very advanced, if in their present state they offer society only weak guarantees, if their imperfection and softness remain so open to charlatanism and ignorance that their actions, committed to the science of healing, sometimes do more harm than good, this is no doubt because of the absence of frequent and sufficiently motivated demands."[34] The problem, in sum, with the advancement of public health was that the calls for its transformation were not forceful enough, since administrative officials too often sought the preservation of private interests first. A more organized push for an improved public health system would bring important changes.

Democratizing Public Health

Starting timidly in the 1820s and gaining steam in the 1830s and 1840s with a crescendo in 1848, a concerted attempt to politicize questions of medicine and public hygiene was nurtured within a broader democratic movement. Trélat captured the spirit of this movement during his participation in the famous trial of *Nineteen Citizens Accused of Plotting to Replace the Royal Government with a Republic*.[35] He stated his ambition in the plainest terms: "The longest possible existence under the happiest conditions for the greatest number of men." This was to be achieved by coming together to share in the happiness and suffering of all to ensure "the law of sociability," which Trélat defined as "equality among men." Currently, he argued, one portion of society was at war with the other because it suffered from misery. "Who has a better understanding of the problem than a doctor, the privileged witness to all pain?" he asked. Some people had poor health because they could only eat once every three days, while others simply died of malnourishment. But "in a well-constituted order, improvements would be made every day." The relationship between "the governing and the governed is broken due to a servile subjugation to pernicious traditions," Trélat insisted. "The fact is, [administrative] power and those administered have been considered two different entities, with diverging and even opposing interests." In such a context, the only way to improve the administrative situation was through revolution: "The absence of insurrection results only in the diversity of malheur experienced by men."[36] Trélat's speech unflinchingly called for a popular uprising to improve the sanitary and public health conditions of the poor. Through insurrection, the people's voice would be heard by the administration, forcing it to expand and improve care for the poor.

Flora Tristan highlighted the health problems of the working poor with her characteristic charisma and rhetoric when she cried out: "Workers, your condition in contemporary society is miserable, painful—in good health, you lack the right to work—ill, invalid, wounded, old, you don't even have the right to a hospital!"[37] Building on the legacy of using public health to alleviate the conditions of the poor, new popular pressures were being placed on public authorities from multiple directions. Democratic almanacs considered it their duty "to make the ideas of good and progress penetrate into the most isolated places." Among the areas that needed to be showered with new ideas was public health. "The best way to increase appreciation of the importance of a new system, among the inhabitants of the province who do not yet enjoy its benefits, is by putting before their eyes some of the general observations which accompany its practice."[38] To do so, the almanacs explored the actual practices of medicine, sanitation and public hygiene.

Three major themes emerge out of the democratic almanacs' treatment of the health question. First, the almanacs insisted that the medical profession had abandoned those who were in the greatest need, and they placed workers at the heart of their critiques of medical care and public hygiene. Generalizing out of the specific cases of "the life of a worker," fictionalized accounts insisted on horrible living and working conditions, long hours, and their consequences: "The worker will have no choice but to heal himself in the hospital, in the common room where the doctors have so many ailments to treat that they have but a few minutes to deliver care; in the hospital, he will be surrounded by students for whom his tortured body will serve as a piece of study; where the iron will be turned in his wound, to make the apprentices understand the theory of their art."[39] The conditions of sanitation and hygiene necessarily forced workers into a state of ill health, while the hospitals, the accounts insisted, were closed to those most in need. Similar fictionalized accounts recounted that "we began our apprenticeship of misery at an early age, and it was never ending! The health of my father could not resist continuous privations. He died, without a single day of his life being free of worries."[40] There was little hope that workers and the urban poor would receive the care they needed, the accounts argued, since the hospitals themselves at worst simply refused to care for them or at best became sites of administrative corruption. "The hospital administration publishes every year an account of its operations. For those who know how to read it, this enormous quarto volume is certainly curious, bristling with figures and calculations, which the most trained mind does not always grasp. What one glimpses through the golden veil which supposedly demonstrates public charity, behind all these millions lavishly spread at their feet, there is a deep misery which is far from being relieved."[41] The winner of the worker's poetry contest for the almanac penned his own contribution to the complaints about public health:

> When your fever comes, sad and slow,
> Tie its burning tunic to your side,
> If the door to the overflowing hospital is closed,
> Your cry, alas! all help will refuse,
> Especially the man in the black frock, the misery-phobic man
> We call the doctor.[42]

This wretched health situation, the authors of the almanac argued, was not due to a mere lack of regulations or laws. Articles in the almanac recognized that there had been great strides made in the realms of hygiene and health administration since the 1820s. The problem with the hospitals and medical police was, rather, their inability to execute the laws and regulations effectively:

> It is insufficient to discuss laws and to make them. It is still necessary to see them through in practice, to know if they are applied and if they can be applied, and to descend from the heights of philosophical and political speculation into real life, which, if it offers a less vast field to the imagination, imposes a great work on reason and great duties on the conscience. Neither politics nor economics nor philanthropy are abstract sciences; if they are based on general principles, like the truth, of which they must be the expression, they are summarized, in the end, in acts or social facts, and these facts are well worth studying.[43]

By politicizing the question of hospital administration, these leaders of the democratic movement pushed beyond the mere creation of regulations, insisting that democracy was a product of effective and practical execution in the name of the public good. They recognized "public relief legislation," "the considerable number of provisions it contains," and the necessity of "conscientious study, knowledge of the needs of the working classes, and a firm determination to meet them." The problem, therefore, was not in the ambition and the letter of the law, but in its execution. "Does it meet current requirements as implemented? Are the funds voted for charitable institutions sufficient and properly used?" The food within the hospitals, for example, was "overseen by good regulations, which were not executed."[44]

This critique pushed beyond the hospital, out into the dangerous everyday sanitary conditions of the industrial city. Again, the almanac recognized and even encouraged the ambitions of the Conseil de salubrité. Specifically targeting the unfulfilled promise of the Conseil, the almanac argued that it was necessary to take "precautions at every moment." The growth of industry "enveloped us in poisons. Our decorations, our clothes, our wallpapers, the covers of our books are impregnated with it. . . . The linen of the sick infests the healthy, even when it is washed," it argued. It continued highlighting the effects on poor children: "It is enough for them to chew on a strip of these bits of wallpaper painted with green copper arsenic. The child suddenly falls into fits. The symptoms escape diagnosis, and the remedies are administered blindly, no one being able to recognize the cause of terrible evil." Those responsible for the situation could be found among those "manufactures that poison streams, wells, nearby springs." Recognizing that there was an administrative authority of public hygiene, the articles cried out against its inaction: "The public health committee could not be more careless."[45]

A tireless critic of the sanitary and medical conditions of the poor, the democratic almanacs insisted on two means of responding to this situation. First, they argued for the importance of a new education for workers and those in need who were being ignored by doctors and hospitals and were suffering from the ineffective application of health regulations. Continuing education for the urban and industrial populations was one of the almanacs' central goals. An article on education published in 1847, on what its authors referred to as the "People-Method" of teaching, insisted that "the human soul is able to learn on its own and without the help of explanatory masters."[46] Pushing beyond methods involving a traditionally vertical interaction between the teacher and the student, the almanac professed a horizontal mode of apprenticeship for "those who want to learn and those who want to contribute to the education of others."[47] One area where this horizontal mode of self-teaching was most imperative was the realm of public and personal hygiene. Amid its critiques of the execution of regulations by administrative bodies, the almanac therefore provided essential information to educate on the promotion of health and well-being. "We shall go into further details on hygiene," explained the almanac, "so that our readers may find in our little book even the simplest notions which may, whatever their nature, contribute to the well-being besought by all."[48]

As part of the call for a new public education on health, an article in the almanac criticized the existing organization of the medical profession. Seeking to reduce the mysteries of medical knowledge that ensured a monopoly on the well-being of the population in the hands of a few elite individuals, the article stated: "Like all the other sciences, medicine must make its doctrines and its means of applying them more and more popular."[49] The article went so far as to insist that even dissection in amphitheaters should be open to the public instead of excluding those who were wrongly considered "lazy, turbulent or incapable."[50] In another article on hygiene, "written to be in everyone's hands," the almanac divided the question into three parts: public hygiene, "which examines man living in society" and is necessary for "sound administrators"; standard everyday hygiene; and special or exceptional hygiene in the case of illness or epidemic. Having treated the problem of public hygiene and administration elsewhere, the article focused on everyday private hygiene, providing medical advice on diet, ways to organize one's home, and activities to maximize health under the basic categories of quotidian life. The section subtitled "Atmosphere" signaled the importance of clean air, ventilation, and sunlight. Under the subtitle "Clothing," the article explained the advantages of wool, silk, and cotton in conditions of cold, heat, or rain, insisting that "ties should not be knotted too tightly and one's belt should be fastened too tightly. The next section, "Food," was divided into categories of "refreshing," "soothing," "enervating," and "tonic," offering the useful advice that if one were particularly hungry, "it is necessary 15 minutes before eating to drink a glass of sugared water or a little bullion to calm the stomach." Under the subtitle "Sleep," the article recognized differences between individuals, but suggested that eight hours of sleep per night was generally recommended.[51]

While the almanac sought to educate the wider public, it also called for reforms to the medical profession. A long article on the organization of medical treatment asked, "Do you want to restore dignity to your profession, confidence in the opinion of the administrators, faith in the patients within the sanctity of an institution that takes care of them?" If so, the article argued, it was necessary to democratize not just access to public health but the medical profession itself. There were multiple dimensions to this democratic reform. The article proposed first transforming doctors into elected "magistrates." The medical officers should "be voted into office by their peers." Second, they should be paid "at the expense of the State, to watch over public health."[52] Third, medical students should be sent into each neighborhood in numbers based on the number of sick people, to care for them and at the same time observe as many cases as possible to improve their medical knowledge through practice. The article also argued for a neighborhood board to oversee medical practice. Each evening the doctors were to present their observations and treatments to the board, which would consist of their superiors and fellow doctors, and recount the number and status of sick patients, in order to receive advice from the board. In turn, medical inspectors would ensure that care was properly delivered. The president of the board would present a statistical report to the committee of the arrondissement every eight days, and then the delegates of the arrondissement would report to a higher body every month to propose reforms and prevent any corruption or abuse of power.

The democratic almanacs proposed a revolution in the administration of public health and medical care. First, the very nature of the almanac meant that articles on health and medicine were published alongside others on political and social issues, thus suggesting that health was not the remove of distant experts who were beyond questioning, but rather should be subject to the same political pressures as those experienced by forest guards and municipal administrators. Second, the reformers who wrote for these publications kept a watchful eye over the execution of public hygiene regulations. That is, they did not trust neutral judges to ensure that new regulations were respected, but sought the intervention of the local populations through elected neighborhood committees. Third, by making doctors civil servants, they aimed to remove financial pressures from the delivery of health care. And finally, by cultivating public knowledge on health and medical administration, they hoped to reduce inequities and ensure proper knowledge about the specific circumstances of each patient.

A Social Contract for Public Health

La Berge has suggested that the reforms of the revolutionary period "incorporated the social contract idea into their theory of public health" through the notion that "health was a natural right to which all citizens are entitled."[53] Across the first half of the nineteenth century, the idea that health was central to the social contract gained new momentum, pushing far beyond basic notions of natural right. At the heart of this new contract was a reform movement on medical education and practice that sought to make health a public good. Examining the general conditions of public hygiene in his own work, Ulysse Trélat echoed the ideas presented in the democratic almanacs on reforms of the medical profession by arguing there were three primary reasons why the system failed to deliver public health adequately: "the general ignorance of society," "the imperfection of medical education which does not offer sufficient guarantees," and "the impotence of the laws and regulations as they exist, and applied as they are, to help the action of science and to exclude everything that can harm its beneficial results."[54] Trélat's book placed particular emphasis on the final point: the ineffective execution of laws and regulations. There was simply no guarantee that the legal and regulatory reforms of medical practice were being followed. "Today, all public functions are overly monopolized; the same men are part of almost all the committees of improvement, health, manufactures, arts and crafts, etc., and have been there more or less since the Constituent Assembly or the Consulate."[55] Trélat insisted that promoting a more meritocratic and accountable medical profession should become an administrative priority. A new medical exam, open to a much wider group of individuals, would ensure that regulations were learned and followed. Furthermore, such a system would guarantee that medical practice improved and changed with society instead of ensuring the often hereditary and self-serving positions of a medical aristocracy that neglected the public's best interests. With a more meritocratic and accountable medical profession, doctors would gain influence "and would expand their impact on the movement of the progress of society," because their mission was not "concerned only with the preservation of individual lives."

Rather, doctors would "modify and improve the collective life as well" while "presiding over the improvement of morals and legislation." In Trélat's view, such collective aims could only be achieved through "representative" medical institutions.[56]

At the heart of this new, more social approach to medicine was an emphasis on public hygiene. Philippe Buchez and Ulysse Trélat authored a book called *Précis élémentaire d'hygiène*, explaining that while the art of medicine required education, expertise, and experience, hygiene was of a very different nature. "Its study can only be useful; its principles are accessible to everyone, and its precepts are easy to observe," they explained. In the opinion of Buchez and Trélat, ensuring public health through hygiene required, first, a profoundly sociological conception of individual subjects: "Its rules are based on the knowledge of man and the relations between him and the outside world."[57] To understand hygiene, one needed to investigate social relations to grasp the "the organization of man, the things surrounding him and how they affect him." Out of this sociological approach to individual health, one could develop a "consistent application of an appropriate system based on general laws of economy." That is, a sociological study allowed for the discovery of general social laws. Buchez further developed the fundamentally social character of medicine and hygiene in his *Introduction to the Study of Medical Science*.[58] "Science must be represented by social institutions," he wrote, arguing that in this regard "the institutions representing the medical sciences are extremely flawed."

Perhaps foremost among these democratic medical reformers was François-Vincent Raspail. As one his earliest biographers referred to him in 1848, he was "the very portrait of the democratic party and one of its national glories."[59] Born in Carpentras, in the French department of Vaucluse, in 1794, Raspail began his education in Avignon before moving to Paris to pursue his studies at the beginning of the Bourbon Restoration in 1816. Throughout the 1820s, '30s, and '40s, his democratic politics and scientific study in the realms of organic chemistry and medicine developed in tandem. Presenting his ideas in their first mature form and accelerating his political engagement in the early July Monarchy, Raspail published his *Essai de chimie organique* in 1830, the same year in which he took an active role in the Revolution of 1830. Disappointed like so many of his political allies by the instauration of a new constitutional monarchy, Raspail pursued his radical political agenda on the Paris streets until he was sentenced to fifteen months in prison. During his confinement he refined his ideas on organic chemistry, publishing his *Nouveau système de chimie organique* in 1833 while also cultivating his radical political agenda, which culminated in the creation of his publication

Le réformateur, which began to appear in 1834. Raspail became a central figure of the democratic movement throughout the 1830s and 1840s. He ran for president in the Second Republic, produced some of the most original and groundbreaking scientific work in the field of organic chemistry, and led the reform of the medical profession and public health.

A self-styled inheritor of Marat, Raspail sought to channel the spirit and ideas of that eighteenth-century revolutionary luminary in a new democratic era. In a long article dedicated to his forebear, Raspail disguised his self-portrait in a historical study divided into two parts, defined by his roles as "savant" and as "revolutionary." In the field of science, he lauded Marat's creativity and commitment to "overturning many accepted systems and elucidating many anomalies previously unexplained."[60] He established an implicit parallel with his own tumultuous relationship to the scientific and medical community by portraying Marat the scientist as an "inventor who elicited rival and hateful passions, since one only invents by refuting, and one can only build after one has demolished."[61] For Raspail, this scientific intransigence complemented Marat's political heroism. "A man of science, he had treated politics in the manner of science; radical logician, he had pushed the demonstration to its last consequences; a passionate lover of truth."[62] Marat's weapon of choice in this revolutionary tumult, Raspail insisted, had been the printed word: "Jean-Paul Marat threw himself into the revolutionary torrent which was about to swallow up the entire past that the spread of enlightenment had been undermining since the day when the invention of printing had brought the encyclopedia of human knowledge and the discoveries of each day within the reach of everyone at low cost. Glory to the printing press, this great school of human progress!"[63] Raspail's account of Marat highlighted his own conception of democratic action: he understood himself to be a scientific and political revolutionary who used his pen and his genius to challenge the scientific and political status quo. His biographical self-portrait was successful enough that others echoed this nineteenth-century incarnation of Marat: "Monarchs! leave for a moment the royal purple, and come to throw some gold coins on the Raspaillian path."[64]

For Raspail, the democratic revolution in scientific knowledge was to be put in the service of a more effective and responsive public health system. As in the democratic almanacs, in which he wrote articles on public hygiene, hospital, and political reform, his ideas on medicine and hygiene included making doctors civil servants, to be called upon to advise in the creation and execution of laws and regulations pertaining to public health. The doctors were also to expand public knowledge through publications and education for a wide audience, and to practice a new kind of medicine accessible to all social classes. Raspail placed a more popular and accountable politics at the center of this call for health reform. For him, politics, social policy, and public health were all of a piece.

Building on the arguments presented in the democratic almanacs for a medical magistrature, Raspail argued that public health would best be served by a transformation of the relationship between doctors and the administrative state. He demonstrated the tension between the extreme limits of the current administrative system and the necessity of a robust and more democratic administration in his prison notebooks. In a compelling account of his interactions with the prison inspectors and the need for penitentiary reform, Raspail presented his ideas on equality and public authority. Prison, he argued, had the effect of reducing every individual to the most base conditions. They had "nothing less than a body, a mind, a stomach, and their health."[65] The prison, in turn, "distributes to all of them, with the same measure, and the same mass of light, and the same amount of breathable air, and the same dose of food, and the same weight and nature of bread, and the same clothes and the same bedding."[66] Presenting the dark side of the conditions of equality that characterized the imprisoned body in a democracy, Raspail entered into a sustained dialogue to improve and transform the regulatory conditions of the prison where he was condemned.

"Monsieur l'inspecteur," said Raspail in his account on attempts to ameliorate the quality of the bread served to inmates, "please tell me what the conditions of the auction are, and what the successful bidder is obliged to do, so that I may have a basis for assessing how far he has deviated from them."[67] The inspector responded: "The notarized and accepted conditions are delivered to the bakery, that is, 13 percent reduced mercury and pure wheat flour of fourth quality." Raspail exclaimed in astonishment that such quality was simply impossible, since at that rate the boulanger would go out of business. He then asked the inspector if the Conseil de salubrité had not signaled the impossibility of such high-quality flour for the nourishment of so many inmates: The "administration seemed to take as keen an interest in the results of my research as I did; it provided me with a laboratory."[68] After demonstrating that the flour delivered for analysis was not the flour used to make the bread for prison inmates, and facing the incredulity of the inspector, Raspail turned to Vivien, the prefect of police. He recounted the prefect's response that he would assign the Conseil de salubrité to the task of investigating the bread more thoroughly. And yet no new inspector came to the prison.

The central theme of Raspail's account is not that the administration was necessarily intent on doing harm, nor that it was by nature corrupt and abusive. Raspail staged a very different tension between an inspector who was under the ill-informed orders of a new prefect who meant well but was unfamiliar with the realities of the bureaucratic machine, and a distant Conseil de salubrité that had established entirely acceptable regulations but suffered from a complete inability to execute them properly. The critique thus focuses on the distinction between the positive attempts of the administration to establish regulations, and the inertia of what Raspail called "bureaucracy" as opposed to "administration." "Everything ends up in bureaucracy, as soon as things stop working for the administrators," he argued.[69] Young prefects arrived with great intentions, but the problem was the long-serving employees in the various offices. The bureaucracy, Raspail recounted, generated a system in which "the report, for the police, becomes law; the prefect's decree is only its promulgation." Under such conditions, "the prefect reigns, which can be done while sleeping; it is the report that governs. . . . Brave lazy kings, all these ministers and prefects, who, once buried in the depths of their cabinets, can no longer see anything except through the glasses of their advisors, and who seem to be held in a private cell, like machines fit for signing, and broken piggy banks, after having thrown into them, penny by penny, at the expense of taxpayers, a few hundred thousand francs!"[70] At the heart of Raspail's prison notebooks was therefore a critique of bureaucracy, its ineffectiveness and profound limitations, and a call for a more democratic and effective administration.

Thus, Raspail did not respond to this bureaucratic weightiness with a simple critique. Rather, he argued for the necessity of democratizing administrative action, the proper execution of regulations, and a more transparent and accountable choice of the administrators.

> One is never so well cared for as by oneself or by one's own; do by yourselves the business of your well-being and your health. Do not take to heart the interests of the citizens who live in Montmartre, neglecting those of the inhabitants of Bercy, your neighborhood. Help each other with your cooperation and your advice, in your respective neighborhoods; entrust the care of the cleanliness of the streets, of the sanitation of your atmosphere, of everything that concerns your health and that of your children, to the supervision of a certain number of you, as interested as all of you are in bringing a prompt and decisive remedy to the ills that afflict you, and from which they are not immune. Let each district have its own council of public health, appointed by you, and which will last a time short enough not to confer privilege, long enough not to interrupt the series of operations. In order to regulate the relations of influence from district to district, organize a general council composed of delegates of each particular council, and where everything is finished amicably, and in virtue of the principle: that in the matter of sanitation, what

harms others can benefit no one. You do not need a law to be authorized to proceed in this way; *the law leaves at your disposal all that does not go beyond the limits of the contract; and the association of which I speak to you is only a simple contract to be signed.*[71]

Echoing ideas he would promote throughout the 1830s and '40s, Raspail drew on the theme of a new social contract to define how health inspectors should be chosen and their proximity to the population. At the heart of this social contract was not a recognition of new rights or even new laws, but a more effective administrative system. Learning the essential precepts of hygiene and sanitation, each individual was to take responsibility for ensuring that their neighborhood was salubrious and clean. But this expanded education and individual responsibility did not obviate the need for an administrative power. To the contrary, such public knowledge would be translated into a new local administrative body, consisting of well-informed delegates who would serve on a new local council and inform decisions on public sanitation.

"What could it mean for the State to take care of public health, if it abandons the citizen to the caprice of charlatans as soon as he feels sick?" Raspail asked. "The citizen, by the fact of his tax, has the right to be protected as much against the one who murders him as against the one who lets him die without help." Raspail argued that the only way to build a reliable and affordable public health system was to transform doctors into civil servants paid by the state. This reformed public health service would expand beyond doctors to include "the pharmacist, this doctor's assistant. The citizen [doctor] who cares for everyone in the city, no longer sells health, but teaches and administers it, supervises and imposes it, in the name of all, and to everyone, at everyone's expense." The "pharmacist and the physician should be magistrates, nobly paid by the State, and receiving nothing more, on pain of concussion, from the scarcity or munificence of diseases." Moreover, the hierarchy of doctors was to be established through "free and competent election." These new public offices were to be paid for by "a few additional cents," ensuring that "the poor would be just as well cared for as the rich." By transforming public health into a public service paid for through taxes for all citizens, "the lack of profit within the profession makes the dedication to the patient uniform."[72] With these ideas, Raspail became one of the first to sketch the foundations of a public health system paid for by the whole population and accessible to all.

Raspail's push to democratize access to medical care and proper hygiene also included a commitment to public education. A regular contributor and then editor of the democratic almanacs for questions of personal health and public hygiene, Raspail also authored a series of inexpensive works and then a yearly publication—initially published in two volumes in 1843 and then reedited every year into the twentieth century—titled *Manuel annuaire de la santé, ou médecine et pharmacie domestique: Tous les renseignements théoriques et pratiques nécessaires pour savoir préparer et employer soi-même les médicaments, se préserver ou se guérir ainsi, promptement et à peu de frais, de la plupart des maladies curables, et se procurer un soulagement Presque équivalent à la santé dans les maladies incurables* (A Handbook on health, domestic medicine, and pharmaceuticals: All the theoretical and practical information you need to know how to prepare and use medicines yourself, to preserve or cure yourself, promptly and inexpensively, from most curable diseases, and to obtain relief almost equivalent to good health in the case of incurable diseases).[73] Explicitly written to improve the state of medical "administration,"[74] the book was one of the growing number of publications meant for working-class audiences in the 1840s. Its pocket size, lightweight paper, price, and descriptive (lengthy!) title all directed it toward a wider audience looking for relief and knowledge on how to self-medicate inexpensively. The book was a tremendous success by any standard, selling almost 200,000 copies in the first five years—and, as one of its publishers, Dentu, recorded, 322 copies in the first six weeks.[75] The opening lines of the book insisted, "This book is written in the interest of the greatest number,"[76] encouraging those who could afford its modest price to purchase it for others. Raspail's stated ambition was to "teach the sick how to heal themselves without my aid; I no longer address myself to the clientele, but to readers." Convinced that the medical profession had been captured by professional secrets and obscure doctrines, "unintelligible to the patient that his means of healing are alternately preached and criticized by the pontiffs of the temple,"[77] he explicitly "put the theory and practice of my medicine within the reach of all intelligences, and the preparation of my medicines within the reach of all pockets."[78]

Raspail's educative mission was filled with the language of the democratic movement. Critiquing the "arbitrary" and "capricious" power wielded by doctors, Raspail sought to create a new "reciprocal" relationship between medical authorities and the sick. The patient should not be asked to "profess a blind faith in the doctor"; the patient "should be free to choose a doctor in whom he or she has confidence."[79] The client was now to offer an "enlightened control" over the work of medical authorities. Beyond checking on the "despotic" power of traditional medicine, "popularizing" access to medical knowledge also prevented the "irrational practices" of certain doctors, and thus guaranteed a faster road to good health. Arbitrary authority was therefore to be overcome through what Raspail explicitly referred to as popular "practice." Exploring the "art of medicine and healing," he insisted, "We should only ask of theory what is practically possible." This emphasis on practice ran throughout Raspail's oeuvre. Practice was essential to one's self-education—it was important to depend neither on blind faith nor on overly complex and remote theory in a new democratic age—just as it was essential for improving the medical profession itself. As Raspail argued in his plans for neighborhood administrative councils, the more patients that a doctor saw and treated, the better their methods and knowledge. This was still an original idea in the 1840s, when medical teaching remained largely based on theory and dissection. Raspail was one of the strongest voices within a movement that called for medical education reform grounded in firsthand experience. For him, the emphasis on practice would also have the positive effect of opening the medical field to more practitioners. A more accessible medical education could, as he argued, "provide people, even those most unfamiliar with medical studies, not only with the means to control wisely the doctor's prescriptions, but also to maintain good health, to treat themselves and others, in the greatest number of cases, by simple and easy means, and without needing to have recourse to the doctor."[80] The educative mission further infused Raspail's medical and political preoccupations. By 1848, Raspail's "club" provided him with the opportunity to speak to large gatherings of workers on questions of health and politics interchangeably: "an exposé of doctrines and the illustration of these principles in practice."[81] Raspail argued that these public clubs were "the preparatory meetings of the city, . . . its advanced sentinels, the mutual school of patriotism, the crucible of reputations, the nursery of young devotion and of unrecognized or ignored talent."[82]

Alongside providing education, Raspail also dedicated an important part of his time to treating working-class patients who previously had lacked access to medical care. Offering to see patients for an extremely low price, he developed an overwhelming clientele first in the Montsouris neighborhood and then in a small office in the Marais, on the rue des Francs Bourgeois. Since he had refused to pursue the medical degree of his day, he was not able to prescribe medicines or perform acts as a doctor himself. He therefore served as an "assistant" to a Doctor Cottereau, who wrote all official prescriptions. Raspail's practice was sufficiently well known—as was his hostility to the elite medical establishment—that he was brought to trial for illegal practice of medicine in 1846. Having set aside much of his direct political engagement since his imprisonment to focus on providing health and hygiene relief to as many people as possible through his books and his practice, he used the trial as an opportunity to speak about the corruption of the contemporary medical and judicial system.

Raspail heralded the "the influx of patients who come to us on the day of the free consultations, and whose number rose one day to six hundred," before explaining that more than six thousand sick people had come to seek care since the previous October.[83] Raspail attempted to turn the trial into a battle between his own attempts to help the sick and poor and the "police of diploma merchants, who defend the material and purely arbitrary privileges of the profession."[84] In a final harangue, he announced to the audience and the readers of the publication:

> You want to forbid me from entering your hospitals! I will organize one for me, for you, for everyone. I have power too! My sceptre is a tiny pen! My friends are my readers; my rooms are the garrets of the poor and the golden paneling of the rich. . . . Well, I will cure by correspondence! . . . The medical police, in spite of its slogans, is overwhelmed by the 80,000 copies sold in France, without counting the counterfeits and the translations abroad [of my *Manuel annuaire de la santé*]. Panic is spreading: the leaders see their influence declining; the politicians understand that they will lose votes in the elections if they do not come to the aid of the voters in need of medical care. Time is short; the ministry is testing us.[85]

As his biographer, Dora Weiner, has argued, considering that Raspail had turned away from direct engagement in politics for almost twelve years by the Revolution of 1848, it was no doubt his ability to present and defend his cause of caring for the health of the working class that played an essential role in his huge popularity on the democratic left in 1848.[86]

The connection between Raspail's ideas on medicine and his politics were deeply intertwined. He had referred to himself explicitly as "the man of resistance in the name of the people and the man of the people's moral and political instruction."[87] In another famous trial, the "Lafarge affair" of 1840,[88] which further contributed to his fame, Raspail tirelessly reminded the public that political and scientific questions were of the same piece. "As for the public's riveted attention on these very sad debates," he argued, "it is justified by the interest of the moral questions raised by this affair; social institutions, jurisprudence, procedures, expertise in general, all led to the proclamation in full audience in support of these reforms of which the electoral reform is only a particular case and an imponderable detail, in the midst of the immense mass of our social shortcomings."[89] Indeed, Raspail's democratic politics and medical practice walked hand in hand.

Most importantly, while Raspail was a dedicated revolutionary, he insisted on the importance of a democratized administration as one of the essential outcomes of revolutionary action. This democratic administration would execute the regulations necessary for the public good in general, including those in the realm of strong public health and improved domestic hygiene.

In his periodical *Le réformateur*, he explained the contributions that would come with the creation of a transparent and popular administrative authority. While he sought to "fight against the government of one," he nonetheless was far from refusing the "magistrature of one or many." He rejected the idea of kingship, or of dictators appointed for life. Instead, his administrative ideal was grounded in "temporary magistrates, elected, revocable, and accountable."[90] He clearly stated his understanding of the role of administration, arguing that "the highest magistrate executes the law which is the expression of the general will." He then outlined the ideal administrator:

> The head of the administration would be only a passive and not a blind instrument, a devoted and responsible servant and not an exactor; where the will of all, as widely represented as possible, would regulate in advance the use of the funds and the destination of the resources; where everything would be done in the interest of the greatest number, and for the greatest possible happiness—it would matter little whether the tax were 1 or 2 billion and absorbed all the money of the country. The happiness of the people would always be directly related to the increase of the number. It is obvious, in fact, that the aim of administration as we define it, being to procure for men the greatest sum of enjoyment, the greater the social fund, the more progressive the result.[91]

Using increased taxes to fund ambitious public policy revealed how favorable Raspail was to the expansion of public services. Throughout his publications, he insisted on the fundamental necessity "to organize a humanitarian administration, whose paternal solicitude, watching day and night over all the branches of our occupations, penetrating everywhere, into the living room as well as into the workshop, into the factory as well as into the garret, had as a constant goal in all its efforts: to improve, to relieve, to educate, to harmonize the conditions, to balance the sum of the needs and the resources, to adapt work to physical organization, and to provide occupation according to intellectual capacity."[92] Summarizing the essence of his ideal for a democratic administration, he argued for "the election of a temporary administrator, and establishing limits within which his arbitrariness would be confined."[93] A more complete statement of the ideal of the new relationship between the administration and a democratic society in the nineteenth century is difficult to imagine.

So the danger of administration lay in a distant autonomous bureaucracy, which was guided by its own rules and its own goals, divorced from those of the population. Such an autonomous bureaucratic power, Raspail argued, would necessarily end by provoking a revolution. The result of revolutionary activity was not to bring an end to administration and regulatory power, but to bind the administration more tightly to the demands and needs of the public. "A revolution must consist in proclaiming the progressive law of reform, in supporting its development, in promoting the daily applications of its innovations," he demanded.[94] For it was precisely through revolution that the administered could reassert their ideals.

For Raspail, "the mass is always right in the end; this is the day of a revolution, of a great epoch in history." Society was forming a "new social pact under new conditions." The new social contract was to guide the administration according to two central principles. First, Raspail argued, a democratic pact between administrators and the administrated could not "last eternally," because a population was always changing. The new pact was therefore intended to "establish a governmental form which, successively preparing itself for the march of all these progressive modifications, marches with civilization."[95] Or, as he argued in the next issue, "the administrative organization changes as the population grows."[96] In other words, the new social pact had a profoundly historical nature, since the population and its demands changed over time. The most effective means to ensure that the administration would remain in contact with its population was through delegation and election.

Importantly, in his articles on universal suffrage, Raspail insisted that the realm in which universal suffrage was perhaps most important was that of administration and not legislation. "What do we mean by universal suffrage?" he queried. "Is it the suffrage of all on every administrative and governmental question, on every current event of the administration?" He responded with a restatement of an essential theme that could be found throughout discussions of democratic administration in France:[97]

> Nature has from time immemorial led men assembled in the same enclosure and living on the products of the same soil to distribute work among themselves and to choose a delegate, an administrator who takes charge of the interests of the masses, who regulates current events and decides, at least by provisional execution, on the appropriateness of such and such an urgent measure, who takes such and such a course of action, finally who administers alone by conforming to the wishes of his constituents. But the idea of administration implies that of election, because the talent to administer is not transmitted by inheritance, is not presumed by induction; it is recognized; it is chosen.[98]

Universal suffrage provided the best means of choosing delegates for key administrative functions. Once again, Raspail's essential aim was to reduce bureaucratic autonomy while preserving the essential functions of a popular administration and regulation. This allowed him to conclude: "We want an administrator who does not reign without governing, nor who governs without reigning, but who administers and is accountable for his administration to those who appoint and supervise him."[99]

Second, Raspail argued that administrators should take action according to general social rules. "Society grows according to unquestionable laws," he stated. Magistrates should not "make orders based on the rules of their own logic, which is most often, and among many self-proclaimed geniuses, simply their bon plaisir."[100] Instead, it was necessary to learn the basic laws of guiding a society through social scientific study, and to adapt the administration to these laws as they changed over time. Without a clear understanding of social science, "the administration was organized without rules and without system," leading to a bureaucratic system in which "social organization accommodates the encroachment of the administrative power, [and] the man ends up putting himself in place of the masses." In such a context, there could only be "struggle between the governed and the administrators." In the context of adapting to the needs of a population over time through clear social-scientific understanding, however, "societies have organized their administration in such a way that the agents, who hold the reins of the State, take it upon themselves to lend a hand to the natural course of human affairs, then, by virtue of their mutual affinity."[101] Raspail's conception of a democratic administration seized upon and articulated in the clearest sense the ideals of the democratic revolution that was underway. Revolution should give birth to a more just popular administrative power that would be grounded in a historical and social-scientific understanding of society to solve the most fundamental aspects of citizen's lives.

Finally, this new mode of administration required a holistic understanding of the individual which reached not only into historical context and a sociological understanding of general needs but also into the care and understanding of individual needs. Disease needed to be understood as a field in which the well-being of individuals and that of the community were intimately bound. Disease did not stop on the doorstep of any one group. To "guard the health of the people," a socialist reformer would later argue in terms that Raspail had imagined in the first half of the century, "look on them as being one whole, not as being several communities."[102] Raspail offered a particularly sophisticated interpretation of this doctrine, grounded in the need for modern politics to occupy itself with the most concrete aspects of the everyday life of its citizens. "Man is certainly not an ideality that can be fruitfully studied in isolation from his physical organization. We cannot relieve him in this way any more than we could cure him with abstractions and metaphysics."[103] The practical attention to medical and hygienic needs of individuals pushed administration out of the realm of the abstract "natural" individual and into the most basic, concrete social demands. "Raspail wrote, establishing a parallel between the works of biological science and government of the eighteenth century, "When one reads carefully the books that have been composed on the greatness of Nature, that have multiplied on the art of governing individuals, one is tempted to believe that the art of governing was considered by their authors without man, who is everything in government, and without whom there is no government."[104] Raspail's own scientific and medical practice pushed him out of the "science of the salons and the Bourse." In both medical and administrative practice, he was concerned with "man on earth and in society, the man of pleasure and pain, man with and without needs, man of hate and love, that malady destroys, or good health inspires." This actually existing human being was the object of an administration that sought to "protect, nourish, enlighten, and console while also conforming to the special laws required for the organization of governance."[105]

The arbitrary will of individual administrators was to give way to a new sociological pact in which general laws discovered through social science guided administrative decisions and actions, which were to be wedded to the development of a specific social milieu that was understood to change over time. The object of administration was then to be transferred from the abstract individual of natural law to the concrete individual of medical practice, and bureaucratic autonomy was to be replaced by popularly elected magistrates. With this medical-administrative model, Raspail—"one of the luminaries of democratic France,"[106] as he was known in 1848—captured the core of the democratic revolution in public health.

When Raspail ran for president of the Second Republic in 1848, his views were clearly established in his resurrection of Marat's revolutionary periodical, *L'Ami du peuple*. In the issue of March 12, 1848, Raspail explained: "The Republic we have dreamed of (and our dream will become a reality) will not be a Republic of thrones and sinecurists. Jobs will be duties and not dignities...; and the president, a mere crank in the administrative machinery, will often say to someone more fortunate than himself: Do you want my place?"[107] Raspail's ideal of public service and democratic administration guided his candidacy. And while his bid for the presidency was unsuccessful in the face of Louis-Napoleon, the ideas he and many of his fellow democrats had defended on public health and hygiene would later find their way into the policies of the Second Republic and establish a new model for public health, hygiene, and sanitation.[108]

Erwin Ackerknecht revealed long ago that "it is generally and rightly assumed that the years around 1848 are the starting point of modern hygiene, public and private."[109] This chapter has placed the spotlight on a series of democratic reforms and reformers who explicitly rejected the primacy of commercial and individual interest over the public good at the same time as their conception of new and more robust administrative capacities rejected an elitist approach of public health. Summarizing the influence of those engaged in the battle for democracy in the previous decades, the doctor Louis Delasiauve wrote: "There was, as we have said, no uniformity in the systems. There were notable differences between Pierre Leroux, Buchez, Considerant, Proudhon, Louis Blanc, Jules Lechevalier, Dupoty, Lamennais, Émile Barrault, the advanced democrats, and the socialists. But although they disagreed on the means, they agreed at least on the goal, that is to say on the necessity of radical modifications in the political and civil organization."[110] In the realm of public health and hygiene, these efforts contributed to a sea change in and after 1848.

Indeed, during the Second Republic, a battery of new public health and hygiene measures were implemented. On August 10, 1848, the Conseil supérieur de santé was replaced by the new Comité consultative d'hygiène publique, under the Ministry of Agriculture and Commerce. On December 18, 1848, the creation of the Conseil d'hygiene publique et de salubrité was extended to all departments. The law of January 10, 1849, established the Assistance publique in Paris, while the law of January 19, 1850, created the first law against "insalubrious housing." And in 1851, laws were passed on March 10, 19, and 27 against the trafficking of merchandise that could have ill effects on the health of consumers. The Second Republic undoubtedly marked a watershed in public policy on health and sanitation questions.

Here the 1850 law on insalubrious housing is particularly telling. Inspired by the critiques leveled against the insufficiencies of the Conseil de salubrité during the July Monarchy, the law provided the Parisian administration with ample new means to intervene and improve the living conditions and public health of working-class Parisians. Discussions of the law explicitly stated that "its purpose was to put an end to a cause of weakening and mortality of the population, and its effect was to arm the public authorities with new means of action on private property." As a result, its article 1 declared "insalubrious all dwellings that are in conditions likely to affect the life or health of their inhabitants."[111] The push for greater administrative capacity in public health in the name of the public good, and against the "liberal" ideals of private property, marked a key victory for the democratic movement of the previous decades grounded in local knowledge and the power of municipal councils.

5

Workplace Democracy

Equity and Popular Arbitration

After climbing a staircase in a provincial porcelain factory, the radical democratic socialist Sénécal opened a door to find a room filled with women workers. In the corner, and despite factory regulations, which forbade "eating in the workshops, for reasons of cleanliness and hygiene for the workers," he saw a woman with an open bottle of wine and some charcuterie on the table beside her.

Sénécal, "either out of duty or despotism," cried out to the woman, and pointed toward a placard on the wall with a list of regulations. "Read article 9 out loud to me," he shouted.

"What for?" she responded proudly.

"So that you know why you will be paying a three-franc fine!"

Bemused, the woman responded: "Why should I care? When the owner returns, he'll remove your fine. I don't give a damn about you, my bonhomme!" She quickly returned to work, snubbing the arbitrary intervention of this awkward visitor.

Having witnessed the exchange, Sénécal's friend Frédéric looked at him and exclaimed, "You are quite severe for a democrat!"

Sénécal responded, "Democracy is not wanton individualism. It is equality before the law, the distribution of work, and order!"

Recognizing Sénécal's democratic convictions, but still unimpressed, Frédéric quickly added: "You forgot about humanity."[1]

This scene from Flaubert's *L'Éducation sentimentale* offers a surprising account of promoters of radical democracy in the 1840s. Indeed, Sénécal is the most revolutionary of the circle of young friends at the center of the novel, giving long harangues on the reconstruction of a new order and the destruction of the old. And yet here he is, in a factory, attempting to impose regulations on a room of women workers. There are two essential themes in this scene that sit at the core of this chapter and a more thorough understanding of the relationship between democratic society and regulatory power in the workplace. First, worker regulations were understood to be a part of the democratic revolution underway in the middle decades of the nineteenth century. Second, beyond the mere fact of expanding and implementing further regulations, workplace democracy also depended upon *how* these regulations were enforced. The woman's refusal to recognize Sénécal's authority, her conviction that the owner himself would not enforce Sénécal's intervention, and Frédéric's surprise at Sénécal's despotism captured essential elements of the debates on how to regulate the workplace democratically. To be sure, in question was neither the regulations nor their democratic nature, but the arbitrary way in which they were being enforced.

This chapter focuses on the invention and elaboration of new, shared practices of regulatory power in the workplace, and their relationship to larger processes of democratic administration in the first half of the nineteenth century. It explores attempts in the postrevolutionary period to construct a more participatory, nonarbitrary, egalitarian, and collective mode of protecting individuals who worked in factories. Once again, as in the case of forests, municipal power, and health care, there was a need not only to adjust and reinvent rules and regulations that managed the workplace after the Revolution, but also to reconsider how such public authority was practiced.

The creation of new Prud'hommes councils was one of the principal ways in which this was achieved. These new modes of regulation and arbitration were designed to limit efforts to accumulate excessive regulatory or administrative power in the hands of central authority, arbitrary local officials, or autonomous corporations. The councils were jurisprudential, focused on practical concrete issues, and sensitive to the particularities of context. As such, they attempted to manage everyday problems on the workshop floors and beyond as closely as possible to their source.

Historical studies of the Prud'hommes councils during this period have already noted their democratic nature. The Prud'hommes were one of the institutions that best captured Sydney and Beatrice Webb's ideal of the experiments in "industrial democracy" that thrived in the nineteenth-century workshops and factories.[2] "It is of interest as an early illustration of democracy in industry and as the institution which filled, in a sense, the gap between the guild system of the ancien regime and the modern trade union," Chester Higby and Caroline Willis argued in 1948.[3] Françoise Fortunet has referred to the Prud'hommes of 1848 as a "democratic utopia,"[4] Claire Lemercier has highlighted Victor Hugo's assessment that it represented a "justice démocratique,"[5] and Jean-Pierre Royer's *Histoire de la justice en France* notes that persuant to "a law of 1853, the Second Empire wished to recover an authority judged too democratic by appointing the presidents from among supervisors."[6]

Historians' references to the democratic nature of the Prud'hommes have largely focused on the fact that the council members were voted into office, with limited mandates to represent workers and masters, making the councils institutions in which individuals were judged by their peers. This is certainly an essential aspect of their democratic nature. What follows argues that these councils also played an essential role in democratizing essential modes of regulatory policymaking and social provision in the workplace. In other words, their role as "democratic" institutions was limited not only to the source of their power or how they were chosen—although that too was essential—but also in the way they contributed to elaborating technologies of democratic governance in which the traditional paternal and providential responsibilities of the state were shared by turning to those who were most directly concerned. It was precisely in the attempts to redefine the means and ends of regulatory police that these councils helped forge a new ideal of democratic government.

The End of the Guilds and the New Challenges of Workplace Regulation

The first years of the Revolution famously transformed the regulation of work. Following the abolition of privileges on August 4 and the signing of the Declaration of the Rights of Man and Citizen twenty-two days later, the social, political, and economic regulations bound to the guild system were turned upside down. After almost eighteen months of confusion about the impact that these declarations of liberty and equality should have on the guild system, the Decree of Allarde in March 1791, followed a few short months later by the Le Chapelier Law on June 14, 1791, provided one of the most radical solutions imaginable, destroying the corporate organization of work. The decrees were slathered in language of commercial, industrial, and individual liberty, which was to serve as a new foundation for professional activities. The famous article 7 of the Decree of Allarde stated: "Any person shall be free to engage in such trade or practice such profession, art, or craft as he may think fit." Similarly, article 4 of the Le Chapelier Law stated: "If, against the principles of liberty and the constitution, citizens attached to the same professions, arts and trades, were to take deliberations, or make agreements among themselves tending to grant only at a determined price the assistance of their industry or their work, the said deliberations and agreements, accompanied or not by the oath, are declared unconstitutional, infringing on liberty and the declaration of the rights of man, and of no effect." The bonds of employment were therefore to be determined by individual choice. Nonetheless, the idea of individual "liberty," a constant leitmotif for rethinking the organization of work during the short but monumental half decade stretching from the summer of 1789 to the summer of 1794, posed more questions than it provided answers. Article 3 of the Decree of Allarde left the issue of what kind of regulation could be reasonably pursued in this context almost entirely open, stating simply that it was necessary to "comply with any police regulations that are, or may be, made." As Philippe Minard has noted in his commentary on these laws: "Confusion remained; what regulations were they talking about? Who was to enforce them?"[7] Furthermore, the importance of the Allarde and Le Chapelier laws became even more outsized in postrevolutionary French politics as one of the most symbolic bodies of legislation of the early Revolution.[8] This meant that any discussion of how to regulate the workplace conjured up images of revolutionary transformation. And considering the importance of the guilds for workplace regulation prior to the Revolution—involved in everything from working hours to wages to product quality to promotion—replacing them was a cornerstone in a social order no longer bound to privilege.

The challenge of regulating work following the first years of the Revolution could therefore be presented in the following terms: the ideals of individual freedom and equality so cherished by the declarations of 1789 and reforms of 1791 forced the dismantling of the semi-autonomous self-regulating corporations on the one hand while encouraging the reduction of any arbitrary exercise of regulatory police on the other.

While we are certainly not without our share of historians who have recounted the contributions of the Napoleonic Empire's juridical geniuses— Portalis, Tronchet, Maleville, Bigot, the emperor himself—the creation of a new regulatory model in the wake of the Revolution and the Empire also emerged out of another, deeper history that reached back into the question of regulatory police since the middle of the eighteenth century.

Historians of police powers have highlighted a gradual but profound shift across the second half of the eighteenth century that pushed in two opposing directions. On the one hand, the police, as Steven Kaplan argues, were increasingly regulating forms of economic and social life. At the same time, they were also developing a growing concern for the well-being of the king's subjects: "Royal paternalism and policy of social control were two sides of the same coin; both dealt with the relationship between the ruler (or his deputies) and the ruled. But whereas social control spoke the chilling language of *raison d'état* and stressed the checks placed upon the people and the supremacy of the State, this brand of paternalism exuded the compassion characteristic of familial ties, emphasized not the constraints upon the subjects but their claims upon the State, not the prerogatives of the government but its obligations."[9] Across the eighteenth century, the elaboration of a more effective regulatory police adhered, then, to this double imperative of social control on the one hand and paternalistic demands and obligations to oversee the welfare of the king's subjects on the other. In his "Mémoire sur la police de Paris," the commissaire Jean-Baptiste Lemaire summarized these twin objectives by suggesting that the police were to play the key role of "governing men and doing them good." These interventions were part of a larger engagement with "providing aid, protection, and relief that they must expect [*à leur accorder les secours, la protection et les soulagements qu'ils doivent attendre*]."[10] These dual motors for the expansion of regulatory police could be found throughout texts in the cameralist and police traditions in France, as well as in Germany and elsewhere. As the police brought an extraordinary range of social activities under the control of the state to ensure the efficient management and wealth of the state itself, they effectively found themselves responsible for a host of new daily activities. In its article on police, the *Encyclopédie* of Diderot and d'Alembert provides a relatively clear perspective on the scope and functioning of regulatory police powers by the mid-eighteenth century, noting that it managed domains ranging across society, including religion, discipline of *mœurs*, intemperance, commerce, arts, health, security and public order, roads, buildings, workers, and the poor.

The legacy of this social provision and obligation into and beyond the Revolution remains fundamental for understanding the regulation of work in the nineteenth century. This is because, paradoxically, while old regime corporations and police were legislated out of existence in the Revolution, the ideals of social provision—"providing aid and doing them good"—were reinforced. By 1802, for example, Günther von Berg could argue in his handbook on police that regulatory power "cleans the air one breathes; secures the villages and holdings in which one dwells, and the streets along which one walks; protects the fields that one cultivates; secures homes against fire and flood, and against illness, poverty, ignorance, superstition, and immorality; even if it cannot prevent all accidents, [the police force] seeks however to diminish and ease their consequences, and offers refuge in time of need to every pauper, casualty or person in need."[11] In other words, the scale and extent of public provision increased in many areas over the last decade of the eighteenth century, raising the stakes of reinventing regulatory power on the ashes of old-regime corporations and administrative despotism even further, at precisely the moment when the means through which such regulation was administered came under attack, especially in the workplace.

Under Napoleon, numerous proposals emerged to manage the tension between the means and the ends of regulatory power in the world of work. Most commonly, legislators, jurists, and merchants argued that for all of its possible flaws, the only reasonable remedy for fulfilling the regulatory duties of the state in the realm of work was a return and an updating of the guild system.[12] Merchants complained of bad product quality; apprentices complained of working conditions; master workmen complained of broken contracts, false trademarks, and problems of using raw materials procured by theft. One of the fervent supporters of reestablishing the guilds, Antoine Levacher-Duplessis, depicted the impact of the abolition of the guilds in the darkest terms, arguing that "the first effect of this absolute independence was to inspire a multitude of simple craftsmen with the desire to establish themselves as masters." As a result, he insisted, "the regulations which fixed, in the factories referred to as regulated [réglées], the manner according to which one was to manufacture no longer existed."[13] Other consequences brought on by this "unlimited liberty," he argued, were the "destruction of all discipline in the workshops and of the authority of the masters"; "the conditions stipulated for apprenticeships, the rules established in this respect by the statutes, [ceasing] to be followed"; the foremen "[giving] up training workers without profit for them"; and "the apprenticeship, so important and so necessary to the maintenance and promotion of the mechanical arts, [being] almost abandoned."[14] With this long list of complaints, Levacher-Duplessis captured a common set of arguments in favor of a return to the guilds. In his case, he hoped to capitalize on the return of the Bourbons to present the case of those merchants and laborers for whom a return to corporations was the only effective means of reestablishing an effective system of police in the postrevolutionary workplace. The watchmakers to the king signed a position making a similar statement: "The experience of twenty-five years of revolution has shown us the need to reestablish the guilds and masteries, which were only abolished as a consequence of a destructive system that was already well known in 1793, a system that wanted to divide everything."[15] Levacher-Duplessis was therefore able to conclude: "La France, once covered with useful establishments, stripped today of all the benefits that the spirit of religion and the patriotism of the bodies had granted it, can still recover all that it has lost; but it is necessary to renounce these disastrous systems that isolate men and dry up hearts; to bring together, on the contrary, those whom similar occupations and interests bring together."[16] Arguing before the Chamber of

Deputies in March 1816, Étienne-Antoine Feuillant summarized his position on the importance of reestablishing the guilds. Not only would "fraud . . . become impossible" but, because the foremen and the heads of the guilds would constantly survey their workshops and workers, the guilds "would render the action of the police easier and consequently less severe."[17] In short, Feuillant and many others argued that the guilds would provide much-needed oversight at the same time as they reduced the arbitrary power of the police. Little surprise, then, that this approach received such a wide audience throughout the first years of the Restoration.

But as widespread as it may have been, the idea of restoring the guilds ran up against a second, seductive conception of work in the postrevolutionary world, which fully embraced the ideals of the Revolution—although not necessarily toward the same ends. Generally gathered under the heading of "liberalism," this approach proved far more tenacious. For while the ideal of returning to the old-regime guilds was never realized, the liberal ideal would enjoy a long, committed following in both government and commerce. Though they did not necessarily refer to themselves according to the blanket term "liberals," those who supported some form of what would later come to be referred to as economic liberalism were committed to a radical critique of the arbitrary nature of police regulation in the name of individual liberty in the realm of the economy. Emphasizing the unwavering necessity of respecting individual liberty, this school rejected any return to the old corporations. Jean-Baptiste Say argued, summarizing the ambitions of this camp, "You can easily imagine that corporations result in an increase in the price of products, which is prejudicial for consumers." Emphasizing the new regime of rights and natural order, Say insisted that "the public is entitled to obtain the objects of its needs in the least expensive way. In the natural order, competition guarantees that the profits of the producers are only just wages, the equitable compensation for productive services. With competition removed, this guarantee no longer exists." According to this "liberal" perspective, presented by such figures as Say, liberty did not necessarily come at the expense of any regulatory force. Rather, the claim was that if industry were organized according to the ideals of liberty, it would self-regulate in the name of the public interest. "In many cases," Say asserted, "the monopoly is detrimental to the public without being profitable to the monopolists. For if an exclusive privilege preserves them from the competition of the nonprivileged, it does not preserve them from the competition of their fellow members. Each of them, moreover, is exposed, in his capacity as consumer, to suffer the prejudice which the corporations inflict on the public. If he sells the objects of his trade at a slightly higher price, he pays a little more for the objects of his consumption." Say's work was saturated with language of ensuring the public good through full-throttle competition, and it warned of the dangers that any form of corporation or monopoly would ultimately pose for the public prosperity.[18] In this sense, even an economist as fervently anticorporatist as Say remained committed to the ideal and obligation of providing for the public. He also remained convinced, however, that such provision could only be achieved at the expense of corporations and any form of arbitrary police.

It is worth noting that this ideal of liberty had a correlate in the political realm, which placed a renewed importance on the limits of government intervention: the idea of founding a new regime on formal constitutionalism and natural rights developed a vast audience in this period. From this liberal perspective, the key ambition was to determine the proper balance of governmental powers and the formal constitutional organization of a state that would preserve individual natural rights and limit state power by carving out large realms of social and economic activity outside of any government control.[19] The return to the corporations of the old regime and the postrevolutionary discourse of liberalism thus confronted each other head-on, especially in the waning years of the Empire and the Restoration.

A Nondespotic Management of the Workplace

By the early nineteenth century, gradually a new set of principles based on individual liberty and nonarbitrary intervention emerged to accomplish the ever-growing list of ends and ambitions attached to the idea of public welfare. The abolition of the guilds and the critiques of an arbitrary old regime police took on a new salience precisely *because* the tasks they had performed did not disappear, even as the essential vehicles for ensuring them came under fire. If agents of old-regime police intervened into almost every region of social activity to preserve social order and encourage the health and prosperity of the state, it was in the name of the prince. That is, the prince (through the police) acted as a paterfamilias "who seeks to maximize the welfare of his—or rather its—household."[20] The new imperatives of liberty, equality, and fraternity that had fueled the dismantling of the guilds and critiques of old-regime police during the Revolution, however, effectively reversed in whose name such social provision was to be pursued. It was no longer in order to ensure the prince's metaphorical household that social provision was ensured; it was no longer a question of pleasing the paterfamilias or even guaranteeing the opulence of the state in the abstract, as theorists of old regime police had argued. Gradually the idea came forward that it was necessary to ensure that social provision would ultimately serve those who needed it by making it more responsive to individual needs, assessing particular dangers, and responding to the most contingent and extreme circumstances. The administration was now to act not through some suspended ideal of natural order, but according to the specific circumstances in which individuals found themselves as a result of an ideal in which individuals should be able to choose their livelihoods and professions. So, as comforting as the calls for a return to old-regime corporations were, and as far-reaching and impactful as a liberal school might have been in other contexts, it was not the dominant path out of the critique of arbitrary police power in the name of liberty and equality.

A new mode of regulation challenged the ideals of unlimited freedom and limited government in the name of the social, cultural, and economic imperatives of regulation for public welfare. Michael Fitzsimmons has noted that some of the first legislation proposed by Jean-Antoine Chaptal for regulating work in March 1802 followed precisely such a logic: "On the one hand, [the Napoleonic regime] was not prepared to return to the structure and regulated economy of the Old Regime. On the other, it was unwilling to continue the unfettered, laissez-faire policies inaugurated by the Revolution, as evidenced by its intervention to assure the quality of products."[21] How was it possible to regulate in the name of the public interest without returning to old-regime corporations or leaving everything up to the individual interests of competitors in civil society? How could new regulations be established which were grounded neither in the particularity of a given industrial sector nor in the abstract interest of economic actors? And how could such regulations not be the product of an arbitrary state interest that ignored the well-being of the people? Solving this fundamental problem of public life required a rehabilitation of regulation as a means of serving both particular interests and the public good more generally.

Sismondi captured the spirit of this approach in the immediate wake of the Empire when he wrote: "The fundamental dogma of free and universal competition has made very great progress in all civilized societies; it has resulted in a prodigious development in the powers of industry; but often it has also resulted in appalling suffering for many classes of the population." As a result, Sismondi insisted, emphasizing the practical nature of his observation, "it is by experience that we have felt the need of this protective authority which we invoke; it is necessary to prevent men from being sacrificed to the progress of a wealth from which they will not profit."[22] Here, liberty and equality (for "civilized societies")[23] became the foundation for at once reinforcing the value of individual lives and redefining the reasons why those individual lives should be looked after.

This was not solely a problem of theory. The practical consequences of a new regulatory worldview grounded in liberty, equality, and fraternity also transformed and in some cases even expanded the providential function of regulation, increasing the wide range of exigencies falling under the heading of social provision. Alain Cottereau has shown how the Declaration of the Rights of Man and Citizen, as well as the early revolutionary legislation on work, radically transformed the very relationship between merchants, workers, journeymen, and apprentices, revealing that the postrevolutionary workplace hardly witnessed a new era of blanket laissez-faire. The Revolution, Cottereau argues, "was not simply a question of new formal civil rights but [one] of actually achieved possibilities, which were used on a massive scale."[24] The imperatives of regulation that emerged on the other side of the revolution therefore directly prolonged and even expanded the very practical aims of old-regime regulatory police and corporations, even as they were built on a radical critique of the means by which regulation in the name of public welfare had previously been pursued. The means and scale of this ambition had therefore shifted: the extensive reach of regulatory power was now possible because it was neither tethered to tightly controlled guilds nor performed in the name of the prince or the distant bureaucrat in the service of a well-ordered abstract state. It was instead the actual workers and those they encountered every day who were to be the subject and object of regulatory power. Workers themselves were now expected to play some role in negotiating and shaping the rules and guidelines according to which individuals would exercise and manage their newfound liberties.

Regulating for Liberty

Even in the early years of the revolutionary decade of the 1790s, individuals and groups on all levels of the production, distribution, and consumption chain expressed a growing concern about the impact of deregulation on manufacturing and markets.[25] As the revolutionary dust settled, the question of how to manage and regulate work came rushing back in on the Directory and then on Napoleonic France, especially during two key moments around 1799 and between 1803 and 1806.[26] The challenges were compounded by the fact that the industrial needs of war were pushing production to new levels at the same time that they brought the necessities of effective regulation to the fore. As Napoleon consolidated his power and set off to war with much of Europe, the problem of regulation became even more pressing.

"The trade has asked the government for a law to maintain apprenticeship contracts, the agreements made between workers and the manufacturers who employ them, and to guarantee the manufacturer ownership of the particular mark that he prints on the products of his factory. On the other hand, it is proposed to reestablish the communities of arts and crafts. It is thus a question of knowing whether the regulatory system will prevail over that of freedom."[27] With these words, spoken in January 1803, a deputy in the legislative assembly captured the essential terms through which regulation of work was understood in the early Empire. The necessities of regulation made themselves felt on a quotidian basis: apprentices complained of abuses, masters decried ruptures of contracts, and producers faced fraudulent products and breeches of brand names. The problem with how to respond in these first years of the new century was presented as a battle between the old regulatory system and a new kind of regulation that was consistent with liberty. While new versions of some of the old guilds were ultimately recreated, any massive return to the guilds was rejected. The potential restrictions on who could work and where directly contradicted the ideals of liberty celebrated by the revolution; restrictions on work based on privilege, age, and heredity were insufferable. So as evident as the need for regulation was, the Conseil d'état refused to return to an old guild system, and sought to update the powers of regulatory police without falling into the trap of corporate limits on individual freedom: "In a word, one should not confuse what is called *maîtrise* and police; these ideas are quite different, and one should never lead to the other. Therefore, the origin of the *maîtrise* offices should not be considered to be the same thing as an improvement of the police, nor even the needs of the State, but merely the spirit of monopoly, which usually reigns among the workers and merchants."[28] Police could be reinvented, and could be perfected without recourse to guilds.

The jurist Henrion de Pansey framed this problem in more straightforward terms when he posed the question: "So what is the best way to provide for this important part of public administration?" Pansey responded to his own rhetorical question by explaining that even if corporations could no longer provide the essential regulatory functions, "the reasons which have established the corporations have lost nothing of their force."[29] It was therefore a problem of extracting from the old system those elements that were necessary for good manufacturing and commerce while excluding the elements that were despotic or which hindered liberty. "Several useful institutions were attached to the regime of corporations," explained Regnaud de Saint-Jean-d'Angély, member of the Conseil d'état, to this end in 1806. "The privileges of which they availed themselves, the impediments they put to the exercise of industry, the tributes they levied on those who received the aggregation, disappeared without return. Freedom in the exercise of professions is a benefit that will be preserved for the French, and it will continue to favor the improvement of our arts, the restoration of our manufactures, and the reestablishment of our commercial relations with foreign countries."[30]

This process of conserving and even expanding many of the essential regulatory functions while transforming the means through which they were accomplished pushed statesmen, jurists, merchants, and workers to redefine regulatory power by considering what liberty could mean in the context of a well-regulated workplace. At a general level, one sees as early as 1803 a gradual move away from any straightforward opposition between the guilds, police, and regulation on the one hand and individual liberty on the other. At that time the relationship was growing increasingly less hydraulic; less regulation no longer necessarily meant more liberty, and vice versa. Again, the point was not that there had previously been no discourses of regulation, nor that the discourse of liberty was new. The novelty resided in the slow emergence of an idea that regulation was necessary in order for the freedom to work to be maintained. Regnaud insisted that guaranteeing liberty in the realm of work required some form of regulatory intervention. "Among the manufacturers and the workers, the craftsmen and their companions, freedom has also had its license which had to be repressed: it still has its abuses which must be destroyed."[31] Or, as one of the key texts on the Prud'hommes would summarize about the situation a few decades later: "After the abolition of the old regime of arts and crafts, the unlimited freedom of trade and industry, which the law left to themselves without rules or restraint, had produced by reaction many of the opposite excesses."[32] So while there was a wide-ranging consensus that old-regime corporations and regulatory police hindered liberty, by the early years of the Empire it was also clear that what was referred to as "unlimited liberty" without any regulation in the realm of work produced the opposite result. "Freedom once had too many fetters; since then, license has been unbounded. Everything was subjected to rules that were too narrow, everything was left to absolute arbitrariness." Or, as Francis Demier has suggested: "In the circle of the great notables of the Empire, the unfettered liberalism promised by the revolutionary legislation carried great risks for the economic and social balance of the nation."[33]

The shift in policy in the final moments of the Consulate and early years of the Empire was therefore brought on not by a new unbridled liberalism, but through a series of interrogations on how to articulate a revolutionary conception of individual liberty, work, and regulatory power. How could a new form of regulation that guaranteed individual liberty be achieved? At what level should the administrative regulation be organized, and according to what principle?

Creating the Conseils des Prud'hommes

The creation of the Conseils des Prud'hommes was one attempt to form a nondespotic mode of regulation that respected liberty. As early as 1803, the Consulate attempted to respond to the growing insistence of new modes of regulation by reintroducing some forms of police regulation that were reminiscent of the old regime. By reestablishing the worker's passport (the *livret ouvrier*), forbidding any form of worker coalition, and giving the employer the full right to establish workshop regulations (*règlements d'atelier*), the law of April 12, 1803, took a first step in navigating between older mechanisms of regulatory power and the postrevolutionary emphasis on individual liberty.[34] But such legislation, even as limited as it was, quickly raised another issue that was bound to the postrevolutionary critique of regulatory despotism: How should such regulations be executed and enforced?

In theory, responsibility for administration and application of rules and regulations was given to local police, but their capacity to intervene, especially in the traditional industries with their complex sets of rules and regulations, quickly proved infeasible. Within a few years, Napoleon offered a more thorough response with the law of March 18, 1806, creating the first Prud'hommes council for the silk workers of Lyon. Two laws followed on June 11, 1809, and August 3, 1810, which allowed the institution to spread to other industries and towns. The institution spread rapidly. By 1814 there were already twenty-six new councils.[35] And by 1845, Prud'hommes councils existed in sixty-eight cities, with Paris finally benefiting from the legislation in 1844.

The jurisdiction of the Prud'hommes in this period emerged precisely from the fact that, despite some claims that the first half of the nineteenth century was a heyday of laissez-faire industrial capitalist liberalism, industrial workshops were actually rife with regulations, which only mushroomed across the first half of the nineteenth century.[36] As the scene recounted by Flaubert that opened this chapter attests, individual workshops each had their own regulations, often established by the owners and foremen themselves. Initially, the Prud'hommes councils tended to side with the workers who claimed ignorance of the regulations. As a result, the regulations were increasingly made public, especially in the 1830s, in posters submitted to the Prud'hommes councils and to justices of the peace and mayors' offices. These regulations became the backbone of working conditions in nineteenth-century France. In 1836 at the workshop of Engelhardt and Heilman, for example, regulations were established and posted: "Art. 16. Any worker who enters our factory must read the present regulation or have it explained to him by his comrades, and his stay for eight days in the workshops will be considered as his adhesion to the regulations. The present regulation will also be deposited at the secretariat of the industrial tribunal." A similar set of regulations was posted under the title "Règlement de police intérieure de la Filature de Monthureux-sur-Saône (Vosges, 1836, R.5)," which stated: "Art. 19. will be read to the workers who will be advised as being subject to it by the sole fact of their participation in the work." In 1845, the regulations in the workshop of M. M. Collier opened with article 1: "Any worker who accepts work in the workshops of the Mechanical Painting Company submits himself to the conditions of the regulations established there."[37] As Flaubert suggested in the passage that opens this chapter, it was often the owners of businesses who considered themselves responsible for establishing and enforcing these regulations. Émile Bères won the Montyon Prize awarded by the Académie française for his work on improving the conditions of workers, arguing in one chapter for the "positive effects of regulations in the workplace": "An industrialist must avoid, as much as possible, sharp words and quarrels with all those under his control; it is also in his interest that good order reigns on his premises. These conditions are easily obtained by establishing a regulation that teaches the worker the obligations he contracts by accepting work, as well as the penalty he incurs for violating them. When this penalty then strikes him, he has only himself to blame."[38]

But workplaces were not the only sites where regulatory police expanded. Across the Restoration and especially the July Monarchy, there was also a growing concern about what were understood to be dirty or dangerous factories. A vast new range of regulations was slowly applied to these factories to improve working conditions and reduce impact on surrounding areas. One of the leading jurists on administrative law, Louis Antoine Macarel, noted that "these workshops can harm individuals, either in their lives or in their property; they can also diminish or destroy those comforts of life which make it sweeter. All these needs of first and second necessity call for a special protection against the dangers which can threaten them. Hence, the regulations on industrial establishments."[39] Macarel added that there were two ways of managing the dangers of such industrial complexes. One could allow individuals the freedom to choose where they wanted to work and live, as well as how they wanted to manage their workplaces. Macarel further argued that such liberty was in some cases necessary for the development of new industries. However, he also insisted that over the long term, no industry could be excluded from regulatory oversight. Hence, he highlighted those who had "thought it necessary to subject the exercise of human industry to certain restrictions which are intended to prevent the harm that might result from it. In the system of the latter, the maintenance of public order requires that the administration supervise the exercise of certain professions that could disturb society. These are, in particular, the workshops that are known as dangerous, unhealthful, or inconvenient."[40] Macarel's assessment once again confirmed the general opinion in the late 1820s that new modes of regulation were necessary.

This new attention to regulation raised the stakes for negotiating the relationship between workers and their employers in two ways. The sheer increase in regulations meant that there were more potential litigations. Consequently, the increase in the number of litigations created a new role for managing and further regulating work through the jurisprudential expansion brought on by the interpretation of such regulations. Claire Lemercier has highlighted the role that the Prud'hommes councils played as regulatory bodies: "These jurisdictions had first and foremost the aim of maintaining a form of discipline, of social order among their litigants—hence the importance of the idea of conciliation. They were institutions of social, economic, and technical regulation."[41] The dynamics which pushed the councils into the center of worker arbitration—the way the Prud'hommes judges were chosen, the principles that animated them, the way they exerted their powers of arbitration, and the decisions they came to—all developed in response to a more general problem of precisely how to manage and implement such regulatory power in a nondespotic way. In so doing, they contributed to this early experiment in the construction of a democratic regulatory power.

The Prud'hommes councils had their origins in the exceptional courts and corporations that had regulated and policed work while settling essential questions on wages, contracts, and quality in the old regime.[42] The creation of the Prud'hommes built, therefore, on many of the old means of managing and regulating work at the same time as they provided a technique for responding to the vacuum left by the interdiction of the corporations. Those in favor of the Prud'hommes councils during this period explicitly highlighted the role they played in providing regulation without old-regime corporations: "The choice of the industries and the Prud'hommes, distributed and mixed in this way, is, moreover, a good, I will even say a necessity, in that it excludes any retrograde tendency toward the system of the old corporations."[43] The Prud'hommes provided specific knowledge of the questions relating to industrial organization, contracts, and other work-related issues, while also ensuring the service that previously had been ensured by local police or justices of the peace. Moreover, a given Prud'hommes council could hear cases from multiple workshops, with members elected from a variety of industrial activities. In this way, the expertise was not confounded with an autonomous privilege of self-regulation by a given occupation. The development of the councils and their relationship to a new regulatory culture therefore joined the ideals of individual liberty and the recognition of common interests across trades and among workers.

The result was a growing awareness about and dependence on regulatory power for understanding key social questions. From their creation in 1806 through the Second Republic—a crucial period for the transformation, mobilization, and politicization of the workplace in France—the Prud'hommes played a fundamental role in mediating the relationships between workers and their foremen and factory owners, and therefore introducing a new emphasis on the role of regulation in structuring and appeasing social relations. Here too, the democratic almanacs provided key information on the lives of workers, presenting quotidian experiences of working life, and entertaining stories as well as useful information. The issue of 1841 argued, "We would like for this new Almanach to serve the moral, political, agricultural and industrial sciences" in an effort to give "democracy the solemn and calm allure that it requires from this point forward."[44] Amid the variety of information the almanac provided to workers were workplace regulations. For example, in 1841, the democratic almanac published "A Brief Code for Workers." The code began: "1. It is a principle of all law is that no one should be ignorant of the law. And yet, institutions seem to have forgotten workers; none seem to have the specific aim of helping workers learn about the law. As a result most of the time, workers are subject to laws they are unfamiliar with. It is therefore useful to indicate the principal laws that concern them directly."[45] The code went on to list more than one hundred specific regulations for different types of workshops: "Thus, there are different regulations for workers in seaports and salt marshes; for silk factories; for workers in inland ports, mines, and quarries; for halls and markets; for butchers, bakers, carpenters, etc.; for workers in all professions in the manufacturing countries. The practice of the trade teaches each worker the prescriptions of the regulation that concerns him."[46] This same issue of the almanac also treated the importance of the Conseils de Prud'hommes, explaining that they were elected officials responsible for "police in the workshops."[47] The almanacs therefore attested to the fact that increased knowledge of the specific regulations of given workshops played an essential role in developing a more just and "democratic" society. A short observation by a "Maitre Pierre" insisted on the importance of informing workers about the growth of regulations: "In these times, a tremendous work of social renovation is being carried out without the knowledge of everyone, poor and rich alike.... The best social form is the one from which the people derive the most freedom and well-being."[48]

The increasing attachment to a culture of regulation was therefore fed by the growing awareness of litigiousness within the workplace and its importance for "social renovation." By the time of the July Monarchy, when the almanacs were being published, Prud'hommes councils were delivering almost forty thousand judgments per year.[49] In 1841, the year in which the almanac cited above was published, one newspaper, *Echo de la fabrique* of October 15, noted that twenty-two cases had been heard over the previous two weeks in Lyon alone.[50] Between 1830 and 1842 alone, the sixty-eight councils heard 184,514 cases.[51] The supposed high point of laissez-faire liberal individualism in fact marked the birth of a new, widespread participative regulatory culture.

The Prud'hommes not only contributed to a growing focus on redefining social relations, but also provided a response to the threat of a despotic mode of police regulation. Article 1 of the law of 1806 established that the council in Lyon would be comprised of nine members, consisting of five commercial agents or producers and four heads or foremen of workshops. According to article 17 of the law of June 11, 1809, these members were to be elected individually by an absolute majority of all votes. By the 1830s the elections for the Prud'hommes had become important events in the daily lives of workers. In 1841, the *Echo de la fabrique* announced that the upcoming elections were of signal importance, because "by receiving this new mandate from the popular vote, the workers have the right to impose conditions on the councils. This imperative mandate gives them the necessary strength to demand the improvements that the factory needs."[52]

The impact of a vote by all "maîtres" and "patented workers" was that workers and merchants were being judged by their peers, instead of by expert judges. As another article in the *Echo* explained in encouraging workers to vote: "The ordinary judge only sees in his courtroom people with whom he has no relationship, shares no interest, affection nor hatred . . . ; the president of the Conseil des Prud'hommes is called, on the contrary, to judge for or against his interests, for or against his friends; I assume he does not have personal enemies, and his decision is sound at the moment, not like those of the other courts, captured by litigious issues; but he comes to a decision that is good or bad for a whole class of traders or workers."[53] In such a context, the elected judges played a dual role as both representatives—since they were chosen from among either the workers or the merchants—and arbitrators. Moreover, the mandates were limited. So while expertise could play a role, legal or judicial expertise was not the foundation for their judgments. In theory, they were to be elected based on their knowledge of the workplace and their sense of public duty, as well as their capacity to resist private interests. As a result, candidates often ran with an emphasis on their practical knowledge and their impartiality.

Once elected, the Prud'hommes were responsible for settling a wide range of disputes between laborers and manufacturers over regulations, wages, and contracts. As elected officials, they settled cases of fraud, infractions against workshop discipline, disagreements between workers or between workers and management, and so on. They could impose small fines, as well as short jail sentences of up to three days. Although they decided cases that resembled civil suits, they were considered not defenders of civil law but agents of the administration. At the same time, even as they served an essential administrative function, they did not operate under the specifics of a preestablished administrative law, and were not appointed by the king or the administration, but were elected by their peers. This hybrid nature was commented upon extensively at the time: "The Prud'hommes move in a triple circle; they are at the same time, arbitrators, conciliators, and judges. As arbitrators, they must know through practice the disputes that are submitted to them; as conciliators, they must present to society and to their litigants guarantees of wisdom and impartiality; as judges, they need knowledge similar to that found among the consular judges, and the code of laws to be applied."[54] As a locally elected board with powers to decide and interpret local regulations, they provided a practical approach to a key administrative problem of postrevolutionary France.

Here too, as a regulatory watchdog, the Prud'hommes were understood to overcome the arbitrary tendencies of previous modes of police. There was no room for "absolute regulations" that were "unlimited in duration, either on the part of the worker or on the part of the manufacturer," stated Mollot. "Man's freedom is a sacred right; he is not permitted to alienate it at any price." Elsewhere, Mollot highlighted a similar argument: "By confining oneself to the law, even though it may seem severe, one avoids arbitrariness, which is the worst of all abuses."[55]

Through this antidespotic ambition, the Prud'hommes were able to provide an essential resource for commenting on, augmenting, and interpreting regulatory expansion within the workplace in the first half of the nineteenth century. Within this approach, several general trends can be identified. First, at the heart of the Prud'hommes system was a principle of equity that was grounded in individual liberty. Mollot went so far as to argue, "The science of the Prud'hommes is EQUITY."[56] This ideal of equity functioned at multiple levels. First, reciprocity between the workers and their employers animated the entire process of arbitration. Their role in this case was bound to the fact that in legal terms, workers were "lessors of labor" to a given workshop. They therefore remained proprietors of their own labor even as they performed work on behalf of another. As Alain Cottereau has highlighted, all forms of "legal obligations of subordination implicit in the regulatory decisions of the kind and the courts" were challenged in this new context.[57] Second, since the judges were elected by workers and employers and represented both groups, the Prud'hommes courts were making their decisions on the basis of what they considered to be an equitable arrangement of a given contractual relationship. As Mollot presented this distinction: "To judge the law strictly, is to apply the provision of the law, the regulation, or the convention, however hard they are." He then opposed this vision to the principle that he argued should motivate the Prud'hommes councils: "To judge in equity is to admit a temperament in the application of the law or regulation, when the strict meaning of its provision may present some ambiguity.... Between these two modes of pronouncing, the Prud'hommes must not hesitate. In their eyes, equity will always prevail." It is for this reason that Alain Cottereau speaks of "the Prud'hommes regulations as another historical case where political economy and equity interpenetrate."[58]

Second, as wide-ranging as their responsibilities were, the emphasis on equity within the councils did not derive from a formal lawmaking capacity in the legislative sense. They were rather jurisprudential: "In the case of regulatory institutions, it is clear that the authority that created them always has the power to make such improvements as it sees fit."[59] Since they were bodies for interpreting regulations, they were called upon to improve regulations that already existed. In this capacity, decisions made by a given council could be used to justify a decision in another context. The *Echo de la fabrique* regularly published the decisions made within the councils. Similarly, by the 1830s and 1840s regular publications of Prud'hommes decisions fed an increasing appetite for what was referred to as a "Code de Prud'hommes."[60] The idea of a "code" was something of a misnomer, since it was in no way a straightforward legal code like the civil or penal codes. Rather, such codes were hybrid documents which—in the code published by M. A. Franque, for example— included a wide range of information pertaining to the Prud'hommes: legislation regarding the organization of the Prud'hommes, "complemented by jurisprudence and formulas," as well as laws that might be useful in the making of Prud'hommes decisions, and lists of the councils in the various departments. All of it was designed to be of "great practical utility."[61]

Finally, the councils were concerned with questions of social provision, or with ensuring that the workshops were not simply orderly and making profits, but were providing a social good: "Considered from the point of view of the legislator, the institution of the Prud'hommes was founded on organic conditions which affect the well-being of society as much as the prosperity of the manufacturing industry."[62] These courts provided a means of increasing social welfare by peacefully managing social relations and therefore increasing the potential productivity of given workshops. "The initiative left to the Prud'hommes, as an exception to the rule, is a consequence of the principle of public health which motivates the essential provision of the decree."[63] Moreover, the Prud'hommes councils were presented as offering a less arbitrary means of looking after public health and ensuring safe working conditions. The *Echo de la fabrique* argued in its first issue of September 1841: "Whenever any authority refuses something to a citizen, he suffers in his private interest; but it is to be applauded in the general interest because this refusal gives reason to examine the right by virtue of which one is able to proceed."[64]

The Prud'hommes councils thus provided a model of regulation that was grounded in the participation of those directly concerned and based on a principle of equity. They radically outstripped the old-regime corporations in their openness and nonhierarchical structure at the same time as they turned their backs on the liberal ideal of unrestrained liberty. Their structure was designed to remain as close as possible to the people who were affected by their decisions. Moreover, the judges were to pay specific attention to the particular circumstances of each individual and case. As they found their way into the center of workers' everyday experiences, they opened new possibilities for thinking about the relationship between free individuals and a state that was committed to public welfare and social provision. By the 1830s and especially the 1840s, such commitment to participatory regulatory power only increased. It was within a new school of activists, journalists, jurists, and social theorists that many of these ideas were explicitly brought under the broader ideal of democracy.

Toward a Democratic Regulation of Labor

As emphasized in the introduction of this chapter, the Prud'hommes councils were understood by the second half of the nineteenth century and then throughout the twentieth century to be ideal examples of a specifically "democratic" mode of regulation and judgment. Indeed, the Prud'hommes undoubtedly opened the door sociologically and procedurally to a democratic mode of regulatory power in the workplace by turning their back on the semi-autonomous control and hierarchical model of the old-regime corporations, as well as the overwhelming emphasis on individual liberty at the expense of regulatory police. Though the exact moment when the Prud'hommes councils themselves acquired their "democratic" appellation is difficult to determine, there was a general shift in the terms used to describe the kind of regulatory police that operated in the name of the public welfare in a nondespotic mode across the 1830s and 1840s.

This growing interest in nonarbitrary social regulation for the public good was driven by an inversion of the terms according to which the old-regime corporations and the liberal market presented the problem. Beyond the back-and-forth between liberal ideals and old-regime solutions in the first half of the nineteenth century, the danger of a modern regulatory intervention for liberty was slowly inverted from the way it had been posed by the late eighteenth and early nineteenth century by those in favor of either the guilds or liberal laissez-faire. Starting in the 1830s, and more prominently by the 1840s, regulation was no longer perceived as a counterbalance to liberty (as it was for those in favor of a return to the old-regime guilds) or as an enemy of liberty (as it was for liberals). Instead, for some, nondespotic regulatory police slowly came to be understood as the best way to ensure modern liberty through regulation. While the inversion was gradual, it was largely established among those who considered themselves to be democratic.

This inversion was perhaps first introduced as a key element of modern democracy by Louis Blanc. One of the most famous fighters for the workers' cause in the 1830s, Blanc developed a vision of work that hugged closely to the terrain opened by the Prud'hommes. His best-selling work *Organisation du travail*, (Organization of labor) first published in 1839, rang out across both intellectual and political circles on the left. And yet, his adherence to both democratic and socialist ideals led him to push neither for an overarching centralized state apparatus that would remedy the condition of workers nor a refusal of regulations in favor of an autonomous, self-regulating civil society. Blanc argued that to deliver workers from the ravages of competition, it was necessary to build the future workplace on associations between workers. These associations, he clearly stated, would require the impetus of the state to overcome the deep-seated drive toward competition. And although the state's role would be reduced as the associations became the foundation for industrial production, regulations would continue to be necessary even in the most ideal of associational contexts. Language of regulation can be found throughout his classic text. "The role of the government would remain limited to supervising the maintenance of the relations of all the centers of production of the same kind, and to prevent the violation of the principles of common regulation," he argued.[65] Far from arguing for a self-regulating social utopia, Blanc insisted that regulations would be a necessity. The question, then, was how the regulations should be established and by whom.

Blanc responded that for the rules and regulations guiding these associations, or "social workshops," to remain fair, just, and effective, they had to be organized through the participation of the workers themselves. To promote this participation, he suggested an electoral system. However, it must be noted that even though he was committed to democracy, Blanc did not see elections as a straightforward solution; he was already attentive to the potential problems that elections could introduce. Citing one of his critics, he recognized what he called "electoral anarchy," in which elections could provide an apparent legitimacy for those leaders who mastered "intrigues, lies, slander, false promises, [and] immoral threats."[66] For this reason, he argued that introducing elections into the associations of workers required that the workers accurately understand their own interests and vote accordingly. He asked: "Would it be possible that instead of voting according to their instinct, or at the whim of the blindest passions, they vote according to reason and that the voters choose based on knowledge of their interests, based on the sphere from which their whole life flows—in a word, under the influence of their interest well understood?" He then concluded: "To make a good choice, two conditions are necessary: interest and ability. Well, the members of the social workshop obviously meet these two conditions. . . . Is a worker in a position to appreciate his foreman? Will a worker, who must reap the fruits of his boss's skill, willingly give himself an unfit boss?"[67]

Mollot showed the compatibility between Blanc's ideas and the Prud'hommes when he referred directly to Blanc's opus, stating that "by the organization of labor (a delicate theory which so vibrantly animates public opinion today) . . . I mean not the absence of any repressive authority, but the impartial power which maintains these rights and duties by enforcing, with strength and equity, the laws and conventions by which they are established."[68] Blanc's work demonstrates that he shared a number of positions with the organizational and decision-making structure of the Prud'hommes. In the introduction to the ninth edition of *Organisation du travail*, for example, he argued in no uncertain terms: "It is therefore in the name, it is for the sake of freedom, that we ask for the rehabilitation of the principle of authority." He then concluded, "We want a government that intervenes in industry."[69] By the mid-1840s, Blanc could not conceive of liberty in the world of work without government intervention. By the time of the Second Republic, the fear of despotic regulatory power in the workplace, acting as a paterfamilias taking care of his flock regardless of its liberties, had been replaced by a vision that sought participatory modes of government intervention into worker's daily lives.

In his history of the 1830s, Blanc highlighted the role he thought the Prud'hommes should play. Recounting the difficulties confronted by the Lyonnais silk workers following the Revolution of 1830, he explained how competition had become too severe and the workers were no longer paid a living wage. He insisted on the important role the Prud'hommes played in attempting to establish a minimum wage: "On October 11, 1831, the council of the

Prud'hommes had drawn up the following declaration: 'Considering that it is public knowledge that many manufacturers actually pay too little, it is useful that a minimum tariff be fixed.'" He then explained that the Prud'hommes were not only responsible for giving a voice to the workers, but were given the authority to execute and oversee the new wage regulations. "The tariff was signed on both sides and the council of the Prud'hommes was charged to supervise its execution, and one day per week was fixed to hear the complaints to prevent the possibility of bad faith." When a few of the owners refused to implement the new wages, Blanc explained, "the council of the Prud'hommes condemned them." The owners' representative responded with a letter to the Prud'hommes: "One read in the council of the Prud'hommes a letter in which it was said that, since the wage never had force of law, it was not obligatory for anybody, and could at most only serve as an honorable commitment and be used as a basis for the transactions between the manufacturer and the workman."[70] Blanc's account clearly sided with the delegated administrative power of the Prud'hommes against the formal legalism of the owners and the merchants.

One could find a growing critique of formal legal power in favor of regulatory effectiveness throughout discussions of the Prud'hommes. Their regulatory effectiveness required a move away from an ideal of formal liberty and toward a more realistic conception of how liberty could be achieved in specific circumstances through regulation. While the Prud'hommes councils obviously never theorized this critical conception of law themselves, some of the authors who wrote about them did. For example, Mollot introduced a version of this when he argued, "If equality must be the sovereign rule of Prud'hommes in their judgments, it must be recognized, according to the same principle, that they are invested by the law with a great latitude on the choice of the appropriate means to ensure its good and prompt execution."[71] In other words, within this context of equity, the Prud'hommes had a wide range of possibilities for action based on what they considered to be the most effective and executable judgment. In this sense, they were agencies for interpreting regulations that already existed in specific sites and circumstances. Or as Mollot noted: "A regulation is understood to be an act issued either by the King as head of the Government and the administration of the State, or by the various agents of the King, by virtue of the power he has delegated to them; it must be the execution of a preexisting law. There is this crucial difference between law and regulation, that law is obligatory for all citizens, without exception and everywhere, such as in the Civil Code, the Commercial Code, etc.; whereas regulation obliges only the persons and localities it determines, such as in a royal ordinance, an ordinance of the prefect of police, the decree of a mayor, etc."[72]

Regulatory decisions and enforcement therefore necessarily operated with a wide latitude. Their decisions were grounded in a whole host of local practices and individual cases as opposed to generalizable formal rights claims about how work should be protected in general.[73] For example, when it came to wages, "they cannot fix the prices, to the extent the parties did not determine them themselves, and they must take into account the age, the capacity of the workman, the nature of the work, and especially the usage."[74] Each decision needed to take into consideration the specific contract and the particular circumstances under which it was drafted and agreed upon.

This informal interpretation and enforcement of the law was supported by a broader critique of legal formalism among workers and those who fought for them in the 1830s and 1840s. Examples of the critique of legal formalism were ubiquitous. In his *Organisation du travail*, Blanc condemned those who hid behind a formal conception of justice: "Now, power is organized force. Power relies on chambers, on courts, on soldiers; that is to say, on the triple power of laws, rulings, and bayonets. Not to use it as an instrument is to confront it as an obstacle."[75] The commitment to a realist conception of the law was echoed by Pierre Leroux, who argued: "You have not realized the equality you have proclaimed; so I am not familiar with this abstract sovereign that you refer to here and there, in the form of a lie, as the nation, the people, or by another fiction, the law."[76] A well-argued form of legal realism also spread into democratic almanacs. The almanac summarized the view of the democratic socialists: "What is law? Law is nothing more than the interpretation of those who apply it; its meaning and its impact is as variable as those who interpret it."[77] Hence, as critical as these democratic socialists were of formal legal claims, their support of realistic and pragmatic interpretations of the regulations based on contingency and necessity flourished. So while more formal notions of law could and often did oppose state order to sociological reality, during the Restoration and the July Monarchy, the Prud'hommes largely operated under very different ideals that were supported by those behind the workers' movement.[78]

But it was perhaps Blanc's colleague Alexandre Ledru-Rollin, one of the leaders of the democratic socialist movement of the July Monarchy and the Second Republic, who presented the clearest account of this critique of formal legalism. He openly asserted in his work *Jurisprudence française*, published in 1845, that "a philosophy that cannot be realized in social fact is by definition false."[79] Ledru-Rollin offered a thorough critique of a formal conception of law, arguing that what he referred to as the "French school of law" combined two principles. On the one hand, he explained, "the history of law is only, properly speaking, a history of modifications of a contingent principal in its relationship to the principle of necessity."[80] On the other hand, he argued, any true legal principle also had to respect the eternal truth of the individual's natural right. Ledru-Rollin concluded: "Thus, the individual is protected by what is divine in the law, while at the same time submitting to what is human."[81] The conclusion to be drawn from this "French" school in his account was that law was profoundly political at the same time as it needed to respect the eternal abstract ideal of individual liberty, which could not be achieved solely by freeing individuals from the forces of exploitation within society; its achievement required a thoroughgoing political conception of freedom. Another way of making this claim would be to argue that law was a political instrument even as it obeyed natural right: "Any modification to human society is a social reform, from the lowering of the electoral census to the raising of the salary, from the overthrow of a throne to the establishment of the industrial tribunal."[82] With this argument, Ledru-Rollin demonstrated two essential ideas. First, he confirmed his claim that it was through the political that social justice could be achieved. And by extension, he suggested that Prud'hommes councils were a political reform with social consequences alongside the overthrowing of kings.

By the 1850s and 1860s, the idea of a democratic regulatory police reached new heights in the work of Étienne Vacherot. Vacherot's book *De la démocratie* (On democracy) included chapters on every aspect of political and social life from the perspective of a democratic society that he argued was the definitive form of organization in the modern age. In his chapter on justice in democracy, he reserved a special place for the Prud'hommes councils. "In spite of the perfection of the legal forms with which the science of the legists has enriched the justice of modern societies, the practice of this justice could give rise to criticism,"[83] he argued, noting the tendency to make the system overly complex through centralization. Vacherot suggested that in a democratic system, justice should be more local and be managed by less lofty and formal judicial systems. "In this respect, the institution of free jurisdictions, such as justices of the peace, commercial courts, and industrial tribunals, is of capital importance."[84] He recognized the dangers within such a model. There were occasions, he argued, when professional judges were necessary. Nonetheless, he asked, "does this mean that civil justice must be entirely removed from the action of citizens?" Certainly not, he responded. In a democracy there was another model situated between citizen juries and professional judges that would be most effective: "In the absence of the ordinary jury, whose incompetence is obvious, special judges can be instituted, such as the commercial courts, the industrial tribunals." Essential to these systems was that they were "composed of citizens elected by merchants, workers, and bosses, and at the same time rendered judgments that are binding decisions." Vacherot did not think that such legal systems could be used to solve important large-scale cases, which would require professional judges. But in a democracy, he argued, they could have a role even if "they decide in the last resort only on cases of little importance. It should be noted that these form the vast majority of cases, and offer abundant material for the judicial activity of citizens. This is the essential point ... With few exceptions, the people will be able, with sufficient education, to do justice for themselves."[85] Vacherot's thoroughly democratic conception of the Prud'hommes found an echo in the passage by Victor Hugo quoted at the beginning of this chapter. Explaining the impact that "Paris, under democracy,"[86] could have, Hugo argued that the Prud'hommes should become one of the models for a more just judicial system across Europe alongside a vast number of other reforms—"to practice the absolute freedom of publicity, of posting and peddling, of association and meeting, to refuse the jurisdiction of the imperial magistracy, to establish an elective magistracy, to take the commercial court and the institution of the industrial tribunals as an experience made to serve as a basis for judicial reform."[87]

Like the introduction of administrative elections during the July Monarchy, the Prud'hommes councils participated in attempts to create a more democratic regulatory power and public administration during these key decades. The councils themselves and the discourses surrounding them unlocked a new dimension of democratic practice by reintroducing regulatory power, overseen by elected peers who would judge according to a basic principle of equity. As the Prud'hommes gained ground in the 1830s and 1840s, they became increasingly associated with democracy because they provided a means of solving social problems that was grounded in public knowledge and popular participation.

6

Capital Democracy

A Very Social Contract

> Democracy must be made a reality through an economic revolution.
> ÉTIENNE VACHEROT, *De la démocratie*[1]

> A collective act [*Gesamtakt*] is a contract if it has as its object the constitution of a democratic power. The foundation of a corporation, of a joint-stock company, of a cartel, of a trade union, or of a party, by mutual agreements between the members concerned, constitutes such a collective agreement.
> FRANZ NEUMANN, *The Rule of Law*[2]

As we have seen, a new democratic regulatory practice and ambition on factory floors, in health care, on city streets, and in forests filled the void left by the destruction of natural privilege as the foundation for social and political order. Urban and rural environments as well as homes and workplaces became key sites for the elaboration of a new mode of administrative authority, grounded in popular demands and public responsibility. But the advance of a new regulatory power did not stop with the consequences of industrialization, for such enterprises also required new financial and commercial tools, and, principally among them, the need to provide unprecedented amounts of capital for larger and larger ventures.

Business regulation in the first half of the nineteenth century was at once startlingly new and rooted in centuries-long tradition. While the first regulatory commercial code, established by Colbert under Louis XIV, had been original, unique, and ambitious in its time, it was rendered impracticable by the massive commercial expansion of the eighteenth century and the Revolution. During the 1790s, attempts at commercial deregulation targeting old-regime monopolistic models combined with the shutting down and reopening of the bourse and the increasing pressure of industrial and capitalist development generated deep questions about how to regulate businesses. Once again, Napoleon's regulatory ambitions stepped in to fill the void, establishing the new Commercial Code of 1807 during the Empire. But while that code offered an important foundation, it also left many of the most important administrative and regulatory details vague. As a result, regulation across the first half of the nineteenth century was largely decided through jurisprudence and legal practice.

At the center of this regulation was the *société anonyme* or joint-stock company. The history of joint-stock companies during the first half of the nineteenth century has tended overwhelmingly to be written in a liberal key. The argument that large corporations marked the advent of a new, rapacious liberal capitalism, however, has not always been so plain. When A. V. Dicey set out to understand what had given "additional force and influence of more or less socialistic ideas" in the beginning of the twentieth century, he looked back to the preceding century to highlight the trend "to place the conduct of business in the hands of corporate or quasi-corporate bodies" that were "wholly in the hands of masses of shareholders who for some legal purposes may well be considered one person, though they constitute in reality many thousands of persons."[3] In Dicey's view, it was precisely the possibility of collective ownership of capital that prepared the foundations for a modern socialism. Just a few years later, Franz Neumann insisted on the profoundly democratic nature of joint-stock companies—which, he argued, were fundamentally distinct from individual entrepreneurial endeavors because they offered collectivist solutions to large public problems. They were therefore democratic to the extent that they distributed the resources, returns, and responsibilities of the investments deep into society.

This chapter builds on these earlier assessments to explore the radical reconceptualization of the social functions of capitalist activity that would allow it to productively shape democratic social life. Indeed, the emergence of a democratic society confronted a fundamental problem amid the growth and development of industrial capitalism: the necessity of ensuring the public good through economic development while preventing the naturalization of social inequalities—or the creation of a "new aristocracy," as Tocqueville called it—through nondespotic regulatory powers. The result, then, much as Oscar and Mary Flug Handlin demonstrated in their magisterial study of corporations in American history, was that early nineteenth-century corporations in France may be "conceived as an agency of government, endowed with public attributes . . . and designed to serve a social function for the state."[4] Large joint-stock enterprises were invented to provide essential services in the name of "public utility," which could not be managed by individual entrepreneurs or by public authorities alone. As such, the *société anonyme* diffused ownership of a given enterprise into society. Hence, business corporations in the first half of the nineteenth century also participated in a broader attempt to harness social resources toward the development of projects that potentially contributed to the public good. Paradoxically, it was only much later that such modes of corporate organization, especially banks and insurance companies, would become hallmarks of unbridled capitalism in the service of shareholders alone.

For in the first half of the nineteenth century, as Karl Polanyi so famously highlighted, capitalist enterprise was deeply embedded in a political conception of social interest and public utility.[5] Across the first half of the nineteenth century, the creation and regulation of joint-stock companies refused any clear opposition between commercial enterprise and the public good.

Democratic Society and the Dangers of Capitalism

For all we have learned about the essential roles of the classical republican paradigm and the birth of liberalism for the development of early modern commerce, the question remains regarding whether these two paradigms were alone in political economic thinking in the wake of the French Revolution. Witnesses of early capitalism in the first half of the nineteenth century also understood the new forms of commercial capitalist activity to be an integral part of the tectonic shift toward a democratic society. Like many who authored large volumes on democracy during this period, James Fennimore Cooper included a chapter titled "Commerce" in his *The American Democrat* that argued for a new understanding of commercial activity within a specifically modern *democratic* life. "It is a mistake to suppose commerce favorable to liberty," Cooper argued, making reference to the Italian republics and England. "Its tendency is to a monied aristocracy, and this in effect, has always been the polity of every community of merchants."[6] In spite of this long tradition of a monied aristocracy that thrived in both republics and regimes founded in liberty, Cooper argued, such an oligarchic accumulation of wealth remained unacceptable in a modern democratic society. "Commerce is entitled to a complete and efficient protection in all its legal rights, but the moment it presumes to control a country or to substitute its fluctuating expedients, it should be frowned upon," Cooper insisted. Commercial activity, he went on to show, could certainly enrich individuals, but needed to "depend on certain great principles"; and among them was the refusal to be governed by an established, minted aristocracy.

Cooper was certainly not alone in trying to conceive of a new democratic approach to commercial activity. In his own writings on the United States, *Lettres sur l'Amérique du Nord*, Michel Chevalier titled his chapter on democracy "La Démocratie—La Banque." His discussions of American democracy—in a clearly Tocquevillian mode—were centered on his analysis of the banking question that had erupted in the United States under President Andrew Jackson. Highlighting the potential dangers of "despotism" and "tyranny" on the part of banks, Chevalier argued that "politically speaking, in fact, the existence of an institution as powerful as the bank in a country such as the United States can present disadvantages," because "self-government is the only political regime."[7] Restating—and simplifying—the arguments of Jacksonians for a French audience, Chevalier argued that "self-government" needed to be free of the control of banks. Chevalier then turned back to France, suggesting that the Revolution of 1830 might provide a response to the Jacksonian banking crisis. He insisted that the new regime, which he suggested offered some essential democratic guarantees, would promote healthy capitalist development because "a people will only engage in commerce and manufacturing with ardor and success when they feel free from political or religious despotism." "Democracy," therefore, was the frame he used to argue for the development of commerce.

Tocqueville provided one of the most sophisticated analyses of the new relationship between commercial practices, industrial development, and modern democratic society. He captured an essential role of commercial activity when he argued that in a democracy, those who wanted to benefit from the equality of conditions within society also needed to assume responsibilities within it. The stakes of this development were even higher since, like Chevalier, he argued that democracy favored commercial and industrial development: "Almost all the tastes and habits that arise from equality naturally lead men to commerce and industry."[8] The result was that commerce and industry would flourish in a democratic society. "In democracies, there is nothing greater or more brilliant than commerce; it attracts the public eye and fills the imagination of the crowd; toward it all energetic passions are directed."[9] For Tocqueville, the individualism and condition of equality inherent in modern democracy as a social form logically and historically preceded the new commercial revolution.

Tocqueville did recognize, however, a structural problem in the commercial and industrial development of a democracy: the push toward a new industrial aristocracy. "Thus, as the mass of the nation turns to democracy, the particular class that deals with industry becomes more aristocratic. Men show themselves more and more alike in the one and more and more different in the other, and inequality increases in the smaller society in the proportion with which it decreases in the larger."[10] Working counter to the drive toward equality within a modern democratic society, Tocqueville described this new aristocracy as a "monster," "an exception in the whole of the social state," and "one of the most brutal forms of aristocracy that ever appeared on earth." The result, he concluded, was that "the friends of democracy must constantly turn their eyes with concern." Within a democracy, the danger of extensive commercial and industrial development was neither individual nor public enrichment, but rather a new kind of aristocracy that would become a form of despotism in modern society. In short, the great threat born of the democratic impetus to industry and commerce was the despotism of a commercial class.[11]

Tocqueville, Chevalier, and Cooper were not alone. Almost every writer who provided an analysis of democratic society during these years felt obliged to explain how it would build on and potentially be transformed by commerce and industry. Central to their concerns was an emphasis on the economic and social possibilities unleashed by a democratic organization of the economy, *and* a deep concern that, precisely because the equality at the heart of democratic society provided such fertile ground for economic development, it would generate a new kind of aristocracy that undermined its own foundations. Indeed, a whole range of social and political theorists attempted to anchor the new democracy in the commercial and industrial success of a growing middle class. In *The New Democracy*, Edouard Alletz insisted, like Tocqueville, that democracy was rooted in a rejection of natural hierarchies like the aristocracy of the old regime. "The nobility has been destroyed," he argued. In such a context, it was merit and wealth that would be the only distinctions. In Alletz's view, wealth in itself did not run in contradiction to a democratic regime in his view; to the contrary, the egalitarianism and freedom afforded by democracy were essential to allowing individuals to accumulate wealth. But as much as Alletz favored the new bourgeois class, he still recognized a potential problem: the possibility of passing such wealth from one generation to the next. Like Tocqueville, he recognized that this possibility ran the risk of creating a new nobility and inherited privilege. He responded that, while he was far from embracing some of the radical ideas of redistribution that were quickly developing on the left, "observing the spirit of equality at work among us, I cannot say that one day it should not be forbidden to the father to leave, in favor of his children, beyond a certain limit fixed by the law."[12] Even Alletz recognized that there might need to be legal limits on wealth inheritance.

Alletz further highlighted the role of commerce in his *The New Democracy*, in a chapter titled "Du commerce français" and a following chapter called "De la liberté commerciale."[13] Commerce in the new democracy, he argued, should be governed by three principles: "ambition, interest, and justice." Up to the present, he argued, France's "only compass had been its ambition. It has sacrificed everything to vainglory."[14] Alletz's notion of democracy fell squarely within the doctrinaire tradition, according to which the extension of the vote beyond a strict limit determined by individual wealth was of little importance. Instead, he placed a great deal of emphasis on the destruction of a natural inherited aristocracy and of old-regime social and land structures. For figures like Alletz, as well as François Guizot, the July Monarchy was democratic not because individuals voted, but because it opened the doors to equality of condition. Guizot argued before the Chamber of Deputies on May 5, 1837, "In our Charter there are public rights that have been conquered by everyone, that are the price of everyone's blood. These rights are the equality of public offices, the equal eligibility to all public jobs, the freedom of the press, and individual freedom!" For Guizot, it was precisely this equality that marked the foundations of the new democratic society: "They speak of democracy, they accuse me of ignoring rights and the interests of democracy. Ah, gentlemen, yesterday I tried to answer this objection in advance." In his view, the ultimate risk for a democracy was not limiting the vote—he remained adamant on this point right up to the Revolution of 1848 and beyond. However, he did express an essential critique that had nourished the democratic tradition since the eighteenth century: the danger of "creating a closed and privileged hierarchy," one that denied "the perfect liberty of individual rising and falling and the constant *concours* between individuals according to each one's merit." He concluded: "I want that wherever these causes meet, wherever there is capacity, virtue, and work, democracy fills up to the highest functions of the State, and from this platform, makes its voice heard, speaking to the whole country."[15] It goes without saying that Guizot's understanding of democracy offered a justification for bourgeois rule. But at the same time, what is striking here is how he built his conception of government out of his ideas on democratic society.

This democratic tradition also animated the other side of the political spectrum. Those who pursued the ideals of democracy similarly recognized the potential for industrial development and its potential dangers for creating a new, more dangerous aristocracy. Figures like Louis Blanc insisted that despotism was not merely a problem of government, and aristocracy not merely a problem of inheritance. The danger of creating a new monied nobility sat at the heart of a capitalist competition in which there would necessarily be those who were exploited and those who accumulated capital. He decried the possibility that those who had acquired wealth "want to perpetuate their names, to survive through an heir. It is a secondhand aristocracy."[16] For Blanc, the inequalities generated by this competitive system were also unacceptable because the control over others that such wealth afforded to some individuals generated a new form of social despotism. Building on his own interpretation of the positive aspects of the system of the eighteenth-century speculator John Law, Blanc argued that credit had to be sponsored and provided by the state; otherwise, "the credit of the bankers, [would be] deadly for the industry, because these greedy lenders exercised a real despotism on all the workers."[17] Blanc's works of the late 1830s and 1840s clearly built on the central themes of a critique of the aristocracy and the danger of despotism in the name of a substantial reduction in social inequalities.

On the other side of the 1848 Revolution, Étienne Vacherot similarly considered the question of the commercial economy important enough for his understanding of democracy that in his book *De la démocratie* he included a long chapter titled "The Economic Conditions of Democracy." Here he argued that during the eighteenth century and the revolution, "the thought of organizing and regulating industry and commerce was unknown, since freedom was sufficient for everything and everyone."[18] By the nineteenth century, however, "what was true for the past may not be true for the future."[19] Vacherot suggested that commercial activity was slowly turning its back on the ideals of democracy and ceding to the dangers of speculative and expropriative capitalism. "If the progress of democracy is still so slow in modern societies," he argued, "the fault lies neither with science nor with industry, but with human justice." According to his analysis, the problem was not so much commercial or capital activity in itself, but the unjust ways in which commerce was being used against social interests. Vacherot predicted that under these new conditions, "barons of finance, industry and capital" would govern, leading to "a new financial, industrial, commercial, agricultural feudality by means of the concentration of capital." This new world would no longer be an economy fit for a democracy; "the only government that suits it is a despotism."[20]

These accounts from across the political spectrum suggest a general set of ideas about the relationship between commercial and industrial capitalism from the perspective of democracy as a mode of social organization. First, none of these accounts suggest that personal enrichment was perceived in itself as a problem for democracy; there even seemed to be a certain agnosticism regarding individual profit. There was, however, a problem with the concentrations of capital that could be generated by a system grounded in equality of conditions. First, there was the constant risk that such a system would create a new aristocracy, which in turn would be perpetuated across generations. Even those theorists and politicians who were great apologists for bourgeois government, like Alletz or Guizot, considered the creation of a new aristocratic class to be unacceptable. Of course, how much of a role the state should play in leveling the playing field depended on where one was located on the political spectrum—but the general critique of a new aristocratic capitalist class and its dangers for a democratic society was widely accepted. The theme of what Tocqueville and many others referred to as a new financial and industrial "aristocracy" was therefore regularly pointed out as the great danger inherent in commercial activity that was not properly democratic. The risk was unequal wealth distribution would undermine the imperative of relative equality that stood at the core of a modern democratic society.

It was not regulation and administrative intervention by the people on themselves that was to be feared, but the creation of a new aristocracy that would remove the very possibilities of self-government and the possibility of generating social wealth for the benefit of society as a whole. Thus, a new democratic commercial ideal accepted individual profits as long as they were spread widely enough to contribute to the general wealth and welfare of society, and were not funneled into the hands of a few. The great danger to be avoided was the tendency to take advantage of the liberty offered by a democratic regime for one's own personal interest—"to the detriment" as Vacherot argued, "of the bourse and public health."[21]

Capitalist Enterprise and the Public Interest

This conception of how democratic society shaped commercial activity developed within a specific juridical context, grounded in the Commercial Code of 1807. Its origins, like many of the codes developed during the Empire, were to be found in the first commercial code written by the financier Jacques Savary for Colbert in 1673. Already by the second half of the eighteenth century, the code was increasingly outdated, ill-adapted to the growing size and ambitions of commercial enterprise. Hence, in 1778 Armand Thomas Hue de Miromensil began preparing a new code, and finally presented a draft in 1782. While this code never took effect, the idea that a new code was necessary remained. By the beginning of the nineteenth century, observers and administrators regularly commented on the void left by the old code's inadequacies. The renowned jurist and commercial trader Vital Roux noted in 1800: "Colbert, always attentive to all that could favor the progress of manufactures, wanted to give regulations a more determined consistency, by preventing infidelity or alteration; he thus offered a guarantee to public faith, and the consumer was less exposed to deception or distrust." Vital Roux then posed the question that had been raised by the Revolution: "Has the abolition of these regulations, which, according to many people, hindered the industry, produced happy results?" His answer was clearly negative; a new, updated code was necessary along with the institutions that would advise and enforce it like Chambers of Commerce and Commercial courts.

Within a few short years, the new Commercial Code was being prepared. It was ratified by the Conseil d'état and voted on by the legislature in 1807. Central to this push was an updating and reinvention of a wide range of juridical controls on commercial activity. One of the most important among them was the legal foundations for profit-making companies. First, the code maintained two common forms of corporations that were variations on old-regime predecessors: a regular partnership (*société en nom collectif*) and a limited or silent partnership corporation (*société en commandite*). The regular partnership was a standard form of corporation in which two or more partners joined their resources to create a common enterprise. The silent corporation was usually for enterprises requiring greater capital, and included a manager or active partners who had full liability, and then some number of silent partners who received a regular return on their investment and had limited liability. But the Commercial Code also included a third type of corporation, the *société anonyme* or joint-stock company, in which a large number of individuals could purchase a variable number of shares to create a company that required large amounts of capital. Over the course of the nineteenth and into the twentieth century, the *société anonyme* became one of the central legal forms for the development of large capital-intensive businesses. It was an essential force in what Maurice Levy-Leboyer and François Bourguignon refer to as the period of "the creation of a market economy."[22] Simply put, it was to become one of the key juridical forms for the development of modern capitalism.

Amid the financial technologies of commerce in the first half of the nineteenth century, perhaps none was more important than the emergence of the joint-stock company. While chartered *société anonyme* or joint-stock companies had existed under the old regime, they were rooted in monarchical privilege and monopoly. One of the most well known early versions of this kind of enterprise was the East India Company, which was granted a monopoly on Eastern trade. One could hold shares in these companies because they required large amounts of capital. They were exceptions to common law, however, to the extent that they were a privilege granted by the king. John Law's famous boom-and-bust bank and trading company in the Americas in the eighteenth century expanded this model to show its potential, both for the state and for private individuals. However, its disastrous end darkened impressions of joint-stock ventures.

While the memory of John Law remained vibrant in the postrevolutionary period, the legacy and nature of the joint-stock company was slowly reinvented. Joint-stock companies became an essential asset for economic development, but it was widely recognized that such corporate entities could not and should not be monopolies. For, there remained misgivings that such massive leverage of wealth in the hands of one company could potentially crowd out future competition, lead to speculation, and massively raise the stakes of commercial fraud. As one commentator argued: "Independently of general and limited partnerships, there is another kind of partnership called a joint-stock company, in which all the partners work under their own names, without the public being informed of their association; as this may result in monopolies, fraud, agiotage or other abuses pernicious to trade, it is prohibited by law."[23] The statesman Jean-Jacques-Régis de Cambacérès argued in the debates on the new code that joint-stock companies touched directly upon "the public order." "The public order," he continued, was directly "involved in every company that issues shares, because far too often these enterprises are only a trap set up for trusting citizens."[24] The question for those who reinvented the joint-stock company in the early nineteenth century concerned how to extract the social benefits of such an enterprise without suffering the social consequences. Hence, the creation of a new legal form of *société anonyme* that issued stock to shareholders to raise large amounts of capital shifted it from being an exception granted by the king to becoming one of the basic forms of commercial activity. This change was a product of the French Revolution's impact on commercial activity, and especially its ambitions to deregulate and destroy the monopolies that had managed large commercial activities during the old regime. Under the new regime it was no longer possible to guarantee effective commercial activity through monopolistic privilege. Commercial activity needed to be open and free to those who chose to pursue it. As Vital Roux explained in his arguments for the creation of a new commercial code in 1801: "When, in addition to a considerable pool of capital, they add the right of privilege, they destroy competition by making themselves arbiters of prices; this monopoly is always dangerous, especially when it can be exercised on objects of necessity."[25]

It was widely recognized, however, that the creation of large businesses that drew on vast amounts of capital needed to "be justified to society." As Franz Neumann argued in his analysis of joint-stock companies, they introduce a profoundly sociological component into capitalist enterprise, since they "shift the risk to others, especially to the state, be it through direct or indirect subsidies."[26] Out of this sociological imperative emerged the necessity for government authorization. The code thus called for an elaborate process of government approval for large-capitalist enterprises to modernize a system inherited from the old regime. This authorization was rooted in the potential dangers and need to guarantee the social utility of large corporations. "In another era," commented Delaporte in his own commentaries on the commercial code published in 1808, the year after its ratification, "public companies for large undertakings, which almost always enjoyed exclusive privileges, could only be fixed by the authority of our Kings; and even their existence was established according to the solemnities required for the formation of law." But in this new age, Delaporte insisted paradoxically, "the Government has a more extensive power." As a result, "it can create joint stock companies or authorize them." For Delaporte, government had an obligation to authorize major capitalist activities and provide oversight, because such corporations were directly tied to the public good and public order: "Indeed, joint-stock companies can be as harmful to the public good by the nature of their enterprise as they can be favorable to it if the purpose of their enterprise is useful. It is therefore important to society that these large establishments can only be made under the authority and supervision of Government."[27] By creating the category of joint-stock company and insisting upon governmental authorization and close regulation, the Commercial Code of 1807 was therefore an attempt to create a new kind of business activity that could provide essential public goods by tapping into social resources, which were "anonymous"—that is, without a specific legal mention or limitation on the number of partners—and at the same time respect the fundamental rules of competitive markets.

Hence, even as these enterprises were private, they were perceived to be directly bound to the public interest. The general recognition of this public role of the joint-stock enterprise was clearly established in the observations on the Commercial Code of 1807 provided by local commercial courts and offices as well as municipalities throughout France. For example, the city of Caen responded to the project for a commercial code by arguing that "the rules to be established for these large joint-stock companies, which may be considered in some sense as national," were necessarily distinct from other types of small businesses "of which freedom is the first element, and of which nothing should delay the progress." What was specific about the joint-stock companies, the merchants of Caen argued, was that "by the extent of their operations and their direct influence on national credit, political relations, and their place in the public order, they call the attention of the Government, and must obtain its admission."[28] The commercial court of Rouen made a similar argument. The use of joint-stock companies, it argued, was necessary for major projects of inland navigation, such as the building of canals and the ensuring of the navigability of rivers. Such corporations worked on behalf of "the interest of the nation and by the intention of the Government."[29]

The language of public interest saturated discussions of joint-stock companies. The city of Aubenas insisted that in the case of *sociétés anonymes*, "the public interest must prevail over a momentary and misunderstood interest of the creditors."[30] Jurists from Le Havre agreed, employing once again the language of public interest for the role of large capitalist enterprises, and observing that "the authorization of the Government, which is referred to in this article, is probably required only for large enterprises which might have some connection with the public interest."[31] The city of Geneva provided the most elaborate response on the question, attempting to explain why government authorization was necessary in the context of capital-intensive projects, and less important or even dangerous in others. It recognized that it was often the case that smaller enterprises might be pursued "when the interest is circumscribed in a narrow circle of businesses and individuals, . . . which, therefore, no longer belong to the public interest." In these cases, which were largely private affairs, the city argued that "the intervention of the Government would be detrimental to the freedom of action and the liberty that commerce must enjoy." On the other hand, however, there were those projects that did require government authorization and oversight, specifically because "support through shares cannot take place without the authorization of the Government." Echoing the general opinion of other cities, the city of Geneva argued that government authorization and oversight was "wise and beneficial in all cases where large-scale, general-interest enterprises are involved." By its estimation, there were then two fundamentally distinct types of capitalist enterprise: those sufficiently circumscribed in their aims that they were merely a private matter, and those that were vast enough to touch upon the public interest.

Building Administrative Oversight over Large Businesses

The idea that there were clearly two types of businesses further raised the question of how to distinguish between those businesses that were primarily of private interest and those that touched upon the public interest. The principle proposed in Geneva was for "government intervention to be limited by the number of shareholders and by the sums involved. Thus, for example, it would not be necessary for any company that had less than two hundred shareholders, and whose capital did not exceed one million."[32] For the commercial authorities of Geneva, it was necessary to establish a principle according to which the degree of public interest of a given company could be determined. Beyond a certain size, government authorization and regulation were required. Otherwise, it could be considered a purely private affair.

The emphasis on governmental authorization was born of a deep-seated assumption that joint-stock companies had a public function and therefore needed to be consistently subject to public regulation. Instead of being a hindrance to their development, however, the result was a steady growth in the number of joint-stock companies across the first two-thirds of the nineteenth century. Between 1807 and 1867, six hundred forty-two joint-stock companies were authorized by the government.[33] The overwhelming majority of these companies fell broadly into five types: public works and transportation, especially bridges, railroads, and canals (146); insurance and banking (105); public utilities such as water and street lighting (15), and a more miscellaneous grouping of capital-intensive industries such as mines (46), chemical companies (3), paper factories (8), sugar refineries (7), and glassworks (8).[34] The use of capital-intensive corporations was therefore largely reserved for areas that touched upon the public interest and public utility, including key areas that would later form the foundation of nationalization as the French attempted to reinforce the welfare state in the twentieth century.[35] In 1837, Emile Vincens—a member of the Conseil d'état (and father-in-law to François Guizot's brother, Jean-Jacques)—explained the importance of joint-stock companies for the development of these key industries. "For some years now, banks and insurance companies, canals, bridges, railroads, docks, all enterprises that require the assistance of pooled capital, have occupied public attention and aroused private interest."[36] He insisted that these projects were driven by "a noble emanation of patriotism which is skillfully used to endow the country with vast and useful creations." Furthermore, Vincens argued, these projects could only be achieved through a combination of private interest and public effort. "Most of the great works that the state of civilization and industry requires cannot be accomplished, especially not in a reasonable amount of time, without the zealous assistance of men capable of founding vast conceptions, who are skilled in finding the right moment, and who are in a position to carry them out. Unquestionably, the State and its government owe them assistance, and their fellow citizens recognition and favor."[37]

During the first half of the nineteenth century, these enterprises remained in private hands and subject to market competition, but the commercial code established the strict modes of their founding, as well as extensive procedures of authorization and oversight. The procedures for government authorization and oversight were established by the Commercial Code. Vincens argued: "The law which fixes the consequences of the obligations of the citizens, which, in the general interest, regulates and sanctions more precisely the commitments of the tradesman, could not dispense with ruling on the scope of these same commitments when several persons contract them in common."[38] The first round of authorization was to be handled by the local prefecture in whose jurisdiction the company was located. Those who sought the creation of the company would submit a petition signed by all potential shareholders. If accepted by the prefecture, the petition was then submitted to the ministry—the Ministry of the Interior until 1828, and then the Ministry of Commerce afterward. If approved by the minister, the petition was then sent to the highest administrative court, the Conseil d'état. The historian Bertrand Gille notes, "One feared the examination of the Conseil d'état, which was always severe and whose opinions were scrupulously followed by the government."[39] The process came to an end with an ordonnance published in the *Bulletin des lois*. The average time necessary for the process was approximately from eighteen months to an average of two years during the supposed *enrichissez-vous* years of the July Monarchy.

The petitions and authorizations themselves were filled with language on the public interest and public utility as part of the arguments in their defense. Providing a useful metaphor for the relationship between large capitalist corporations and government in overseeing public interest during this period, the application for the creation of the Compagnie du Pont de Bordeaux in 1818 decreed that the share of the profits generated by the bridge for maintenance was to be kept locked away with two keys: one for the prefect and one for the company's directors.[40] In 1822 the creation of a mutual insurance company for the departments of the Drôme, l'Isère, and l'Ardèche stipulated that if the company closed, any remaining funds could be recovered by the department's general council, which would "be able, on the proposal of the board of directors, to employ these funds toward objects of public utility of interest to humanity, trade, industry, the sciences, or the arts."[41] The ordonnance for another company founded in 1819 for fire insurance asserted, in a somewhat philosophical tone: "The ESTABLISHMENT of which the said *comparans* have long conceived the project in view of beneficence and general utility presents, by its nature, advantages which are of essential importance to political economy as well as philanthropy, and results in which the particular interest of the citizens is closely linked to the public interest."[42]

Throughout the first half of the nineteenth century, jurists mobilized arguments precisely along these lines to emphasize the importance of joint-stock companies for serving the public good. In 1841, the jurist J. V. Molinier wrote a new treatise on commercial law, arguing, for example, that commercial law and regulation were even more important in an age when rampant industrialization was opening up a "new future" by harnessing a new "social power [*puissance sociale*]."[43] With his use of the term "social power" to describe *sociétés anonymes*, Molinier was insisting that such enterprises were a means of channeling the resources within society toward an improvement in the public welfare. Justification for the creation of capital-intensive companies, including insurance companies and banks, was founded upon an unbreakable bond between the private and public interest.

In the authorization process, no matter the ambitions of the capitalists themselves, it was necessary to demonstrate the social value and utility of the companies they were creating. In 1822, for example, a joint-stock enterprise submitted a petition with more than fifty pages of testimony describing how "for two years, this process has been tried in all climates, and has incessantly given useful results: experience has shown that it is especially suitable in countries where the grapes are difficult to mature, and in those where the wine cannot be kept."[44] Another company, designed to improve the system of hydraulic locks on the Rhone River, insisted that "the upstream navigation of the Rhone is extremely important for trade in France in general."[45]

The language of public utility legitimized administrative oversight over these companies. The public authorization for the Bordeaux Bridge Company, for example, included an extremely elaborate and detailed table of fees for almost everything and everyone imaginable who might cross the bridge. The company regulations elaborated distinct fees for such details as a person on foot without a load; a person with a load exceeding kilograms; a horse or mule carrying a rider; a horse or mule on a leash; a donkey or ass carrying a load; a pair of geese or turkeys; an uncovered wagon with one, two, or three horses; a cart with four wheels pulled by one horse or multiple men (driver included); a portable chair with two wheels and two horses including the "*postillon et le retour des chevaux, pied levé*"; an empty cart pulled by one horse or two bulls, including the conductor; a small cart or wheelbarrow carried by an individual; and so on.[46] One ordonnance on the creation of a fire insurance company established the minimum amount of liquidity the head of the corporation needed to have at any given time.[47] Phénix, another fire insurance company, was created in 1819 with the provision that "a commissioner for the said company will be appointed by our minister, secretary of state of the interior. He will oversee the operations of the company and of the observance of statutes and will report to our Minister of the Interior."[48] The ordonnance further established that the government could suspend the company's activities if it engaged in activities that appeared contrary to public safety. Another ordonnance for the creation of a fire insurance company in the Loire-inférieure stated in no uncertain terms that "the members shall comply with the laws and police regulations concerning fires." If they did not obey these regulations, the government reserved the right to suspend the company's activities: "The present authorization being granted to the aforementioned company on the condition that it complies with the particular laws and statutes which must serve as a rule for it, we reserve the right to revoke it in the event that these conditions are not fulfilled, without prejudice to the actions to be brought by individuals before the courts, on account of the infringements committed to their detriment."[49] In the ordonnance establishing a chemical company in the Bouches du Rhône, it was stipulated that the corporation would provide a report to the prefect of the Seine and the Commercial Court every six months. This precaution was inserted almost systematically in the ordonnances establishing these companies.

Jurists recognized that such governmental authorization and oversight could be interpreted as running counter to the ideals of individual freedom as well as the spirit of *enrichissez-vous* that supposedly guided the July Monarchy. "At first sight," stated a treatise on commercial businesses written in 1833, "one might have been astonished that the legislator gave the government the right of examination over the contracts of joint-stock companies, and invested it with the unlimited power of granting or refusing authorization for the establishment of joint-stock companies; this power might have been regarded as a hindrance to the free exercise of industry and to the freedom of commerce." But, the treatise continued, there were ample reasons for such authorization. Among them, it argued, was the fact that the shareholders were unknown to one another and served the public interest. "The founders of a joint-stock company request an exemption from personal liability for themselves and for those with whom they will associate; it is therefore fair that they present guarantees in lieu thereof, and as a sort of surety for the commitments that the company will contract."[50] The government's intervention was necessary precisely because no single individual or clearly defined set of individuals could be held responsible for potential wrongdoings. In this way, authorization and regulation were a means of ensuring that a given collective enterprise would fulfill its social function.

Another reason offered for government authorization and oversight was the influence that such large businesses could have on markets more generally. In his treatise on public and administrative law, Émile-Victor Foucart explained, "There are commercial enterprises that can only take place if they are authorized by the administration, either so that they do not become traps set for credulity, or because of the influence they could exert on credit: these are joint stock companies in general, and certain financial enterprises, such as banks, discount banks, insurance companies, etc. As we shall see, the public interest provides sufficient justification for this derogation from the general law."[51] Major financial institutions required special modes of oversight and authorization precisely because of the potential influence of marketizing such areas as credit and money. There was, of course, the fundamental problem of fraud and corruption. As the minister of justice, Félix Barthe, argued before the Chamber of Deputies in 1838, the aim of government authorization and intervention was to ensure the public against corrupt schemes or vehicles for illicit speculation. "This is not a vain prospectus on an idea without consistency, but a social act, a fund which ensures the commitment of the company."[52] The goal of establishing such companies, Barthe concluded, was not simply to be profitable, but to preserve "public morality."[53]

Emile Vincens explored the importance of government authorization and intervention for preventing individuals from taking advantage of the new capitalist opportunities at the expense of others. Writing on the question of government authorization and oversight, he recognized that "some people may feel that this is a lot of governing, that it is too much to involve the public administration in the examination of privately owned businesses." But he insisted that such intervention was fundamental not only for the services the businesses provided but also because of the potential dangers they posed to the public:

> It could be said that in large cities, where many capitalists are greedy for dividends, commit venal actions, are susceptible to speculating on the stock exchange, and are pressed into all kinds of engagements, he who takes one share out of a thousand of which a business is composed, follows with confidence the guarantees he has been given. In this instance, he does not pay much attention to the articles of incorporation to which he offers subscriptions, and certainly not a fraction of the attention he would give to a business which would be his sole interest. It is not out of place for the government to be in a position to give the public some moral guarantee on associations of this kind.[54]

It was, as another commentator argued, a question of not sacrificing the public good to private interest: "It is necessary to sacrifice often the particular interest to the general interest: or there would be nothing more contrary to the general interest of the trade than that the quality of a good be constant."[55] Fears of fraudulent production and corruption ran throughout the processes of government authorization, and were used to motivate arguments for government intervention in corporations. As the petition on the part of the hydraulic locks on the Rhone argued: "Ignorance, presumption, charlatanism, and bad faith have in turn abused the use of associations; they have discredited them by diverting them from the wise directions which should have been given to them. . . . Mr. Bourbon has done everything to defend himself from this: before presenting his project, he has neglected neither precautions, nor care, nor work, in order to be better enlightened; and he has given himself over to considerable expenses in order to acquire for himself, and to be able to communicate to the others, a real certainty of success."[56] Hence, at the same time as joint-stock companies provided essential services to the public, the sums involved and their potential profits augmented the danger of counterfeit and corruption. The process of government authorization, it was argued, provided an essential bulwark against such abuses, and was necessary for ensuring that joint-stock companies served the public good.

Claude-Alphonse Delangle provided perhaps one of the best summaries of the necessity of government authorization when he argued:

> Without individuality, so to speak, without responsible managers, and administered by agents whose ruin of the company's affairs does not compromise their own fortune, the joint-stock company could be a source of abuse and fraud; it could become a means of minting money at the expense of the public. The law has provided for this, placing it under the immediate control of the authorities. The joint-stock company cannot exist without an authorization of the government. The elements of the proposed association, its basis, its status, its means of execution, its chances or probabilities of success, everything is the object of a severe and enlightened appreciation; and so that the faith of third parties cannot be misled, a complete publicity is given to the act of the company.[57]

With this argument in his *Commentaire sur les sociétés commerciales*, Delangle concluded that individual commercial action required responsible management to avoid corruption as well as abuse of public trust and fraud, all of which would come at the expense of the public instead of working toward the public good. The law therefore placed the corporations under the control of an authorizing regulatory power, which then further required full public disclosure of the companies' activities. Delangle claimed, then, that large capital enterprises would thrive under the umbrella of public responsibility.

The economist Louis Wolowski similarly argued that joint-stock companies provided essential social goods with a specifically democratic vocabulary:

> This new force is expanding and growing every day. It derives from the most imperative needs of our social order. At the same time as the democratic influence of institutions fragments patrimonies and subdivides fortunes, the genius of man opens wider paths for industry, which solicit powerful efforts; nothing is more effective, to destroy the dangers of this opposition, than to make fractioned, scattered elements flow back toward a common center, which, isolated and disunited, would be consumed in sterile attempts and would not be long in fading before the energetic and absorbing influence of major capital.[58]

With this analysis, Wolowski outlined a relatively common way of thinking about the problem of capitalist enterprise in a democracy. In his view, democracy had had the effect in France of subdividing property and therefore effectively distributing land much more evenly across the population. At the same time, this "democratic" conception of property divided and fractured land capital. In such a context, associations between large numbers of small capital owners helped provide investment in projects of social utility.

Arguing for greater regulation even among smaller corporations that sometimes had chosen the legal framework of limited liability partnership, Wolowski insisted that precisely because of their contributions to society and the dangers of fraud, greater regulation was necessary.

> But when one finds oneself in the presence of a social act, the terms of which have not been debated between the co-interested parties, an act imposed by the joint partner on those who wish to participate in the enterprise as shareholders; when the latter has been able to fix at his will the advantages which he stipulates in his favor and to estimate the value of his contribution as he sees fit; when, finally, it is aimed at small amounts of capital, unpredictable by their nature and easy to invite to the perilous chances of a new kind of lottery, laissez-faire and laissez-passer would not be appropriate, and this brand new situation strongly calls for new regulations.[59]

Laissez-faire was dangerous in joint-stock companies precisely because the resources and consequences were so deeply embedded into society. While associations of capital were essential for providing public goods, they needed to be under the close supervision of the administration.

Social Science and the New Associative Ideal

But there was also another, deeper, social reason for creating and therefore regulating large capital corporations: their role as a fundamentally social enterprise. Among those jurists who defended the importance of the joint-stock company, there was a general understanding that these enterprises required some level of cooperation between freely acting individuals. Delangle offered a historical account of the rise of the contract to demonstrate this idea: "Contracts are born, so to speak, with man; who was obliged to fight against the obstacles that a rebellious nature opposed to the satisfaction of his needs, and despaired overcoming them alone. He came closer to his fellow man to fight, and then share with others the results of their common efforts."[60] These businesses were grounded in the cooperation necessary between individuals to achieve mutual benefit. Through such common efforts, individuals formed into associations to benefit society as a whole. Delangle then expanded this idea: "Nowadays, forming an association means creating an instrument of social renovation." He concluded that "individual wealth, following a development parallel to that of public power, rapidly increases and extends to all conditions, so to speak. With wealth comes the love of well-being and all the enjoyments that constitute it; the arts, industry, and commerce, charged with satisfying these new needs, face the insufficiency of individual action and resources."[61]

This profoundly social approach to capitalist enterprise developed through a specific vocabulary in which corporations were understood to be a social form that benefited both the individual and society. The term most employed to capture the social ambitions of these enterprises was *association*. Throughout the Restoration and the July Monarchy, the term "l'esprit d'association" (the principle of association) appeared across French economic works.[62] Indeed, this period may be understood as a golden age of associational experiments. Vincens referred regularly in his writings to "the spirit of association" that motivated the creation of joint-stock enterprises. Another author, in an 1834 piece on associations titled "Science sociale" in the *Revue du progrès social*, observed: "We have commercial companies in limited partnership or in participation, joint stock companies; we have learned societies, political societies, religious societies. Especially in recent times, attempts at association have multiplied, and the idea itself has been elaborated, to such an extent that there exists today a science whose entire effort is directed toward the research and application of the laws of association."[63]

By understanding joint-stock companies as one type among many different kinds of associations, jurists, social theorists, and political activists were able to define these profit-making ventures as entities that were socially embedded, and which thus had a role to play in preserving the public good. The article in the *Revue du progrès social*, for example, attempted to define associations in the most general possible terms: "Considered in all its breadth and depth, the idea of association expresses the regular coordination of several different, unequal, or even divergent forces, and the direction of these forces toward a single goal. . . . The use of all the different and opposing characteristics for the maintenance of order and harmony; the direction of the isolated efforts of each individual toward a goal useful to all; the direction of the work of the masses toward the good of the individual: these are, for human society, its true conditions of stability and perfection."[64] By defining *sociétés anonymes* as ideals for *social* progress, these definitions embedded them into a broader set of social aims and hence provided a new, more robust rationale for administrative authorization and oversight.

Alexandre de Laborde, already discussed for his major treatise on the Parisian municipal administration, captured the spirit of this associational ideal in his own work on associations, which included an extended discussion of joint-stock companies. In his view, since it was a kind of association, a joint-stock enterprise "is not only an association of profit; it is also a company of insurance of these same profits. It has political relations with the other companies as neighbors. It especially has relations with each of the members who compose it, to unite their efforts in the common interest, and to distribute them toward social responsibilities."[65] Because of the political and social impact of these associations, they were in direct contact with "the general interests of society." At the same time, Laborde insisted upon the "effects of this same principle on the private interests, or otherwise the different branches of industry of men."[66] The consequence of this alignment of general and private interests was that joint-stock companies had to be understood as entities through which society provided for itself. In Laborde's view, this deeply social conception of joint-stock companies revealed precisely how individuals came together to act upon and shape themselves: "The authority of a king over his subjects has limits; that of individuals over themselves has none; it includes all that they have and all that they can acquire, their fortune and their privation."[67] He continued in this same vein, arguing that "what I consider to be the principle of association is a tendency of enlightened and industrious men to come together for any operation that is of great interest to society."[68] A better presentation of how a democratic society could be self-governed is difficult to imagine.

Laborde then listed a whole range of types of large corporations which had direct relationships with the general interests of society, citing all those businesses directly relating to civil and military administration as well as industrial development, including "creation of products" and "commercial associations for the development of products."[69] In this view, the role of government authorization was to "put the finishing touches to this great work, which can, by consideration and honors, be more powerful in France than the [individual] interest, and inspire useful works to the highest degree."[70] The development of these enterprises was therefore to be pursued freely by private individuals in the name of the public interest, and it was up to the government to lift them up and ensure that they provided utility.

The *Dictionnaire analytique d'économie politique* seconded Laborde's assessment. A strong capitalist industrial sector, it argued, required a transformation in government. "It is certainly not to be found in the power of nature which so long founded its dominion on the scourges of war, slavery and the degradation of the human race," it argued, adding that "such a power has nothing in common with one that lives on the contributions of the whole population." Once a public authority was established, then useful commercial enterprises could be more thoroughly developed: "They are formed at a time when governments have acquired stability, power and a kind of public confidence."[71]

Observing the impact of the Revolution and the Empire on the development of the economy and civil society across Europe, Hegel had provided the most elaborate understanding of the ideas Laborde and other associational theorists were putting forward. Completing in these same years—1817 to 1821—his courses on the *Philosophy of Right*, Hegel offered his own interpretation of the new relationship between free-willing, profit-seeking individuals who animated civil society through corporations, and their relationship to the general interest through the state. Hegel argued that corporate activities in the postrevolutionary world were distinct from royal companies and privileges of the past. "Privileges, in the sense of the rights of a branch of civil society organised into a Corporation, are distinct in meaning from privileges-proper, in the etymological sense." While kings had created corporations in the past as "casual exceptions to universal rules" in the postrevolutionary world, corporate activities were "the crystallization, as regulations, of characteristics inherent in an essential branch of society itself owing to its nature as particular." In the new regime, then, corporations were not dispensations on the part of royal authority that granted monopolistic control over a given activity, but rather a common grouping of individuals congregating freely together to pursue their common interests. Hegel therefore defined corporations as "associations" in language that was strikingly similar to that of Laborde. "The implicit likeness of such particulars to one another becomes really existent in an association, as something common to its members," he argued. In this context, the activities that brought individuals together were indeed driven by "a selfish purpose, directed toward its particular self-interest."

However, even as a product of free-willing self-interested individuals gathered toward a common particular purpose, large corporate activities were not purely private enterprises. Instead, because individuals gathered into associations and provided important services to society, the association "apprehends and evinces itself at the same time as universal." What Hegel meant by this was that through the pursuit of individuals' interests in the context of groups, these associations, "under modern political conditions," also played a role in ensuring well-being for the individuals who were involved in the association, and for society more broadly. "The citizens have only a restricted share in the public business of the state," wrote Hegel, "yet it is essential to provide men—ethical entities—with work of a public character over and above their private business. This work of a public character, which the modern state does not always provide, is found in the Corporation." In a modern "ethical life," the corporation therefore allowed the individual to thrive in his or her private pursuits while also ensuring essential public services that the state could not afford to pursue. And, as Hegel highlighted, it was precisely because of this public nature that "it is only by being authorised that an association becomes a Corporation."

In an issue of the *Revue du progrès* that included an article on Hegel,[72] the author of the previously mentioned article "Social Science" argued, in language that echoed Hegel's, "Each profession concentrates its action and its interest on one of the particular spheres of social work; and the sum of all these partial activities constitutes, in a given territory, the general system of the production of wealth, the improvement of enlightenment, and the development of enjoyment."[73] Others in these years used a similar framework for understanding the role of the state: "The means of ensuring the prosperity of commercial industry are derived from two sources held in hand by individuals and the state."[74] Speaking in very similar terms, the jurist Frémery highlighted the importance of understanding the proper relationship between the particular and the general interest: "In the first place, there are the truly commercial operations with their primitive purity; if they serve the particular interest, they also serve the general interest: the state prospers by imports, by manufactures, and by exports; its strength is in work and circulation." He distinguished these activities in which both the private and the general interest benefited from those in which solely private interests prevailed: "There are the operations of pure speculation; their purpose is to serve the particular interest of the speculator; but they are, by their nature, of no use for the general interest."[75] Frémery captured an essential foundation for capital-intensive enterprise in the first half of the nineteenth century: individual private profits were positive, as long as they also served the general interest.

Social and Historical Obligation as Modes of Commercial Action

Now, there is little doubt that such an elaborate process of authorization and regulation also served as a gatekeeping mechanism to control access to the creation of joint-stock companies.[76] But extensive efforts were made to provide a more just foundation for processes of government authorization. One of the leading jurists of commercial law in the July Monarchy, Raymond-Théodore Troplong elaborated a theoretical foundation for this social conception of business. First, he highlighted that the word *société*—as in *société anonyme*—contained a vast range of social relationships, from the most basic to the most elaborate: "All these societies, some elementary, others artificial, whose bundling forms political society; all these aggregations so varied in their purpose, from marriage to the commune, scale up by degree." While they were all grounded in a common principle of association, a variety of these *sociétés* had developed to satisfy an increasingly greater range of social functions. It was necessary then to understand the specificities of a corporate *société* as opposed to others. "Starting from a common principle, religious, friendly, political, literary, or economic associations: those animated by a conservative spirit, those bubbling with the spirit of opposition and reform: those organized for the development of private and public wealth."[77] In Troplong's view, certain kinds of associations were designed to produce private and public wealth; these were the *sociétés anonymes*. In this way, Troplong argued:

> The word *société* not only applies to assemblies of men, living as a body of nations, under the influence of the same laws and the same civilization; it also includes all sharing of material or intellectual things, all participation in interests, affections, and pleasures put in common. . . . But within this common ground, there is a relationship which stands out from all the others, as the species stands out from the genus, and whose place is marked by its own and salient signs; it is the combination by which two or more persons agree to put something in common, with a view to making a profit and sharing it. Hence the contract known in the science of law as the partnership contract. It is of considerable importance; it plays a principal role in the development of civil and commercial interests. It is a powerful auxiliary for industry, trade, agriculture; it favors the exploitation of all our territorial and manufacturing wealth by forming a fruitful union of movable and immovable property, of capital and labor.[78]

In short, the business corporation was a socially embedded and a morally charged mode of associative action. These joint ventures were a means for multiple individuals to come together to profit, and to share the profits toward civil and commercial interests. These "social contracts" allowed for the development of territory and industry by bringing together resources that would otherwise lay fallow.

The deeply social conception of joint-stock enterprises made them similarly dependent on historical development. Troplong offered a historical account of corporate law, arguing that it had evolved alongside and out of previous modes of social organization to fulfill specific social purposes. He traced the origins of commercial law back to the ancients, insisting that it was the Romans who had provided the foundation for contemporary legal outlines of business activity. His ambition in providing such a long and elaborate history was to show that while industrial capitalism was quickly changing and this specific form of the "société anonyme" was new, it was rooted in a much older set of laws and regulations that provided precedents for legal action.

Troplong insisted on the tradition of commercial practices and regulations to suggest that the law was insufficient at times, but not because it was new or ill-conceived. Against those who argued that the Commercial Code was already outdated by the end of the 1830s, and that this was why there had been so many cases of fraud, especially in the realm of the limited silent partnerships, Troplong argued for a more elaborate understanding of the history of commercial law. "It was thus a question of reversing the combinations of our commercial code, of inventing new principles for a commercial era that was believed to be new," he wrote. In this context, "what one was especially wrong to forget was the history in which one would have seen that the past is not as small, as devoid of great economic facts, as one imagines." He then noted how strange it was that "we marvel at the fact that mines, factories, patents, newspapers are sold in shares; but two centuries ago, islands, kingdoms, almost a whole hemisphere was sold in shares!"[79] For Troplong, what was new in the nineteenth century was the object toward which these enterprises were oriented and the services they provided, not the law and oversight necessary to manage them. To properly regulate these businesses, it was necessary to understand their historical development in a long, socially embedded past.

A social-historical approach to corporate life in these early decades of capitalist development could be found among economists, politicians, and political theorists alike. Jérome-Adolphe Blanqui wrote his *History of Political Economy* in the July Monarchy with the intention of integrating the contemporary transformations of economic life toward a more complex mode of capitalist investment in a long historical trajectory. Guaranteeing effective regulations and responsible economic development, he insisted, could be found in the practices of the past. Looking at Colbert for an example, he argued: "He pushed the regulatory mania too far, and we find it difficult to understand today this luxury of penalties applied to errors in chemistry or mechanics, as if they were attacks on morality. However, such rigor was perhaps necessary to the success of industry, like the severity of rules in nascent communities."[80] Blanqui did not therefore seek the foundation for regulations in a naturalized market that contained its own rules. Rather, he looked to past experiences.

Politicians used this historical and social conception of capitalism to make policy as well. Although he was a firm believer in private property and great proponent of various forms of capitalist investment, Adolphe Thiers regularly demonstrated his commitment to a more socially embedded and historical conception of capitalist enterprise. Thiers's ambition can be summarized by the objective of ensuring effective government intervention in a capitalist economy without undermining capitalism itself. "Such is the beautiful argument of laissez-faire and laissez-passer, which has never produced anything in the world,"[81] he declared. Turning his back on "this empty, unfruitful and sterile theory of laisser-faire," Thiers argued that government should intervene to prevent and respond to crises, make strategic investments, and protect key industrial and agricultural sectors. While he shared with some of his French liberal counterparts an emphasis on individual liberty in commercial development, he nonetheless inserted this liberty within its specific historical moment and the society within which it took place. For Thiers, the state, society, and the economy were part of one larger system; and as a result, "what is indispensable everywhere, what we do everywhere . . . is to intervene."[82] In his book *De la propriété*, Thiers argued that no law on commerce could be understood as a transcendent, natural given, even in its relationship to individual property. He therefore dismissed those he referred to as "the philosophes of a century gone by," who, "wanting to distinguish between the natural state and the civil state, liked to imagine an epoch when man wandered in the forests and the deserts, not obeying any fixed rule, and another epoch when he had assembled and was bound by contracts called laws." He insisted that such ideals of natural property rights were a "pure hypothesis." To the contrary, he argued, it was necessary to observe society when making commercial law, to inspect the positive and negative effects and then respond accordingly.

As a result, for Thiers it was the social impact of a given law that determined its value: "Let us therefore start from the principle that property, like everything else that belongs to man, will become a right, a right that is well demonstrated, if the observation of society reveals the need for this institution, its suitability and its utility."[83] "Utility" was the term Thiers used to understand the social consequences of commercial law. As he put it: "Social utility is the question considered from the point of view of society itself. A law, and even property itself, need be seen as a social product." It was impossible to judge utility based on the lone individual. It was necessary to approach such questions from the perspective of the individual's relationship to society more broadly. In this vision, the individual had a right to his or her property not as a natural right, but in the name of society.

It was precisely through this idea of utility, which gained in importance across the first half of the nineteenth century, that government intervention into the economy was ensured. Thiers testifies to the usage of the notion of social utility to justify a massive expansion in state intervention into the economy. "It is necessary to pursue numerous attempts, it is necessary to verify all the facts," he explained in speaking of the various forms of state intervention, for example, "when the utility of the railroads is demonstrated."[84]

This same notion of utility opened opportunities for the state to invest. "The state, too, has ongoing maintenance and improvement expenditures ... nor am I unaware of the utility of these expenditures."[85] Indeed, it was through the ideal of social utility that a figure like Thiers attempted to sponsor capitalist development for infrastructures and at the same time regulate commercial enterprises. The idea of "social utility" carried with it a kind of principle for state intervention embedding major capitalist enterprises in a thick web of historical and social obligation.

A spectrum emerged within which socially bound associational activity for the public good was understood. On the far left one may place the work of Louis Blanc, and in particular his arguments in favor of industrial association in *Organisation du travail*. Building on the public outrage that followed a series of scandals involving limited silent partnerships, and responding with his own conception of associational action, Blanc argued that association was indeed the proper way to organize all socioeconomic resources for the public good. What was unacceptable and even self-contradictory, however, was the idea that association could take place among one sector of the public and be in competition with other associations. He argued that this form of competition between associations, or between commercial enterprises, only shifted the dangers of individual competition to a more dangerous level of intensity, which would ultimately undermine the well-being of workers. "In recent years, we have seen the establishment of many limited partnerships. Who does not know of these scandals? Whether it is an individual fighting against an individual; or an association against an association, it is always war, and the reign of violence."[86] Blanc argued that to avoid this form of constant violence generated by capitalist competition between associations, it was necessary to create much more expansive associations and to apply the associational ideal evenly across society. For the latter, he argued that associations could be expanded by including not just capitalists but also workers who would manage these associations. In this conception, it would not be only capitalists who would receive the benefits of the associational activity at the expense of the workers. Instead, the workers and their labor—or human capital, if you will—would be considered on an equal footing and be presented as a foundation for associational activity. Furthermore, the associational ideal would be expanded to understand the society as one large association. In this context, different productive associations would not compete with one another, but would work together for greater social benefit. Blanc recognized that in attempting to launch this process, the question of credit would be a challenge, because banks would lend to those companies that were more profitable—that is, those that relied on the traditional competitive system of capitalist associations. He therefore argued that the state should play a fundamental role as the bank of this associational regime. The state in this context was not to dominate industry; it was to allow individuals to gather into self-governing associations in which each was rewarded as a full associational member.

On the other end of the political spectrum were those who embraced the capitalist form of competition and management by leading capitalists. But even here, among those who embraced the profit-making and exploitative form of associational enterprise, there was a recognition that these commercial businesses played an essential role in the development of democratic society. Charles Coquelin, who favored key policies for the liberalization of markets and free trade between France and England, opened one of his most important essays stating, "Man is a social being." He continued, "Yes, man is a sociable being; he is more so than any other sentient being: this is his most distinctive attribute and his most noble privilege."[87] But for Coquelin, this social condition should not bind the individual to one form of activity or overdetermine his relationship to a given enterprise. He used a metaphor surprisingly similar to Marx's argument for the relationship between the peasant and the state in the "theft of wood" articles written just a few short years earlier (discussed in chapter 2): "Instead of binding himself once and for all, in a single society, by a heavy chain that would hinder the freedom of his movements, he must rather bind himself by thousands of light threads which, by attaching him on all sides to his fellow creatures, nevertheless respect the play of his mobile nature. This is what reason commands; this is progress."[88]

It is important not to understate the massive gulf that separated a democratic socialist like Louis Blanc and a free-trade capitalist like Coquelin or a liberal politician like Thiers. These men disagreed in very profound ways on who should administer socially responsible industrial associations, how they should be organized, the nature of the bonds between individuals within them, and the relationships between the associations themselves. They indeed sat on opposite sides of the political spectrum during the July Monarchy—Blanc in favor of a democratic socialist republic, while Coquelin's ideas were compatible with those of King Louis-Philippe and Guizot. At the same time, however, they all understood the individual and his or her associational activity to be socially bound. Whether one was a democratic socialist or a supporter of the doctrinaires, there was an implicit assumption that commercial and industrial activity was grounded in a new social contract.

7

Substantive Democracy

The Nonsecular Foundations of a Democratic Social Science

> Did you, too, O friend, suppose democracy was only for elections, for politics, and for a party name? I say democracy is only of use there that it may pass on and come to its flower and fruits in manners in the highest forms of interaction between men, and their beliefs.
>
> WALT WHITMAN[1]

Popular decision making, public oversight, and a social conception of individual rights were the core elements of democratic state building throughout early-nineteenth-century France. However, even as these arguments ushered in new calls for vigorous administrative action, they raised new questions. The central challenge may be stated in the following terms: Any robust administrative intervention in favor of the public welfare necessarily carried with it assumptions about what kind of public life was socially acceptable and desirable. The realization of a thriving substantive democracy thus unavoidably carried moral assumptions regarding how society should be organized. And yet the dangers of such an enterprise were immediately obvious. In the first decades of the nineteenth century, it was sufficient to mention the Terror to unlock the fear of state-led moral tyranny. Balzac captured the rapprochement most present to the minds of thinkers and politicians of the early nineteenth century when he staged an oneiric meeting between Catherine de Medici and Robespierre, establishing a parallel between the treacherous excesses of religious zeal during the religious wars and the supposed moral dictatorship of the Terror.[2] Such comparisons helped fuel liberal critiques of robust administrative action just as they pushed individuals back behind the high-walled safety of individualism and formal legal protections from government.

Constituting the demos—or the historical and sociological construction of the political—consistently confronted this basic challenge to public authority and collective obligation. The consequence, however, was not a renunciation of a more forceful regulatory power, but, as we have seen, the contrary. Piercing this mystery requires an investigation of another essential feature in the construction of a self-governing democratic society: the invention of a new "social science" and "sociology" that was tightly bound to demands for substantive social transformation. Social science buttressed the search for a substantive democracy by generating an unprecedented and nonarbitrary investigation of the social structures that *should* guide action toward the collective good.

It did so, however, in an unexpected way.

Indeed, looking back from the other side of our democratic modernity, no doubt one of the most surprising—and most suggestive—features of the wide-ranging meta-discourses on the social in the first half of the nineteenth century was that they were so often couched in nonsecular terms.[3] While many during this transformative moment turned their backs on traditional religious systems and dogma, key democratic actors and theorists investigated the normative foundations and practical consequences of democratic life by reformulating the relationship religious belief and effective social action in order to increase administrative capacity.[4]

Toward a Sociologization of the Sacred

In his history of public law, Martin Loughlin has highlighted the role of the Protestant Reformation and the corollary cultivation of self-discipline in the expansion of regulatory police in the early modern age. Drawing on the work of Philip Gorski, Loughlin argues that "whereas the authority of medieval government had been anchored by a transcendent figure with the power to issue commands (the sovereign), these early-modern disciplining processes emphasized the necessity of instilling self-government. Flowing from the Protestant Reformation, the impact of social discipline on governmental practices was most pronounced in Calvinist regimes."[5] Culminating in what Gorski refers to as "the disciplinary revolution," the Protestant Reformation prepared the foundations for a new more "disciplined" individualism, which expanded the infrastructural capacity of the administrative state. Across the early modern period, those European countries which largely converted to Protestantism were therefore able institutionalize social discipline with the effect of "enhance[d] efficiency in government" and the promotion of "a more orderly private existence, one that government can more effectively control."[6] In so doing, they inaugurated a renewed ambition to shape political and social life, "establishing a well-ordered commonwealth at the heart of public law."[7]

Not surprisingly, perhaps, historians of the first half of the nineteenth century intimated these essential contributions of the Protestant Reformation to the development of the modern state. In Tocqueville's account, the long process of democratization which began in the medieval period, giving birth to individualism and equality as a social condition, was accelerated by the Reformation. In language not dissimilar to that of Loughlin and Gorski, Tocqueville insisted in the notes in the second volume of the *Democracy in America* that religion serves "to purify and regulate the love of well-being, without attempting to destroy it." He sought to explore "God's relationships with humanity, the nature of their soul, and their duties toward their fellows."[8] Convinced that religious beliefs "were necessary to all men and that each man needed them daily in order to solve the smallest problems," he similarly recognized that the absolutist state had taken over a range of responsibilities that limited the kind of liberty and regulation brought on by Protestantism. However, his focus on democracy in the nineteenth century also led him to a further observation: that alongside the decrease in liberty afforded by the absolutist state, there had been a paradoxical increase in equality. It was then, during the Revolution, that the kind of discipline promoted by Protestantism came to join the fashioning of social equality promoted by the absolutists' war on the nobility. "Who does not see that Luther, Descartes, and Voltaire used the same method, and that they differed only in the greater or lesser use they claimed to make of it?"[9] But if the Reformation and the secular philosophy of the Enlightenment had contributed to the leveling of society, "the political laws, the social state, and the habits of mind which flow from these first causes were opposed to it."[10] The Revolution, in Tocqueville's view, had inaugurated a new role for religion. In this new context, it was no longer Protestantism and its focus on individual liberty and responsibility that were to pay a central role in the process of regulation. Rather, in Tocqueville's view, it was a renewed Catholic commitment to social equality, combined with individual liberty, that was to play a central role in granting greater power to the administrative state.

In the first volume of his history of the French Revolution, written in 1847, Louis Blanc offered a similar narrative. He solemnly opened his history stating that there had been three great revolutions in the creation of modern rule: the ages of authority, individualism, and fraternity. "Authority was wielded by Catholicism with an astonishing brilliance; it prevailed until Luther," he argued. He then suggested, like Tocqueville, that while Luther had attempted to combine authority and individual liberty, in doing so he had dismissed solidarity. Only the French Revolution had been able to combine all three:

> Individualism, inaugurated by Luther, has developed with an irresistible force; and, freed from its religious elements, has triumphed in France thanks to the publicists of the Constituent. It governs the present; it is the soul of things.

> The Fraternity, announced by the thinkers of the Mountain, disappeared in a storm, and appears to us today only as a distant ideal; but all the great hearts call for it, and it already occupies and illuminates the highest spheres of intelligence.[11]

Recognizing that Luther continued to operate as the "soul of things," Blanc argued nonetheless that the French Revolution marked a new "fraternal" moment that was profoundly social. "Robespierre was the heir to Jesus and the apostle Rousseau: the truth of his utterings made him a true prophet."[12] But Robespierre's sacrifice on the guillotine cut short the prophecy's fulfillment. Fulfilling the prophecy was to be achieved through a just popular authority that respected individual liberty and social fraternity.

So while figures like Blanc and Tocqueville emphasized the role that Protestantism had played in destroying medieval forms of social and political hierarchy and introducing self-government, they remained convinced that this initial social and political transformation brought on by the Reformation was only one step in the construction of a modern state, and that the next step would require a very different set of religious ideals. In short, they suggested that if Protestantism had provided an essential contribution in introducing individual liberty and self-government at the local level, only a renewed set of religious ideals could provide a foundation for the social cohesion necessary for a democratic authority. As the famous theologian of the period, Henri Lacordaire, argued, a renewed Catholicism "allowed the nations to give themselves leaders, to govern each individual by its laws and its magistrates."[13]

The problem for which religion, and specifically a redefined, democratized Catholicism, provided a potential response was clear.[14] As critics had argued, an overemphasis on individual liberty from authority in favor of personal flourishing and self-discipline may have helped challenge the abuses, inefficiencies, and overcentralization of absolutist decision making, but it had also played an important role in the atomization of society and generated the deep-seated inequalities of the modern age. Such an approach simply could not provide the solidarity necessary for ensuring social obligation through public authority.[15] It was in this context that a new conception of religion developed, this time focused largely on society, solidarity, and equality toward an examination of the possibilities for understanding society as a structural force in which individuals were embedded and through which they could be emancipated. The individual would now be governed more justly through the elaboration of a new system of belief that drew its legitimacy from social equality and a need for a social and political authority that would address social needs.[16]

In the third letter of his *Lettres d'un habitant de Genève à ses contemporains*, published in 1803, Saint-Simon shed early light on this investigation by interrogating the kind of belief system that could guide the reinforced political institutions of his young century: "I will consider religion to be a human invention; I will consider it to be the only kind of political institution that tends to the general organization of humanity."[17] Looking to build the foundations for a thorough intervention toward the construction of a new social and political order, Saint-Simon shared with his conservative, antimodern contemporaries like Joseph de Maistre and Louis de Bonald a concern for rebuilding social unity, though from a very different point of view,.[18] Like them, he held the conviction that the uncompromising secularism and radical individualism of the philosophes of the previous century had left the postrevolutionary world adrift. He therefore sought, like Maistre and Bonald, a response in the recomposition of social life toward a renewed moral commitment. However, Saint-Simon drastically departed from these antimodern Catholics when he turned his back on previous dogma and initiated the idea that even the most fundamental religious foundations of social life—those aspects of social and political organization that were to be the most sacred and the most implicit in every individual action—were to be entirely reinvented. By integrating scientific methods into a new faith, Saint-Simon's religion shifted the terrain of technical and practical study in two directions at once: first, from the natural world toward society, and second, toward a deep engagement with the beliefs that underpinned any effective administrative system of social reconstruction.

Saint-Simon argued that his proposed "New Christianity" would build on the progress of the ages.[19] At the same time, however, it would overcome the disaggregating tendencies of early modern Protestant, scientific, and political thought by reassembling the broken pieces of revolutionary society through the creation of a new "social science": This would be a "science that constitutes society," he argued. "It is the science that serves as its basis."[20] In his view, this new social science would reinvest the spiritual realm that had been so doggedly under attack by prerevolutionary thinkers. Discovering "the regulatory principle of the human species"[21] was only possible, he argued, by "listening to the voice of God."[22] A new spiritualism would allow social scientists to comprehend society as part of an organic whole. A universal religion would bring together the seemingly disparate scientific discoveries in each realm of knowledge and overcome the chaos brought on by the tensions between scientific rationality and social improvement. Social regulation could no longer be left in the shade of mysticism; a new "clergy" of social scientists was necessary to bring it into the light. "What God has spoken is certainly not ameliorable," Saint-Simon acknowledged in his manifesto *Le nouveau christianisme*, published in 1827; "but what the clergy has said in the name of God is a science that can be perfected, just like all the other human sciences. The theory of theology needs to be renewed at certain times, as does that of physics, chemistry, and physiology."[23]

Saint-Simon therefore argued that he was inaugurating a third moment in the history of social organization. The first moment had been captured by the universal and unified vision of Catholicism. But by the late Middle Ages, Saint-Simon argued, the Roman Church had been reduced to purely political and material interests, focused on maintaining its grip over the faithful through a denial of the great technical discoveries and scientific progress. So with the end of the rise of a new age, "the force that this association possesses is only a material force, and it is only by means of cunning that it manages to sustain itself."[24] The spiritual consequence of this decline, Saint-Simon argued, was the Protestant Reformation. "It is to Luther that we owe the dissolution of a spiritual power that was no longer in touch with the state of society."[25] This second moment began just as the age of scientific discovery was blossoming. The Reformation and scientific materialism therefore filled the void created by the decrepitude and decadence of the Catholic faith.

While Saint-Simon recognized the legitimacy of Luther's critique of the Church, he in turn blamed the Reformation for misunderstanding the consequences of its critique of Catholic decadence. Inaugurating the definitive end of any organic relationship between social organization and religion, he argued that "Luther's reformation has missed its mark." In his view, "this reformation has been incomplete; it needs to undergo a reformation itself."[26] He saw Protestantism as insufficient because it was built on a critique of social unity through its blind commitment to individualism. The critical and individualist nature of the Lutheran and Calvinist legacy left little means to build a positive, solidaristic set of human relationships based on the well-being of all. It was therefore necessary to inaugurate a third moment out of the critical spirit of Protestantism and scientific discovery while reconnecting with the organic, universal, and unified vision of early Catholicism.

There was nonetheless a profound difference between Saint-Simon's "New Christianity" and those religions that preceded him. Saint-Simon's new system of belief was designed to integrate the critical discourse of Protestantism and the scientific revolution back into a conception of a unitary society. He therefore opened the path to a scientific—and in this sense progressive and critical—conversation about the very moral underpinnings of state action toward specific social aims. The new religion had as its central ambition the advancement of equality and the alleviation of poverty. "The new Christian organization will deduce temporal institutions, as well as spiritual institutions, from the principle that all men should behave toward one another as brothers. It will direct all institutions, of whatever nature, toward the increase of the welfare of the poorer class."[27] The ultimate goal of this one new great faith was, then: "Religion must direct society toward the great goal of improving the lot of the poorest class as quickly as possible."[28] If early Catholicism had invented an overarching vision that ordered the individual's place in a spiritual conception of the universe, it had done so only in abstract uncritical terms, Saint-Simon argued. Moreover, it had proved unable to hold up its universal doctrine in the face of Luther and the extraordinary progress in science that began with the Renaissance, and therefore had been unable to build a new system of authority capable of realizing the promise of scientific thought on this earth. The great unifying and administrative power of a universal system of belief had been lost. The new Christianity, oriented entirely toward the improvement of the condition of the poorest members of society, "must make men happy, not only in heaven, but on earth."[29]

While Saint-Simon's legacy was as complex and sinuous as his doctrine, his nonsecular approach to the social would have an outsized influence in the decades that followed. First, one can trace the development of a social science and the invention of sociology in the 1830s and 1840s directly out of his doctrine. Auguste Comte, who began using the term "sociology" in the 1830s, was a student of Saint-Simon in his youth, as were such key figures as Philippe Buchez, who set out to create a new practical science of political action. Second, Saint-Simon insisted on the importance of a profound historicization of religious belief, returning to an earlier, "primitive" Christianity for finding a unified doctrine in which earthly concerns were given a universal significance. It was only by understanding the history of this early church that a new universal religion could be achieved. Finally, Saint-Simon placed an overarching emphasis on mobilizing this new universal religion, which brought together spiritual doctrine, technical progress, and a scientific understanding of society, to ameliorate the conditions of the poor. The practical consequences of Saint-Simon's extraordinary flights of spiritual fancy were undeniable. As a growing awareness developed of the consequences of industrialization and urbanization, the idea took root of a consistently critical discussion of the moral foundations of social and political action needed to combat the destructive forces of modern capitalism.

And yet, as influential as Saint-Simon's social thought was, he almost systematically avoided the language of "democracy" as the means for putting into place his new organic society. Writing from 1803 through the mid-1820s, Saint-Simon's philosophy and spiritualism were presented as a means of escaping the political radicalism of the last decade of the eighteenth century. Bringing new harmony to France and even to the world through an investigation and administrative organization of commercial and industrial life, Saint-Simon sought social harmony in a new unity of all social interests backed by the state. The religious, in his conception, was therefore a means of providing a new substantive foundation for social action that culminated not in politicking but in a depoliticized scientific study of things. As a result, democracy as such did not feature prominently in his writings. It was only with the following generation that a democratization of this debate on the moral foundations of public action would come.

Politicizing a Nonsecular Conception of the Social

The religious turn among postrevolutionary thinkers and politicians provoked a radical reversal in the relationship between public authority and religion: it brought into broad daylight the ways in which politics was necessarily grounded in belief systems, while at the same time subjecting these belief systems to new social scientific investigation. Edgar Quinet succinctly summarized this key question of his age in his best-selling *Du génie des religions*, first published in 1842, less than two decades after Saint-Simon's death. "For a long time, dogmas were considered the work of politics," he argued in the opening pages of his pathbreaking work, "whereas the opposite proposal is the only true one."[30] Opponents of religion in the Enlightenment, Quinet argued, had critiqued religious doctrine as the plaything of states and their earthly political ambitions. Capturing the new religious ideas swirling around him, Quinet insisted that in fact quite the opposite was true. An investigation of the world religions of antiquity—including ancient India, China, the Middle East, and Greece—showed that politics had in fact been derived from and motivated by religious doctrine: political and institutional organization grew, he argued, out of the belief systems that formed the foundations of each society. He sought to recount the variety of ways in which political systems had been born of their socio-religious orders, and in so doing he explored their radical political consequences.

In the moment surrounding Quinet's work, intellectuals, politicians, activists, and clergy revisited a variety of religious questions, practices, and dogmas. In some cases they wrote new histories of Catholicism, and some even invented entirely new religions. In each instance, however, these investigations of a new spiritualism shared an ambition to surpass what they presented as a dead-end of radical secular Enlightenment thought, liberal critiques of authority, and the legacy of individualism. In so doing, this nonsecularism provided a new social foundation for regulatory action. Where the investigations differed, however, was in the effort to elaborate the political consequences of these new religious doctrines. They therefore increasingly politicized this powerful new social vision. The consequence was a profound democratization of religious discourse and practice that provided a new social foundation for political action.

This democratization of new religious ideas and practices exploded onto the scene in the July Monarchy. The radical religious journal *L'avenir* stated in no uncertain terms on October 22, 1830, in its editorial entitled "Our Duty in the Moment": "We live in a vast democracy."[31] The political activist, democrat, and later socialist Charles-François Chevé captured the spirit of the age with his book *Catholicisme et démocratie ou le règne du Christ*, in which he argued that the democracy developing all around him was the final great stage in the development of Christianity.[32] Flaubert captured this democratic spirit when his inflamed revolutionary in *L'Éducation sentimentale*, Sénécal, smashed his wine glass and shouted, "The popes who, after all, defended the people were slandered" during the Reformation. In response, Senecal called for "the dawn of democracy, a great egalitarian movement against the individualism of the protestants.'"[33] Tocqueville provided a characteristically sanguine view of the impact of democracy on religion in his *Democracy in America* when he argued, "I think it is wrong to look at the Catholic religion as a natural enemy of democracy." Reversing the assumptions of the previous century, he argued that if Protestantism had been the religion behind the liberal individualism of the Revolution, a renewed Catholicism could rightly be considered the religion of democracy. No doubt, he conceded, Protestantism had paved the way for a new emphasis on individual liberty; but "Protestantism, in general, carries men much less toward equality than toward independence." Capturing the core of arguments on religion and the construction of democratic society, Tocqueville further argued, "If Catholicism disposes the faithful to obedience, it does not prepare them for inequality. I would say quite the opposite, in fact." In the postrevolutionary democratic world he examined, a renewed Catholicism could therefore provide an important resource for preserving democratic society: "Among the various Christian doctrines, Catholicism seems to me to be one of the most favorable to equality of conditions."[34] Just as absolutism had forged a new condition of equality among French subjects, Catholicism had prepared the people for an egalitarian society: "Catholicism is like an absolute monarchy. Remove the prince, and conditions are more equal than in republics." In parallel terms, he argued that in the realm of religion, all that was necessary was to remove the Church's traditional hierarchy. In similar terms to those of Quinet, Tocqueville rendered explicit the dimension of democratic society that had remained hidden, the religious fashioning of the social.[35] Inspired by his work, Louis de Carné summarized Tocqueville's contribution when he argued: "Christian doctrines alone can prepare other destinies for democracy, by quieting the incessant activity and by implanting in souls a principle of dedication."[36]

It was precisely this task that many of Tocqueville's contemporaries undertook. Catholicism, it was argued, understood the individual as a fundamentally social being. Balzac captured this idea in his improbable study of Catherine de Medici, when he argued (in language reminiscent of Hegel): "Opposition in France has always been Protestant because it has only ever had *negation* as the foundation of its politics." He continued arguing that instead, "Catherine de Medici, like anyone committed to a well-regulated society, recognized the *social man* [*l'homme social*] as its subject."[37] "Man is not a solitary being," concurred Henri Lacordaire. "He is not flung at random to live and die in the unknown shade of a rock or a forest; he is born in the midst of society."[38]

Investigations of the social individual were thus built on religious grounds as early "social scientists" sought resources in the universal, egalitarian, and solidaristic revision of Catholicism. The challenge, however, was in overcoming the hierarchies of the Roman Church as it had developed since the early modern period. Louis Rousseau,[39] who converted to Saint-Simonianism in the wake of the Revolution of 1830, presented his ideas for a new social science in his book *The Nineteenth-Century Crusade*.[40] Insisting on the "degrading theories of the school of Adam Smith," Rousseau called for the creation of a new social science, which he called "social economy." The shift from "political economy" to a "social economy" would help build "a capacity for synthesis, experience, and analysis through the compass of faith."[41] Rousseau's critique of eighteenth-century economic thought focused on replacing possessive individualism in favor of a new social investigation to guide public action. "Liberalism," he argued, "had only been able to create institutions founded on slavery." True freedom in the new industrial age, he argued, would come from a search for "laws of unity, justice, and charity."[42]

Philippe Buchez, a former student and follower of Saint-Simon, and later president of the National Assembly in 1848, declared, "No one today is happy with what exists in politics; the rulers, because they fear; the contented, because they doubt; the men of heart, because they desire; the masses, because they suffer."[43] The principal cause of this generalized discontent was the impasse of secular thought. "All political doctrines that have been taught to men are exhausted," Buchez argued, concluding that "all known political forms have been put into practice and tried."[44] The revitalization of a new politics with a wholistic conception of society grounded in religion was the only way forward. Incarnating "the theological age of sociology,"[45] Buchez derided radical secularism, "as if between God and us, there was no society, as if man were the only being that God had created."[46]

Buchez sought the renewal of political education for magistrates, politicians, journalists, and judges in a vast revision of Catholicism. His multi-volume project *A Complete Treatise of Philosophy from the Point of View of Catholicism and Progress* proposed nothing less. Like Saint-Simon, he had an overarching ambition to create a unified doctrine that would reinvent the foundations for society and for ensuring social welfare. Buchez sought to elaborate a complete philosophical system grounded in a new universal faith that integrated all human understanding. The problem was that every political leader "had their own particular philosophy." Moreover, science had been split into so many different areas that works by savants were "unfortunately incomprehensible if one were not already a specialist in the area."[47] Overspecialization had reduced politics to a series of decisions solely concerned with solving immediate problems. All attempts to respond to "great political problems" of the day therefore confronted only "incapacity, inertia, and repugnance."[48] In response, this new system was designed to provide "a common method and a common scientific language" to overcome a politics of individualism, liberty, and formal rights.

Like so many of his contemporaries, Buchez argued that the Protestant Reformation had rightly challenged the staid moral foundations of a moribund Catholic Church. But while it had marked an important step forward, it had left social and political authority aimless: "Protestants argued that the reason of each individual was sovereign." For all of its contributions, the end result of the Protestant reformation had been to splinter society. Buchez argued that the dangers of such radical individualism could be seen in the politics of the Doctrinaires. "Protestantism has ended in individualism and the federalism of interests," he argued. Without a philosophy of society, the regime of Louis-Philippe was reduced to atomistic inequality. A new social-philosophical foundation was necessary.[49] Building on the critical capacities of Protestant individualism on the one hand and the unity inherent in Catholicism on the other, Buchez proposed a new religious approach to social progress.

Pierre Leroux, philosopher, journalist, democratic theorist and one of the first to elaborate the idea of "socialism," similarly insisted on the institutional empowerment inherent in a religious approach to the social. For him, a new universal religion ensured that politics would serve society as a whole instead of the aristocratic few. "Outside of religion," he explained in his work on a new religion of humanity, "we cannot find that solid point, which is necessary to us, and without which our internal strength remains dormant."[50] Leroux borrowed from new social Catholicism and from Saint-Simonianism to propose a religion in favor of equality for all. The birth of this new religion inaugurated nothing short of a new Renaissance. "We are now in an era similar to that of the Renaissance."[51] Enlightenment and revolutionary ideals provided the means "for shaking feudalism and a ruined Catholicism."[52] Leroux's ideal also pushed beyond what he presented as the untrammeled individualism of Protestantism and formalist discourses on citizenship and individual rights that he traced back to 1789.[53] He instead examined society in search of a new moral condition that could provide the foundation for a generous, capacious, and substantive public policy. This "religion of humanity" would create a novel political authority built on radical egalitarianism and self-administration: "No one today can, without folly, resist the fact that all minds legally participate in the administration of society, that each one's right to a share of public intelligence forms the foundations of society, and that thus, in the intellectual field, the principle of Equality triumphs."[54] Pushing beyond the institutional confines of the Roman Church, Leroux argued that his religion of humanity was the true heir of Christianity. "Christianity has always been democratic," Leroux argued; "if it has assumed, in the course of the centuries, a different form, this form is repugnant to its true nature."[55] The institutions built by the Church had buried Christianity's universal, egalitarian, and democratic message. Luther had been right to attack the Church. But his doctrine, Leroux argued, ultimately "weakened religious sentiment."[56] As a great accelerator of this slow disenchantment of modern society, the Enlightenment had been as damaging as it was emancipatory. "The critical philosophy of the eighteenth century has only half emancipated us, because it has been unjust, because it has denied instead of explaining, because it has taken a blind and antisocial hatred against all religions and against all religion."[57] Leroux's new universal religion would reenchant postrevolutionary society by showing its common interests. A rejection of political and religious hierarchy in the name of a religion based on social equality was to give birth to "a truly democratic spirit at the time when democracy is proclaimed."[58] The consequences would be a renewal of the original democratic ambitions of the early church: an egalitarian vision for humanity in which the people not only were constituted through a system of beliefs but also acquired the means to govern and regulate themselves.

The democratization of social life through religious renewal was not solely the project of Saint-Simonians and early democratic socialists. One of the most promising and conservative Catholic theologians in his youth,

Lamennais steadily radicalized, moving away from the established Church, and ultimately providing one of the most democratic conceptions of social Catholicism of the post-revolutionary world.[59] Félicité de La Mennais, later simply Lamennais, began his theological studies alongside conservatives like Maistre and Bonald. Gifted with a vibrant written voice and dogged conviction, his early conservative theological writings made him an instant success. By the latter part of the Restoration, however, Lamennais's theology showed a new interest in the social and political questions of his day, marking a shift toward what one historian has referred to as "the affirmation of the primacy of the practical over the speculative."[60] In 1826 he echoed an entire generation of democratic thought when he stated: "It is impossible to understand any aspect of the present society if one ignores that France is a vast democracy."[61] While recognizing the foundational importance of this new democratic society, its consequence was not entirely felicitous. In words that would be echoed by Tocqueville, he argued that this generalized democratic condition shook all social foundations to the point that "an irresistible force pushes and agitates men; whatever is in their way is trampled underfoot: they advance, return, advance again, and the whole social order becomes for them like a path through a narrow passage."[62] For Lamennais, the response to democracy was therefore a reinvention of religious doctrine that would provide new substantive underpinnings for postrevolutionary society. In words that captured the essence of what Quinet would argue a decade and a half later, Lamennais stated his ambition: "Any revolution always and necessarily begins in the church, then passes to the state."[63]

Lamennais's personal and political trajectory captured a larger transformation in the relationship between the political and social. In the final years of the Restoration, he still saw a reinvented Catholicism as the means for overcoming the disaggregating tendencies of democratic society; faith remained an antidote to democratic dilution. By the eve of the Revolution of 1830, however, Lamennais increasingly understood democracy and a reinvented Catholicism as part of a common project of social and political renewal. As he democratized his theology and theologized democratic theory, he increasingly came into conflict with the Roman Church. In 1829 he boldly announced his democratic conversion: "Everyone now sees that France and Europe are moving toward new revolutions. The most intrepid hopes, nourished for years by interest or imbecility, are giving way to facts. It is no longer possible for anyone to be under the illusion. Nothing can remain as it is; everything wavers, everything tilts.[64]

Grasping the full impact of the democratic revolution a half decade before Tocqueville, Lamennais gave witness to the ways in which democracy radically reshaped the underpinnings of all social and political activity. Following the Revolution of 1830, Lamennais diagnosed the battle taking place both within himself and within the Restoration as a battle over what kind of public authority, monarchical or democratic, would serve this new democratic society. The Restoration, he argued, "was the last fight between two irreconcilable principles armed one against the other by the law, the monarchic principle, and the democratic principle, and the latter possessing a force in all respects incomparably greater."[65] For Lamennais, democracy had triumphed. And as a result, it was now necessary to uncover "the essential laws of society" and establish a correlate political system. The foundations for democratic government could be found in a new Catholicism rooted in radical equality and solidarity. "To develop according to one's own particular laws, in harmony with universal laws, to fully possess the gift of God, to enjoy it without disturbance, that is the right, without which there is no order, no progress, no existence."[66]

By the 1840s, Lamennais had become the "proven apostle of democracy."[67] His political theology grappled with the consequences of a fully egalitarian society for the construction of a democratic state. His *Book of the People* offered a new Gospel designed "to teach an abridged account of democratic rights and obligations."[68] Religion was to provide the fiber that connected a politically constituted society of equals into a self-governing power: "You can ask for your share of influence in the administration of the public good, which is above all your good."[69] In an article published in *The Democratic Almanach of France* in 1841, Lamennais reinterpreted and relativized sovereignty in a democratic age. Sovereignty, he argued, was in no way the right to command. Rather, it should be understood as complete liberty and independence. From this perspective, only God was sovereign, because only God was infinitely free. As a result, no individual was absolutely sovereign, since in Lamennais's view everyone ultimately drew their power from God and from the laws that God provided. Earthly sovereignty grew out of these laws. An individual, Lamennais argued, "is sovereign in the sense that neither his reason, nor his will, nor consequently his acts depend by right on any man; that, the prior and superior law of justice being his rule, he is primitively and completely free with regard to beings similar to himself, and owes obedience to none of them."[70] This spiritualized notion of sovereignty therefore defined individuals as independent from arbitrary authority *and* interdependent upon others: brought by God into a society of equals, each individual was intrinsically bound and fully free through spiritual bond. Democracy recognized the common interests born of equality, the power of individual obligation to the community, and the necessity of governing in the service of both.

Building on a classic theme of early modern social contract theory—most reminiscent of Rousseau—Lamennais argued that the only way to preserve the radical independence within community granted by God was to join together on the basis of the mutual preservation of individual liberty under God's sovereignty, which was by nature collective and binding.[71] At the same time, however, he "sociologized" Rousseau's social contract in his search for the values that structured social action.[72] In a democracy, government would be built upon these moral configurations that were to be discovered and cultivated within society itself. As a consequence, the state was not sovereign; it was instead "a simple function." Individuals did not and in fact could not delegate sovereign power, since it was given by God. They could only preserve the right of individuals to ensure interdependency and prevent exploitation or any form of modern slavery—that is, they could preserve their right to freely participate and serve the general sovereign will of God. People joined together and deputized a power that was "essentially revocable. It does not make the law; it provides for its execution." From this, Lamennais drew the essential conclusion of the democratic state that "the people do not exist for the sake of power, but power for the sake of the people."[73] His political theology therefore freed individuals through a justly governed society under the sovereign will of God.

It was perhaps the economist and activist Henri-Robert Feugueray who best summarized the impact of this democratization of Catholicism: "Many great things have already been accomplished in the nineteenth century; but we do not know of any greater or more recent than the reconciliation of Catholicism and democracy, which is taking place before our eyes and which no one will be able to prevent from happening."[74] Together these theorists and practitioners grappled with the possibility of establishing new normative foundations for a social democracy that pushed far beyond purely formal notions of individual rights, voting procedures, or legislative representation. These theorists, administrators, theologians, and social scientists united science, philosophy, and religion to create "a religion of immanence."[75] While they understood that any political intervention necessarily carried with it implicit moral and ethical ideals, they sought a more explicit and critical relationship to these belief systems. In so doing, they attempted to reinvent the religious function of social belief and come to grips with how greater social cohesion could guide administrative action. Turning their backs on the opposition between the secular and the religious that they argued had plagued the eighteenth century, their commitment to a universal religion of humanity proposed a new society founded on solidarity, in which individuals recognized one another as equal and free. This society of liberty and interdependence in turn provided the social foundations for self-government. If a democratic society preceded—both logically and historically—the creation of democratic government, it was because in a true democracy, social needs came first and public solutions were required to address them.

Historicizing the Nonsecular Foundations of Democratic Life

If Catholic theology had been broadly marked by an "unconditional obedience owed to a foundational past and to the dependency on tradition,"[76] the democratic approach to religion reorganized belief around needs of contemporary society. Instead of a search for origins and a lost ideal order, historicization of the religious subjected belief to temporal development. In so doing, it undermined an obscurantist mystification of a collective past as well as any eschatological futurity. Fulfilling a new role in a specific historical moment, it became the force that animated democratic society, and thus the legitimate foundation for democratic rule.

It is for this reason that in spite of his commitment to upending the secularism of "Voltaire's century," François-René de Chateaubriand refused to turn his back on democracy. Enjoying the authority of a leading voice of Christian renewal thanks to his *Génie du christianisme*, his *Mémoires d'outre tombe* revisited the history of Catholicism in explicitly democratic terms. "At just the moment when liberty, equality, and the republic were eclipsed by Augustus, the great representative of equality, liberty, and republic on earth, that is, Christ, transmitted his power," Chateaubriand recounts. This transfer of power gave birth to a "temporal power and democratic order" that established "the social equality of men and women." For Chateaubriand, "the history of modern society begins at the foot and on this side of the Cross."[77] Chateaubriand's social history of religion captured the ideals of a new democratic society and inspired a whole generation.

"Separated from the past, the present can say nothing of the future."[78] With these words, Lamennais illustrated a widespread investigation into novel interpretations of the early church, and the process whereby a radical historicization of the religious bolstered democracy. By the early years of the July Monarchy, Lamennais increasingly repudiated the traditionalist ideals of the Roman Church, in particular the papal rejection of liberty of association and freedom of conscience best represented in the encyclicals by Gregory XVI, *Mirari vos*, of 1832, and *Singulari nos*, which had been written directly against Lamennais and his support for the revolts of 1834. Refusing Roman authority, Lamennais encouraged his readers, "Lend an ear and tell me where this confused, vague, strange noise which is heard on all sides is coming from."[79] The popular revolts of the early years of the July Monarchy were a call for a new social reform; the people were the voice for realizing the ideals of a new faith. These revolts did not however emerge spontaneously, Lamennais argued. They were deeply bound to their historical moment and the realization of an immanent social transformation that had come of age.[80] "Humanity does not turn in a fatal circle," Lamennais argued; "it develops incessantly, incessantly it passes from an imperfect state to another which is less so."[81] Lamennais believed that the popular revolts of the 1830s were thus forces of history, pushing for a more just and equal society "so that you constantly walk toward the goal assigned to you by divine laws."[82] He found a precedent for this popular movement in the religious practices of the first political societies. He followed the development of the monotheistic religions up through Protestantism to argue for a general law of progress. The people, he suggested, were the force of social justice. It was through their rising up and the satisfaction of their needs that the ideals of a unified faith could be realized. The ultimate revelation of this progress would come in a democratic government: "Freedom depends on two inseparably linked conditions, property and participation in government, in the power of legislation and in the administration of common affairs."[83] Lamennais's historical reinvention investigated the early moments of Christianity, the Reformation, and the French Revolution, making historical interpretation itself the foundation for a new society with great political consequences for self-government.

Saint-Simon similarly offered a history of Catholicism in his *New Christianity*. Having condemned the Roman Church since the Middle Ages while appreciating its universal message, he sought inspiration in the Church's earliest moments. "Leaders of the early church preached frankly the union to all peoples," he argued. Prior to the expropriation of dogma by a papal monarchy and an aristocratic clergy, Christianity had attacked the powerful in the name of the many: "They declared positively and with the greatest energy to powerful men that their first duty was to employ all their means for the most prompt possible improvement of the moral and physical existence of the poor."[84] The lot of the poorest, most vulnerable members of society had been the specific concern of an early church that was not yet erected into a means of institutional and political oppression. Recovering this original message would provide the means for building a new universal faith to help administrations combat the inequities of the new postrevolutionary industrial age.

A wide variety of thinkers developed similar arguments on the democratic origins of Christianity across the 1830s and 1840s. A review of François Dominique de Reynaud de Montlosier's *De l'origine, de la nature et des progrès* suggested that "we learn first that the Church began as a democracy; that it became an aristocracy through the usurpation of the bishops; and that finally, the ascendancy of the bishop of Rome made it a pontifical monarchy."[85] While Montlosier was a conservative, he too had argued for the democratic influence of the early Church. It was, however, up to the more radical democratic reformers to elaborate how these popular origins of the Church and its doctrine could be applied positively to the present. One of the most original religious reformers to propose the democratic nature of the early Church was Bernard-Raymond Fabré-Palaprat. A prominent surgeon, Fabré-Palaprat attempted to reestablish the order of the Templars in the nineteenth century. He claimed to have acquired a text written in Greek entitled the *Lévitikon*, which he presented as a previously undiscovered version of the Gospel according to John. According to Fabré-Palaprat, this work contained "the fundamental and indispensable principles of the primitive Christian religion.[86] The book was filled with references to the popular foundations and ambitions of the early Church. "The church of Laodicea means people's court," he surmised. "It is democratic like the church of Sardis, and is quite similar to the Protestant church."[87] Fabré-Palaprat's writings contributed to a whole range of voices that placed religious history in the service of democracy.

In *La femme et la démocratie de nos temps*, Hortense Allart argued that a "model democracy existed and dominated Europe." The leaders of this democracy were "recruited from all ranks of society," she argued, just as "the lowest ranks of the hierarchy could attain the highest throne through talent alone." She then revealed that "this democracy was the Roman Church," and that "this was the true form of government; in which all were called." However, she added, "Today all that remains of this government is a cadaver."[88] More radical political figures like Pierre Leroux also explored the history of a lost primitive Church to push for the spread of democracy under the banner of a new universal humanistic religion. According to Leroux, not only was the message of early Christianity concerned with the poor masses, but its original structure was also democratic. "I say that the spiritual power began democratically," he insisted in his history of the origins of Christianity. In his view, Catholicism's democratic origins were attested to by the system for choosing the early bishops. "Who was a bishop then? By whom was he instituted, if not by the suffrage of the clergy and the people? The bishops were thus the elected representatives of the Christian people."[89] Even the top of the church hierarchy and the decisions it made on dogma were decided democratically, Leroux argued:

> Spiritual power began with the Councils, that is to say, the first time it appeared in our world was in democratic form. When, at Nicaea, the nature of

Jesus Christ was decided and the symbol was drawn up which has always been considered the foundation of the Catholic faith, who drew up this symbol and who decided on the nature of Jesus Christ? It was an assembly of three hundred and eighteen bishops, not a Pope.[90]

Democracy offered the means of choosing officeholders, made doctrine through a committee of elected officials, and was concerned with the condition of the poorest members of society.

Among the most famous Catholic theologians to pursue a democratic history of the early Church in the 1840s was Frédéric Ozanam. A theologian and faculty member of the Sorbonne, Ozanam professed an increasingly egalitarian and radical social policy in the name of a renewed Church. Looking back to the low Middle Ages, Ozanam argued: "The Popes of the eighth century found in France liberators who founded the temporal independence of the Holy See. They found thousands of heroic men to go and evangelize the Barbarians of the North, to give them not only faith, but laws, cities, and schools." It was through these "barbarians" that "the modern pontificate" could draw more faithful into its ranks. Ozanam insisted that it was time to embrace those who had also been pushed out of the Church, both intellectually and materially. "It is time to sacrifice the old resentments and to turn to this democracy, to these people who do not know us." Ozanam concluded with his famous call "*Passons aux Barbares* [Let us turn to the Barbarians],"[91] begging the Church to reach out to the new democratic society to build the faith of the future.[92]

Alongside attempts to return to the early Church was a profound interest in the moment of the Reformation. Many of those who saw in religion the means of consolidating democratic society in the first half of the nineteenth century considered the original critiques of Luther against the Roman Church entirely justified. They were also convinced, however, that Reformation had not succeeded in replacing the cohesive universal vision it had set out of destroy. The Reformation had generated not a founding moment but a historical shift that opened new possibilities for liberty. By integrating itself into a history, the Reformation participated in the progress and possibilities of self-government without becoming an end in itself.

If the Reformation had marked an important step forward, it was not until the French Revolution that the true promise of liberty—initially offered by Protestantism—was actually achieved by society as a whole. Religious readings of the French Revolution abounded in this golden age of revolutionary historiography. Among the most powerful—and extensive—histories of the French Revolution from a religious perspective was Philippe Buchez and Vital Roux's forty-volume parliamentary history of the French Revolution, which developed many of Buchez's religious ideas. For Buchez and Roux, the Revolution played the role of a revelation, the culmination of a prophecy that had begun in Europe with the birth of Christianity. They opened their masterful opus declaring:

> The French Revolution is the last and most advanced consequence of modern civilization, and modern civilization came entirely from the Gospel. This is an incontrovertible fact, if one consults history, and particularly that of our country, studying not only the events, but also the ideas that led to these events. It is also an incontrovertible fact, if one examines and compares with the doctrine of Jesus, all the principles that the Revolution inscribed on its flags and in its Codes; these words of equality and fraternity that it put at the head of all its acts, and with which it justified all its works.[93]

Like Blanc, Buchez and Roux argued that the egalitarian and fraternal ideals of the Revolution had realized a renewed Christian ideal under the banner of social justice. In so doing, they rejected secular readings of the Revolution. "How was our revolution presented?" they asked.[94] Regrettably, some "writers invoked natural law." But such analyses were short-sighted, they argued, for it was impossible to found a cohesive society on a formal conception of law. "Law is unfit to found a society. Has it not been repeated many times that, from the point of view of nature, each person is interested in his own private interest, and that from there he can justly repel any social duty?" The history of social solidarity in the French Revolution could not be told as a story of individual rights from social obligation. It was instead a history of the realization of a new regulatory principle designed to ensure individual liberty through society. The foundations for this regulatory principle were to be drawn from a renewed concept of religion. It was by openly asserting and accepting the tenets of this new religion that the acts of the Revolution could be justified. "The events of the revolution, as soon as they are understood in these terms, are justified in the eyes of all, people, kings, and priests; they change their nature; because one is obliged to see in its axioms laws long taught and long pursued, and which are almost realized."[95] The Revolution had been the first event, they argued, to recognize the social ideals and realize its political consequences for humanity on the scale of a sovereign people. As Feugueray explained, it was thanks to Buchez that a new relationship between democracy and religion had been established through his history of the French Revolution: "It was he ... who had the merit of reconnecting the chain of time by linking democracy to Christianity as its principle. Before him, it had never been taught with such authority that the French Revolution is a consequence of the Gospel."[96]

The journalist and historian Barthélemy Hauréau wrote a series of articles offering a similar interpretation of religious history and democracy for a massive collective editorial project, le *Dictionnaire Politique*, published by Pagnerre in 1842.[97] Offering his own politico-religious history, Hauréau argued that the Protestant Reformation had marked an essential moment in the realization of individual liberty, but had been unable to match this new social condition with a common public authority. In his encyclopedia entry on "Protestantism," Hauréau wrote:

> We must conclude that Protestantism, in its most absolute formula, which is individual rationalism, is not a principle hostile to Catholicism. We see, on the contrary, that these two principles tend to make more and more perfect the unity in which they coexist. What is democracy? . . . Democratic government has the advantage over other constitutions of being at once the expression of each and all, of reconciling order and liberty, Protestant anarchy and Catholic authority.[98]

Only a democratic government could unite the two great principles of religious development, individualism and public authority.

This combination of liberty and authority in democracy had taken root in the French Revolution, Hauréau argued. "The victory of the revolutionary party reestablished the unity of the executive power. . . . The power of individuals prevailed over the authority of representation."[99] By uniting the principles of authority and individual liberty, the Convention during the Revolution provided an "admirable understanding of democratic organization."[100] The challenge in recovering the moral message of the Revolution in the early nineteenth century was, of course, the Terror. If the Revolution, and in particular the Convention, had been a moment of moral unity, how was it possible to explain the horrible acts of 1794? Here too Hauréau turned to religious history. In a weakly disguised parallel between the Terror and the Inquisition, he argued that the horrors of the auto-da-fé could not be used to dismiss the historical contributions of Catholicism. Likewise, the Terror could not be used to dismiss the democracy born of the French Revolution. New Catholics, he argued, "had to recognize the more or less direct participation of the Roman Church in all the autos-da-fé that bloodied France, Spain, and the Germanic states."[101] Hauréau embraced the critiques of the Inquisition, claiming that they needed to be understood and integrated into any future religious practice. But they could no longer be used as a blanket dismissal of all religious belief: "The Terror was barbaric, the punishments were merciless! We certainly do not intend to justify the acts, even less to excuse the crimes." On the other hand, however, these practices had been sufficiently denounced.

In Hauréau's mind, there was no danger that such an intolerant Catholicism could ever return. "The enemy it has defeated will not rise again, and we have nothing more to fear from such a history. All grudges are now stale."[102] The spread of Protestantism and then Enlightenment ideals had definitively undermined any possibility that the Inquisition could return. Old Catholicism was dead: "Temporally and spiritually, the power of the pope is today only a fiction."[103] Drawing out the conclusions of this argument for democratic government after the Terror, Hauréau argued that absolute monarchy had been destroyed and that there was no risk that democratic government of a democratic society would lead to Terror. "What proves that the democratic party would not be reduced, even in the hypothesis of a new revolution, to the sad necessity of terrifying its adversaries in order to make its reforming work respected, is that the revolution of 1789 has so weakened the conservative elements of the monarchical order that they can no longer offer any serious resistance to the progress of minds and institutions."[104] The Revolutionary moment had its excesses, but it had also fulfilled its office. It was now possible to build on its moral ideals without fear that it would disintegrate into Terror.

This historicized conception of religion turned its back on the supposed "corrupt" institutions of the Church; it integrated the Protestant affirmation of individualism and self-government while also critiquing its supposed "anarchism," and it interpreted the French Revolution as the realization of a social ideal that far outstripped formal notions of natural liberty and constitutionalism. These historical renderings helped clear the space for the construction of a more substantive administrative action that was neither purely formal nor arbitrary. It also pointed to the historical necessity of a new system of belief that would provide the foundations for nonarbitrary substantive administrative action.

Grounding a Democratic Political Practice

How to provide a legitimate foundation for substantive public action beyond a mere formal recognition of private interests and individual rights? As we have seen, this question, which animated debates on democratic action across the first half of the nineteenth century, found an answer in attempts to interrogate the moral foundations of public action. As we have also seen, by the 1820s, those who pursued the construction of a new *democratic* public authority argued that regulation of everyday life could not be adequately ensured by a commitment to formal law and legal procedure. Nor, however, in a democratic society could public intervention be solely based on the will or supposed expertise of specific administrators. Finally, in a deeply historicized and politically constituted society, natural, eternal, and unchallenged religious dictates were equally unacceptable. Slowly, a new nonarbitrary foundation for public action on the social took shape.

Like so many of his contemporaries, Henri Lacordaire embraced the contributions of Protestantism, while arguing that it could not ground a new political system in a democratic age. Protestantism had contributed to the modern age as it "sowed the Bible in the world, and, with the Bible, certain ideas that are abundant there," Lacordaire argued. But it was weakest in providing a new footing for a modern public authority. Protestantism, he argued,

> would not have universally established a hierarchy, since it has none; a legislature, since it has none; a judiciary, since it has none; an administration, since it has none. They have made an intellectual masterpiece, but one that has nothing to compare with that of Catholic society, establishing everywhere, with its doctrine, its hierarchical, legislative, judicial and administrative unity.[105]

Catholicism provided the conditions for unity *and* for an administrative power that could both capture the ideals of modern society and act upon it in return. Instead of combating the state, a modernized faith could provide the "legislative, judicial and administrative" powers necessary for a democratic society to govern itself democratically.

Interrogations on the legitimate foundations of regulation saturated writings on democracy throughout the July Monarchy. In his article on "sovereignty and power," Lamennais argued that there were rules supporting all forms of social action, which were necessary for "the full enjoyment of freedom, modified only by voluntarily accepted rules; rules necessary for the achievement of the purpose of the association."[106] Lamennais then posed the fundamental question of how such regulation could operate and be executed in a democratic context. "How to achieve the social association's goal?" he asked. How was it possible not simply to protect individuals from the intervention of public authorities, but to ensure that a given community could achieve specific social ends? Once the people came together around a common system of beliefs, they needed to be engaged in ensuring the realization of their shared public aims.

Lamennais therefore entirely rejected the idea of elite or expert administrators. In his view, "the people do not make classes, they do not create privileges, they delegate functions."[107] In a democratic state, the people delegated specific administrative roles without losing any of their fundamental control. "One entrusts care to this or to that individual; he entrusts them with the execution of his decisions, which he has regulated for the common good according to the forms established by him, and which he can always modify or change."[108] The people never alienate their ability to supervise and oversee administrative action.

In his 1848 response to the Catholic liberal Charles de Montalembert in the Christian-democratic periodical *L'ère nouvelle*, l'abbé Henri Maret argued in similar terms: "In this account, we had only one thought, only one desire; to see Catholicism frankly allied with democracy, in order to settle it."[109] While the abbé Maret was committed to a reinvented Catholicism, he shared the conviction that religion offered a foundation for democratically regulating a democratic society.[110] In his "Letter on Religion," Raspail argued that it was precisely the destruction of dogma in the postrevolutionary age that opened the path to democratic government. He separated out three aspects of religious practice: "The congregation speaks to the eyes, dogma to the mind, prayer to the heart; these are the three parts of religion," he argued. Among the three, only "the congregation belongs to the city, organizes itself within it, disappears with it, and engages only those who incorporate themselves into it." While dogma could divide individuals and even provoke social decomposition, for Raspail, the general religion or "congregation" of any given political society or *cité* was "its constitution, which serves to regulate the most sacred relations of citizens, to remind them that they are brothers from cradle to grave."[111] Raspail therefore sought to make a clear distinction between any particular belief and the general function of social belief for ensuring the solidarity and fraternity of a given society. For him, the very role of religion therefore needed to change: it needed to be subject to the same fundamental debates that surrounded scientific knowledge. While Europe had experienced fierce battles between natural science and religion in the previous century, it was now necessary to give religion a new face and function: "Religion, in Europe, will only regain its empire the day it seeks to be what it was in infancy: the science of laws and their application, the science of the good that we are happy to do, of the evil that each of us seeks to avoid."[112] In this context, he asked, "What is left for the priest? . . . He is nothing more, if he does not get out of the stalemate and the impasse in which canon law has cornered him."[113] A postrevolutionary religion had to embrace the critical ambitions of science instead of combating it. This new pact between scientific inquiry and public ethics would assess public action according to a new standard: how it could be applied toward the good of society and the prevention of social and individual harm.

Underlying all the arguments for the new moral foundation of an egalitarian and interdependent society was a deeply pragmatic understanding of the impact of religion and public action. Religion gained in social value as it helped society realize and govern itself in the name of equality, liberty, and fraternity: "Now that equality is established before the temporal law, is the thought of Christianity exhausted? No, undoubtedly, for equality only half exists; there are still poor people to love, to help, to raise up."[114] As François-André Isambert highlights in his study of Buchez, "It should be noted that the justification of Christianity here is historical and pragmatic."[115] Christianity was the religion that best served the social project for the moment, but the achievement of this new social justice was not to be achieved for the sake of Christianity. To the contrary, Christianity served a specific purpose. "This is not to say, of course, that the day will not come when a new moral thinking will descend among men; but it will come, as in the past, when mankind has completed the last consequences of the previous doctrine."[116] Once Christianity had fulfilled its purpose, a new source of moral transformation might emerge. For the time being, a renewed religion provided one of the best means of educating the people toward understanding their social interdependence and equality.

Buchez referred to this practical function of religious belief as a "positive politics applicable to the present." Uniting the people under a common set of democratic values made it possible to devise what he considered a new mode of practical administration deducted from a "general thought of action, the plan, the system according to which it is necessary to act."[117] Buchez maintained the fundamentally practical nature of all morality as its ability to direct immediate political and administrative action. "For social man," explained Buchez's student Ott in the introduction to his *Treatise on Politics and Society*, "what is the great practical law [*la grande loi pratique*]? Morality."[118] These practical consequences of morality occupied a central place in Buchez's writings. "All science and all theory conclude in practice,"[119] he stated clearly. Buchez criticized what he referred to as the "abstract" philosophers of the previous century, in favor of a new kind of practice: "Indeed, although social science always leads to an application, and that is its practical utility, it is far from giving us everything that constitutes politics."[120] Social science, he argued, would offer insight into basic questions of government: "Government is needed, and even what seems to be the best form of government." The new "social science" that would include an understanding of the ethical underpinnings of modern society should guide administrative action. What was needed in the new century was an understanding of what "principles government should follow, what direction it should give to affairs, what beliefs education should inspire, what rights and duties justice it should guarantee." This was the role of a study of social beliefs. "Practice in politics consists precisely in doing certain acts and using institutions in the interest of those acts," Buchez argued.[121] What he referred to as a "political practice," then, required a new kind of understanding of the specific kinds of acts and the value of such acts within any given governmental structure. In other words, it was a question of coming to terms with what was to be regulated, and how this regulation was to be pursued on the basis of a sociological and historical understanding of social values: "So there is always a certain idea, a certain doctrine, a certain belief, a final view, in a word, which is destined to preside over the activity of all constants and to direct them." All intervention on the part of public authorities, Buchez recognized, was rooted in a belief system or a doctrine. "This final view, this doctrine precedes the practice as the idea precedes the act." His practical theory was therefore designed to uncover, examine, and make sense of these underlying values that shaped public decision making and policy. All political questions were bound up with an explicit and critical examination of the aims of society:

> Since social organization is a means to an end, it must fit the result one hopes to achieve. Otherwise it would be an obstacle and an evil. It is not acceptable, in this respect, to remain too general or to avoid proposing solutions. Philosophy is the highest form of education for those who govern society; it is from it that they must learn their positive duties in this area.[122]

In other words, for Buchez the practical means of public action had to be clearly aligned with a proper understanding of social ends. Administrators therefore needed to be at once social scientists and philosophers in order to understand the social good. In turn, they needed to shape society according to this understanding.

Among the creators of a new "social science" and its practical consequences, Auguste Comte was no doubt the most important. Comte's invention of "sociology" in the 1830s following his break with the Saint-Simonians ushered in a new general understanding of the organic and structural content of modern society. It was not until the Second Republic, however, that he invented his own "religion of humanity." Comte divorced religion from a transcendent God, focusing on channeling social energies in one direction toward a common goal.[123] Though his proposal for a social religion was only one among many in his century, Comte's efforts stand out because of his pioneering role in the field of sociology. Within this new sociological approach to religion, Comte offered a "positivist catechism" to replace what he considered the worn-out traditional Catholic dogma. Summarizing the ideals of his age, and his ambitions for the establishment of a new society, he opened the work stating that it was dedicated to "the servants of theory and the practical servants of HUMANITY [*les serviteurs théoriques et les serviteurs pratiques de L'HUMANITÉ*]."[124] True to his positivist rejection of metaphysical ideas, he insisted that those who sought the construction of modern society would need to look to society itself to find principles of reconstruction. "The retrograde nature of the exhausted doctrines which our conservatives temporarily employ must render them essentially unsuitable for directing politics." A new moral system, entirely in keeping with the ideals of a new century, would "realize at last the noble vow of a demonstrated religion directing peaceful activity."[125] This religion would frame "that happy instinct according to which practical wisdom often precedes sound theoretical indications."[126] Instead of the political theories inherited from the early modern era, the nineteenth century required a new faithful foundation for public action and practice. "Religion therefore consists in regulating each individual nature and in rallying all individualities."[127]

While Comte recognized that there were values implicit in public action toward social goals, there was nonetheless a twofold danger. First, it was of primary import that such values could not serve purely personal or private interests, but were reserved for the common social good. Second, there was the danger that the belief system would harden, and slowly distance itself from the actual organization of society, as Christianity had done. Instead, a universal social religion should hug as tightly as possible to society as it self-reflexively understood itself. Its doctrine should be shaped by the social discoveries made by social scientists. In turn, it could prepare minds for collective action. This new religion therefore served to improve the effectiveness of administration by preparing minds for the common goals being pursued.[128] Comte's universal religion bolstered the capacity of society to shape itself.

This chapter has explored how the creation of modern social science provided a nonarbitrary foundation for administrative action. A new scientific understanding of society obviated reliance on sovereign will as the foundation for governmental decision, and offered instead a "sociologization" of the social contract. In other words, as discussed in chapter 1, social science ushered in a transition from the contractualization of sovereign wills checked by individual and collective consent to a democratic society that mediated self-government through investigations of social structure. Administrative despotism was limited not only by popular sanction but by actual social conditions and needs.

But as we have also seen, the first self-designated "social scientists," from Saint-Simon and Buchez to Balzac and Comte, understood that for social science to guide administration decisions effectively, it also had to articulate a set of common values underpinning its investigations and conclusions. This discussion of common beliefs took the shape of an immanentized political theology, which, they argued, was proper to their historical age and social condition. In that sense, the nonsecular debut of social science offered a means of publicly debating the values that would guide public action toward a common good. As Jules Michelet argued in his *Bible de l'humanité*, where he recounted how "each people wrote a chapter of a common Bible" across history, he would have liked to write such a book "without a word of critique." But "in the final chapters, critical reflection came rushing back in" as he explained the transformation of modern thought.[129] Historico-sociological religiosity was understood to be liberatory to the extent that it provided a new foundation for collective obligation, and thus for substantive social action. The sum of this extraordinarily wide reinvention of belief, then, was not a standard, conservative, traditionalist religious ideal. To the contrary, it added up to a critical sociological and historical examination of how the community could reflect on the common values that undergirded nondespotic public power and administrative practice.

8

Imperial Democracy

Colonial Empire and the Limits of the Demos

"Democracy that fills the world. It is the only door open in the future. . . ."
ALEXIS DE TOCQUEVILLE[1]

In previous chapters we have explored how a democratic society tackled problems of democratic governance in key sites of social activity: forests, cities, public health, the workplace, and large corporations. We have also investigated the surprising role that a nonsecular social science played in creating the conditions under which collective obligation could be mobilized by public administration. There remains, however, another essential element of postrevolutionary French politics that is even more difficult to square with our normative conceptions of contemporary democracy: imperial conquest. Any study of this period is confronted with the basic fact that the rise of the modern demos was accompanied by the demise of one empire, that of Napoleon, and the rise of another, overseas colonies in Algeria, which would define modern French politics well into the next century and beyond.

Histories of the political thought of colonization in the first half of the nineteenth century have made plain the inherent contradictions and normative weaknesses of liberalism in an imperial context.[2] We have garnered essential insights into the justification of brutal colonial practice by learning how liberalism, correctly understood, offers the most pertinent place to start for a critique of the European imperial project. Tocqueville's writings on Algeria—a privileged site for writing the history of liberal empire—forcefully demonstrate the profound contradictions in his dedication to individual liberty and protections against despotism at home, and his support for brutality and violence on the imperial periphery.[3]

And yet, as much as we have learned about the legal and normative contradictions of liberal empire, we know much less about the fraught relationship between empire and democracy. This is particularly surprising in the context of Tocqueville's work on Algeria. While the author of *Democracy in*

America was working on the colonial question, he was above all celebrated as one of the principal theorists of democracy. To cite one of his earliest official biographers, Tocqueville was celebrated on the basis of the "inspiration and thought in his book on modern democracy, a book which placed him, still so young, among the ranks of established writers and thinkers of his day."[4] It would be no exaggeration to suggest that exploring the consequences of democracy was far more central to his thinking in this period than any conscious attempt to define liberalism as such.[5] From our contemporary perspective, the fact that a leading theorist of democracy was also one of the principal supporters of imperial expansion is at once surprising and challenging. This chapter seeks to elucidate that mystery by investigating how the relationship between empire and democracy was understood in the first half of the nineteenth century, with a particular focus on Tocqueville's writings on Algeria.[6]

To begin to understand this relationship between democracy and empire, it is necessary to return once again to the kind of problem democracy was in the first half of the nineteenth century. In this book I have shown how, during the first half of the nineteenth century, an expanded, exceedingly capacious definition of democracy took root—the idea of democratic society. In this context, in which it was widely accepted across the political spectrum that France was becoming a democratic society, the dominant question remained: Was a modern democratic society best served by a democratic government or by some other form of institutional organization, and what were the conditions according to which a democratic society could govern itself? Starting from this point of departure allows us to read Tocqueville's writings on Algeria in a new light, just as it accounts for the expansion of administrative capacity in the other realms of social and political life discussed in this book.

Tocqueville's writings on Algeria were overwhelmingly concerned with observations on the kinds of government, administration, and political economic regulation necessary for managing these societies on the imperial frontier. Hence, his writings on Algeria focused on the relationship between the development of a modern society and the form of government appropriate to it—questions that in the metropole were bound to democracy. Importing these ideas into the colonial context necessarily added an entirely new dimension to the already complex problem of democratic administration. On the one hand, from the perspective of the metropole, Tocqueville argued that colonial conquest—like administrative elections, the creation of joint-stock companies, or the collective belief systems discussed in the previous chapter—could contribute to a common sense of purpose for citizens in the metropole, and therefore help build the administration's infrastructural power—that is, the ability to enact the administrative policies through society instead of despotically lording over it. At the same time, on the imperial periphery the administration faced a profoundly different situation, posing a specific set of questions about the relationship between a collective mode of governance and the people impacted by it.

There were three layers to this problematic in Tocqueville's treatment. First, there was the basic process of establishing a French presence in Algeria. This required military conquest, or "domination," as Tocqueville chillingly referred to it. The second question, which he referred to as "colonization," focused on how it was possible to move from military conquest to civil rule, and in some cases how to introduce self-government on the imperial periphery. Within these two parts of his Algeria writings, political economy played a particularly important role. Indeed, it was through the economic management of colonization that Tocqueville entered its finest details.

There was, however, a third essential issue: the problem of boundaries. As civil rule of French nationals was established, the constant question emerged of where the agentive subject of their administration should start and stop. Should all those affected by the demos be a part of it? Or was participation in the demos reserved for citizens of the metropole? If so, on what specific grounds was this boundary to be established? These questions sat at the heart of Tocqueville's writings on Algeria, pushing the question of who administered, governed, and regulated and how they did so to the center of the imperial enterprise. This revealed fundamental limits of democratic administration as it was conceived in the nineteenth century: if a modern administration were fashioned by democracy, then it would necessarily be opposed to the very military rule imposed on the imperial periphery. Democratic administration, or democracy tout court, would prove impossible in the context of empire. This was a lesson Tocqueville would learn too late, under Napoleon III.

Civil Society and Democratic Society

To begin to understand how Tocqueville came to terms with problems of administration on the colonial periphery, it is necessary to understand how he situated the French expansion into Algeria within what he understood to be the structural dynamics of democratization. In keeping with his larger theory, democratization included two dimensions: on the one hand, a transformation in the modes of social organization toward an equality of condition, and on the other, the modes of government and administration adequate for that society. Somewhat surprisingly, while civil society was an essential concept in Tocqueville's writings, an examination of Tocqueville's work on Algeria reveals his special interest in the notion of "democratic society" and its relationship to administrative power.

While Tocqueville recognized the conceptual importance and interpretive power of civil society, he makes an important distinction between the notions of "civil society" and "democratic society." He shared his conception of civil society with many of his contemporaries. There were two quite distinct ways of using the term "civil society" in French during the period when he was researching and writing his *Democracy in America*. First, civil society was understood to encompass one dimension of social activity among others. Bonald, with whom Tocqueville was certainly familiar,[7] conceptualized his "theory of political and religious power" under the triple headings of *société politique, société religieuse*, and *société civile*.[8] This was notably the original tripartite structure Tocqueville had sketched for his *Democracy in America*.[9] Guizot, whom Tocqueville read assiduously, used the term similarly, writing that "*la société civile* and *la société religieuse* were necessarily the dual subject" of his *History of Civilization in France*.[10] According to this usage, civil society was thus juxtaposed with "religious society" or "political society." To the latter, Tocqueville adds other cognates such as "political world" and "political mores." These categories were not completely isolated, and did overlap with one another. For example, activities and structures within civil society could have political consequences. Nonetheless, the notion of civil society describes a set of phenomena that complement but remain logically distinct from other broad categories of social action.

More importantly, according to this usage, civil society itself was not a product of history. That is, it did not emerge or disappear at a given historical moment. Guizot, for example, used the term "civil society" to describe activities that took place as early as the seventh century.[11] It was therefore an analytical category used to make important distinctions between different types of human activity within which social change could take place over the longue durée. The concept of civil society was useful for structuring a sociological or historical study, but was not a social form that emerged at the end of a historical process.

This was one of the essential ways in which Tocqueville used the concept. The term "civil society," in his usage, is not itself a product of historical development. Like "political society," it is a conceptual category useful for bundling certain activities of social life. This is not to say that the nature of activities within civil society do not change over time. Tocqueville clearly explains that in the new condition of equality, "the appearance of civil society has been no less changed than the physiognomy of the political world."[12] In other words, a civil society can be egalitarian or not, and it can function according to aristocratic or democratic principles; but in Tocqueville's account, it is not itself a product of history.

There was, however, a second usage of the term "civil society" in the first decades of the nineteenth century, one most commonly found in the realm of political economy. Jean-Baptiste Say's *Cours complet d'économie politique pratique*, which Tocqueville read,[13] used the term to build on some of the essential arguments of Adam Smith and the Scottish Enlightenment. First, Say argued that civil society comes into being through the accumulation of capital:[14] "It is a constant that no civil society could subsist without the accumulation of capital, that is, the fruit of labor and the instruments of industry." He then claimed that the "economy of nations" demonstrates that "in nature, the father is superior to his children" while "in civil society it is an entirely different situation."[15] For Say, then, civil society was the busy realm of productive life that had acquired autonomy in "a century that has achieved maturity."[16] In this conception, the economy slowly moved out of the realm of the family (both literally and figuratively, by moving out from under the control of the prince) and into capitalist civil society, where it then thrived outside both the household and the state. This idea was reproduced and attributed directly to Smith in a political economy textbook from the 1840s in France, which argued that "the State . . . would have no means of satisfying the needs of civil society." To argue the contrary, the author added, "would overthrow the economic order recommended and prescribed by Adam Smith."[17] According to these political economists, civil society emerges at the end of a historical process brought on by modern capitalism. Transformed by the rise of a new form of capitalist exchange, civil society becomes an autonomous realm of individual liberty and fulfillment outside the traditional authority of the sphere of the family or the administrative state.

Tocqueville shared elements of this political economic conception of civil society in his *Democracy in America*. He concurred that civil society had become the bustling realm of industriousness and economic vitality described by the political economists. And he further agreed that this had become a sphere of individual liberty and personal fulfillment. At the same time, however, he disagreed with the political economists on how this autonomous civil society had come to be. For him, it was neither the rise of capitalism nor new modes of commercial exchange; rather, in his account, civil society had always existed. What had changed was its democratization. It was this *democratized* civil society, characterized by individualism, equality of condition, and industriousness, that he called "democratic society."

Juxtaposing the term "democratic society" with "aristocratic society," Tocqueville defines the former as being founded on a basic "equality of condition." In his *Democracy in America*, he argues that this democratization of the social has occurred in several ways. There are those who have "arrived at equality by a long and difficult social effort"—for which the archetype is France—and another, rarer mode, in which "from the beginning, citizens have always been equal"[18]—for which the archetype is the United States. In France it was the leveling effect of absolutism that slowly eroded the power of the aristocracy; or, as Tocqueville remarks in the introduction to the *Democracy*: "In France, kings showed themselves to be the most active and most constant of levelers."[19] In Tocqueville's account of the long-term historical achievement of democratic society, for which France was the ideal type, he explains that "an aristocracy usually succumbs only after a prolonged struggle."[20] This struggle, he argues, leaves deep social tensions in its wake that in turn influence the early moments of the emergence of democratic society and contribute to the general sense of confusion and constant movement that thrives within it. However, "little by little the last traces of the struggle fade," Tocqueville argues, as "the remnants of the aristocracy finally disappear." Repose follows upon class war, and "the dominion of rules is reborn within the new world. . . . Men finally come to the same level; democratic society is finally established."[21] It is important to note that whether by revolution or by the slow construction of the centralized monarchical state, democratic society does not just happen; it is made by public power. Democratic society is therefore a historical process in which the social is constituted. As Cheryl Welch has put it, Tocqueville describes a democratic society in which the social is saturated with the political.[22]

This democratic society, which emerged in the old regime and took root in the wake of the French Revolution, replaced the traditional values and boundaries that had previously shaped individual action in aristocratic society. The condition of equality that characterized democratic society ushered in a new set of social interactions that lessened the grip of the family and pushed individuals to seek fulfillment in their private interests and in the material world. It was a world in which "everyone works, and work leads to everything," Tocqueville argued.[23] The very self-interest that was so central for the political economists' civil society had in fact surged forth from a newfound unshakable faith in the individual's power to shape his or her life: "They all conceive of the idea of increasing it, and, if they are free, they all try to do so."[24] In turn, this new democratic condition drove the economic growth characterized and described by Smith and his progeny: "Each man is in motion; some want to attain power, others to take hold of wealth. Amid this universal tumult, this repeated clash of contrary interests, this continual march of men toward fortune."[25] In the notes of his manuscript, Tocqueville was even more explicit: "In a democratic society the only *visible* advantage that you can enjoy over your fellows is wealth. This explains the desire for riches."[26] He then concluded: "You cannot cultivate industry without forming a small or large democratic society. When men cultivate industry, they are democratic, and when they are democratic, they necessarily cultivate industry."[27] Tocqueville therefore subsumed a key theme of the political economists' interpretation of civil society into modern democracy, and not into economic structure: the self-interest, productiveness, and activity of civil society that constitutes a vital realm of liberty and allows for unprecedented opportunities to pursue individual well-being was made possible by the structural drive toward the condition of equality within modern democratic society. In other words, since democratic society was forged by a political process—either a spontaneous revolution, as in the United States, or a long-term historical and political process, as in France—the peculiarly modern form of civil society in which individuals sought their private material well-being was in fact a result of the political process of constructing a democratic society, which in turn pushed individuals to pursue private economic interests. For Tocqueville, the structural drives of democracy hold primacy over the economic.

As a result, Tocqueville recognized with other political economists that this new civil society was the realm in which individuals could realize their personal liberty and take full possession of themselves. However, unlike others who celebrated this sphere as the sole sphere of freedom, Tocqueville argued that the equality and constant social movement that characterized democratic society could also limit liberty and personal happiness.

The Antinomies of Democratic Society

Tocqueville's understanding of the challenges posed by democratic society drew upon the critiques of eighteenth-century liberal political economy, and especially those of Adam Smith, which had been elaborated by Sismondi. So not only did Sismondi shape Hegel's ideas on political economy, but, as Helmut Pappe has noted, Tocqueville and Gustave de Beaumont read Say's *Cours complet d'économie politique pratique*, and Beaumont later promised an abstract of Sismondi's work to Tocqueville. Pappe argues that Tocqueville was inspired by Sismondi's critique of an overemphasis on individual well-being and happiness at the expense of the preservation of a healthy "love of country."[28]

At the core of Sismondi's *Nouveaux principes d'économie politique* was his claim that, while Smith's basic principles were sound, he had overstated the role of the individual. "We concur with Adam Smith that work is the sole source of wealth, and that economy is the only means of accumulating it," he argued; "but we add further that benefiting from such wealth is the only motivation for its accumulation and that national wealth is only truly augmented when it is accompanied by an increase in the ability to benefit from it."[29] Sismondi placed a direct emphasis on the need to balance individual interest and social obligation. Accumulating wealth for society as a whole, instead of for a few individuals, could only be achieved by regulating the proper distribution of work and reward: "We have seen that the principal difference between our opinions and those of Adam Smith is that the latter rejected government intervention in all things related to the wealth of nations whereas we have regularly insisted upon it."[30]

Tocqueville integrated this critique of laissez-faire individualism, adapting it to his theory of a democratic society. Throughout his *Democracy*, he highlighted structural drives within democratic society that undermine its very foundations. For example, he insisted on the risks of atomization: "It is above all at the moment when a democratic society finally takes form on the debris of an aristocracy that this isolation of men from each other, and the egoism that follows, are most easily seen."[31] The dangers of radical individualism hang over democratic society; or, as Tocqueville wrote in his notes for the manuscript, "You isolate yourself by instinct and by will."[32] Tocqueville drew out the consequences of this isolation by arguing that it could in turn lead to social and political polarization. Throughout the book, he highlighted "the tumultuous and revolutionary movements that almost always accompany the birth and development of a democratic society."[33] Finally, he insisted on how isolation and polarization could contribute to greater alienation from one's social surround. He reserved one of his more extraordinary literary flourishes to describe this state of alienation: "When I come to imagine a democratic society of this type, I immediately think I feel myself in one of these low, dark, and suffocating places, where lights, brought in from outside, soon grow dim and are extinguished. It seems to me that a sudden weight overwhelms me, and that I am dragging myself along among the shadows around me in order to find the exit that should lead me back to the air and daylight."[34]

Perhaps most importantly, Tocqueville aligned his thinking on political economy with that of Sismondi in his discussion of what he called "the greatest question of our time": that the democratization of social organization could in fact produce its opposite: radical new inequalities. "Fortunes become unequal," he argued, "from the moment when each man makes use of all his abilities in order to grow rich."[35] As Tocqueville demonstrated in his *Democracy in America*, the drive for individual wealth brought on by the democratization of civil society had the paradoxical effect of creating a new industrial aristocracy: "As the mass of the nation turns to democracy, the particular class that is concerned with industry becomes more aristocratic. . . . In this way, when you go back to the source, it seems that you see aristocracy come by a natural effort from the very heart of democracy."[36] He then concluded: "I think that, everything considered, the manufacturing aristocracy that we see arising before our eyes is one of the harshest that has appeared on the earth."[37] So in Tocqueville's account, democratic society produces its opposite: isolation, polarization—and, most of all, massive inequality.

Social scientists and political theorists have certainly recognized these antinomies within Tocqueville's account of democratic society. Ironically, it has been precisely in response to this inequality, atomization, polarization, and alienation that some important political theorists have leaned on a neo-Tocquevillian notion of "civil society" as an antidote to these nefarious tendencies.[38] As inspired and useful as these interpretations have been, however, it would seem that the actual language employed by Tocqueville himself also offers other avenues of investigation. For it is at this moment in his argument that Tocqueville turned away from the idea of an "autonomous" civil society to ensure liberty and toward a related but ultimately very different question that was posed by Sismondi but never settled by him: In the face of such antinomies, what kind of government is necessary to maintain democratic society grounded in the equality of condition?

For Tocqueville, the structural contradiction toward inequality within the process of the democratization of modern civil society meant that an inflated administrative and governmental power was at once an ineluctable product of and a necessity for preventing the otherwise necessary rise of inequalities and alienation. The constant mobility, individual drive to work harder, and desire for material goods in a democratic society carried within it the development of an increasingly powerful centralized state. The tireless aspiration for property and "love of well-being" also generated "a fear of material disorder." As a result, the administrative state grew, since it "alone seems to them to have the interest and the means to defend them from anarchy while defending itself."[39] Tocqueville further specified in his notes to the manuscript that this was "why in democratic centuries centralization and unity are loved so much. . . . Centralization is the means of attaining quickly and without difficulty the results they desire."[40] This desire for a centralized administrative state, Tocqueville argued, was therefore a structural tendency in democratic societies raised by the constant clashing of individual interests. Tocqueville made this dynamic plain in this important passage:

> Since a multitude of men has this particular view at the same time on a host of different matters, the sphere of the central power expands imperceptibly in all

directions, even though each one of them wishes to limit it. So a democratic government increases its attributions by the sole fact that it lasts. Time works for it; it profits from all accidents; individual passions help it even without their knowing, and you can say that a democratic government becomes that much more centralized the older the democratic society is.[41]

We must carefully reconstruct Tocqueville's argument here. First, the central administrative power expands in every direction to limit the multitude of views that compete with one another but which, because of their unlimited reach, must be regulated. As a result of this dynamic, the very persistence of a democratic government over time will lead to its growth. Tocqueville thus concludes that democratic government will naturally become more centralized the longer a democratic society lasts. So state power is both a necessity and a consequence of the democratization of civil society.

Of course, Tocqueville can hardly be considered a naive supporter of a strong centralized administrative state. An essential ambition of his whole enterprise is to preserve individual liberty in a democratic society even as the structural push toward a centralized state can have dire consequences—in particular, a new despotism. Indeed, the central character of that despotism is that it slowly draws all authority toward itself, turning its back on public pressures by accumulating all responsibilities in the hands of a unified authority and achieving an unprecedented control over every aspect of individuals' daily lives. Tocqueville argues that the only force to counterbalance this tendency in previous centuries was aristocracy, but he also clearly states that he is "persuaded that in the centuries which we are entering, all those who try to base liberty on privilege and on aristocracy will fail."[42] So the democratization of civil society would seem ineluctable, even if it mechanically increases the reach of government and thus opens up the constant potential toward despotism.

Once again, our analysis at this point crosses the path of the liberal civil society reading of Tocqueville, which has argued that his response to the tendency toward despotism is precisely to reinforce associative life. Again, it is both a creative and tempting interpretation, and certainly not unfounded. Tocqueville does explicitly claim at one point that "if [those who govern] always want to take the place of great associations, they prevent the spirit of association from developing and they take on a burden that weighs them down." But it would seem that this is not the entirety of his response, since he immediately adds that "if they rely only on associations, very useful and often necessary things are not done by anyone." He then concludes that "men who live in democratic centuries have more need than others to be allowed to do things by themselves, and more than others, they sometimes need things to be done for them. That depends on circumstances." Associations, Tocqueville clearly states, are essential. That much is clear. But he also states that associations are ultimately insufficient in themselves to guarantee the effective organization of democratic societies. Interpreting when to turn to associations and when to turn to government is what Tocqueville refers to as "the greatest art of government in democratic countries [which] consists in clearly distinguishing the circumstances and acting according to how circumstances lead it."[43] So for Tocqueville, the "art of government" is precisely the art of determining when associations may manage on their own through popular participation, and when the administration must take over. Or, as he stated in the notes to the original manuscript: "In democratic societies not only is the government stronger [illegible word] than the citizens, but also it alone has duration, foresight, extended plans, profound calculations. It surpasses the citizens as much in quality as in strength."[44]

For Tocqueville, the problem of despotism in democracy cannot be treated by handing over power entirely to associations and free self-interested individuals while weakening government. As he says, "Everything is unstable and fleeting among democratic peoples, outside of the government."[45] Democracy therefore requires government; or, as Tocqueville explains in no uncertain terms: "It is at the very same time necessary and desirable that the central power that directs a democratic people be active and powerful. It is not a matter of making it weak or indolent, but only of preventing it from abusing its agility and strength." He even goes so far as to argue in the original manuscript:

> Unique and central government [power] charged with dispensing the same laws to the entire State and with regulating in the same way each one of those who inhabit it, an intelligent, far-sighted and strong administration that enlightens, aids, constantly directs individuals, such is the ideal that in democratic times will always occur by itself to the imagination of men as soon as they come to think about government.[46]

If government is a necessity, however, then the danger of despotism necessarily—and always—lurks in the wings of democratic society. In other words, a central conundrum for democratically governing a democratic society is how to overcome its disaggregating, isolating, and unequal tendencies through the very conditions and institutions that create it.

Tocqueville offered two responses to these structural antinomies of democratic society. On the one hand, he argued that the drive within a democratized civil society toward inequality, isolation, and despotism could be managed over time through the democratization of administration. By grounding the expansion of the administrative state in modes of popular participation through both administrative surveillance and regular public consultation, the menace of a new kind of tyranny could be avoided. To assuage the alienation, isolation, polarization, and inequality generated by a democratized civil society, further democratization of administrative power was necessary, giving particularly poignant meaning to the fact that democracy is at once a social form and a political regime.[47] There was, however, a second way of managing these structural contradictions, and there is room to suggest that this second response provided a foundation for Tocqueville's enthusiasm for imperial conquest.

Inequality, Alienation, and the Imperial "Spatial Fix" of Democratic Society

Tocqueville posed the problem of inequality brought on by modern democratic society as "the greatest question of our time." As important as it was for him, however, in his comments on the chapter on salaries in his *Democracy in America* he offered a detumescent characterization of his treatment of the question: "This chapter has the disadvantage of posing the greatest question of our time without even trying to resolve it. . . . You are disappointed after reading it." No doubt his most complete treatment of the question of administrative regulation of poverty came in his *Mémoire sur le paupérisme*, in which he clearly demonstrated his conviction that it is impossible to create a permanent public system of social aid based on distributing long-term monetary benefits for the poor. It is therefore helpful in understanding Tocqueville's treatment of the problem of inequality to also look elsewhere, and in particular to Sismondi and the central role he played in shaping Tocqueville's ideas on the structural tendency toward inequality and poverty in modern democratic society.

Even as he criticized what he referred to as Adam Smith's skepticism toward government intervention, Sismondi insisted that such intervention should come in the form of providing work instead of a blanket distribution of property: "It is not through distributing property that happiness will be gained, because it will destroy all desire to work, and desire should be the only motivation for work and the only means of creating property, since it finds its stimulant in the very inequalities that are constantly renewed by work. It is rather by always guaranteeing that all labor has appropriate reward."[48]

Like Sismondi, Tocqueville argued that it was necessary to provide work for those who were without resources. In terms similar to those of Sismondi, he further suggested that the dangers of doing otherwise, of providing aid without work, would generate further isolation and social alienation on the part of those who were already excluded from the social fabric. However, at the end of his first *Mémoire sur le paupérisme*, Tocqueville arrived at the obvious question raised by such a policy: "We would like charity to come from work. But is there always work to be done?" He then continued with an intriguing follow-up question: "Is such work not unevenly distributed across the surface of the country such that one sees a great deal of work to be done in one district and few people to do it; and in another a great deal of people needing work and no work to be done?" Tocqueville then concluded this thought with more challenging interrogations: "Having thought of alleviating evils, would it not be useful to seek to prevent them? Could we not prevent the rapid displacement of the population, so that men only leave the land and move into industry to the extent that the latter can easily meet their needs? Can't the sum of national wealth continue to increase without some of those who produce it having to curse the prosperity they bring about?"[49]

To begin to understand how Tocqueville responded to these questions, we must understand their spatial implications. Tocqueville was arguing that a key part of the problem of poverty came from the lack of available land, and hence the concentration of propertyless industrial laborers around industry. "The most effective means of preventing pauperism was the division of land," he argued. He added that it was "the duty of government and of all good men to work toward this goal."[50] So Tocqueville invited his reader to understand this problem of social policy—that is, of maintaining a democratic society and avoiding its internal drive toward inequality and despotism, in spatial terms. In other words, he suggested that a "spatial fix" could provide a means of preventing massive inequalities and alienation that plague modern democratic society.[51] Where might one look, then, for a discussion of the spatial fix Tocqueville had in mind?

No doubt the place to start is with his treatment of imperial peripheries, starting with his discussion of the American frontier in his *Democracy*. Tocqueville highlighted in numerous places that the frontier provided a particularly propitious environment for the development of a healthy democratic society. In the opening of the conclusion to the first volume, after announcing that he wanted to return to first and general principles to bring his study to a close, he lamented that "a combination of circumstances that would be too long to enumerate deprived [France] of this magnificent heritage." In a note, however, he did gesture to some of these circumstances: "Free peoples accustomed to the municipal regime succeed much more easily than others in creating flourishing colonies. The habit of thinking for yourself and governing yourself is indispensable in a new country, where success necessarily depends in large part on the individual efforts of the colonists."[52] In this context, Tocqueville argued further, "the men of the United States will penetrate these uninhabited areas even before those who have the right to occupy them."[53] And then he reminded his reader: "You imagine that the prodigious movement that is noted in the increase of the population of the United States dates only from independence. That is an error. The population grew as quickly under the colonial system as today; it doubled the same in about twenty-two years. But then it applied to thousands of inhabitants; now it applies to millions. The same fact that passed unnoticed a century ago strikes all minds today."[54] So Tocqueville drew a direct parallel between the colonial settlers of the seventeenth century and the pioneers of the nineteenth.

Some of Tocqueville's most elaborate discussions of democratic administration are reserved for the development of a democratic society among the early colonial settlers. He highlighted the profoundly democratic nature of the early colonial system, and how its expansion into the territories of New England had generated prosperity while fostering an unprecedented democratic experiment of regulation. "The English colonies, and this was one of the principal causes of their prosperity, always enjoyed more internal liberty and more political independence than the colonies of other peoples," he wrote; "but nowhere was this principle of liberty more completely applied than in the states of New England." Tocqueville explained that there had been different ways of governing these early colonies. "In certain cases, the king subjected a portion of the New World to a governor of his choosing." In other cases, "he granted ownership of certain portions of the country to a man or to a company." But what interested Tocqueville was the "third system," which "consisted of giving a certain number of emigrants the right to form a political society, under the patronage of the mother country, and to govern themselves in everything not contrary to its laws. This method of colonization, so favorable to liberty, was put into practice only in New England."[55]

Recounting how the New England township favored democracy for white settlers, Tocqueville emphasized "the most characteristic law code that the small state of Connecticut gave itself in 1650." Describing the code, he highlighted the impact of frontier democracy on the construction of an extraordinary expansion of regulatory powers: "Above all, in this body of penal laws, the legislators are preoccupied with upholding moral order and standards of good behavior; they constantly enter, therefore, into the realm of conscience. There is hardly any sin that they do not manage to submit to the censure of the magistrate."[56] He continued highlighting that "the Code of 1650 abounds in preventive measures. Laziness and drunkenness are severely punished.

Innkeepers cannot provide more than a certain quantity of wine to each consumer; a fine or a flogging cracks down on a simple lie when it might be harmful. In other places, the legislator . . . forces by threat of fines, attendance at divine worship. And he goes so far as to impose severe penalties and often death."[57] Tocqueville then recounted "the fervor for regulations" this democracy created, including "a law that prohibits the use of tobacco" or "the worldly luxury of long hair." As extraordinary as these regulations seemed to Tocqueville, what was fundamental to his analysis was the fact that "these bizarre or tyrannical laws were not at all imposed; that they were voted by the free participation of all those concerned."[58] Moreover, alongside these abundant social regulations, the colonial settlers also promulgated "political laws" for "the intervention of the people in public affairs, the free vote of taxes, the responsibility of the agents of power. . . . The electoral body was comprised of all citizens; individual liberty and the jury trial were established without argument."[59]

Central to Tocqueville's observations was the fact that this democracy was not a system of "representative government" grounded in a parliamentary system, but rather a system of self-administration: "The town names its magistrates of all sorts; it taxes itself; it apportions and levies the tax on itself." Highlighting the importance of administration in this democratic colonial settlement, Tocqueville explained: "In Connecticut, at that time, all the agents of executive power were elected, even the Governor of the state."[60] He even went so far as to explain that "the law of representation is not accepted," drawing a parallel to ancient Athens: "As in Athens, matters that touch the interests of all are treated in the public square and within the general assembly of citizens." He then concluded: "The law gets into a thousand different details to provide for and to satisfy a host of social needs."[61]

For Tocqueville, democracy and colonization could favor one another. It was on the imperial periphery that a democratic administration, in which executive power and government were in the hands of the people, had found its fullest realization. In his view, colonial New England offered a model "democratic society" to the extent that it was marked by an equality of condition and had also chosen to self-govern—not through representation, but through the distribution of executive and administrative offices into the hands of the people. Perhaps even more importantly, the result of this democratic government of a democratic society in the distant colonies was not a utopian social state of individual liberty to pursue one's own private interest on some distant frontier, but, to the contrary, an extraordinary proliferation of laws, regulations, and demands of public office. It was the opposite of license. Pursuing democracy on the imperial periphery required the construction of a public authority.

A Political Economy of Imperial Possession

The idea that seventeenth-century colonial empire offered an example of the development of a democratic society that governed itself democratically provided Tocqueville with a compelling starting point for thinking about Algerian colonization. He had argued for a spatial fix to the fundamental contradiction operating within democratic society according to which the structural drive toward social leveling would produce a new brand of individualism that would increase the drive for material well-being and the accumulation of wealth, and in turn generate concentrations of resources that would generate poverty and lack of opportunity for others. The question facing Tocqueville in the first half of the nineteenth century, then, was whether or not colonial empire could help overcome the challenges inherent in a democratic social state.

Here too, Sismondi offered an important contribution. Sismondi viewed the conquest of Algeria as an opportunity to overcome some of the structural deficiencies of modern industrial capitalism. "The Kingdom of Algiers will not only be a conquest," Sismondi argued; "it will be a colony, a new country, over which the surplus of French population and activity will be able to spread." He further argued that from this perspective, Algeria differed fundamentally from the French overseas empire of the eighteenth century: "Often in economic calculations colonies have been valued far beyond their importance; Saint-Dominque, for example, has been represented." But he insisted that any comparison with these former colonies was ill-conceived, since they "were not worth a tenth of what Algiers might be worth." This increased value was bound to the extraordinary opportunities that Algeria presented for absorbing population from the metropole and providing economic opportunity for common French people, and not simply wealthy merchants and landed interests. "The old nations of Europe, like those of antiquity, need outlets where they can pour all the surplus population and life that civilization creates within them. Undoubtedly, France is large enough and fertile enough to be able to feed twice as many inhabitants and employ twice as much capital as it has; but property is chained in the present order, the proportion between products and needs is recognized, and cannot be changed without suffering."[62] For Sismondi, the Algerian conquest would provide the land and opportunity necessary to accommodate the needs of an excess population.

Providing access to property and work for the growing working class was a central feature of Sismondi's economic theory, and it provided the backdrop for his support of the Algerian conquest. In his view, excess population and overproduction were the essential problems generated by modern industrialization. The problem, as he saw it, was the basic misapprehension by eighteenth-century political economy and its inheritors that man was an isolated individual who could simply accumulate as much wealth as possible without it influencing the general well-being of society as a whole. "The solitary man's aim had been only to amass, so as to be able to rest afterwards," wrote Sismondi. As a result, "he had before him a ready stage in the accumulation of wealth, after which it would have been folly for him to accumulate further, for he could not proportionately increase his consumption."[63] For Sismondi, any accumulation of wealth needed to be placed in the context of "the needs of the social man" instead of an abstract isolated individual. From this point of view, he argued, "it is a great mistake, into which most modern economists have fallen, to imagine consumption as a boundless power, always ready to devour infinite production."[64] Instead, the consistent push toward technological innovation necessarily required fewer and fewer workers at the same time as it produced more and more goods, which could only be purchased by the ever-narrowing group of wealthy who accumulated wealth. This dynamic necessarily produced a mass of impoverished workers who produced goods they could not consume. And since consumption would slowly be concentrated at the top of the economic pyramid, overproduction would generate unemployment and a class of poor.

This dynamic had been poorly understood by Adam Smith and his colleagues, Sismondi argued, because they didn't understand the underlying reasons for the creation of a class of impoverished individuals in industrial society. They wrongly "point out those who are idle for public humiliation, and, in a nation where the powers of the workers have been increased a hundredfold, they would like everyone to be a worker, everyone to work for a living." Sismondi therefore concluded that "the indefinite multiplication of the productive powers of labor can only result in an increase in the luxuries of the idle rich."[65] He boiled his argument down to a more socially embedded conception of production: "Isolated man works so that he can rest, social man works so that someone else can rest; isolated man hoards so that he may then enjoy, social man sees the fruit of his sweat hoarded by the one who should enjoy it; but as soon as he and his equals produce more, and infinitely more than they can consume, what they produce must be destined for the consumption of people who will not live as equals, and who will not produce anything."[66] The social individual produced for society as a whole, not simply for his or her own benefit. The problem, however, was that it was precisely because the social individual produced for society that there was an excess of production, which low-wage-earning individuals could not absorb.

This problem of overproduction was a structural inevitability as long as one remained within the strict confines of the nation-state. For social man would produce for too few consumers, driving down wages and at the same time forcing workers to seek whatever opportunities they could find. Sismondi argued that Algeria offered a solution to this problem. By providing, in his words, "outlets that the excesses of population and life can be poured into," Algeria could ensure more land and new markets. Colonial conquest therefore created the conditions through which overproduction and workers without jobs could be absorbed. In so doing, it also remedied one of the most basic problems plaguing the French industrializing economy: structural inequality and overproduction. These ideas influenced Tocqueville's writings on Algeria.

It must first be noted that Tocqueville's works on Algeria provide an exceptional window into his political economy.[67] To read the notes from his trips to North Africa is to discover a voyager who was almost obsessed with the everyday economic functioning of the colonies. His observations on the life and customs of the local populations have been amply noted, as have his political and legal arguments in favor of French rule. But in many parts, it is the very concrete minutiae of political economic mechanics and techniques of coloniziation that occupy Tocqueville's observations.

Tocqueville's notes are filled with remarks on what kind of public works would be necessary to make the colony function properly: "Civil engineering costs in Oran. A quay to be built: 200,000 F., I think. Jetty to build: 600,000 F., I think."[68] He notes the extraordinary efforts that will be necessary for public works: "Village built from nothing by the administration: houses, 4 hectares cleared, 12 hectares of concessions."[69] Throughout his work, Tocqueville insisted on the role the government would have to play in providing essential services and in building on the ground to ensure the proper functioning of the colony after settlement. He stated in no uncertain terms the essential role the administration was to play in the economic development of the North African colony. "When I ask myself what part the particular circumstances of our colony oblige the administration to play, I find that this part is as follows," he observed, providing an extraordinary list of administrative responsibilities, including "carefully survey[ing] the country to be colonized"; "acquiring it in order to sell it cheaply to the colonists"; "fixing the location of villages"; "fortifying them"; "arming"; "creating lots"; "making a fountain, a church, a school, a common house and providing for the needs of the priest and the master"; and "[forcing] each inhabitant to lodge himself and his herd within the enclosure and to fence his field." The administration needed to "subject everyone to the rules of guarding and defense that security requires"; "put at the head of their militia an officer who maintains in the population some military habits and can command it outside"; and "provide the colonists either with animals or instruments, or with food, in order to facilitate and ensure the birth of the establishment." Moreover, Tocqueville called it "crucial" to "impose, if you wish, very narrow obligations, but let them not vary according to your whims." Such was the task of the administration, he argued, concluding: "It is necessary to give a head to the administration which must supervise and create this new company."[70]

These public administrative projects would, in turn, provide the framework for the development of economic opportunity. Tocqueville consistently focused on how it was possible to succeed economically on the colonial periphery. He was convinced that "to bring inhabitants to such a country, they must first be given a good chance of making their fortune; secondly, they must find a state of society in keeping with their habits and tastes."[71] It was "unreasonable to imagine that a large number of men will leave their homeland" if they were "masters neither of their persons nor of their property, and [were] to find fixed limits to all their expectations."[72] To develop a thriving economy on the imperial periphery, "it takes nothing less than all the energy of the passions that individual property gives rise to."[73]

Tocqueville therefore observed which properties provided the best model for economic development and success. "We found ourselves on the edge of a vast property planted with mulberry and olive trees, under which vegetables such as potatoes and onions grew in many places." Describing the size of the properties, the number of trees, their nature, and their development, he argued that "all of this admirable plantation belonged to its owner, including the acquisition of the land, which the administration had sold at a very high price, 48,000 F."[74] To make sense of these observations, he gathered personal testimonies to help inform himself on the best policy—recounting, for example, "M. Baudier le colon paysan," who explained to him that "if hay were bought by the administration at 8 F per quintal on a regular basis every year, and if we were sure of selling when we brought good merchandise instead of being exposed to a thousand ruinous hassles, we'd be well served."[75] He recounted " M. Borelli," with a "concession of 500 hectares. Conditions to place 20 families." After four years of settlement and farming, they were "property owners of 5 hectares." However, "the house is not paid for." As a result, "the farmer who becomes the owner will either have to buy it in annual installments or build another one."[76] This system had an advantage over the villages built by the administration, Tocqueville argued, since "instead of having to feed himself, provide for part of his house and his work tools, which presupposes a capital of 3,000 F, he can enter here without a penny to his name."[77]

Insisting further on the role the state should play in offering concessions to workers, Tocqueville also observed that it was "impossible to compete with the Arabs for wheat," highlighting such details as "last year wheat at 10 francs per hectoliter, 2 million exports for France. Also very difficult to compete with them for livestock." For this reason, it was particularly problematic that "no concessions have yet been made in the civil territory of Bone. The state owns at least 20,000 hectares of admirable land in this territory alone."[78] Tocqueville concluded, with words that directly responded to his ideas in the *Memoir on pauperism*, that the administration needed to step in to provide land for those willing to colonize, because "land is useful for everyone, but a necessity for the poor."[79]

Because of its importance in alleviating inequalities in the metropole, Tocqueville showed regular concern that the imperial project would reproduce the kinds of structural inequalities that existed in the metropole. There was a great danger for "small landowners and workers" on the imperial periphery. In particular, the concentration of capital characteristic of a democratized civil society in the metropole needed to be avoided. "Almost all the land belongs to large landowners," Tocqueville argued. There would be hope, however. if the administration effectively distributed the concessions and provided the right conditions, since unlike in the metropole, the consequences of this concentration would not entirely dispossess the workers to create an impoverished class, because the labor market would remain far more competitive. "As soon as you bring in a good worker, he's immediately hired out by another owner."[80] The challenge, therefore, would be to ensure that these workers could remain competitive and ultimately accumulate enough capital to participate as relative equals in the economic system. These guarantees were to be provided by the administration. In this vein, Tocqueville quoted "M. Gentet. [1846] Nothing can be done here without capital. But with capital one can get by very well." He succinctly summarized the problem: "Men are insufficient to colonize. So is capital. You need both."[81] And it was up to the administration to make sure that both would be available to those who arrived.

By carefully planning public works, ensuring provision, and organizing the distribution of land, workers, and capital on the imperial periphery, the colonial administration could at once ensure the development of the colonies and alleviate poverty in the metropole. Providing an important outlet for capital and social development that escaped the structural tendency of democratic society to generate inequality, individual isolation, and alienation, the imperial adventure would also provide a means for reinforcing and recompensing individual effort. In this way, Algeria would play an essential role in solving the problems generated by a democratized civil society. Through the expansion into Algeria, democracy in the metropole could be strengthened because the political economic opportunities it provided would reduce the negative structural contradictions within the process of democratization.

The Boundary Problem of the Imperial Demos

While the imperial solution would help manage the contradiction produced by the antinomies of a democratic society, there remained the significant problem of what type of administration would be instituted and how it would operate on the imperial periphery. For Tocqueville it was insufficient to merely distribute land and provide a vast number of public services to ensure that colonial settlers had access to land, capital, and work. If the administration on the ground in Algeria was itself despotic, then these opportunities might offer some economic relief, but would not be able to overcome the potential dangers of a democratization—that is, isolation, alienation, and ultimately inequality. Tocqueville spent the better part of his first and second memoirs on Algeria discussing the type of government that should be established there. He insisted, "We won't succeed just by digging pits, opening streams, building walls, granting land, and laying out villages." The task at hand was at once more difficult and more ambitious; it was of primary importance to "profoundly change the institutions that currently govern the country."[82] Tocqueville condemned in no uncertain terms the fact that "the Algerian government has several contradictory defects that are rare to find in the same power. It is violent, arbitrary, and tyrannical, and at the same time weak and powerless."[83] As one of Tocqueville's Algerian interlocutors explained the problem to him: "There is no *gouvernement* here to speak of."[84] Or, as Tocqueville stated in his own words: "The government in Algeria is weak and impotent."[85]

To remedy this situation—and it is important to note that creating a strong administration in Algeria was one of Tocqueville's central concerns—three steps were required. First, it was necessary to establish the proper balance of centralization and decentralization. These themes formed the backdrop to his *Democracy in America*, and provided the essential narrative thread of the *Old Regime and the Revolution*—which was prefigured in the July Monarchy in his essay "État social et politique de la France avant et depuis 1789" (1836), and briefly in his article "La centralisation administrative et le système représentatif" (1844).[86] They also formed the basis for the debates, treated in chapter 4 of this book, on administrative elections. In his writings on Algeria, Tocqueville developed these arguments in a different register. On the one hand, he took an interest in the process of elaborating an entirely new administrative structure at multiple scales on conquered lands; and on the other, the development of administrative centralization as an essential force in the construction of a modern democratic society on the imperial periphery.

In keeping with his treatment of the problem in these other works, however, centralization was not understood as a linear process. Instead, building an effective government and administration in Algeria required establishing the proper dosage of centralization and decentralization. Tocqueville demonstrated his concern with establishing the proper balance on several occasions. "Centralization is excellent, but must be in Algiers,"[87] he noted, similarly stating elsewhere: "The first cause of weakness and impotence for our colonial government is the lack of centralization in Algiers. The second is the absurd centralization that exists for the same matters in Paris."[88] He stated his point most clearly when he argued: "As a result, there is both too little and too much centralization."[89] At the same time, however, reminiscent of the argument for the balance of centralization and decentralization in the state of New York in his *Democracy*, he cautioned against overcentralization within Algiers: "After the excessive centralization of Paris, the greatest flaw in the administrative organization of Africa is the excessive centralization in Algiers."[90]

In his discussion on the impotence and sluggishness of the colonial administration, Tocqueville noted that the central problem was the lack of a clear division of labor between relatively minor regulations that should be decided locally and the most ambitious issues of colonial expansion that needed to be centralized in Algiers. "As centralization knows no bounds, and local and municipal life is nonexistent, the smallest matters arrive jumbled up with the biggest, under the eyes of the main civil servants." As a result, he argued, the administrators in Algiers were overwhelmed with minor details: "Administrative details distracted them from the main interests of society. After exhausting themselves solving questions of paving and lighting, they neglect, for lack of time, the great works of European colonization."[91]

It is important to note, then, that the problem with colonial government, or what gave Tocqueville's interlocutors on the ground the impression that there simply was no government, was hardly a lack of regulation: "Everything regulated in France is regulated in Africa," he pointed out, even suggesting that "the administration is also involved in many things it has never been involved in before. The police decrees issued by the Director of the Interior in Algiers alone would fill a volume." The problem was instead that all kinds of issues were mixed and pushed in different directions, and that "with so much movement, nothing moves forward."[92] The extraordinary mélange of regulations and lack of capacity to implement them correctly gave the impression on the ground that there was in fact no government at all; and as a result, in spite of the overwhelming numbers of regulations, all important matters were delegated to distant decision makers in Paris. "Nothing could be more wretchedly anarchic than the civil government of Algiers," Tocqueville concluded.[93]

What was needed was not simply greater centralization or decentralization, but a proper balance between the two to produce greater government capacity. Reminiscent of the debates on administrative elections in the metropole, which Tocqueville had summarized in his 1846 article on centralization when he wondered, "With the help of what precautions, what guarantees, following what rules would it be possible to combine for the first time in a democratic society a vast centralized system and a serious representative system?" Tocqueville argued that the civil administration in Algiers must have a capacity to make decisions on the local village level, as well as a strong central office: "There must be a man in charge of ensuring that all the various agents of this administration work together to carry out either its projects or those of the general government."[94] Indeed, as far as Tocqueville was concerned, without administrative capacity, the entire colonial operation would collapse and become "impracticable."[95]

With this assessment we come to an essential thesis in Tocqueville's oeuvre: the role administration played in crafting a modern society. As he stated on a number of occasions in his notes and writings on Algeria, it was a "small and new society,"[96] because "the very foundations of society are not solid."[97] Or, as he noted more eloquently further on, "The truth is that Africa does not yet have what Europeans understand by society. There are men, but no social body."[98] How was it possible to "make society" then, or to create a "social body," as he understood it? Tocqueville's response was clear, and reminiscent of his conclusions in his *Democracy* and in his *Old Regime*. "The administration must be given a leader to oversee and create this new society," he argued.[99] Such is the essential claim: Creating a proper administration is essential to the process of creating society. Modern society, in Tocqueville's view, was crafted by the administration. It was precisely for this reason that a proper balance of centralization and decentralization was necessary. In such a context, the stakes of ineffective, tyrannical, and chaotic administrative decision making were raised to the highest level.

It is precisely for this reason that it was so imperative to establish the second essential element of the colonial administration: the transition from military to civil government. This problem had its roots in Tocqueville's analysis of Napoleon. Tocqueville had already discussed the problem of shifting from a military administration to a civil and increasingly participative one in a context of prolonged conflict in his assessment of the first empire. In his view, the French revolutionary wars and Napoleon's empire had been fundamentally about defending and spreading emancipatory principles beyond the Hexagon, and marking a radical shift in the very nature of imperial expansion. Since the French Revolution, France's glory, as Tocqueville himself argued, now came in part from its ability to fearlessly spread emancipation through military conflict. The challenge for Napoleon, however, was that he was unable to transform the supposedly "emancipatory" thrust of his imperial expansion into any serious form of democratic administration—that is, any form of rigorous self-government. This was one of the processes that Tocqueville had explored in his work on American democracy, and it re-emerged as central in the context of Algeria. "It is obvious that the men least suited to organizing and even designing a civilian society and a colonial civilian society are the clerks of the Ministry of War."[100] If it was up to the administration to organize and even create a society on the imperial periphery, such a task was impossible under military rule. The essential problem with creating an effective administration was that the governor of Algeria was "a general with no clear, practical notions of civilian administration," Tocqueville insisted—adding that he was "very preoccupied with military ventures, and more often than not . . . engaged in distant activities at the head of armies." As far as Tocqueville was concerned, a military general was entirely ill-equipped to "conceive administrative plans and, even if the idea presented itself to his mind, his ignorance of the details, his military preoccupations, and his remoteness would almost always render him incapable of translating his ideas into practice." Furthermore, it was precisely this lack of "practice" that made it impossible for the general to create administrative capacity by ensuring that "different department heads work assiduously and in concert on their implementation."[101]

The challenge in creating civil government was that in the state of social infancy of the colonial settlements, the colons would constantly be looking to the administration for help, surrendering themselves potentially to the chaotic and despotic decisions of the military. "The circumstances in which Algeria finds itself, the small number of colonists, their isolation, the strength of the army, the inevitable predominance of the spirit of military government will always give an irresistible force to power there."[102] Once again, Tocqueville understood the construction of administrative capacity to be the product of a more nuanced, proper dosage between military and civil government. He recognized the importance of having "a delegate of the military power in each village." But, he insisted, "this does not mean that the administration of communal property, the care of public works, and the city's internal police force are in its hands."[103] Problems of regulatory police, public works, and management of property needed to be managed by the administration, and this administration needed to be headed by civilians under the protection of the military.

It was, then, in this realm of civil government that the third equally essential step in creating an effective administration came to the fore: including the population in the decision-making process. For if the proper dosage of centralization and decentralization and the necessary balance of military protection and civilian government were essential for building a colonial society, the process could not be completed without introducing some means of popular influence over decision making. It is important to note that Tocqueville had a relatively instrumental vision of popular participation in the colonial context. Far from arguing that it would provide procedural legitimacy, he was once again primarily interested in expanding administrative capacity—that is, the ability to properly execute and make effective the laws and statutes that were decided upon. It was in this context that he favorably quoted M. Lepécheux, the director of public education in Algiers, who explained that while he was not overly committed to regular elections, he did think it was necessary and even urgent to "create something that can at least make the needs and wishes of the country known to both local and central authorities. If you want to have only public servants, at least have public servants who don't have the power to make decisions but who are responsible for preparing local by-laws of a general nature, and who have an overview of the situation."[104] If the process of decision making was prepared through an understanding of the terrain and local problems, the administrative decisions would be more effective. As Tocqueville noted in this passage, as long as this was not the case, the population would lack "the guarantees most necessary to man in society."[105] This was fundamentally a question of building greater administrative capacity to construct an Algerian society of colons. Tocqueville is quite clear that neither the Europeans nor the Arabs were living in a democratic society according to the standards he had set in his previous work. However, it was through an effective and attentive administration that a colonial society could be constructed.

Algerian conquest therefore provided numerous essential antidotes for the potentially decomposing effects of democracy in the metropole: it offered new commercial and scientific opportunities to reinforce the nation's wealth; it allowed for the distribution of land and labor and thus prevented the spatial concentration of inequalities generated by a democratized civil society; and through the creation of an efficient government and administration on the imperial periphery, it provided the means to preserve democratic society.

The problem, of course, was that it ran into the fundamental and structural contradiction that the more it consolidated the demos, the harder the boundaries became vis-à-vis those who were outside it. And since the very consolidation depended upon the nation's ability to take over lands that were already occupied, the demos would run into constant contact and would necessarily have to govern and administer those who were not a part of it. The aporia was patent: by reinforcing the demos's ability to remain unified and alleviate its internal contradictions, Algerian conquest hardened the social and political boundaries of the demos against those outside, even as those areas were still to be governed by it. Being governed by a unified demos of which one was not a part was no more democratic than being governed by the Ottoman autocracy. And yet, the very language of democracy allowed for a profoundly ambiguous relationship to indigenous populations on North African soil. For if France was a demos, then the problem was that the majority of the people in North Africa were not, according to Tocqueville.

For Tocqueville, the notion of a "democratic society" introduced structural contradictions into life in the metropole. The equality of condition, as Tocqueville demonstrated time and again, could lead to unprecedented social domination through the emergence of an industrial aristocracy and a new despotism. Tocqueville provided a range of responses to this general problem, and colonization was one of them. Nonetheless, he confronted the constant contradiction that creating these opportunities required an abundant administrative authority that could only ever be very partially democratized on the imperial periphery. And even as he considered ways of democratizing the administration of the colonial settlements, he was still left with the basic fact, which he recognized, that any form of participatory government would be reserved for the colonial settlers themselves. In other words, even if the democratic administration were expanded to include all European settlers, and a colonial "society" was created, they would still be ruling and imposing their administration on conquered subjects. In short, members of the demos would necessarily be governing those who were not a part of it. And it was in this basic fact that Tocqueville confronted the profound limits of democratic administration in the context of empire.

CONCLUSION

The Mixed Social Constitution

Car, il faut en ce siècle que la révolution soit partout.
VICTOR HUGO, *Les Misérables*

Revolt, uprising, and insurgency have constituted a new global landscape for democracy in the twenty-first century. But as waves of popular outcry have focused the world's gaze on ecological, political, social, sanitary, gender, and racial injustices, their extraordinary proliferation has also met with a profound pessimism about our political present. These pages have sought perspective on this condition through a critical investigation of democracy's past. Though the time has been largely forgotten, it was during the first half of the nineteenth century that collective action, popular mobilization, and recurrent revolution invented a democratic society, the foundations of which remain today.[1]

The story recounted here of how this democratic society came to govern itself pushes us to revise some contemporary theoretical assumptions on democracy and democratization. First, this book has deemphasized suffrage as the essential indicator of democratic life. While elections, especially for legislative representatives, have come to be seen as the cornerstone of popular democratic politics, some historical dilemmas remain with this paradigm. For example, as Bernard Manin has noted, it is of no small consequence that the representative government generated by this suffrage was not considered democratic during the French Revolution but was understood as its opposite, thus creating the paradox that "modern democracies are the product of a form of government that its founders opposed to democracy."[2] More troublingly, in recent decades we have increasingly witnessed how elections can be used to mask deeply antidemocratic political systems rather than support them. Such practices have a history, since universal suffrage became the foundation for one of the most normatively unacceptable "democratic regimes" of modern France, the Second Empire of Napoleon III.

CONCLUSION

The limited impact of suffrage on the democratic revolution described in this book is at least partially historically determined. The popular uprisings and the massive expansion of administrative action and regulatory power described here thrived in France in the context of two constitutional monarchies that became increasingly conservative and rigid while clinging to drastically limited suffrage. During this period, democratic society constantly flooded beyond the narrow confines established by the political regime, necessarily sidelining the centrality of the vote in the invention of a modern democratic authority. Through this constant process of overflowing, democratic society spilled over into the vast range of social activities and concerns treated in the chapters of this book, creating a new social and political order that remains to this day. The legacy of this extended revolution was therefore not the mere expansion of suffrage, though it did achieve that as well. Nor was its actual historical success measured by an insurrectional moment outside the state.[3] The legacy of this moment was the possibility of justly organizing a society of equals through self-government across a full range of social activities.

Second, this book has offered a historical alternative to civil society as the cornerstone for the transition to and maintenance of a strong democratic polity. Anchoring the essential critical power of social action outside government, theorists and historians of the late twentieth century gave civil society tremendous analytical purchase and liberating potential in a context of single-party rule, authoritarianism, global pressure groups, and nongovernmental interests. But as the late and post–Cold War era recedes into the past and the bold experiment in hyperliberalism to which it gave birth confronts new democratic aspirations, the civil society paradigm has left intellectuals, activists, and policymakers increasingly dissatisfied. As early as 1993, Krishan Kumar proposed "an inquiry into the usefulness of a historical term," noting that while "the revival of the concept of civil society is a self-conscious exercise in remembering and retrieval," it nonetheless "offers little guidance to societies seeking to construct a genuine political society."[4] Kumar was hardly alone. Michael Walzer sought to "warn against the antipolitical tendencies that commonly accompany the celebration of civil society,"[5] and Sheri Berman demonstrated how important civil society was in undermining the democratic experiment of the Weimar Republic.[6] Simone Chambers and Jeffrey Kopstein similarly introduced the normative possibility of "bad civil society," especially in our post-antitotalitarian moment.[7] And, revisiting the very terrain of Tocqueville's initial study of democracy, William Novak revealed the deep limitations of our legal historical renderings of the associative life of early America, skewering civil society approaches that "revitalized a privileged, normatively charged language to describe an apolitical society."[8]

At the heart of these critiques have been what are referred to as the "apolitical" or even "antipolitical" tendencies of civil society. This book offers an alternative by arguing that civil society was neither the only nor perhaps the most common mode of social organization to have fostered the development of modern democracy. In the first half of the nineteenth century, the consequences of the slow and then sudden demise of a social organization rooted in natural aristocratic privilege transformed every aspect of society. It was argued that the rise of an equality of condition in the form of a democratic society rose up from the long battle against the nobility. As George Sand wrote, already by the eighteenth century "even in the most backward provinces of the Centre, the feeling of social equity reigned."[9] This democratic society was understood to have been prepared in the fiery cauldron of the Reformation, made by absolutism's tireless war against the nobility, consolidated by solemn declarations of civil equality in 1789, and brought to fruition in the visionary constitution of 1793. To the extent that democratic society had been fashioned, it was also understood to have been politically constituted. So as the full force of a new democratic society was felt, the essential question became how to ensure that this politically constituted society of equals was conserved despite its own internal contradictory drives to produce unprecedented inequalities and fall prey to more sinister forms of despotism. This was above all an administrative problem.

I have shown how this problem of justly governing a politically constituted society of equals provided the backdrop for the massive expansion of administrative capacity in the first half of the nineteenth century. In this period, Victor Hugo and Karl Marx explicitly referred to this self-governing democratic society as a *demos*. The demos, in this usage, was not a constituent power. Instead, a given society's very status as a demos depended on a constant political process of instituted self-fashioning. The moment the people ceased to govern themselves democratically, they might remain a democratic society, but would be subject to unmatched inequalities and new forms of tyranny. Moreover, since the demos's very existence depended on its ability to govern itself, it was hardly autonomous from government. To the contrary, as it rose, the demos built the modern administrative state, warts and all.

I have argued that this new relationship between democratic society and democratic government emerged within a process of democratizing the social contract. In this conception, the demos had not formed in a hypothetical, originary, and idealized social contract imagined out of a state of nature. To the contrary, while the demos legitimately self-governed according to a contractual relationship, this process of collective actualization, and the endless demands and shortcomings it produced, took root in an iterative process

CONCLUSION 241

of popular practice, demands, and administrative responses. This study has explored the concrete elaboration of this democratic social contract as a historical, sociological, and pragmatic process through confrontations with problems that were identified as being of public importance. As varied as the problems and solutions were, they were driven by a conviction that the state could hardly be reduced to the elaborate trappings of ceremony and the heteronymy of sovereign authority. In a democracy, government and administration needed to address specific public problems and provide clear responses. The regulatory and administrative drive of modern democracies contained a profoundly pragmatic necessity to address the basic problems faced by their communities. It was out of the popular demand for public solutions and the development of responses on the part of public authorities that the foundations of the modern democratic state was constructed.

So while this book has followed the growth of administration in a historical register, it may also offer some perspective for contemporary theoretical considerations on the democratic social contract. Essential to this contribution is to understand how the revised contractualism of the nineteenth century took aim at what was considered a basic shortcoming of previous social contract theories in which free-willing individuals joined together, creating a sovereign general will, and in turn, forming a government to ensure that the will was effectively executed. In his *Social Contract*, Rousseau concluded that no doubt a mixed constitution including some forms of aristocratic and democratic government would most effectively execute the general will.[10] In other words, as John Rawls characterized this tradition, we could think of "the original contract as one to enter a particular society" and "to set up a particular form of government."[11]

Nineteenth-century revisionism of the contract radically inverted this process. Instead of starting from individuals who used a contract to enter society and set up a government, it started from society. Essential to this view, however, was the idea that democratic society was not transparent to itself. That is, a democratic society had to be analyzed and understood to be governed. As we have seen, such an ambition was structured around three imperatives inherent in democratic society: it was made (1) over time, (2) through social structure, and (3) via reflexive self-orientation. These three imperatives of *history*, *sociology*, and *pragmatic reflexivity* were considered essential to the good governance of modern society. They formed the backdrop for the actions and responses of those who sought to build modern administrative power in the first half of the nineteenth century.

In some essential ways, this conception of a cumulative and organic contractualism provided a precedent for what Jeremy Waldron describes as an "anthropological" contractualism. As opposed to the classic, hypothetical, and normative criteria of a classic state of nature, in Waldron's anthropological alternative, "the whole course of the evolution of political institutions out of prepolitical society cannot be seen as a single intentional or consensual process." Instead, "individual steps in that process can be analyzed and evaluated in contractualist terms."[12] The revisionism discussed here shares Waldron's fundamental argument for a processual contract, exploring the actual historical, sociological, and pragmatic constraints and obligations that shaped our ability to self-govern.

One of the essential lessons of the story told here, which can be profitably deployed within contemporary democratic theory, is the idea that democratic society formed through a *mixed social constitution*. Such a constitution is not designed to establish a specific type of institution or government. Rather, it structures *how* democratic society may legitimately understand itself in its aim to self-govern. The mixed social constitution pushes for a revision of the social contract in three ways. First, in response to the social contract's hypothetical one-time collective covenant between individual wills, the democratized social contract regulates through a historical process of resistance, provisional consent, revision, and accretion. Second, in response to the social contract that posits the formation of a given society as an assemblage of abstract free-willing individuals, the democratized social contract recognizes the structural constraints and opportunities of socially-embedded individuals. Third, in response to the early modern social contract's focus on rights preservation, the democratic social contract emphasizes the ends of administrative action, regulatory intervention, and social obligation. These branches of the mixed social constitution provide a foundation for the legitimate exercise of public power in democratic society. Legitimate governance, in this view, is neither the product of a formal agreement between wills nor a hypothetical compact to preserve abstract rights. It is, rather, a general disposition to legitimately guide and regulate a democratic society toward its own self-determined ends.

So while it goes without saying that the history of modern democracy rests on a story of formal rights and the civil and political expansion of popular power, the question remains: Do these dimensions encompass the whole history of the democratic as it developed in the modern age? This book has suggested that they do not. Another indispensable revolution was necessary for modern democracy to take shape: the democratizing of the social contract. While the origins of the new social contract can also be found in the early modern period and the Revolution of 1789, it was in the wake of the Terror and the First Empire that it took shape as the rights of abstract sovereign individuals were given specific content. Individuals and groups rose to make new demands on government, and their claims were increasingly read through the lens of a new contract that attended to a society of equals who were agents of their own self-government. The democratic social contract respected the mixed social constitution based on historical obligation, social scientific observation, and a pragmatic approach to governing toward the public good.

It was therefore precisely—and, from where we stand today, paradoxically—by focusing democratic activity entirely on the practice of universal suffrage while simultaneously capturing and dismantling the vast array of democratic social practices and projects for increased self-administration supporting it that Napoleon III brought an end to the demos revolution. Following his coup in 1852, Napoleon III claimed the mantle of modern democracy, putting his empire before the sovereign people and basing his legitimacy on a plebiscite of universal manhood suffrage. Over the next eighteen years, he built his democratic despotism on the regular exercise of the vote and his claim to be incarnating the sovereign will of the people. At the same time, in every realm of social action and administration discussed in this book, he attempted to centralize, capture, and de-democratize what had been birthed through the iterative exchange between the public and the public authorities, making abstract sovereignty and occasional voting the sole emblems of democratic life.

It is difficult to imagine a more extreme attempt at state capture of democracy than the one set in place by the Second Empire. Napoleon III embarked on a massive reforestation, managed by the central government at the expense of participation by peasants, mayors, and communal lands. According to the law of June 19, 1857, each commune was required to sell one-twelfth of its commons to private owners every year, and the new owners were required to plant trees on the land. The cost involved prevented the peasants from purchasing the land, which primarily fell under the control of partisans of the regime and major landholders.[13] In the capital, Napoleon III's extraordinary reconstruction of Paris was achieved by ending all local elections at the same time as his appointed prefect, Georges-Eugène Haussmann, rebuilt the city through the massive set of planning innovations spawned by the participatory administrative culture of the 1840s.[14] In the domain of public health, as the historian Florence Bourillon has pointed out, laws designed to improve insalubrious housing were manipulated by promoters looking for redevelopment during the massive reconstruction under Haussmann.[15] Napoleon III similarly transformed the Prud'hommes councils with the law of June 1, 1853, in which it was stipulated that the emperor would directly appoint the president and the vice president of each court.[16] The legal foundations of *sociétés anonymes* were also undermined with the law of May 23, 1863, which dismantled the administrative control over the functioning of these companies.[17] At the same time, the emperor sought the consolidation of a conservative, patriarchal Catholicism designed to ensure social order.[18] And in the realm of empire, the administrative and semimilitary centralization that had been necessary to establish the Algerian expansion became the foundation for governing the metropole itself. As Tocqueville had suggested, empire could be a means of reinforcing national grandeur; but as Napoleon III channeled a discourse of popular sovereignty into his very person and consolidated a top-down administration, he realized Tocqueville's greatest fears of a democratic society that no longer governed itself.

But if Napoleon III brought an end to the demos revolution by fetishizing the vote and further centralizing administrative decision making, his ascendency hardly destroyed the democratic society that had risen up in the first half of the century. Nor could it demolish the legacy of this period for the construction of a new administrative power. Indeed, the demos revolution recounted in this book has remained a structural feature of modern governance far beyond the Second Empire to this day. Defining a new democratic practice, and thus marking an essential moment in the constitution of modern democracy, the first half of the nineteenth century not only inaugurated a new social conception of the democratic, but also prepared the foundation for a new moment in the history of democracy.[19] After rising out of the ashes of Napoleon's empire, the demos could be assembled.

Acknowledgments

As this second volume of genealogical inquiry digs further into democracy's past, the question of how democratic states have been understood, what they actually do, and what they are capable of in the present has taken on a new gravity. When I started the first volume of this project, *Demos Assembled*, a decade ago, it was still difficult to imagine the challenges that lay ahead for our contemporary democracies. But as new opportunities and challenges arise today, the sustained push backward in the hope of offering a perspective on our democratic future would seem as urgent as ever.

One advantage of working on a long-term multivolume project of this kind is the chance to return to conversations, comments, and critiques that have accumulated over years and even decades. Some of the origins of this book can be found in my graduate work, so I'd like once again to thank Jan Goldstein and William Sewell for their guidance. I would also like to thank those who took the time to write reviews of the first volume of this project, especially Robert Tombs, Jennifer Pitts, Sophia Rosenfeld, Cheryl Welch, Serge Audier, Michael Behrent, Philip Nord, and Max Skjönsberg, among others. Their comments and insights on *Demos Assembled* helped establish the groundwork for this volume. I would like to extend a particularly warm thanks to Darrin McMahon for his insights, his support of this project, and the invitation to contribute to his book series.

This book took shape thanks to a year at the Center for Advanced Study in Behavioral Sciences at Stanford University. It is in no small measure thanks to CASBS that this book was completed. While there, I had the pleasure of enjoying the intellectual camaraderie of many colleagues, especially Dominique Lestel. I'd also like to thank Margaret Levi for her support. CASBS, and then a term as Kratter Visiting Professor in the History Department at

Stanford, allowed me to share ideas with Stanford faculty, in particular Keith Baker, Jim Sheehan, Bernie Meyler, and Priya Satia. I'd like especially to thank Dan Edelstein, who has been an *interlocuteur extraordinaire*. Through our many stimulating discussions and shared projects, not to mention his all-around intellectual bonhomie, this book and my ideas on democracy have been deeply transformed.

The American University of Paris has continued to provide an exceptional institutional context for developing this project. That one might enjoy the advantages of an American-style liberal arts college along the Seine would seem improbable. And yet, thanks to my extraordinary students and colleagues, and the university staff and administration, that improbable ideal has become my intellectual home. Without the continued encouragement and distinctive leadership of Celeste Schenck, this book would not have been possible. Among my many wonderful colleagues, I'd like to give special thanks to Miranda Spieler, Oliver Feltham, Peter Haegel, Jayson Harsin, Albert Wu, Michelle Kuo, Rebekah Rast, Sofia Voleonti, and Russell Williams.

I would also like to thank AUP and the Horizon Europe program for its support of the Center for Critical Democracy Studies. This project has been sustained by conversations with the dozens and dozens of guests who have graciously accepted invitations to speak at the center. Its remarkable community has continued to shape my ideas on the history and theory of democracy, particularly thanks to Roman Zinigrad, Julian Culp, Zona Zariç, Nathanael Collin-Jaeger, Zach Freig, Kendra Mills, Shane Mclorrain, and Kira Minvielle. I'd also like to thank Valérie Fodé, Brenda Torney, Stéphanie Buisson, Christine Tomasek, and Jean-Charles Khlaut for their extraordinary administrative support. Elizabeth Ballantine's generous dedication to my academic work has been indispensable, as has Ray Henze's sustained interest in my scholarship. It is always a pleasure to exchange with Tim Rogers, and I'd like to thank provosts Scott Sprenger, William Fisher, and Hannah Westley, as well as offer a special thanks to AUP's president, Sonya Stephens.

I have also benefited from comments and conversations on democracy and the themes in this book with Colin Jones, Nicolas Delalande, Quentin Deluermoz, Stéphane Van Damme, Larry Norman, Jim Kloppenberg, Michael Behrent, David Bell, Bernard Harcourt, Dilip Gaonkar, Ed Berenson, John Shovlin, Anna-Louise Milne, Daniel Stockemer, Umut Korkut, Alex Kirshner, Hasret Bilgin, Paul Godt, Fabienne Serrand, Kesi Mahandran, Noam Maggor, Pierre Singaravélou, Jean-Numa Ducange, Silyane Larcher, Allan Potofsky, Greg Conti, Steve Pincus, Beppo Cocco, Barbara Szanieki, Alexandre Mendes, Dominique Spada, Cross Lawrence, Allan Potofsky, Paul Cheney, David Todd, Danny Steinmetz-Jenkins, Romain Richy, Jon Levy, Emilia Palonen, and Michael Sonenscher. Special thanks to Thomas Dutoit for so many wide-ranging and stimulating conversations, and to Vincent Duclert for being a model of intellectual vitality. With Andrew Jainchill, I have enjoyed the camaraderie of so many shared interests.

Demos Rising ends and *Demos Assembled* begins with a discussion of Tocqueville. My heterodox Tocquevillianism has been nurtured by the intellectual companionship of the editorial board of the *Tocqueville Review/La revue Tocqueville*, in particular François Melonio, Art Goldhammer, Catherine Audard, Michel Forsé, Alan Kahan, Olivier Zunz, Simon Langlois, and Laurence Duboys-Fresnay. The editorial board of the *Annales* has continued to provide an exceptional context for sharing ideas on history and social science. Anne Simonin's intellectual camaraderie has consistently enlightened this scholarly adventure. My conception of historical scholarship has benefited from the social scientific acumen of Étienne Anheim.

I'd like to extend a particular thanks to Antoine Lilti, who graciously accepted to serve as *garant* for my habilitation at the École des hautes études, and to share the hallowed halls of the Collège de France for my *soutenance*. His comments throughout the process shaped the manuscript into the book it has become. I'd also like to thank the other members of the Habilitation à diriger des recherches jury (whom I have not already thanked), Bruno Karsenti and Céline Spector, for their careful reading of my work over the last ten years, and for their extremely helpful reports following the defense. I'd like to thank Dylan Montanari, Fabiola Enríquez Flores, and Renaldo Migaldi for their expert editorial work on this book at the University of Chicago Press.

Persistent, precise, and refreshing exchanges with Alain Chatriot have nourished this project since its earliest moments. Conversations with Jim Sparrow have continued to be a prized part of this endeavor. Bill Novak's friendship, intellectual companionship, academic insight, and overall generosity have continued to be an indispensable guide as I have pursued this history of democracy.

I'd like to thank the Wrights—Deb, Mick, Kyle, and Avery—and my father, William Sawyer, for their support. Thank you to Paul Dude, and I cherish the encouragement and love of my mother, Carol Dunn, who unwittingly provoked my dedication to the study of France and its history. And thanks to Le Roc—Jean-Pierre and Geneviève Roudeau, Claire, Julien, et le petit Anatole Debet—where so many of these words were written. This book is dedicated to my wife, Cécile.

Notes

Introduction

1. François-René de Chateaubriand, *Mémoires d'outre tombe*, vol. 1 (Paris: Gallimard, 2015), 150. All translations are my own unless otherwise noted.

2. Royer-Collard, *De la Liberté de la Presse, Discours* (Paris: Collection Le Jardin du Luxembourg, 1949), 47.

3. Here I am narrowly referring solely to those studies that have explicitly cited "democracy" as the core of their study of the late eighteenth century. The great dean of French revolutionary studies, Alphonse Aulard, famously presented his political history of the French Revolution as a history of the origins and development of democracy and the republic. *Histoire politique de la Révolution française: Origines et développement de la démocratie et de la République, 1789–1804* (Paris: Armand Colin, 1901). A half century later, R. R. Palmer confidently stated that it was "no anachronism to apply the word 'democratic' to the eighteenth-century revolution." *The Age of Democratic Revolution: A Political History of Europe and America, 1760–1800* (Princeton, NJ: Princeton University Press, 1954). Marcel Reinhard offered a course at the Sorbonne titled "La Révolution démocratique"; it was published in three volumes as Marcel Reinhard, *La Révolution démocratique* (Paris: Centre de documentation universitaire, 1959).

4. See, for example, Manuel Covo et al., "Les révolutions Atlantiques: Une vague démocratique," in Ludivine Bantigny et al., eds, *Une histoire globale des révolutions* (Paris: La Découverte, 2023), 223–63; James T. Kloppenberg, *Toward Democracy: The Struggle for Self-Rule in Europe and American Thought* (New York: Oxford University Press, 2016); Marcel Gauchet, *L'Avènement de la démocratie*, vols. 1–4 (Paris: Gallimard, 2007–16); Joanna Innes and Mark Philp, *Re-Imagining Democracy in the Age of Revolutions: America, France, Britain and Ireland, 1750–1850* (Oxford, UK: Oxford University Press, 2013) and *Re-Imagining Democracy in the Mediterranean, 1780–1860* (Oxford, UK: Oxford University Press, 2018); Sophia Rosenfeld, *Democracy and Truth: A Short History* (Philadelphia: University of Pennsylvania Press, 2018); James Livesey, *Making Democracy in the French Revolution* (Cambridge, MA: Harvard University Press, 2001).

5. David Thomson forcefully titled his seminal work in French political history *Democracy in France: The Third Republic* (Oxford, UK: Oxford University Press, 1946). See also Sudhir Hazareesingh, *From Subject to Citizen: The Second Empire and the Emergence of Modern French Democracy* (Princeton, NJ: Princeton University Press, 1998); Philip Nord, *The Republican*

Moment: Struggles for Democracy in Nineteenth-Century France (Cambridge, MA: Harvard University Press, 1995).

6. Albert L. Guérard, "Honoré de Balzac," *Southwest Review* 10, no. 3 (1925): 109–24.

7. Charles Breunig, *The Age of Revolution and Reaction, 1789–1850* (New York: Norton, 1970); André Jardin and André-Jean Tudesq, *Restoration and Reaction, 1815–1848*, trans. Elborg Forster (New York: Cambridge University Press, 1983); Roger Price, ed., *Revolution and Reaction: 1848 and the Second French Republic* (London: Croom Helm, 1975); Ted Margadant, "Tradition and Modernity in Rural France during the Nineteenth Century," *Journal of Modern History*, December 1984.

8. On the supposed liberal revival of this period, see Stephen W. Sawyer and Iain Stewart, *In Search of a Liberal Moment: Democracy, Anti-Totalitarianism, and Intellectual Politics in France since 1950* (New York: Palgrave, 2016).

9. For just a glimpse into how generative this scholarship has been since the 1970s, see Pierre Rosanvallon, *Le Moment Guizot* (Paris: Gallimard, 1985); Louis Girard, *Les Libéraux français, 1814–1875* (Paris: Aubier, 1985); André Jardin, *Histoire du libéralisme politique de la crise de l'absolutisme à la constitution de 1875* (Paris: Hachette, 1985); Pierre Manent, *Histoire intellectuelle du libéralisme: Dix leçons* (Paris: Hachette, 1997); Annelien de Dijn, *French Political Thought from Montesquieu to Tocqueville: Liberty in a Levelled Society?* (Cambridge, UK: Cambridge University Press, 2008); Lucien Jaume, *L'individu effacé ou le paradoxe du libéralisme français* (Paris: Fayard, 1997); Helena Rosenblatt, *Liberal Values: Benjamin Constant and the Politics of Religion* (Cambridge, UK: Cambridge University Press, 2011); Aurelian Craiutu, *Liberalism under Siege: The Political Thought of the French Doctrinaires* (Lanham, MD: Lexington Books, 2003); Alan S. Kahan, *Aristocratic Liberalism: The Social and Political Thought of Jacob Burckhardt, John Stuart Mill, and Alexis de Tocqueville* (New York: Oxford University Press, 1992); Cheryl Welch, *Liberty and Utility: The French Idéologues and the Transformation of Liberalism* (New York: Columbia University Press, 1984); K. Steven Vincent, *Benjamin Constant and the Birth of French Liberalism* (New York: Palgrave, 2011); Stephen Holmes, *Benjamin Constant and the Making of Modern Liberalism* (New Haven, CT: Yale University Press, 1984). For a summary of some of this important work, see Michael Behrent, "Liberal Dispositions: Recent Scholarship on French Liberalism," *Modern Intellectual History*, February 2015, 1–31.

10. The literature on French republicanism in the first half of the nineteenth century is extensive. See, for example, Jeane Gilmore, *La Republique clandestine, 1818–1848*, trans. Jean-Baptiste Duroselle (Paris: Aubier, 1997); Samuel Hayat, *Quand la république était révolutionnaire: Citoyenneté et représentation en 1848* (Paris: Seuil, 2014); John Merriman, *The Agony of the Republic: The Repression of the Left in Revolutionary France, 1848–1851* (New Haven, CT: Yale University Press, 1978); Douglas Moggach and Gareth Stedman Jones, eds., *The 1848 Revolutions and European Political Thought* (Cambridge, UK: Cambridge University Press, 2018); Claude Nicolet, *l'idée républicaine en France: Essai d'histoire critique (1789–1924)* (Paris: Gallimard, 1982); Pamela Pilbeam, *Republicanism in Nineteenth-Century France, 1814–1871* (London: Macmillan, 1995); Michele Riot-Sarcey, *La démocratie à l'épreuve des femmes: Trois figures critiques du pouvoir, 1830–1848* (Paris: Albin Michel, 1994); Pierre Rosanvallon, *Le sacre du citoyen: Histoire du suffrage universel en France* (Paris: Gallimard, 1992); I. Tchernoff, *Le Parti Républicain sous la Monarchie de Juillet: Formation et évolution de la doctrine républicaine* (Paris: Pedone, 1901).

11. Stephen W. Sawyer, *Demos Assembled: Democracy and the International Origins of the Modern State, 1840–1880* (Chicago: University of Chicago Press, 2018), 3.

12. For an international history of democracy in this period, see Joanna Innes and Mark Philp, *Re-Imagining Democracy in the Age of Revolutions: America, France, Britain, and Ireland,*

NOTES TO PAGES 4–7   251

1750–1850 (Oxford, UK: Oxford University Press, 2013) and *Re-Imagining Democracy in the Mediterranean, 1780–1860* (Oxford, UK: Oxford University Press, 2018).

13. R. R. Palmer, "Notes on the Use of the Word 'Democracy' 1789–1799," *Political Science Quarterly* 68, no. 2 (June 1953): 203–26, here 204–5.

14. Jussi Kurunmäki, Jeppe Nevers, and Henk te Velde, introduction to *Democracy in Modern Europe: A Conceptual History* (New York: Berghahn Books, 2018), 4.

15. Pierre Rosanvallon, "The History of the Word 'Democracy' in France," *Journal of Democracy* 6, no. 4 (Oct 1995).

16. Joanna Innes and Mark Philip, "'Democracy' from Book to Life," in *Democracy in Modern Europe: A Conceptual History* (New York: Berghahn Books, 2018), 18.

17. Oliver Hidalgo, "Conceptual History and Politics: Is the Concept of Democracy Essentially Contested?" *Contributions to the History of Concepts* 4 (2008): 176–201, here 176.

18. James T. Kloppenberg, *Toward Democracy*, 5.

19. Stephen W. Sawyer, "The Forgotten Democratic Tradition of Revolutionary France," *Modern Intellectual History* (2021): 1–29; Dan Edelstein and Stephen W. Sawyer, "Sovereignty and Government in the French Revolution," forthcoming.

20. Richard Tuck, *The Sleeping Sovereign: The Invention of Modern Democracy* (Cambridge, UK: Cambridge University Press, 2016).

21. In *The Social Contract*, Rousseau defines democracy in the following terms: "The Sovereign can, in the first place, entrust the charge of Government to the whole people or to the majority of the people so that there be more citizens who are magistrates than citizens who are simple particulars. This form of Government is given the name *Democracy*." Jean-Jacques Rousseau, *The Social Contract in The Social Contract and Other Later Political Writings*, trans. Victor Gourevitch (Cambridge, UK: Cambridge University Press, 1997), 89.

22. Pellegrino Rossi, *Cours d'économie politique, 1836–1837*, vol. 1 (Brussels, 1840), 341.

23. Friedrich Steger, *Ergänzungsblätter zu allen Conversations-Lexiken* 4, no. 207 (1849): 4. On Steger and democracy as a form of society, see Hans Maier, "V. La démocratie comme indicateur du mouvement historique (XIXe siècle)," *Trivium* 33 (2021): 1.

24. François Guizot, *Cours d'histoire moderne: Leçons du cours de 1828* (Paris: Pichon et Didier, 1828), lesson 14e (July 18, 1828), 6.

25. F. Guizot, *De la démocratie en France* (Brussels: 1849), 9.

26. F. Guizot, *De la démocratie*, 8.

27. On Niboyet, Deroin, and Gay, see Michèle Riot-Sarcey, *La démocratie à l'épreuve des femmes: Trois figures critiques du pouvoir, 1830–1848* (Paris: Albin Michel, 1994).

28. Louis Blanc, *Organisation du travail* (Paris: 1841 [1st ed. 1839]), 161.

29. Étienne Cabet, *Voyage en Icarie, Roman Philosophique et Social*, 2nd ed. (Paris: Mallet, 1842), ii.

30. Hortense Allart, *La femme et la démocratie de nos temps* (Paris: Delaunay, 1836), 106.

31. Allart, *La femme et la démocratie*, 122.

32. Allart, *La femme et la démocratie*, 123.

33. Allart, *La femme et la démocratie*, 123.

34. Indeed, for a whole range of thinkers, the new democratic age, defined as a democratic society, required a radical rethinking of the role of aristocracy as a form of government in the modern era. This partially explains the renewed interest in aristocracy among certain liberals. On aristocratic liberalism, see Alan S. Kahan, *Aristocratic Liberalism: The Social and Political Thought of Jacob Burckhardt, John Stuart Mill, and Alexis de Tocqueville* (Oxford, UK: Oxford

University Press, 1992); Annelien de Dijn, "Aristocratic Liberalism in Post-Revolutionary France," *Historical Journal* 48, no. 3 (2005): 661–81.

35. Pierre Rosanvallon, *Le Moment Guizot* (Paris: Gallimard, 1985).
36. Stephen W. Sawyer, *Adolphe Thiers: La contingence et le pouvoir* (Paris: Armand Colin, 2018).
37. Flora Tristan, *L'Union ouvrière*, 2nd ed. (Paris, 1844), 20.
38. "Profession de foix," *Voix des femmes*, March 20, 1848.
39. Gustave Flaubert, *L'Éducation sentimentale*, in *Œuvres complètes*, vol. 4, *1863–1874*, ed. Gisèle Séginger (Paris: Gallimard, 2021), chapter 4.
40. Nan Zhang and Melissa M. Lee, "Literacy and State-Society Interactions in Nineteenth-Century France," *American Journal of Political Science* 64, no. 4 (October 2020): 1001–6.
41. Jean L. Cohen and Andrew Arato, *Civil Society and Political Theory* (Cambridge: MIT Press, 1992).
42. Philip Nord, "Introduction: Civil Society," *The Republican Moment* (Princeton, NJ: Princeton University Press, 1995).
43. Julien Vincent, "La 'société civile' entre politique et histoire: Discours, pratiques, savoirs," in *La Société civile: Savoirs, enjeux et acteurs en France et en Grande-Bretagne (1780–1914)*, ed. Christophe Charle and Julien Vincent (Rennes, France: PUR, 2011), 9–35.
44. In its common usage in French politics today, the term *société civile* would be more adequately translated as "civilian society." However, whereas in contemporary American English usage this term is reserved for a distinction between military personnel and nonmilitary "civilians," in France the distinction is also applied to mark the difference between those who belong to the central state administration (*grands corps de l'état*) and political parties, and those who are employed in the private sector or are not civil servants. For example, if a CEO of a major company, instead of a professional politician, is appointed minister of finance, the government is mobilizing someone from *la société civile*.
45. Michel Offerlé, introduction to Jay Rowell, Anne-Marie Saint-Gille, eds., *La Société civile organisée aux XIXe et XXe siècles: Perspectives allemandes et françaises* (Villeneuve d'Ascq, France: Septentrion, 2010); Michel Offerlé, ed., *La société civile en question* (Paris: La Documentation française, 2003).
46. Claire Lemercier, "La France Contemporaine: Une Impossible Société Civile?" *Revue d'histoire moderne & contemporaine* 3, no. 52–53 (2005): 166–79, here 172. Alain Chatriot, "La société civile redécouverte: Quelques perspectives françaises," WZB discussion paper, no. SP IV 2009–402, https://www.econstor.eu/bitstream/10419/49614/1/620003847.pdf.
47. Claude Lefort, "Human Rights and the Welfare State," 36.
48. Pierre Rosanvallon, *Le modèle politique français: La société civile contre le jacobinisme de 1789 à nos jours* (Paris: Seuil, 2004).
49. Rosanvallon, *Le modèle politique français*, 425.
50. David Harvey, *Spaces of Global Capitalism: A Theory of Uneven Geographical Development* (London: Verso, 2006).
51. Alexis de Tocqueville, *Democracy in America*, vol. I. Eduardo Nolla, ed. James T. Schleifer, trans. (Indianapolis: Liberty Fund, 2010), 4.
52. On this, see my forthcoming article, Stephen W. Sawyer, "Democratic Society and Political Economy: Revisiting the Tocqueville Civil Society Paradigm."
53. Allart, *La femme et la démocratie*, 27–29.
54. Victor Hugo, *Les Miserables* (Paris: Gallimard, 2018), 1193.
55. Karl Marx, *Critique of Hegel's "Philosophy of Right,"* ed. and trans. Joseph O'Malley and Annette Jolin (Cambridge: Cambridge University Press, 1970), 29.

56. Karl Marx and Frederick Engels, *The German Ideology*, part 1, ed. C. J. Arthur (New York: International Publishers, 1970), 53.

57. For an initial account of this approach, see the introductions to Sawyer, *Demos Assembled*, and Sawyer, *Adolphe Thiers*. For further discussion, see Stephen W. Sawyer and William J. Novak, "Possibilidades de uma História Pragmática do Político," *Revista da Faculdade de Direito da UERJ*, no. 41 (2022): 1–17, where we suggest that such an approach builds primarily on three methodological influences: the pragmatic-hermeneutical approach outlined by James T. Kloppenberg in "Thinking Historically: A Manifesto of Pragmatic Hermeneutics," *Modern Intellectual History* 9, no. 1 (2012): 201–16; the "pragmatic turn" in French social science, and specifically its influence on certain members of the *Annales*, as presented by Bernard Lepetit in *Les formes de l'expérience: Une autre histoire sociale* (Paris: Albin Michel, 1995); and Pierre Rosanvallon's methodological essays on the theme of "Une histoire conceptuelle du politique," which served as his inaugural lecture at the Collège de France. On Rosanvallon's relationship to the *Annales*, see "Face au present: Politique des temporalités," special issue "Autoportrait d'une revue," *Annales: Histoire, Sciences Sociales* 2020, nos. 3–4. For an analysis of Rosanvallon's methodological essays and what I have referred to as a pragmatic approach within his history of democracy, see "Pierre Rosanvallon's Pragmatic Turn," in Oliver Flügel-Martinsen, Franziska Martinsen, Daniel Schulz, and Stephen W. Sawyer, eds., *Pierre Rosanvallon's Interdisciplinary Political Thought* (Bielefeld, Germany: University of Bielefeld Press, 2018).

58. Chateaubriand, *Mémoires d'outre-tombe*, vol. 1 (Paris: Gallimard), 278.

59. Stephen W. Sawyer, "What Is Critical Democracy?" *Tocqueville Review / La revue Tocqueville* 36, no. 2 (2015).

Chapter One

1. John Dewey, *Liberalism and Social Action*, in Jo Ann Boydston, ed., *John Dewey: The Later Works, 1925–1953*, vol. 11 (Carbondale: University of Southern Illinois Press, 1987), 1–65, esp. 25.

2. J.-C.-L. Simonde de Sismondi, *Nouveaux principes d'économie ou de la richesse dans ses rapports avec la population*, vol. 1 (Paris: Delauney, 1819), 7–8.

3. Sismondi, *Nouveaux principes*, vol. 1, p. 9.

4. On Foucart, see Mathieu Touzeil-Divina, *Le doyen Foucart (1799–1860), un père du droit administratif modern*, doctoral thesis, Droit administrative, Paris 2 Assas, defended under the supervision of Jean-Jacques Bienvenu, 2007.

5. E. V. Foucart, *Éléments de droit public et administratif*, vol. 2 (Paris: Videcoq, 1843), 1.

6. Coqueilin et Guillaumin, "Police," *Dictionnaire d'économie politique*, vol. 2 (Paris: 1854), 413–16.

7. M. F. Boeuf, *Résumé de répétitions écrites sur le droit administrative*, 3rd ed. (Paris: Dauvin, 1883), iv.

8. For a history of this distinction in public law, see Martin Loughlin, *Foundations of Public Law* (Oxford, UK: Oxford University Press, 2012). Loughlin argues: "If public law is conceived as a type of political reason that functions to maintain the power of the public sphere, then it becomes necessary also to acknowledge the existence of two different concepts of power: *potestas*, the rightful power of rule, and *potentia*, a source of power drawn from government's actual ability to control the disposition of things" (407). He explains that *potestas* is primarily concerned with constitutional arrangements, while *potentia* is primarily the domain of regulatory police and administration.

9. François Guizot, "L'Autorité," in *Nouveau dictionnaire universel des synonymes de la langue française* (Paris: Aimé Payen, 1822), 103–4.

10. On this problem, see Hayek's *Constitution of Liberty*, where he specifically targets the French case as incarnating the danger of an administrative state that challenges the triumph of liberalism. (Friedrich Hayek, *The Constitution of Liberty* (Chicago: University of Chicago Press, 1960), 193. On Hayek's analysis of the place of France in the history of the administrative state, see Stephen W. Sawyer, "From a History of Liberalism to a History of the Demos: Toward a Democratic Critique of Neoliberalism," *Consecutio Rerum* 5, no. 9 (2020).

11. Contemporary debates on how to keep administration accountable and prevent bureaucratic despotism have been particularly heated in the United States. For a discussion of the myriad critiques of the administrative state, see Gillian E. Metzger, "1930s Redux: The Administrative State under Siege," 131 *Harvard Law Review* 1, 8–50 (2017). American legal historians have understandably focused on the history of the American administrative state. But considering how important France and French administrative law was for the creation of administrative law in the United States, much is to be gained from a better understanding of the French tradition of democratic administration. For a promising investigation of France to reconsider American administrative law, see Christopher S. Havasy, "Radical Administrative Law," *Vanderbilt Law Review*, forthcoming.

12. Loughlin, *Foundations of Public Law*, 431.

13. For a historical account of this process, see "Inequality: Alexis de Tocqueville and the Democratic Foundations of a Modern Administrative Power," in *Demos Assembled*, 22–51. William Novak has noted along similar lines: "In place of administration as antidemocratic threat," we need to locate instead "a much longer history of the crucial role of administration in the actualization of everyday democratic governance." *New Democracy: The Creation of the Modern American State* (Cambridge, MA: Harvard University Press, 2022), 220.

14. For a democratic theory of social contracts grounded in the equalization of power of parties involved, see Albert Weale, *Democratic Justice and the Social Contract* (Oxford, UK: Oxford University Press, 2013), and in particular, chapter 2, "The Democratic Social Contract," and chapter 4, "The Theory of Democratic Social Contracts."

15. See in particular Douglas Moggach, ed., *The New Hegelians: Politics and Philosophy in the Hegelian School* (Cambridge, UK: Cambridge University Press, 2006) and Warren Breckman, *Marx, the Young Hegelians, and the Origins of Radical Social Theory: Dethroning the Self* (Cambridge, UK: Cambridge University Press, 1999).

16. Blake Emerson, *The Public's Law: Origins and Architecture of Progressive Democracy* (Oxford, UK: Oxford University Press, 2019).

17. Ross E. Stewart, "Sismondi's Forgotten Ethical Critique of Early Capitalism," *Journal of Business Ethics* 3, no. 3 (August 1984): 227–34; Richard Arena, "Prix, production et échange dans les nouveaux principes de Sismondi," *Économies et Sociétés* 16, nos. 6–7 ("Déséquilibres et régulation," 1982): 607–20.

18. Gareth Stedman Jones, "Engels and the Industrial Revoution," in Moggach, ed., *The New Hegelians*, 213.

19. "What Hegel took from Sismondi was the need for the regulation of the market, but not a negative of industrialization." Douglas Moggach, "Hegelianism, Republicanism, and Modernity," in Moggach, ed., *The New Hegelians*, 19.

20. See for example, Frank Ruda, *Hegel's Rabble: An Investigation into Hegel's Philosophy of Right* (London: Continuum, 2011).

21. See, for example, David Harvey, "The Spatial Fix; Hegel, Von Thunen and Marx," in *Spaces of Capital: Towards a Critical Geography* (Edinburgh: Edinburgh University Press, 2001). I develop this theme and its influence on Tocqueville's treatment of Algeria in the final chapter of this book.

22. "Unlike the corporation, which has managed to gain substantive scholarly attention in recent years, Hegel's conception of the police is rarely discussed." Zdravko Kobe, "The Interface of the Universal: On Hegel's Concept of The Police," *Philosophy And Society* 30, no. 1, (2019): 101–96, esp. 101.

23. Norbert Waszek, *The Scottish Enlightenment and Hegel's Account of "Civil Society"* (Dodrecht, Netherlands: Kluwer, 1988).

24. Jean-François Kervegan, "Hegel et L'état de droit," *Archives de Philosophie* 50, no. 1 (1987): 55–94, esp. 77.

25. Perpaolo Cesaroni, "Polizia o corporazione: Abitudine, istituzione e governo in Hegel," *Politica & società* 6, no. 3: 443–64.

26. "The ideas of the French Revolution thus appear in the very core of the idealistic systems and, to a great extent, determine their conceptual structure." Herbert Marcuse, *Reason and Revolution: Hegel and the Rise of Social Theory* (London: Routledge, 1941); Joachim Ritter, *Hegel and the French Revolution* (Boston: MIT Press, 1984); Rebecca Comay's, *Mourning Sickness: Hegel and the French Revolution* (Palo Alto, CA: Stanford University Press, 2011); and Terence Renaud, "Hegel and the Revolutions Revisited," *Modern Intellectual History* 13, no. 2 (2016): 525–39.

27. "A large part of the critique of the French revolutionary project that Hegel presents in the *Phenomenology of Spirit* can be read as a summary of the argument against Fichte's police." Zdravko Kobe, "The Interface of the Universal: On Hegel's Concept of the Police," *Filozofija I Društvo* 30 no. 1: 101–21 (2019), 103n.

28. G. W. F. Hegel, *Elements of the Philosophy of Right*, ed. Allen W. Wood, trans. H. B. Nisbet (Cambridge, UK: Cambridge University Press, 1991), §255.

29. As Marc Neocleous has argued, "One of the reasons for the tendency to shy away from fuller discussions of Hegel's concept of police is because it is at odds with modern and essentially liberal sensibilities which treat the police in a decidedly narrow fashion . . . and which considers the other function under more positive headings such as 'welfare.'" "Policing the System of Needs: Hegel, Political Economy, and the Police of the Market," *History of European Ideas* 24, no. 1 (1998): 43–58, esp. 43.

30. On the importance of Hegel for "radicalizing" administrative power, see Christopher S. Havasy, "Radical Administrative Law," 77 *Vanderbilt Law Review* (2024).

31. Hegel has been presented as sitting between liberalism and socialism. "Cette intervention de l'État ne saurait remettre en cause les principes fondamentaux de la société civile. Hegel emprunte ainsi une voie médiane entre le libéralisme strict et sa future remise en cause par le socialisme." Noël Christine, "Hegel et les insuffisances du marché: Le politique face à la pauvreté laborieuse," *Revue Philosophique de Louvain*, (fourth series) 103, no. 3 (2005): 364–89, esp. 365.

32. Intellectual historians have clearly demonstrated the "republican" elements within Hegel's thought and that of his followers, especially among left Hegelians, highlighting a key German influence in modern republicanism. This chapter and book seek to reveal a more explicitly "democratic" interpretation of Hegel by his followers in France. See for example, Kenneth R. Westphal, *Hegel's Civic Republicanism Integrating Natural Law with Kant's Moral Constructivism* (London: Routledge, 2019); Andrew Buchwalter, "Hegel, Modernity, and Civic Republicanism," *Public Affairs Quarterly* 7, no. 1 (January 1993): 1–12.

33. On Hegel's critique of democracy, see W. G. Stratton, "The Problem of Democracy in Hegel's Philosophy of Law," *ARSP: Archiv Für Rechts- Und Sozialphilosophie / Archives for Philosophy of Law and Social Philosophy* 74, no. 1 (1988): 33–41; and Werner Conze, "Demokratie," in Otto Brunner, Werner Conze, and Reinhart Koselleck, eds., *Geschichtliche Grundbegriffe: Historisches Lexikon zur politisch-sozialen Sprache in Deutschland*, vol. 1, (Stuttgart, Germany: Ernst Klette Verlag, 1974).

34. Conze, "Demokratie," 878 and 880.

35. There are social historical and political reasons for this difference as well. Most importantly, local property holders and landed aristocracy had much to lose in the administrative reforms pursued by a unified Germany. Local modes of popular participation were therefore considered an impediment to the creation of a reformed German nation, not only by Hegel but by leading social and economic reformers as well. See Michael Kopsidis and Daniel W. Bromley, "Explaining German Economic Modernization: The French Revolution, Prussian Reforms, and the Inevitable Continuity of Change," *Annales HSS* (2017), no. 4.

36. Warren Breckman, "Eduard Gans and the Crisis of Hegelianism." *Journal of the History of Ideas* 62, no. 3 (2001): 543–64, esp. 548.

37. On other attempts to democratize Hegel, specifically in Ludwig Feuerbach, see Laurence Dickey, "Hegel on Religion and Philosophy," in *The Cambridge Companion to Hegel*, ed. Frederick C. Beiser (Cambridge, UK: Cambridge University Press, 1993), 301–47.

38. On the history of Hegel's reception in France, see Gwendoline Jarczyk, Pierre-Jean Labarrière, "Cent cinquante années de 'réception' hégélienne en France," *Genèses* 2 (1990): 109–30.

39. For a focus on one of the key translators of Hegel's work in this period, see Amaury Catel, *Le Traducteur et le Démiurge: Hermann Ewerbeck, un communiste allemand à Paris, 1841–1860* (Nancy, France: Arbre bleu, 2019).

40. Amédée Prévost, "Hegel," *La Revue de Paris* (1833): 117.

41. Amédée Prévost, "Hegel," *Revue du progrès social: Recueil mensuel politique, philosophique* 1 (1834): 488.

42. Barchou de Penhoën, *Histoire de la philosophie allemande depuis Leibnitz jusqu'à Hegel*, 2 vols. (Paris: Charpentier, 1836).

43. "Crise actuelle de la philosophie allemande," *La revue des deux mondes* 1, year 3 (1843).

44. A. Ott, *Hegel et la philosophie allemande ou exposé et examen critique des principaux systèmes de la philosophie allemande depuis Kant et spécialement de celui de Hegel* (Paris: Joubert, 1844).

45. Louis Prévost, *Hégel: Exposition de sa doctrine, avec une table analytique des matières* (Toulouse, France: Labouisse-Rochefort, 1844).

46. Karl Rosenkranz, *Vie de Hegel* (Paris: Gallimard, 2004 [1st ed. 1844]).

47. Gustave Flaubert, *L'Éducation sentimentale* (1845 version), in *Œuvres complètes*, vol. 1, *Œuvres de jeunesse*, ed. Claudine Gothot-Mersch and Guy Sagnes (Paris: Gallimard, 2001), 991.

48. Charles Rihs, "Lorenz von Stein: Un jeune Hégélien libéral à Paris (1840–1842), observateur du mouvement social dans la France contemporaine." *Revue d'histoire économique et Sociale* 47, no. 3 (1969): 404–46, esp. 404.

49. Warren Breckman, *Marx, the Young Hegelians, and the Origins of Radical Social Theory* (Cambridge, UK: Cambridge University Press, 2001), 177.

50. Heinrich Heine, "Du principe démocratique," trans. Danielle Truchot and Gerhard Höhn, *Revue de métaphysique et de morale* 94, no. 2 (1989): 147–51.

51. Heine, "Du principe démocratique," 150.

52. On the later development of Heine's ideas on democracy, see Warren Breckman, "Heine's Democracy of Terrestrial Gods," in *Marx, the Young Hegelians, and the Origins of Radical Social Theory* (Cambridge, UK: Cambridge University Press, 2001).

53. Moses Hess, *The Holy History of Mankind and Other Writings*, Cambridge Texts in the History of Political Thought (Cambridge: Cambridge University Press, 2004), 59, 84.

54. Avineri, Shlomo. "Socialism and Judaism in Moses Hess's "Holy History of Mankind.'" *Review of Politics* 45, no. 2 (1983): 234–53.

55. Moses Hess, *Holy History of Mankind*, 41.

56. Stein developed extensive intellectual exchanges with French socialists. See Karl Grün, *Die soziale Bewegung in Frankreich und Belgien: Briefe und Studien* (Darmstadt, 1845), 315–16.

57. On the influence of Louis Blanc on Stein, see Diana Siclovan, "Lorenz Stein and German Socialism 1835–1872," doctoral thesis, King's College, Cambridge University, 2014, pp. 54 and 59.

58. Lorenz von Stein, *The History of the Social Movement in France, 1789–1850*, trans. Kaethe Mengelberg (Bedminster Press, 1964), 52–53.

59. Stein, *History*, 52–53.

60. Stein, *History*, 52–53.

61. Stein, *History*, 75.

62. Stein, *History*, 75.

63. Stein, *History*, 75.

64. Stein, *History*, 87.

65. Stein, *History*, 87.

66. Stein writes: "This is the theoretical concept and the meaning-content of the phenomenon of social democracy which constitutes the last stage of the purely intellectual movement of social ideas." Stein, *History*, 87.

67. On Alexandre Ledru-Rollin, see Napoleon Gallois, *Vie politique de Ledru-Rollin* (Paris: Dutertre, 1850); Eugène de Mirecourt, *Ledru-Rollin* (Paris: Havard, 1857); Alvin Rosenblatt Calman, *Ledru-Rollin and the Second French Republic* (New York: Columbia University Press, 1922); Robert Schnerb, *Ledru-Rollin* (Paris: Presses universitaires de France, 1948); Hélène Lemesle, *Vautours, singes et cloportes: Ledru-Rollin, ses locataires et ses concierges au XIXe siècle* (Paris, Association pour le développement de l'histoire économique), 2003.

68. Alexandre Ledru-Rollin, *Introduction: De l'influence de l'école française sur le droit au XIXe siècle* (Paris: Patris, 1845), xxv.

69. Ledru-Rollin, *Introduction*, xxx.

70. Ledru-Rollin, *Introduction*, xxvii.

71. Ledru-Rollin, *Introduction*, xxviii.

72. Ledru-Rollin, *Introduction*, xxix.

73. Ledru-Rollin, *Introduction*, xxix.

74. Ledru-Rollin, *Introduction*, xlix.

75. Ledru-Rollin, *Introduction*, li.

76. Louis Blanc, "D'un projet d'alliance intellectuelle entre l'Allemagne et la France," *La revue indépendante* (1843): 40–67. On this article see Arnold Ruge, *Aux origines du couple Franco-Allemand: Critique du nationalisme et révolution démocratique avant 1848*, trans. Lucien Calvié (Toulouse, France: Presses universitaires du Mirail, 2004), 44–51.

77. Blanc, "D'un projet d'alliance," 67.

78. Blanc, "D'un projet d'alliance," 49.

79. On this text and Ruge's project to unite French revolutionary thought and left Hegelianism, see Lucien Calvié, "Ruge and Marx," in Douglas Moggach, ed., *Politics, Religion, and Art: Hegelian Debates* (Evanston, IL: Northwestern University Press, 2011).

80. Arnold Ruge, *Aux origines du couple Franco-Allemand*.

81. "L'École de Hégel à Paris," *La revue indépendante* (1844): 481–86.

82. "Une des dernières livraisons de cette Revue contenait un long article de M. Louis Blanc sur les rapports de la France et de l'Allemagne et sur l'union intellectuelle de ces deux pays." "L'École de Hégel à Paris," 482.

83. "L'École de Hégel à Paris," 485.

84. "L'École de Hégel à Paris," 486.

85. "L'École de Hégel à Paris," 485.

86. Letter from Ruge to Marx, Paris, August 1843. Cited in Amaury Catel, *Le traducteur et le demiurge: Herman Ewerbeck un communiste allemande à Paris (1841–1860)* (Nancy: Arbre bleu, 2019), 33.

87. Letter from Marx to Ruge, Kreuznach, September 1843. Cited in Catel, *Le traducteur*, 34n.

88. On Marx's democratization of Hegel, see Jacob Roundtree, "Marx's Democratization of Hegel's 'Philosophy of Right,'" *Critical Review* 33, nos. 3–4 (2021): 431–61. All quotations from Marx are from the unpaginated online version: Karl Marx, *A Contribution to the Critique of Hegel's Philosophy of Right*, December 1843–January 1844, first published in *Deutsch-Französische Jahrbücher* (Paris), 7 & 10 February 1844; proofed and corrected by Andy Blunden (February 2005) and Matthew Carmody (2009), https://www.marxists.org/archive/marx/works/1843/critique-hpr/intro.htm, accessed 2019–21.

89. Jonathan Sperber, *Karl Marx: A Nineteenth-Century Life* (New York: Liveright, 2013), 111–13.

90. Patricia Springborg, "Karl Marx on Democracy, Participation, Voting, and Equality," *Political Theory* 12, no. 4 (November 1984): 537–56, esp. 538.

91. Roger Boesche, "Tocqueville and Marx: Not Opposites," *The Tocqueville Review / La revue Tocqueville* 35, no. 2 (2014): 167–96.

92. "In democracy none of the moments obtains a significance other than what befits it. Each is really only a moment of the whole Demos." Karl Marx, *Critique of Hegel's "Philosophy of Right."*

93. Louis Carré, "Hegel penseur de l'État contre la démocratie," *Tumultes* 44, no. 1 (2015): 37–51.

94. Conze, "Demokratie," 889.

95. See in particular Miguel Abensour, *La démocratie contre l'État: Marx et le moment machiavélien* (Paris: Presses universitaires de France, 1997). In his analysis of Abensour's work, Sfez Gérald argues: "Abensour fait sortir Marx de prison, et, en premier lieu, de la prison marxiste." Sfez Gérald, "Notes et lectures: Miguel Abensour, La démocratie contre l'État," *Multitudes*, September 1997, pp. 39–40.

96. Nicolas Poirier, "Politique et démocratie chez Marx," *Cités* 59, no. 3 (2014): 45–59.

97. On this history, see for example Albert Weale's important volumes *Modern Social Contract Theory* (Oxford, UK: Oxford University Press, 2020) and *Democratic Justice and the Social Contract* (Oxford, UK: Oxford University Press, 2013).

98. Weale notes that a key problem utilitarianism posed for contract theory was social obligation: "So the question arises as to whether there is a form of social contract theory that

balances the claims of obligations with the requirement for prudent self-regard." Weale, *Modern Social Contract Theory*, 21.

99. Honoré de Balzac, *Le Père Goriot* (Paris: Gallimard, 1976).

100. Balzac consistently critiqued the notion of a contract based solely on individual will in every aspect of modern society. See for example, his novel *Le contrat du marriage*. One might also profitably read *La peau de chagrin* as recounting the relentless dangers of entering into a contract solely to realize one's will, and the isolation, terror, and death that results.

101. Balzac, *Le Père Goriot*.

102. Jean-François Kervegan, "La théorie hégélienne du contrat: Le juridique, le politique, le social," *Revue germanique internationale* 15 (2001): 127–43; Alan Patten, "Hegel and Social Contract Theory," in *Hegel's Idea of Freedom* (Oxford, UK: Oxford University Press, 2002).

103. Hegel, *Philosophy of Right*, §258 (remark).

104. "Il s'éprit de Jean-Jacques, et s'en fit lire tout ce qu'il lui fut possible d'en écouter. . . . Puis il se fit donner un exemplaire du *Contrat Social*, et alla l'épeler sans relâche." George Sand, *Mauprat*, vol. 1 (Paris: Gallimard, 2019 [1837]), 666.

105. George Sand, *Indiana*, vol. 1 (Paris: Gallimard, 2019 [1st ed. 1832]), 78.

106. Alexis de Tocqueville, "On the Point of Departure and Its Importance for the Future of the Anglo-Americans," in *Democracy in America*, ed. Eduardo Nolla, trans. James T. Schleifer (Indianapolis: Liberty Fund, 2010), vol. 1, chapter 2. See also Tocqueville's "Mémoire sur l'influence du point de départ sur les sociétés," presented before the Academy in 1836.

107. Tocqueville, *Democracy in America*, 58.

108. Tocqueville, *Democracy in America*, 64.

109. Tocqueville, *Democracy in America*, 62.

110. Allart, *La femme et la démocratie*, 61.

111. Allart, *La femme et la démocratie*, 85.

112. Allart, *La femme et la démocratie*, 77.

113. Proudhon refers to Hegel throughout his work. Elsewhere he argued, "Qui a résolu le problème de la certitude? Moi et Hegel." On Proudhon's Hegelianism, see Pierre Macherey, "Le quasi-hégélianisme de Proudhon," *La philosophie au sens large*, https://philolarge.hypotheses.org/875#identifier_0_875, accessed May 2021.

114. Pierre-Joseph Proudhon, *Idée générale de la révolution au XIXe siècle* (1851), 124.

115. Proudhon, *Idée générale*, 128.

116. Proudhon, *Idée générale*, 128.

117. Proudhon, *Idée générale*, 126.

118. Proudhon, *Idée générale*, 129.

119. Jules Simon, *La Liberté*, 2nd ed., vol. 1 (Paris: Hachette, 1859), 154, 156.

120. Auguste Comte, *Cours de philosophie positive*, vol. 5 (Paris: Bachelier, 1841), 752.

121. Guillaume De Greef, *Introduction à la sociologie* (Paris: Alcan, 1886), 139.

122. On the notion of revising social contract theory in early sociological thought based on a "sui-generis" concept of the social, see Michael Follert, "Contractual Thought and Durkheim's Theory of the Social: A Reappraisal," *Journal of Classical Sociology* 20, no. 3 (2020): 167–90.

123. De Greef, *Introduction à la sociologie*, 140.

124. Durkheim wrote explicitly about Hobbes's social contract theory in a course for the French national exam, the *agrégation*. See Émile Durkheim, *Hobbes à l'agrégation: Un cours d'Émile Durkheim suivi par Marcel Mauss* (Paris: Éditions de l'EHESS, 2011); and on Rousseau's social contract, see Émile Durkheim, *Montesquieu et Rousseau précurseurs de la sociologie* (Paris:

Librairie Marcel Rivière et Cie., 1966; 1st edition published in *Revue de Métaphysique et de Morale* 25 (1918): 1–23, 129–61).

125. Émile Durkheim, "La science sociale selon de Greef," *Revue philosophique* 22 (1886): 658–63.

126. Alfred Fouillée, *La science sociale contemporaine* (Paris: Hachette, 1880), 113.

127. Fouillée, *La science sociale*, 113.

128. Fouillée, *La science sociale*, 114.

129. Fouillée, *La science sociale*, v.

130. Bruno Karsenti, introduction to *D'une philosophie à l'autre: Les sciences sociales et la politique des Modernes* (Paris: Gallimard, 2014).

131. Charles Comte, "Considérations sur l'état moral de la nation française, et sur les causes de l'instabilité de ses institutions," *Le Censeur européen, ou examen de diverses questions de droit public, et des divers ouvrages littéraires et scientifiques, considérés dans leurs rapports avec le progrès de la civilisation* (Paris: Bureau de l'administration, 1817–19), vol. 1 (1817).

132. François Guizot, *Essais sur l'histoire de France* (Paris: Briere, 1823), 87.

133. George Sand, "Préface de l'édition Perrotin de 1842," in *Indiana* (Paris: Gallimard, 2019), 248.

134. Victor Considerant, *Manifeste de la démocratie: Première partie, État de la société* (Paris: Librairie Phalanstérienne, 1847), 5.

135. Victor Considerant, *Du sens vrai de la doctrine de la redemption* (Paris: Librairie Phalanstérienne, 1849), 58.

136. Céline Spector, "Aux origines de la sociologie: 'Le Contrat Social de Rousseau' d'Émile Durkheim (1918)," *Les Études philosophiques* 4, no. 184 (2018): 535–68, esp. 536.

Chapter Two

1. Karl Marx, "Proceedings of the Sixth Rhine Province Assembly. Third Article. Debates on the Law on Thefts of Wood," *Rheinische Zeitung* 298, supplement (October 25, 1842).

2. George Sand, *Indiana*, vol. 1 (Paris: Gallimard, 2019 [1832]), 20–21.

3. Fernand Braudel, *Civilization and Capitalism*, vol. 1, *The Structures of Everyday Life* [1967], trans. Sîan Reynolds (Berkeley: University of California Press, 1992), 69–70.

4. Sara B. Pritchard and Thomas Zeller, "The Nature of Industrialization," in Martin Reuss and Stephen H. Cutcliffe, eds., *The Illusory Boundary: Environment and Technology in History* (Charlottesville: University of Virginia Press, 2010), 92.

5. Jurgen Osterhammel, "Deforestation," *Transformation of the World: A Global History of the Nineteenth Century*, trans. Patrick Camiller (Princeton, NJ: Princeton University Press, 2014).

6. Michael Williams, "Forests." in B. L. Turner, ed., *The Earth as Transformed by Human Action: Global and Regional Changes in the Biosphere over the Past 300 Years* (Cambridge, UK: Cambridge University Press, 1990), 180.

7. Andrée Corvol, "L'arbre et la nature (XVIIe–XXe siècles)," *Histoire, économie et société* 6, no. 1 (1987): 67–82.

8. K. J. Kirby and C. Watkins, eds., *The Ecological History of European Forests* (Wallingford, UK: CABI International, 1998); C. Watkins, *European Woods and Forests: Studies in Cultural History* (Wallingford, UK: CABI International, 1998); K. J. Kirby and Charles Watkins, *Europe's Changing Woods and Forests from Wildwood to Managed Landscapes* (Wallingford, UK: CABI International, 2015).

9. Andrée Corvol, *L'homme au bois, histoires des relations de l'homme et de la forêt, XVIIe–XXe siècle* (Paris: Fayard, 1987).

10. Peter Sahlins, *Forest Rites: The War of the Demoiselles in Nineteenth-Century France* (Cambridge, MA: Harvard University Press, 1998), 10.

11. Andrée Corvol, ed., "Les matériaux de la ville: Du bois au béton?," *Forêt, Environnement, et Société, XVIe–XXe siècle* (Institut d'histoire moderne et contemporaine, Centre national de la recherche scientifique), no. 8 (1998): 83.

12. Debate on the "Achèvement du chemin de fer de l'ouest," in *Comptre rendu des séances de l'Assemblée nationale législative*, vol. 13 (Paris: Panckoucke, 1851), 456.

13. Éric Tisserand notes the extensive development of a new industrial sector in the Vosges around sawmills, cabinetmakers, carpenters, luthiers, and papermills that led to the emergence of approximately eight hundred businesses in the middle of the nineteenth century. Éric Tisserand, *La forêt des Vosges Construction d'une filière industrielle, XIXe siècle* (Tours, France: Presses universitaires François-Rabelais, 2018).

14. Jean-Antoine Fabre, *Essai sur la théorie des torrens et des rivières, contenant les moyens les plus simples d'en empêcher les ravages* (Paris: Bidault, 1797), 64.

15. Jean-Baptiste Rougier de La Bergerie, *Mémoires et observations sur les abus des défrichements et la destruction des bois et forêts, avec un projet d'organisation forestière* (Auxerre, France: Impr. de L. Fournier, an IX [1800–1801]).

16. *Discours de Thiers*, vol. 1 (Paris: Calmann Lévy, 1879), 345.

17. M. P. H. Dugied, *Projet de boisement des Basses-Alpes* (Paris: Imprimerie Royale, 1819), 1–2.

18. Corvol, "L'arbre et la nature, 67–82.

19. *Annales forestières*, no. 1, p. 8.

20. *Annales forestières*, no. 1, p. 15.

21. Charles Lardy, *Mémoire sur les dévastations des forêts dans les Hautes Alpes et les moyens d'y remédier* (Zurich: Ulrich, 1842), 39.

22. Alexandre Surell, *Étude sur les torrents des Hautes-Alpes* (Paris: Cabilian-Goeury, 1841).

23. Surell, *Étude sur les torrents*, xvii, 128, 129, 131.

24. Jean-Baptiste Fressoz and Fabien Locher, "Régénérer la nature, restaurer les climats: François-Antoine Rauch et les Annales Européennes de physique végétale et d'économie publique, 1815–1830," *Le Temps des médias* 25, no. 2 (2015): 1, 52–69.

25. Emmanuel Le Roy Ladurie, *Abrégé d'histoire du climat: Du Moyen Âge à nos jours* (Paris: Armand Colin, 2007); interviews with Anouchka Vasak.

26. Jean-Baptiste Fressoz and Fabien Locher, *Les Révoltes du ciel: Une histoire du changement climatique XVe–XXe siècle* (Paris: Seuil, 2020).

27. Rauch has been the subject of some interesting work. See Jean-Baptiste Fressoz and Fabien Locher, "Régénérer la nature, restaurer les climats: François-Antoine Rauch et les 'Annales Européennes de physique végétale et d'économie publique,' 1815–1830," *Le Temps des médias* 25, no. 2 (2015): 52–69; and Diana K. Davis, *The Arid Lands: History, Power, Knowledge* (Cambridge, MA: MIT Press, 2016).

28. Alexandre Moreau de Jonnès, *Premier mémoire en réponse à la question proposée par l'Académie royale de Belgique* (Brussels, 1825).

29. Alexandre Moreau de Jonnès, *Premier mémoire en réponse à la question proposée par l'Académie royale de Belgique* (Brussels, 1825).

30. Alfred Lacroix, "La vie de Moreau de Jonnès," *Journal de la statistique de Paris* 74 (1933): 143–60.

31. De Jonnès, *Premier mémoire*, xix.
32. De Jonnès, *Premier mémoire*, xxvi–xxvii.
33. De Jonnès, *Premier mémoire*, 51.
34. De Jonnès, *Premier mémoire*, 60.
35. Charles Fourier, "Manuscrits de Fourier: Détérioration matérielle de la planète (4ᵉ cahier, 11ᵉ pièce, côté 9)," *La Phalange: Revue de la science sociale* vol. 5 (1847): 402.
36. Fourier, "Détérioration matérielle de la planète," 402.
37. On Fourier's social science, see Mercklé, Pierre. "La 'science sociale' de Charles Fourier," *Revue d'Histoire des Sciences Humaines* 15, no. 2 (2006): 69–88.
38. Fourier, "Détérioration matérielle de la planète," 403.
39. Fourier, "Détérioration matérielle de la planète," 429–30.
40. François Arago, "Notices scientifiques: Sur la prédiction du temps," *Œuvres complètes de François Arago*, vol. 8 (Paris: Gide, 1858), 16.
41. Joseph Jean Nicolas Fuster, *Des changements dans le climat de la France: Histoire de ses révolutions météorologiques* (Paris: Capelle, 1845).
42. Fuster, *Des changements*, 46.
43. Émile Souvestre, *Le Finistère en 1836* (Brest, France: Come, 1838), 126.
44. Émile Mouchon, *Dictionnaire de bromatologie végétale exotique, comprenant en outre de nombreux articles consacrés aux plantes indigènes dont on ignore ou néglige généralement les propriétés alimentaires* (Paris: Baillière, 1848), 341.
45. Dugied, *Projet de boisement*, 80.
46. De Jonnès, *Premier mémoire*, 184.
47. Surell, *Étude sur les torrents*, 220.
48. Adolphe-Jérôme Blanqui, *Du déboisement des montagnes* (Paris: Renard, 1846).
49. Blanqui, *Du déboisement*, 30.
50. Blanqui, *Du déboisement*, 39–40, 41, 51, 61.
51. Blanqui, *Du déboisement*, 61.
52. Vincent Milliot, "Gouverner les hommes et leur faire du bien: La police de Paris au siècle des Lumières (conceptions, acteurs, pratiques)," Habilitation à diriger des recherches, Université de Paris 1, Panthéon Sorbonne, defended in 2002.
53. Paolo Napoli, *Naissance de la police moderne* (Paris: La Découverte, 2003).
54. Markus D. Dubber, *The Police Power: Patriarchy and the Foundations of American Government* (New York: Columbia University Press, 2005), 3.
55. Loughlin, *Foundations of Public Law*, 423.
56. Steven Kaplan, *Bread, Politics and Political Economy in the Reign of Louis XV* (The Hague: Martinus Nijhoff, 1976); Kaplan, *Provisioning Paris: Merchants and Milliers in the Grain and Flour Trade during the Eighteenth Century* (Ithaca, NY: Cornell University Press, 1984); Vincent Milliot, *L'admirable police: Tenir Paris au siècle des Lumières* (Paris: Champ Vallon, 2016); Catherine Denys, *Police et sécurité au XVIIIe siècle dans les villes de la frontière franco-belge* (Paris: L'Harmattan, 2002).
57. For an extended discussion of the lack of any clear boundary between the two, see Steven Kaplan, *The Stakes of Regulation: Perspectives on "Bread, Politics and Political Economy" Forty Years Later* (London and New York: Anthem Press, 2015).
58. Quoted in Jean-Louis Guérin, "Histoire d'une forêt écartelée entre colbertisme et libéralisme: Des capitulaires de Charlemagne au Grenelle de l'Environnement, en passant par Vauban," *Responsabilité & Environnement*, no. 53 (January 2009).

NOTES TO PAGES 52-55

59. Antoine Pecquet, *Loix forestières de France: Commentaire historique et raisonné sur l'ordonnance de 1669, les règlements antérieurs, & ceux qui l'ont suivie; auquel on a joint une bibliothèque des auteurs qui ont écrit sur les matières d'eaux & forêts, & une notice des coutumes relatives à ces mêmes matières*, vol. 1 (Paris, 1753), xiv–xv.

60. The other great ordinances focused on commerce, the navy, the code noir, criminal law, and the census.

61. See "Eaux et forêts" in *L'Encyclopédie méthodique, ou par ordre de matières: Jurisprudence* (Paris: Panckoucke, 1782–89), 144.

62. Michelle Vovelle, preface to Denis Woronoff, *Révolution et espaces forestiers: Groupe d'histoire des forêts françaises* (Paris: L'Harmattan, 1988), 7–8.

63. Le Trosne, *De l'ordre social* (Paris: Debure, 1777), 75n.

64. Martine Chalvet, *Une histoire de la forêt* (Paris: Seuil, 2011).

65. Ch. M. Galisset, *Corps du droit français ou recueil complet des lois . . .*, vol. 1, no. 1 (Paris: Blanchet, 1843), 533.

66. See Sawyer, *Demos Assembled*, chapter 1.

67. Charles Bonaventure Marie Toullier, *Le droit civil français, suivant l'ordre du Code, ouvrage*, vol. 1 (Brussels, 1837), 64.

68. Marie-Noële Grand-Mesnil, "La loi du 29 septembre 1791," in Woronoff, *Révolution et espaces forestiers*, 204.

69. Henrion de Pansey, *De l'autorité judiciaire* (Paris: 1818), 536.

70. P.-Julien Alletz, *Dictionnaire de police moderne pour toute la France*, vol. I (1823), 190–200.

71. This included such figures as W. Gottfried von Mosers, Johann Friedrich Stahl, Heinrich Christian von Brocke, J. Beckmann, Johann Jakob Trunk, Johann Heinrich Jung, and Johann Friedrich von Pfeiffer. On these figures see also Kurt Mantel, "History of the International Science of Forestry with Special Consideration of Central Europe; Literature, Training, and Research from the Earliest Beginnings to the Nineteenth Century," *International Review of Forestry Research*, vol. 1 (1964): 1–37.

72. Gunther Heinrich von Berg, *Hanbuch des Teutschen Policeyrecht*, vol. 1, 2nd ed. (Hannover: Gebruder Hahn, 1802), 1–2.

73. *The Well-Ordered Police State: Social and Institutional Change through Law in the Germanies and Russia, 1600–1800* (New Haven, CT: Yale University Press, 1983), 116.

74. Jean-Claude Richez, "Science allemande et foresterie française: L'expérience de la rive gauche du Rhin," in Woronoff, *Révolution et espaces forestiers*, 238.

75. Richez, "Science allemande," 245.

76. In particular, the work of Louis Duhamel du Mondeau, *Traité complet des bois et des forêts* (Paris: Guerin, 1755–67).

77. In particular, the translation of his work by one of the early adherents of the science of forestry who was employed by the Administration générale des eaux et forêts, Jacques-Joseph Baudrillart (1774–1832). G. L. Hartig, *Instruction sur la culture du bois à l'usage des forestiers* (Paris: Tourneisen, 1807). On the importation of German sylviculture and forest science after the Revolution, see Marie-Jeanne Lionnet, "La Sylviculture à la Conquête de la Planète," *Responsabilité & Environnement*, no. 53 (January 2009).

78. Jacques-Joseph Baudrillart, *Traité général des eaux et forêts, chasses et pêches*, vol. I (Paris: Huzard, 1821), iv.

79. Bernard Lorentz and A. Parade, preface to *Cours élémentaire de culture des bois* (Paris: Huzard, 1837).

80. M. Brousse, *Code forestier, avec l'exposé des motifs, la discussion des deux chambres, des observations sur les articles et l'ordonnance d'exécution* (Paris: Béchet, 1827), 2.

81. Brousse, *Code forestier*, 4–8.

82. Brousse, *Code forestier*, 4.

83. Brousse, *Code forestier*, 3.

84. Brousse, *Code forestier*, 6.

85. Louis Jean Joseph Pierre Cappeau, *Traité de la législation rurale et forestière*, vol. 1 (Marseille: Antoine Ricard, 1824), 123.

86. Brousse, *Code forestier*, 15.

87. Jules Michelet, *Histoire de France*, vol. 2 (Paris: Hachette, 1833), 53.

88. Brousse, *Code forestier*, 2.

89. Brousse, *Code forestier*, 40.

90. Chalvet, *Une histoire de la forêt*.

91. Brousse, *Code forestier*, 61.

92. Brousse, *Code forestier*, 195.

93. Édouard Laboulaye, *Histoire du droit de propriété foncière en occident* (Paris, 1839), 163.

94. Gérard Buttoud, "L'État forestier face au droit nouveau," in Woronoff, *Révolution et espace forestier*, 217.

95. "The state needed to ensure for each individual the right to use their property without being bothered by the action of external agents and to allow for the efficient allocation of resources; legislation and encouragement were its means of action. For the rest, the state needed to go further: to ensure property, and the complete mastery of certain areas of the territory." D. Ponchelet, "Le débat autour du déboisement dans le département des Basses-Alpes, France (1819–1849)," *Revue de géographie alpine* 83, no. 1 (1995): 53–66, here 58.

96. *Annales forestières*, no. 1, p. 4.

97. *Annales forestières*, no. 1, p. 15.

98. Philippe Vigier, "Les troubles forestiers du premier XIXe siècle français," *Revue forestière française*, 32 (Spring 1980): 128–135.

99. Sahlins, *Forest Rites*, 12.

100. *Annales forestières*, no. 1, p. 56.

101. *Annales forestières*, no. 1;56.

102. *Annales forestières*, no. 1, p. 229.

103. *Annales forestières*, no. 1, p. 229.

104. *Annales forestières*, no. 1, p. 230.

105. Soboul Albert. "Les troubles agraires de 1848," *1848 et les révolutions du XIXe siècle* 39, no. 180 (June 1948): 1–20.

106. For the most convincing argument along these lines, see E. P. Thompson, *Customs in Common: Studies in Traditional Popular Culture* (New York: New Press, 1993).

107. Blanqui, *Du déboisement*, 61.

108. Blanqui, *Du déboisement*, 93–94.

109. Blanqui, *Du déboisement*, 93–94.

110. Blanqui, *Du déboisement*, 93–94.

111. Information on this case comes from *Discours à la Chambre des Députés; Dupin, Réquisitoires . . .* , vol. 5 (Paris: Videcq, 1842), and *Annales forestières*, no. 1 (1842).

112. "Affaire des onze communes d'Alsace contre la ville d'Haguenau et le préfet du Bas-Rhin: Droits d'usage," Cour de cassation (présidence de M. Portalis), audiences des 22 et 23 mars, *Annales forestières*, no. 1 (1842).

113. "Affaire des onze communes d'Alsace," 494.

114. "Affaire des onze communes d'Alsace," 494.

115. "Affaire des onze communes d'Alsace," 494.

116. Archives nationales BB18 1460. Pyrénées-Orientales. Canton de Montlouis. Lettre du procureur de la République de Prades au procureur général de Montpellier. 26 juillet 1848.

117. Archives nationales BB18 1460. Rhin (Bas-). Lettre de G. Goldenberg, representant du Bas-Rhin, au ministre de la Justice. 12 juillet 1849.

118. Sahlins, *Forest Rites*.

119. Karl Marx, "Debates on the Law on the Theft of Wood," https://www.marxists.org/archive/marx/works/download/Marx_Rheinishe_Zeitung.pdf.

120. Marx, "Theft of Wood."

121. Marx, *Critique of Hegel's Doctrine of the State*.

Chapter Three

1. J. Gay, *Histoire de l'Administration de la ville de Paris et études diverses sur l'organisation municipale avant et après la Révolution*, ed. A. Astaing and de Fr. Lormant (Nancy, France: Presses universitaires de Nancy, 2011).

2. Jean Tulard, *Paris et son administration, 1800–1830*, Commission des travaux historiques, 13 (Paris: Imprimerie municipale, 1976).

3. On the end of the municipal old regime in the first half of the nineteenth century, see Frédéric Moret, *The End of the Urban Ancient Regime in England*, trans. Melanie Moore (Cambridge, UK: Cambridge Scholars, 2015).

4. See, in particular, Christine Guionnet, *L'apprentissage de la politique moderne: Les élections municipales sous la monarchie de Juillet* (Paris: L'Harmattan, 1997); Charles Pouthas, "Les projets de réforme administrative sous la Restauration," *Revue d'Histoire moderne* (1926); Rudolf Von Thadden, *La Centralisation contestée: L'administration napoléonienne, enjeu politique de la Restauration (184–1830)*, trans. Hélène Cusa and Patrick Charbonneau (Paris: Actes Sud, 1989); Michel Offerlé, "Capacités politiques et politisations: Faire voter et voter, XIXe–XXe siècles," *Genèses* 67 (2007); André-Jean Tudesq, "Institutions locales et histoire sociale: La loi municipale de 1831 et ses premières applications," *Annales de la faculté des lettres et sciences humaines de Nice* 9–10 (1969): 327–63; Philippe Vigier, "La monarchie de Juillet" and "La deuxième République," in L. Fougère, J.-P. Machelon, and F. Monnier, eds., *Les communes et le pouvoir: Histoire politique des communes françaises de 1789 à nos jours* (Paris: PUF, 2002), 203–62.

5. On this point, see Stephen W. Sawyer, "Définir un intérêt particulier parisien: Les élections et l'administration municipal de Paris au milieu du XIXe siècle," *Annales: Histoire, Sciences Sociales* 2, (2019): 407–33.

6. Mauric Genty, *Paris 1789–1795: Apprentissage de la citoyenneté* (Messidor: Éditions sociales, 1987).

7. Stephen W. Sawyer, "Locating Paris: The Parisian Municipality in Revolutionary France, 1789–1852," PhD dissertation, University of Chicago, under the direction of Jan E. Goldstein, 2008.

8. Tulard, *Paris et son administration*.

9. Maurice Felix, *Le régime administratif et financier de la ville de Paris et du département de la Seine* (Paris: La documentation française, 1957).

10. Tulard, *Paris et son administration*.

11. *Correspondance de Napoléon*, vol. 12 (Paris: H. Plon, J. Dumaine, 1863), 38.

12. *Observations et décisions relatives au budget de la ville de Paris*, February 13, 1806, 37–38.

13. Louis Passy, *Frochot Préfet de la Seine: Histoire administrative (1789–1813)* (Paris: Evreux, 1867), 233.

14. Passy, *Frochot Préfet de la Seine*, 233.

15. "Fut-il convoqué au nom de ses fonctions municipales, comme c'est le conseil général qui les exerce, c'est le conseil général que l'on convoque, et c'est le conseil général qui parait" (Passy, p. 247). On the enduring importance of corporate governance in Paris during the Empire, see Claire Lemercier, *Un si discret pouvoir: Aux origines de la chambre de commerce de Paris, 1803–1853* (Paris: La Découverte, 2003).

16. *Correspondance de Napoléon*, vol. 12, p. 56.

17. *Budget de la ville de Paris pour l'exercice 1818 et compte de ses recettes et dépenses pendant l'exercice 1816* (Paris: Ballard, 1818).

18. Geneviève Massa-Gille, *Histoire des emprunts de la ville de Paris, 1814–1875*, Commission des travaux historiques 12 (Paris: Imprimerie municipale, 1973).

19. *Budget de la ville de Paris pour l'exercice 1818*.

20. *Budget de la ville pour l'exercice 1818*.

21. *Budget de la ville pour l'exercice 1818*.

22. See Tulard, "Politique et administration," chap. 1 in part 4 of *Paris et son administration*; and Michel Fleury, "Rapport sur les conférences d'Histoire de Paris," in *Annuaire de la IVe section de l'École pratique des hautes études* (1973–74), 526.

23. Tulard, *Paris et son administration*, 474.

24. Charles Pouthas, "Les projets de réforme administrative sous la Restauration," *Revue d'Histoire moderne* (1926): 351.

25. D'Argenson, *Considérations sur le Gouvernement: With Other Political Texts*, ed. Andrew Jainchill (Oxford, UK: Voltaire Foundation, 2019).

26. "Pour que le public fût admis autant qu'il se peut dans le gouvernement du public." D'Argenson, *Considérations*, 153.

27. Jean-Jacques Rousseau, "Lettres écrites de la Montagne," in *Collection complète des œuvres, Genève, 1780–1789*, vol. 6, letter 8, http://www.rousseauonline.ch/Text/lettres-ecrites-de-la-montagne.php.

28. See Stephen W. Sawyer, "The Forgotten Democratic Tradition of Revolutionary France," *Modern Intellectual History* 18, no. 3 (2021): 629–57; and Dan Edelstein and Stephen W. Sawyer, "Sovereignty and Government in the French Revolution," forthcoming.

29. Royer-Collard, *De la liberté de la presse, discours* (Paris, 1949).

30. Royer-Collard, *De la liberté*, 49.

31. On the history of the word "decentralization," see Pierre Rosanvallon, *Le modèle politique français: La société civile contre le jacobinisme 1789 à nos jours* (Paris: Seuil, 2004). What follows in this analysis breaks partially with Rosanvallon's interpretation of the word "decentralization" in the first half of the nineteenth century.

NOTES TO PAGES 78-85

32. On this point, see the introduction to the second volume of Stefano Mannoni, *Une et indivisible: Storia dell'addentramento ammnistrativo in Francia* (Milan: Giuffre, 1994). Mannoni poses the problem in these terms, "Local democracy responds to the demands of the participation of taxpayers in daily decision making according to the principle 'no taxation without representation.' . . . Why, then, was decentralization so difficult to establish in France as well as throughout Continental Europe during the high point of liberal rule? . . . [It was because] their governmental project attempted to combine the liberties of property holders with administrative centralization" (pp. 3-4).

33. Rudolf Von Thadden, *La Centralisation contestée: L'administration napoléonienne, enjeu politique de la Restauration (184-1830)*, trans. Hélène Cusa and Patrick Charbonneau (Paris: Actes Sud, 1989), 226.

34. Michael Mann, *Sources of Social Power*, vol. 2 (Cambridge, UK: Cambridge University Press, 1993).

35. Louis Blanc, *L'état et la commune* (Paris: 1841).

36. Blanc, *L'état et la commune*, 32. Emphasis in original.

37. Louis Blanc, *L'état et la commune* (Brussels: Lacroix, 1866, 2nd ed.), 61.

38. *Archives parlementaires*, 2nd series, vol. 66, p. 579.

39. *Journal des débats*, January 12, 1833.

40. Quoted in Jocelyn George,"Pouvoir Local ou 'Intérêt Local'?"in Roger Dupuy, ed., *Pouvoir local et révolution: La frontière intérieure* (Rennes, France: Presses universitaires de Rennes, 1995), 467.

41. Von Thadden, *La Centralisation contestée*.

42. *Archives parlementaires*, 2nd series, vol. 81, pp. 624-25.

43. These thirty-six or forty-eight members would be joined by eight more members—including four from the two rural arrondissements, which were also part of the Department of the Seine—to form the General Council.

44. *Archives parlementaires*, 2nd series, vol. 85, p. 623.

45. *Archives parlementaires*, 2nd series, vol. 85, p. 625.

46. *Archives parlementaires*, 2nd series, vol. 85, p. 624.

47. *Archives parlementaires*, 2nd series, vol. 85, p. 625.

48. *Archives parlementaires*, 2nd series, vol. 85, p. 625.

49. *Archives parlementaires*, 2nd series, vol. 85, p. 621.

50. *Archives parlementaires*, 2nd series, vol. 85, p. 622.

51. Charles Pouthas, "Les projets de réforme administrative sous la Restauration," *Revue d'Histoire moderne* (1926): 351. Rudolf Von Thadden, in his work on decentralization during the Restoration, has noted a similar pattern. See Von Thadden, *La Centralisation contestée*.

52. Alexandre de Laborde, *Paris municipe: Tableau de l'administration de la ville de Paris, depuis les temps les plus reculés jusqu'à nos jours, pour servir à l'examen du nouveau projet de loi municipal pour la ville de Paris* (Paris: 1833), 1.

53. De Laborde, *Paris municipe*, 77.

54. De Laborde, *Paris municipe*, 1.

55. De Laborde, *Paris municipe*, 114.

56. *Gazette municipale de la ville de Paris et du département de la Seine*, April 1843. Boldface in original.

57. *Archives parlementaires*, 2nd series, vol. 85, pp. 620-22.

58. *Le national*, January 15, 1834.

59. *Le national*, November 23, 1834.

60. On election day, *Le national* stated clearly, "We hope that the government's ignoble actions will not be supported." November 27, 1834.

61. *Le constitutionnel*, November 25, 1834.

62. *Le constitutionnel*, November 25, 1834.

63. *Le constitutionnel*, November 25, 1834.

64. *Journal des débats*, November 24, 1834.

65. Archives de Paris, D2M2/4.

66. The eleven candidates originally on the municipal council from 1830 to 1834 were Aubé, Besson, Chateaugiron, Cochin, Gerron, Ganneron, Lafoulotte, Lahure, Lebeau, Lehon, and Marcellot.

67. *Le constitutionnel*, November 26, 1834.

68. *Le national*, November 29, 1834.

69. Archives de Paris, VD4/12.

70. *Le constitutionnel*, December 14, 1837.

71. *Le national*, January 16, 1834.

72. Arago and Lafitte were both municipal councillors as well as important members of the opposition throughout the July Monarchy.

73. Pierre Rosanvallon notes that 113,127 signatures were received by the Chamber of Deputies in 1841. Rosanvallon, *Sacre du citoyen*, 277n.

74. Maurice Agulhon has argued that in 1848 the opposition was lacking in any sort of coherent organization "covering a complete and coherent network for France as a whole or capable of establishing links between all republicans." Maurice Agulhon, *The Republican Experiment, 1848–1852* (Cambridge, UK: Cambridge University Press, 1983), 19. This is no doubt true in the strictest sense, but the history of the Central Committee reveals the extent to which the republicans had been preparing a political structure since the 1840s. While there did not exist a clearly defined republican party, which necessarily assumes a corollary "party politics," the organization of the opposition that sought to democratize French administrative and political life was far more structured than Agulhon suggests.

75. In his history of the Provisional Government, Elias Regnault explains that there was a rather high level of organization within the committee and its relationship with the rest of the country. He claims that seventeen thousand individuals participated in the banquet campaign, and that two thousand were in Paris and Rouen. He then states in a note: "The author was the secretary of the central committee and was responsible for all correspondence. He can testify to the exactitude of these details." Regnault, *Histoire du gouvernement provisoire* (Paris: Victor Lecou, 1850), 25.

76. Claire Lemercier, *Un si discret pouvoir*.

77. *Le national*, November 13, 1847.

78. *Le siècle*, November 3, 1847.

79. *Le siècle*, December 8, 1847.

80. *Le siècle*, December 9, 1847.

81. For example, Guionnet cites a republican newspaper in Burgundy in which a candidate argued: "I think that members of the Municipal Council should be chosen according to the different classes and, therefore, it is necessary to choose among those citizens who are part of the commercial enterprises which provide the most wealth for the city. . . . This business is that of

liquids. Therefore, we need a wine wholesaler, a vinegar producer, and an owner of vineyards." Christine Guionnet, *L'apprentissage de la politique moderne*.

82. "Élections du Conseil Général du Département de la Seine," Archives de Paris, VD6/542/4.

83. "Élections du Conseil Général du Département de la Seine."

84. "Élections du Conseil Général du Département de la Seine."

85. "Élections du Conseil Général du Département de la Seine."

86. "M. Considerant, a Messieurs les électeurs du 10ᵉ arrondissement," Archives de Paris, VD6/542/4.

87. *Le national*, November 26, 1846.

88. *Le national*, November 23, 1846.

89. *Le national*, November 23, 1846.

90. *Le constitutionnel*, November 26, 1843.

91. *Le constitutionnel*, November 23, 1843.

92. *Le constitutionnel*, December 9, 1843.

93. *Le national*, November 27, 1846.

94. *Le national*, November 29, 1846.

95. *Le national*, November 26, 1846.

96. *Le national*, November 27, 1846.

97. Charles Merrau, *Souvenirs de L'Hotel de Ville de Paris, 1848–1852* (Paris: Plon, 1875), 347.

98. Louis-René Villermé, *De la mortalité dans les divers quartiers de la ville de Paris* (1830), 295; https://gallica.bnf.fr/ark:/12148/bpt6k81421x.pdf.

99. Joshua Cole, *The Power of Large Numbers: Population, Politics and Gender in Nineteenth-Century France* (Ithaca, NY: Cornell University Press, 2000), 68.

100. Jeanne Gaillard, *Paris, la Ville* (Paris: L'Harmattan, 1998), especially the first chapter "Centralisme et décentralisation urbaine avant 1848," pp. 19–23.

101. "Élections du Conseil Général du Département de la Seine," Archives de Paris, VD6/542/4.

102. *Le national*, November 29, 1846.

103. Nicholas Papayanis, *Planning before Haussman* (Baltimore: Johns Hopkins University Press, 2004), 198.

104. *Le siècle*, July 22, 1843.

105. *Le national*, November 29, 1846.

106. *Le national*, October 19, 1846.

107. *Le national*, November 11, 1846.

108. *Le national*, November 25, 1846.

109. *Le national*, November 29, 1846.

110. *Le national*, November 27, 1846.

111. *Le national*, November 26, 1846.

112. *Le national*, November 29, 1846.

113. *Le national*, November 21, 1846. On November 25 the opposition restated its claim, arguing that for the "freedom from this horrible and often illegally imposed tax, which takes the name of toll-bridges, the restoration of free communications is a contribution to general prosperity."

114. In her history of the Seine, Isabelle Backouche notes the extensive use of private companies for building bridges across the Seine during the Empire, the Restoration, and the first years of the July Monarchy. Thirteen bridges were built between 1802 and 1838 through the use

of privileges granted to private companies, which then had the right to charge tolls. This practice continued in spite of the fact that pay bridges had been abolished during the Revolution. In 1801 the engineer Isnard, head of a commission responsible for building three bridges in Paris, wrote: "We voted in favor of the abolition of toll bridges [during the Revolution]; but in this hour when the public treasury is hardly in a position to make large contributions, public interest requires the help of capitalists in the pursuance of public works." *Archives Nationales*, AD XVI 71, quoted in Isabelle Backouche, *La trace du fleuve: La Seine et Paris, 1750–1850* (Paris: EHESS, 2000), 342. Thus, in spite of the Revolution, the use of private companies for meeting the infrastructural needs of the capital and providing services remained the fundamental means of the local Parisian administration for accomplishing large-scale municipal projects.

115. *Le national*, November 1, 1843.

116. *Le national*, November 29, 1846.

117. Horace Say, *Études sur l'administration de la ville de Paris et du département de la Seine* (Paris: Guillaumin, 1846), 384.

118. Say, *Études sur l'administration*, 385.

Chapter Four

1. Rudolf Virchow, *Collected Essays on Public Health and Epidemiology*, vol. 1, ed. L. J. Rather, trans. Anne Gisemann (Canton, MA: Science History Publications, 1985), 307–15.

2. *Les Misérables* (Paris: Gallimard), 556.

3. Rosen, "Cameralism and the Concept of Medical Police," *Bulletin of the History of Medicine* 27, no. 1 (January–February 1953): 21–42, esp. 21.

4. Peter Baldwin, *Contagion and State in Europe, 1830–1930* (Cambridge, UK: Cambridge University Press, 1999).

5. For his reading of the French case, see in particular Erwin H. Ackerknecht, "Hygiene in France, 1815–1848," *Bulletin of the History of Medicine* 22, no. 2 (March–April 1948): 117–55. On the importance of this period, see also Erwin H. Ackerknecht, "Anticontagionism between 1821 and 1867," *Bulletin of the History of Medicine*, 22, no. 5 (September–October 1948): 562–93.

6. On the question of a liberal approach to public health, see also William Coleman, *Death Is a Social Disease: Public Health and Political Economy in Early Industrial France* (Madison: University of Wisconsin Press, 1982). Coleman also cites the July Monarchy as a high point of liberal approaches to public health.

7. Ann Elizabeth Fowler La Berge, *Mission and Method: The Early Nineteenth-Century French Public Health Movement* (Cambridge, UK: Cambridge University Press, 1992). La Berge argues: "One would get a distorted picture of the public health movement if it were viewed primarily with the context of liberalism. If any one approach dominated the public health movement, it was statism, the notion that it was the responsibility of the state to provide for public health through administrative, legislative and institutional means"(xii).

8. L. S. D. Le Brun, *Traité théorique sur les maladies épidémiques dans lequel on examine s'il est possible de les prévoir, & quels seroient les moyens de les prévenir & d'en arrêter les progrès? Ouvrage qui a été couronné en novembre 1772, par la Faculté de Médecine de Paris, [et] auquel on a depuis ajouté quelques vues relatives à la Pratique* (Paris: Didot, 1776), 125–26.

9. Rosen writes, "The basic problem related to health was the grinding poverty which oppressed a large part of the rural and urban population." Charles Rosen, "Mercantilism and

NOTES TO PAGES 105–110   271

Health Policy in Eighteenth-Century French Thought," *Medical History* 3, no. 4 (October 1959: 259–77, here 267.

10. Henry Ingrand, *Le Comité de salubrité de l'Assemblée nationale constituante. Un essai de réforme de l'enseignement médical, des services d'hygiène et de protection de la santé publique*, doctoral thesis in medicine (Paris: 1934), 174. See "Que sait-on aujourd'hui des comités des assemblées parlementaires?" *La Révolution française*, posted online December 20, 2012.

11. Société royale de médecine, *Nouveau plan de constitution pour la médecine en France présenté à l'Assemblée Nationale par la société royale de médecine* (Paris: 1790), 2.

12. Société royale de médecine, *Nouveau plan*, 104.

13. Société royale de médecine, *Nouveau plan*, 106.

14. "Projet de décret, présenté par M. Guillotin au nom du comité de Salubrité, sur l'enseignement et l'exercice de l'art de guérir, en annexe de la séance du 30 septembre 1791," *Archives Parlementaires de 1787 à 1860, Première série (1787–1799)*, vol. 32 (Paris: Librairie Administrative P. Dupont, 1888). 27–40, here 39–40.

15. "Projet de décret," 39.

16. "Projet de décret," 39.

17. Gérard Jorland, *Une société à soigner: Hygiène et salubrité publiques en France au XIXe siècle* (Paris: Gallimard, 2010).

18. Bernard-Pierre Lecuyer, "L'hygiène en France avant Pasteur," in Claire Salomon-Bayet, ed., *Pasteur et la révolution pastorienne* (Paris: Payot, 1986); Maurizio Gribaudi et Jacques Magaud, *L'Action publique et ses administrateurs dans les domaines sanitaire et social en France, 1800 à 1900* (Paris: Convention de recherche MIRE-INED, 2003).

19. Thomas Le Roux, *Le laboratoire des pollutions industrielles* (Paris: Albin Michel, 2011), 156–57.

20. Le Roux, *Le laboratoire*, 297.

21. La Berge, *Mission and Method*.

22. Bernard-Pierre Lecuyer, "Médecins et observateurs sociaux: Les Annales d'hygiène publique et de médecine légal (1820–1850)," in *Pour une histoire de la statistique*, vol. 1 (Paris: Economica/INSEE, 1977), 445–76.

23. "Le Manifeste," *Annales de l'hygiène publique et de médécine légale*, vol. 1 (1829), 1.

24. Adelon, Andral, Barruel, d'Arcet, Deverge, Esquirol, Keraudren, Leuret, Marc, Orfila, Parent-Duchatelet, and Villermé, *Annales d'hygiène publique et de médecine légale*, vol. 1 (1829), v–vi.

25. Conseil de salubrité, *Rapports généraux des travaux du Conseil de Salubrité pendant les années 1840 à 1845 inclusivement publiés par ordre de M. le Pair de France, Préfet de Police* (Paris: Boucquin, 1847).

26. Conseil de salubrité, *Rapports généraux*.

27. Conseil de salubrité, *Rapports généraux*.

28. Conseil de salubrité, *Rapports généraux*, 2.

29. Conseil de salubrité, *Rapports généraux*, 2.

30. Conseil de salubrité, *Rapports généraux*, 204.

31. Conseil de salubrité, *Rapports généraux*, 72.

32. Conseil de salubrité, *Rapports généraux*, 276.

33. Hortense Allart, *La femme et la démocratie de nos temps* (Paris: Delaunay, 1836), 94.

34. Ulysse Trélat, *De la constitution du corps des médecins et de l'enseignement médical: Des réformes qu'elle devrait subir dans l'intérêt de la science et de la morale publique* (Paris, 1828), 5.

35. The defense is reproduced in *Les Républicains devant les Tribunaux, 1831–1834: Les Révolutions du XIXe Siècle*, vol. 11 (Paris: Edhis, 1974).

36. *Les Républicains devant les Tribunaux, 1831–1834*, 186–88.

37. Flora Tristan, "Aux ouvriers et aux ouvrières," in *L'Union ouvrière*, 2nd ed. (Paris: 1844), 5 (reprint).

38. *Almanach de la France démocratique* (1846), 118.

39. "La vie des ouvriers a Lyon," *Almanach démocratique de la France* (1841), 128.

40. "Histoire d'un Prolétaire racontée par lui-même," *Almanach de la démocratie* (1843).

41. "Le docteur noir, Des hôpitaux et Hospices civils de Paris en 1843," *Almanach de la France démocratique* (1845).

42. "Lorsque chez toi la fièvre arrive, triste et lente / Attache à tes flancs sa tunique brulante / Si la porte est fermée à l'hôpital trop plein / A ton appel, hélas! tout secours se dérobe / Surtout l'homme au froc noir, l'être miseriphobe / Que l'on nomme le médecin." "Le Jury des récompenses pour les ouvriers," *Almanach de la France démocratique* (1847), 134.

43. "Le docteur noir, Des hôpitaux et Hospices civils de Paris en 1843," *Almanach de la France démocratique* (1845).

44. "Le docteur noir," 25.

45. François-Vincent Raspail, "Hygiène ou médecine préventive à observer surtout à l'approche du cholera," *Almanach démocratique et sociale de l'ami du peuple* (1849), 48.

46. "Instruction du peuple-méthode d'enseignement," *Almanach de la France démocratique* (1847), 123.

47. "Instruction du peuple-méthode d'enseignement," *Almanach de la France démocratique* (1847), 124.

48. W. de l'Epine, "Hygiène," *Almanach de la France démocratique* (1845), 128.

49. François-Vincent Raspail, "Projet d'Organisation médicale," *Almanach de la France démocratique* (1845), 112.

50. "Projet d'Organisation médicale," *Almanach de la France démocratique* (1845), 112.

51. W. de l'Epine, "Hygiène," *Almanach démocratique de la France* (1845), 124–28.

52. Raspail, "Projet d'Organisation médicale," 109.

53. La Berge, *Mission and Method*, 16.

54. Ulysse Trélat, *De la constitution du corps des médecins et de l'enseignement médical: Des réformes qu'elle devrait subir dans l'intérêt de la science et de la morale publique* (Paris, 1828), 33.

55. Trélat, *De la constitution du corps des médecins*, 58–60.

56. Trélat, *De la constitution du corps des médecins*, 64.

57. Ph. J. B. Buchez and Ulysse Trelat, *Précis élémentaire d'hygiène* (Paris: 1825), i.

58. Ph. J. B. Buchez, *Introduction à l'étude des sciences médicales* (Paris: 1838).

59. Charles Marchal, *Biographie de F.-V. Raspail, Représentant du peuple* (Paris: 1848).

60. François-Vincent Raspail, "Étude impartiale sur Jean Paul Marat le savant et Jean Paul Marat le révolutionnaire (1836–1863)," in *Nouvelles études historiques et philologiques* (Paris: 1861–64), 243–86, here 248.

61. Raspail, "Étude impartiale sur Jean Paul Marat," 251–52.

62. Raspail, "Étude impartiale sur Jean Paul Marat," 253.

63. Raspail, "Étude impartiale sur Jean Paul Marat," 252.

64. Blanchard et Baulina, *Apothéose de Raspail* (Lyon: 1846).

65. François-Vincent Raspail, *Réforme pénitentiaire: Lettres sur les prisons de Paris*, vol. 2 (Paris: Tamisey et Champion, 1839), 241.

66. Raspail, *Réforme pénitentiaire*, vol. 2, 243.
67. Raspail, *Réforme pénitentiaire*, vol. 2, 253.
68. Raspail, *Réforme pénitentiaire*, vol. 2, 253, 255–56.
69. Raspail, *Réforme pénitentiaire*, vol. 2, 253, 259.
70. Raspail, *Réforme pénitentiaire*, vol. 2, 263–264.
71. Raspail, *Réforme pénitentiaire*, vol. 2, 276. My emphasis.

72. François-Vincent Raspail, *Histoire naturelle de la santé et de la maladie chez les végétaux et chez les animaux en général*, 2nd ed., vol. 1 (Paris: 1845), iv.

73. François-Vincent Raspail, *Manuel annuaire de la santé, ou médecine et pharmacie domestique* . . . (Paris: 1843).

74. "Puisse l'humanite de nos administration doter les hôpitaux de quelque chose d'analogue!" (6); and, further on, "Il est certain, aux yeux de tous les hommes de bonne foi, que lorsque les exigences administratives permettront à notre méthode de s'introduire complètement dans nos hôpitaux, l'administration fera une économie de 50 p. 100; car la moyenne de la durée des maladies diminuera, pour ne pas avoir l'air d'exagérer, des deux tiers au moins." Raspail, *Manuel annuaire de la santé* (1845), 11.

75. For these figures, see Dora B. Weiner, "François-Vincent Raspail: Doctor and Champion of the Poor," *French Historical Studies* 1, no. 2 (1959): 149–71, here 156–57. Weiner points out that "even abroad the Manuel-annuaire was well received. The Preface to an English edition of 1853 urged the British to follow Raspail's therapy. It pointed to his popularity in France: 'M. Raspail's method of preserving health and curing diseases has achieved a most unequivocal and truly legitimate success in France; . . . it has shaken and displaced . . . both the various systems of the old school of medicine, and the more recent importations, Homeopathy and Hydropathy. It is not too much to say that millions have derived solid and lasting benefit from M. Raspail's simple, plain, and lucid insturctions in the difficult art of managing the health.'"

76. Raspail, *Manuel annuaire de la santé* (1845), 1.
77. Raspail, *Manuel annuaire de la santé* (1845), 17.
78. Raspail, *Manuel annuaire de la santé* (1845), 13.
79. Raspail, *Manuel annuaire de la santé* (1845), 18.
80. Raspail, *Manuel annuaire de la santé* (1845), 20.

81. Suzanne Wassermann, "Le Club de Raspail en 1848," *La Révolution de 1848: Bulletin de la société d'histoire de la révolution de 1848* 5, no. 27 (July–August 1908): 589–605, esp. 591.

82. François-Vincent Raspail, *L'Ami du Peuple*, April 23, 1848.

83. *Procès et défense de F. V. Raspail poursuivi le 19 mai 1846 en exercice illégal de la médicine devant la 8e chambre (police correctionnelle), à la requête du ministère public et sur la dénonciation formelle des sieurs Fouquier, médecin du roi, et Orfila, doyen de la faculté de médecine de Paris, agissant comme vice-président et président d'une association anonyme de médecins* (Paris: 1846), 12–13.

84. *Procès et défense de F. V. Raspail poursuivi le 19 mai 1846*, 26–27.
85. *Procès et défense de F. V. Raspail poursuivi le 19 mai 1846*, 44.

86. Dora B. Weiner, "François-Vincent Raspail: Doctor and Champion of the Poor," *French Historical Studies* 1, no. 2 (1959): 149–71, esp. 160.

87. Raspail, *Réformes sociales* (Paris: Bureau des publications, 1872), i.

88. Marie Lafarge was accused of poisoning her husband in Tulle in 1840. Expert witnesses were called in to determine whether her husband had been murdered by cyanide. In Ann La Berge's account, Doctor Mathieu Orfila, a widely respected doctor and public hygienist as well as "statist," spoke for the plaintiff against Marie Lafarge. The defense called upon Raspail

to offer expert counter-testimony. But Raspail did not arrive at the court until the evening, after Lafarge had already been convicted. He thus led a public campaign against Orfila to defend Lafarge, whom he presented as a victim of cold, elite, and ill-informed science. Orfila responded to Raspail's attacks, thus escalating the case's public reception. He then led the trial of Raspail for the unlawful practice of medicine, as discussed above. La Berge, *Mission and Method*. For Orfila's response, see Matheiu Orfila, de Bussy, and Olivier d'Angers, *Réponse aux écrits de M. Raspail sur l'Affaire de Tulle* (Paris: 1840). See Frédéric Chavaud, "'Cet homme si multiple et si di vers': Orfila et la chimie du crime au xixe siècle," *Sociétés et représentations* 2, no. 22 (2006). On the Lafarge affair, see Laure Adler, *L'amour à l'arsenic: Histoire de Marie Lafarge* (Paris: Denoël, 1986).

89. François-Vincent Raspail, "Lettre à M. le docteur Fabre, 26 septembre 1840," *Gazette des hôpitaux civils et militaires* 2, no. 114.

90. *Le réformateur*, no. 172 (March 30, 1835), reprinted in *Réformes sociales*, 206.

91. *Le réformateur*, no. 109 (January 1835), reprinted in *Réformes sociales*, 109.

92. *Le réformateur*, no. 149 (March 7, 1835), reprinted in *Réformes sociales*, 161.

93. *Le réformateur*, no. 74 (December 21, 1834), reprinted in *Réformes sociales*, 222.

94. *Le réformateur*, no. 160 (March 18, 1835).

95. *Le réformateur*, no. 143 (March 1, 1835), reprinted in *Réformes sociales*, 146–48.

96. *Le réformateur*, no. 144 (March 2, 1835), reprinted in *Réformes sociales*, 149.

97. See Stephen W. Sawyer, "The Forgotten Democratic Tradition of Revolutionary France," *Modern Intellectual History* 3, no. 18 (2021): 1–29.

98. *Le réformateur*, no. 72 (December 19, 1834), reprinted in *Réformes sociales*, 213–14.

99. *Le réformateur*, no. 74 (December 21, 1834), reprinted in *Réformes sociales*, 224.

100. *Le réformateur*, no. 172 (March 30, 1835), reprinted in *Réformes sociales*, 207.

101. *Le réformateur*, no. 143 (March 1, 1835), reprinted in *Réformes sociales*, 143.

102. Cyrus Edson, "The Microbe as a Social Leveller," *North American Review* 161, no. 467 (October 1895): 421–26, esp. 425.

103. *Le réformateur*, no. 30 (November 7, 1834), reprinted in *Réformes sociales*, 236.

104. *Le réformateur*, no. 2 (October 10, 1834), reprinted in *Réformes sociales*, 234.

105. *Le réformateur*, no. 2 (October 10, 1834), reprinted in *Réformes sociales*, 235.

106. Charles Marchal, *Biographie de F.-V. Raspail, Représentant du peuple* (Paris, 1848).

107. *L'Ami du peuple*, March 12, 1848. On Raspail's failed bid for the presidency, see Samuel Hayat, "Se présenter pour protester: La candidature impossible de François-Vincent Raspail en décembre 1848," *Revue française de science politique* 64, no. 5 (October 2014): 869–903.

108. There has been a general trend within the history of public health to celebrate the early nineteenth century. "Proponents often refer back to the original public health movement of the nineteenth century as an exemplar for remodeling the 'new' public health, recalling its imputed interest in environmental conditions and improving living standards rather than the emphasis upon the individual which it seems obtained in mid-twentieth century public health." Deborah Lupton, *The Imperative of Health: Public Health and the Regulated Body* (London: 1995).

109. Ackerknecht, "Hygiene in France," 117.

110. Delasiauve, *Un an de révolution ou situation politique et sociale* (Paris: 1849), 15–16.

111. Ferdinand Sanlaville, *Les logements insalubres et la loi du 13 avril 1850* (Paris: 1897), 5.

Chapter Five

1. Flaubert, *L'Éducation sentimentale* (Paris: Gallimard, 2021), 3.

2. Sydney Webb and Beatrice Webb, *Industrial Democracy* (New York: Longmans, Green, and Company, 1897).

3. Chester Higby and Caroline Willis, "Industry and Labor under Napoleon," *American Historical Review* 53 (1948): 465–80.

4. Françoise Fortunet, "D'une république à l'autre: Les conseils de Prud'hommes ou l'institution d'une justice de paix de l'industrie," in *Justice et République*, ed. Jacques Lornier, Renée Martinage, and Jean Pierre Royer (Lille, France: Ester Editions, 1993), 325–33, esp. 326.

5. Claire Lemercier, "Un modèle français de jugement des pairs: Les tribunaux de commerce, 1790–1880" (unpublished manuscript, 2012), 9.

6. Jean-Pierre Royer, *Histoire de la justice en France du XVIIIe siècle à nos jours* (PUF 1995), 621.

7. Philippe Minard, "Le métier sans institution: Les lois d'Allarde-Le Chapelier de 1791 et leur impact au début du XIXe siècle," in Steven Kaplan and Philippe Minard, eds., *La France, malade du corporatisme? XVIIIe–XXe siècles* (Paris: Belin, 2004), 81–97, esp. 83.

8. See Pierre Rosanvallon, *Le modèle politique français* (Paris: Seuil, 2004); and Alain Plessis, ed., *Naissance des libertés économiques: Liberté du travail et liberté d'entreprendre; Le décret d'Allarde et la loi Le Chapelier, leurs conséquences, 1791–fin XIXe siècle* (Paris: Institut d'histoire de l'industrie, 1993).

9. Kaplan, *Bread, Politics and Political Economy*, 5.

10. As Vincent Milliot explains, for example, the changing notions of police "integrated the new 'professional' recommendations on hygiene and health as well as efforts made in favor of those exposed to copper or lead which denotes an increasing interest in public health." From this perspective, according to Milliot, the lieutenant general of the police in Paris in the eighteenth century is best understood "above all as a political figure, a kind of intermediary between the government and different social categories who sees himself as a kind of orchestra conductor." Milliot, *L'admirable police*, 167.

11. Quoted in Loughlin, *Foundations of Public Law*, 442.

12. On the arguments in favor of restoring the guilds, see Michael P. Fitzsimmons, *From Artisan to Worker: Guilds, the French State, and the Organization of Labor, 1776–1821* (Cambridge, UK: Cambridge University Press, 2010), 210. On the various ways that guilds were to be updated, Fitzsimmons explains: "Any restoration of corporations would not be a simple reversion to the status quo ante. . . . The subordination of the proposed corporations to the prefect, and the titular membership accorded to bishops, administrative, judicial and military officials made clear that the 'new corporations' would not have the quasi-autonomous status of prerevolutionary guilds."

13. Levacher-Duplessis, *Requête au roi et mémoire sur la nécéssité de rétablir les corps de marchands et les communautés des arts et métiers* (Paris: Smith, 1817), 23–24.

14. Levacher-Duplessis, *Requête au roi*, 25.

15. A messieurs les members de la chambre des deputes les horlogers du Roi, AN 41, C 2737. Cited in F. Demier, *La France de la Restauration (1814–1830): L'impossible retour du passé* (Paris: Gallimard, 2012), 128.

16. Levacher-Duplessis, *Requête au roi*, 66.

17. *Gazette nationale ou le moniteur universel*, March 13, 1816.

18. Jean-Baptiste Say, "Des apprentissages, des maîtrises et de leurs effets," in *Œuvres de Jean-Baptiste Say* (Brussels: 1844), 256–57.

19. See, in particular, Keith Tribe's argument for the shift from police to an economic rationality in his "Cameralism and the Science of Government," *Journal of Modern History* 56

(1984): 263–84. See also Paolo Napoli's claim that old regime police powers came to an end with the emergence of a generalized theory of adminstration during the Revolution. Paolo Napoli, *Naissance de la police modern: Pouvoir, norms, société* (Paris: La Découverte, 2003). David Lindenfeld has even gone so far as to argue that this new interest in natural rights in the thirty years following the French Revolution was responsible for an unprecedented interest in "what today would be called political theory: the origins of the state, the concept of sovereignty, the various 'powers' of the state (e.g., legislative, executive, etc.), and the forms of the state (e.g., monarchy, aristocracy, democracy)." Lindenfeld points out that no less than 103 books on natural law appeared between 1790 and 1831 which "accepted Kant's notion that the purpose of the state was to protect individual freedom rather than to promote happiness and welfare" David Lindenfeld, *The Practical Imagination: The German Sciences of State in the Nineteenth Century* (Chicago: University of Chicago Press, 1997), 57.

20. Markus Dirk Dubber, *The Police Power: Patriarchy and the Foundations of American Government* (New York: Columbia University Press, 2005), 3.

21. Fitzsimmons, *From Artisan to Worker*, 146–49.

22. J.-C.-L. Simonde de Sismondi, *Nouveaux principes d'économie politique ou de la richesse dans ses rapports avec la population* (Paris: Delaunay, 1827 [1st ed. 1818]), 53.

23. The conequences of Sismondi's theory of civilization and imperialism are the subject of the final substantive chapter of this book.

24. Alain Cottereau, "Industrial Tribunals and the Establishment of a Kind of Common Law of Labour in Nineteenth-Century France," in *Private Law and Social Inequality in the Industrial Age: Comparing Legal Cultures in Britain, France, Germany and the United States*, ed. Willibald Steinmetz (Oxford, UK: Oxford Univerity Press, 2000), 206–7.

25. "As France emerged from the Terror, disaffection with the unregulated market and workplace was widespread." Fitzsimmons, *From Artisan to Worker*, 2–4.

26. Minard, "Le métier sans institution," 88.

27. *Des communautés d'arts et métiers* (Paris: De l'Imprimerie se la République, 1803).

28. *Des communautés d'arts et métiers*.

29. Henrion de Pansey, *De l'autorité judiciaire* (Paris: 1818), 543.

30. M. Regnaud (de Saint-Jean-d'Angély), le Moniteur universel, session of March 8, 1806.

31. M. Regnaud (de Saint-Jean-d'Angély), le Moniteur universel, session of March 8, 1806.

32. Mollot, *De la compétence des Conseils des Prud'hommes* (Paris, Joubert, 1842), 2.

33. Francis Demier, "L'impossible retour au régime des corporations dans la France de la Restauration," in Plessis, *Naissance des libertés économiques*, 118.

34. Law of April 12, 1803.

35. New councils were founded at Lyons and Clermont in 1806; at Nimes in 1807; at Troyes, Thiers, Sedan, Saint-Quentin, Mulhouse, Carcassonne, and Avignon in 1818; at Tarare, Reims, and Limoux in 1809; at Saint-Étienne, Roubaix, Marseilles, Louviers, Lodève, and Lille in 1810; at Saint-Chamond, Orléans, Amplepuis, and Alais in 1811; and at Strasbourg, Bolbec, and Alencon in 1813. See Higby and Willis, "Industry and Labor under Napoleon."

36. More than three hundred samples of workshop regulations for the nineteenth century have been found and catalogued in the *Règlements d'ateliers* at the Bibliothèque nationale. See Anne Biroleau and Alain Cottereau, *Les règlements d'ateliers, 1798–1936*, Collections Études, Guides et Inventaires, vol. 1 (Paris: Bibliothèque Nationale, 1984); and Alberto Melucci, "Action patronale, pouvoir, organisation: Règlements d'usine et contrôle de la main-d'œuvre au XIXe siècle," *Le Mouvement Social* 97 (October–December 1976): 139–60.

37. Biroleau and Cottereau, *Les règlements d'ateliers*.

38. Émile Bères, *Les classes ouvrières: Moyens d'améliorer leur sort sous le rapport du bien-être matériel et du perfectionnement moral* (Paris: Charpentier, 1836), 165.

39. Louis Antoine Macarel, *Manuel des ateliers dangereux, insalubres ou incommodes* (Paris: 1827).

40. Macarel, *Manuel des ateliers dangereux*.

41. Claire Lemercier, "Juges du commerce et conseillers Prud'hommes face à l'ordre judiciaire (1800–1880): La constitution de frontières judiciaires," in Hélène Michel and Laurent Willemez, eds., *La justice au risque des profanes* (Paris: PUF, 2007), 11–27.

42. Amalia Kessler, "Marginalization and Myth: Corporatist Roots of France's Forgotten Elective Judiciary," *American Journal of Comparative Law* 58, no. 3 (2010): pp. 679–720.

43. Mollot, *De la compétence des conseils des Prud'hommes* (Paris, Joubert, 1842), 37.

44. *Almanach démocratique de la France* (Paris: Pagnerre, 1841), 9–10.

45. "Petit code des ouvriers," *Almanach démocratique de la France* (1841), 87.

46. *Almanach démocratique de la France* (1841), 89.

47. *Almanach démocratique de la France* (1841), 65.

48. *Almanach démocratique de la France* (1841), 97.

49. Jean-Pierre Royer, *Histoire de la justice en France du XVIIIe siècle à nos jours* (Paris: PUF 1995), 620–21.

50. *Echo de la fabrique*, October 15, 1841.

51. Higby and Willis, "Industry and Labor under Napoleon."

52. *Echo de la fabrique*, December 15, 1841.

53. *Echo de la fabrique*, December 15, 1841.

54. "De l'établissement d'un conseil de Prud'hommes à Paris," *Echo de la fabrique*, October 15, 1841.

55. Mollot, *De la compétence des conseils des Prud'hommes*, 126.

56. Mollot, *De la compétence*, 10. Caps for emphasis in original.

57. Cottereau, "Industrial Tribunals," 205–6.

58. Alain Cottereau, "Sens du juste et usages du droit du travail: Une évolution contrastée entre la France et la Grande Bretagne au XIXe siecle," *Revue d'histoire du XIXe siecle* 33 (December 2006): 95–115. Cottereau makes a similar argument elsewhere, stating: "La puissance de ces nouveaux impératifs d'équité, généralisés durant les années 1790–1792, nous est aussi accessible, aujourd'hui, grâce aux batailles de conception des droits qui eurent lieu après la Terreur, de 1794 à 1830." Alain Cottereau, "Droit et bon droit: Un droit des ouvriers instaure puis evince par le droit du travail (France, XIXe siecle)," *Annales HSS* 6 (2002): 1521–57.

59. Mollot, *De la compétence*, 31–32.

60. M. A. Franque, *Code de Prud'hommes* (Paris: Paulin, 1842).

61. Franque, *Code de Prud'hommes*, 6.

62. Mollot, *De la compétence*, 9.

63. Mollot, *De la compétence*, 296.

64. *Echo de la fabrique*, September 15–30, 1841.

65. Blanc, *Organisation du travail*, (1845), 123.

66. Blanc, *Organisation du travail* (1845), 149.

67. Blanc, *Organisation du travail* (1845), 151.

68. Mollot, *De la compétence*, 488.

69. Louis Blanc, *Organisation du travail*, 9th ed. (Paris: Nouveau Monde, 1850), 18.

70. Louis Blanc, *Histoire de dix ans, 1830–1840* (Brussels: Société Typographique, 1844), 346–48.

71. Mollot, *De la compétence*, 360.

72. Mollot, *De la compétence*, 94.

73. William Reddy notes a similar quality of the Prud'hommes, pointing out: "Their policies were to be based on what was considered accepted local practice." *The Rise of Market Culture* (Cambridge, UK: Cambridge University Press, 1984), 72.

74. Mollot, *De la compétence*, 112–113.

75. Louis Blanc, *Organisation du travail*, xviii–xix.

76. *Almanach de la démocratie* (1843), 64.

77. *Almanach démocratique et progressive de l'ami du peuple* (1850).

78. Lemercier has also highlighted this point, arguing:

Postuler une équivalence entre culture juridique et identité sociale est souvent un peu facile (Cerutti, 2002). La confrontation entre les discours de certains juristes contemporains sur les compétences des juges du commerce et des Prud'hommes et ce que l'on peut reconstituer de leurs pratiques de jugement souligne que l'on ne peut pas se contenter d'opposer la loi à l'équité, ou le fait au droit. La définition d'une question "technique"—qui pourrait dès lors être renvoyée à une juridiction spéciale, voire à quelque chose d'autre qu'une juridiction—est éminemment relative, fonction de l'état du droit, des moyens de preuve, mais aussi de la distance sociale entre mondes du travail, du commerce et de la justice.

Claire Lemercier, "Juges du commerce et conseillers Prud'hommes face à l'ordre judiciaire (1800–1880)," *La constitution de frontières judiciaires: Hélène Michel et Laurent Willemez; La justice au risque des profanes* (Paris: PUF, 2007), 11–27.

79. Alexandre Ledru-Rollin, *Jurisprudence française: De l'influence de l'école française sur le droit au XIXe siècle* (Paris: Patris, 1845), xiv.

80. Ledru-Rollin, *Jurisprudence française*.

81. Ledru-Rollin, introduction to *Jurisprudence française*, lx.

82. Ledru-Rollin, introduction to *Jurisprudence française*, li.

83. Étienne Vacherot, *De la démocratie* (Paris: 1860), 287.

84. Vacherot, *De la démocratie*, 287.

85. Vacherot, *De la démocratie*, 291–92.

86. Victor Hugo, *Actes et paroles: Depuis l'Exil, 1870–1876*, vol. 3 (Paris: Calmann Lévy, 1876), 108.

87. Hugo, *Actes et paroles*, vol. 3, 118.

Chapter Six

1. Étienne Vacherot, *De la démocratie* (Paris: 1860), 176:

Il faut donc, sous peine de mort pour la civilisation, que la démocratie devienne une réalité par la révolution économique. Cette révolution dont la science sociale cherche à définir le programme depuis trente ans, peut seule préserver la civilisation moderne de la décadence et de la ruine; elle est seule conservatrice, dans le sens profond du mot. La politique au statu quo économique perd les sociétés en servant les intérêts de personnes ou de classes. Voilà ce que l'expérience fera comprendre tôt ou tard aux amis de la liberté, et ce que sentent déjà tous les amis de la vraie démocratie.

2. Franz Neumann, *The Rule of Law: Political Theory and the Legal System in Modern Society* (Berg: 1986), 21.

3. A. V. Dicey, *Lectures on the Relation between Law and Public Opinion in England during the Nineteenth Century*, 2nd ed. (London: Macmillan, 1914), p lv.

4. Oscar Handlin and Mary Flug Handlin, *Commonwealth: A Study of the Role of Government in the American Economy: Massachusetts, 1774–1861* (Cambridge, MA: Belknap Press, 1969), 106. For further study on corporations in the United States in the first half of the nineteenth century, see Eric Hilt, "Early American Corporations and the State," in Naomi Lamoureaux and William Novak, eds., *Corporations and American Democracy* (Cambridge, MA: Harvard University Press, 2017).

5. Karl Polanyi, *The Great Transformation: The Political and Economic Origins of Our Time* (Boston: Beacon Press, 1957).

6. James Fennimore Cooper, *The American Democrat* (New York: Barnes and Noble, 2004 [1st ed. 1835]), 274–76.

7. Michel Chevalier, "La Démocratie—La Banque," in *Lettres sur l'Amérique du Nord*, vol. 1 (Brussels: 1838), 68–69.

8. Tocqueville, "What Makes Nearly All Americans Tend toward Industrial Professions," *Democracy in America*, vol. 2, part 2, chapter 19.

9. Tocqueville, "What Makes Nearly All Americans Tend toward Industrial Professions."

10. Tocqueville, "How Aristocracy Could Emerge from Industry," in *Democracy in America*, vol. 2, part 2, chapter 20.

11. For a more thorough development of this question, see chapter 8 in this book.

12. Edouard Alletz, *De la démocratie nouvelle*, vol. 1 (Paris: Lequien, 1837), 51.

13. Edouard Alletz, *De la démocratie nouvelle*, vol. 2 (Paris: Lequien, 1837), 41–60.

14. Alletz, *De la démocratie nouvelle*, vol. 2, 44–45.

15. This speech was republished in the annex of Alletz, *De la démocratie nouvelle*, vol 1, 348–49.

16. Louis Blanc, *Organisation du travail* (Paris: Nouveau Monde, 1850), 102.

17. Blanc, *Organisation du travail*, 178.

18. Vacherot, *De la démocratie*, 211.

19. Vacherot, *De la démocratie*, 211.

20. Vacherot, *De la démocratie*, 212–14.

21. Vacherot, *De la démocratie*, 212.

22. Maurice Levy-Leboyer and François Bourguignon, *L'Économie française au XIXe siècle: Analyse macro-économique* (Paris: Economica, 1985), 12.

23. Pierre Boucher, *Institutions commerciales traitant de la jurisprudence marchande et des usages du négoce d'après les anciennes et nouvelles lois* (Paris: 1801).

24. Jean-Guillaume Locré de Roissy, *Esprit du Code du Commerce*, vol. 1, (Paris: Dufour, 1829), 92.

25. Vital Roux, *De l'influence du gouvernement sur la prospérité du commerce* (Paris: Dentu, 1981), 248.

26. Franz Neumann, *Rule of Law*, 194.

27. J. B. Delaporte, *Commentaires sur le code de commerce* (Paris, 1808), 159–60.

28. *Observations des tribunaux de cassation . . . sur le Code de Commerce*, vol. 1 (1803), 163.

29. *Observations des tribunaux de cassation . . . sur le Code de Commerce*, vol. 1 (1803), 269.

30. *Observations des tribunaux de cassation . . . sur le Code de Commerce*, vol. 2 (1803), 68.

31. *Observations des tribunaux de cassation . . . sur le Code de Commerce*, vol. 2 (1803), 447.

32. *Observation des tribunaux de cassation . . . sur le Code de Commerce*, vol. 2 (1803), 399.

33. The figure 642 is provided by Charles Freedemen in the appendix to his *Joint-Stock Enterprise in France, 1807–1867*. Anne Lefebvre-Teillard provides a slightly different count by not double-counting businesses that were authorized, then lost authorization and gained it once again. She arrives at the figure 579. Anne Lefebvre-Teillard, *La société anonyme au XIXe siècle* (Paris: PUF, 1985), 64.

34. Lefebvre-Teillard, *La société anonyme au XIXe siècle*, 67.

35. It is worth noting that during the period of nationalization of French industries that followed World War II, these were the primary sectors that were nationalized: especially utilities, banks, and insurance companies. "In 1945–1946, the provisional government headed by de Gaulle had laid the foundations of the French welfare state and established the Commissariat general du plan in charge of national economic planning. A large state-owned sector had been created by the nationalization of utilities, banks, insurance companies and Renault, a car manufacturer."(Yves-Marie Péréon, *Moralizing the Market: How Gaullist France Embraced the US Model of Securities Regulation* (Baltimore: Johns Hopkins University Press, 2018), 16.

36. Emile Vincens, *Des sociétés par actions: Des banques en France* (Paris: Huzard, 1837), 1.

37. Vincens, 2–3.

38. Vincens, 12.

39. Bertrand Gille, *Recherches sur la formation de la grande entreprise capitaliste, 1815–1848* (Paris: SEVPEN, 1959), 35.

40. "Pendant les quatre-vingt-dix-neuf années, il sera prélevé chaque année, pour le Gouvernement, un dixième du produit brut du péage; lequel dixième sera versé, chaque semestre, dans une caisse à deux clefs, dont l'une demeurera entre les mains de M. le Préfet du département, et l'autre dans celles des directeurs de la compagnie." *Bulletin des lois*, 1818, pp. 204–5.

41. *Bulletin des lois*, 1826.

42. *Bulletin des lois*, 1819.

43. "L'importance du droit commercial ne peut qu'être généralement sentie à une époque à laquelle l'industrie absorbe toutes les idées et ouvre aux sociétés un nouvel avenir. La puissance sociale, jadis attachée au sol, passe aux capitaux mobiliers." J. V. Molinier, *Traité de droit commercial*, vol. 1 (Paris: Joubert, 1841), 1.

44. Société anonyme pour l'amélioration des procédés de vinification autorisée par ordonnance royale du 27 février (1822).

45. Aimé Bourbon, *Société anonyme pour l'entreprise des halages hydrauliques accélérés sur le Rhone au moyen des remorqueurs à écluses mobiles* (Lyon: Perrin, 1830), 8.

46. *Bulletin des lois*, 1819, pp. 211–13.

47. "Le cautionnement du directeur de la société ne pourra être de moins de vingt mille francs; et celui du caissier, de moins de huit mille francs." No.7651, Ordonnance du roi portant autorisation, conformément aux Statuts y annexés, d'une Compagnie d'assurances mutuelles contre l'incendie dans le département de la Loire-Inférieu," *Bulletin des lois*, 1819.

48. *Bulletin des lois*, 1819.

49. *Bulletin des lois*, 1819.

50. Léopold Malepeyre and Charles Félicité Jourdain, *Traité des sociétés commerciales* (Paris: 1833), 182–83.

51. Foucart, *Éléments de droit public et administratif*, 361.

52. Exposé on the motives of the bill for joint-stock companies, read before the Chamber of Deputies by Mr. Barthe, minister of justice, in the session of February 15, 1838.

53. Exposé on the motives of the bill for joint-stock companies, read before the Chamber of Deputies by Mr. Barthe, minister of justice, in the session of February 15, 1838.

54. Emile Vincens, *Exposition raisonée de la législation commerciale*, vol. 1 (Paris: Barrois, 1821), 336.

55. Horson, *Questions sur le Code de Commerce*, vol. 1 (Paris, 1829).

56. Aimé Bourbon, *Société anonyme pour l'entreprise des halages hydrauliques*, 8.

57. Claude-Alphonse Delangle, *Commentaire sur les sociétés commerciales* (1843), 429.

58. Louis Wolowski, *Des sociétés par actions* (Paris, 1838), 5.

59. Wolowski, *Des sociétés par actions*, 11.

60. Delangle, *Commentaires sur les sociétés commerciales* (1843), 419.

61. Delangle, *Commentaires sur les sociétés commerciales*, 419.

62. Julienne Laureyssens, "L'esprit d'association and the Société Anonyme in Early 19th Century Belgium," *Revue belge de Philologie et d'Histoire*, Année 2002 80–82, 517–30.

63. "Science sociale: De l'asssociation, et des divers moyens proposés pour la réaliser," *Revue du progrès social* (1834): 302.

64. "Science sociale: De l'association," 302.

65. Alexandre de Laborde, *De l'esprit d'association dans tous les intérêts de la communauté* (Paris: Gide, 1818), 10–11.

66. Laborde, *De l'esprit d'association*, viii.

67. Laborde, *De l'esprit d'association*, 17.

68. Laborde, *De l'esprit d'association*, 60–61.

69. Laborde, *De l'esprit d'association*, 62.

70. Laborde, *De l'esprit d'association*, 329.

71. Charles Ganilh, *Dictionnaire analytique d'économie politique* (Paris: Ladvocat, 1826), 150–51.

72. Amédée Prévost, "Hegel," *Revue du progrès* (1834): 476–89. It is worth noting, as discussed in chapter 1, that the reception of Hegel in these years was abundant and of interest to authors and readers of the *Revue du progrès*.

73. "Science Sociale: De l'association," 304–5.

74. Émile Bères, *Essai sur les moyens d'accroître la richesse territoriale en France notamment dans les départements méridionaux* (Paris: Lassime, 1830), 248.

75. A. Frémery, *Études de droit commercial ou du droit fondé par la coutume universelle des commerçans* (Paris: 1833), 428–29.

76. On this phenomenon in the United States in the first half of the nineteenth century, see Eric Hilt, "Early American Corporations and the State," in *Corporations and American Democracy*, ed. Naomi R. Lamoreaux and William J. Novak (Cambridge, MA: Harvard University Press, 2017).

77. Troplong, "Histoire du contrat de société," *Revue de législation* 16:152.

78. Troplong, *Commentaire du contrat de société en matière civile et commerciale* (Brussels: Meline, 1843), 5.

79. Troplong, *Commentaire du contrat de société*, xxxiv–xxxv.

80. Jérôme-Adolphe Blanqui, *Histoire de l'économie politique* (Paris: Guillamin, 1860), 4.

81. Adolphe Thiers, *Le régime commercial en France* (Paris: Paulin, 1851), 23.

82. Adolphe Thiers, *Le régime commercial*, 75–76.

83. Adolphe Thiers, *De la propriété* (Paris: Paulin, 1848), 21.

84. *Discours de Thiers*, vol. 3, 338.

85. *Discours de Thiers*, vol. 10, 196–97.

86. Blanc, *Organisation du travail*, 95–96.

87. Charles Coquelin, "Des sociétés commerciales en France et en Angleterre," *La revue des deux mondes* 3 (1843): 397–437, esp. 398.

88. Coquelin, "Des sociétés commerciales," 398.

Chapter Seven

1. Walt Whitman, *Democratic Vistas and Other Papers* (London, 1888), 35.

2. Honoré de Balzac, *Sur Catherine de Médicis, la Comédie Humaine*, vol. 11 (Paris: Gallimard, 1980).

3. On this point, see the classic study by François-André Isambert, *Buchez ou l'age théologique de la sociologie* (Paris: Cujas, 1967). Dominique Iogna-Pratt has asked this question in pointed terms: "Pourquoi les reconstructeurs de société des années 1820 font-ils retour au sacré?" Dominique Iogna-Prat, "Religions et utopies sociales (1820–1920)," seminar with Michel Bourdeau (CNRS, Maison Auguste Comte), Patrick Henriet (ÉPHE), and Alain Rauwel (CéSor), École des hautes études en sciences sociales, 2017–19.

4. On the question of the implicit moral and religious foundations of modern politics during the first half of the nineteenth century, see Agnès Antoine, *L'impensé de la démocratie: Tocqueville, la citoyenneté et la religion* (Paris: Fayard, 2003).

5. Martin Loughlin, *Foundations of Public Law*, 409; Philip Gorski, *The Disciplinary Revolution: Calvinism and the Rise of the State in Early Modern Europe* (Chicago: University of Chicago Press, 2003).

6. Loughlin, *Foundations of Public Law*, 412.

7. Loughlin, *Foundations of Public Law*, 408.

8. Alexis de Tocqueville, *Democracy in America*, vol. 2, ed. Eduardo Nolla, trans. James T. Schleifer (Indianapolis: Liberty Fund, 2012), 742.

9. Tocqueville, *Democracy in America*, vol. 2, 704.

10. Tocqueville, *Democracy in America*, vol. 2, 704.

11. Louis Blanc, *Histoire de la Révolution Française*, vol. 1, (Paris: Furne, 1869), 9–10.

12. Jean-François Jacouty, "Robespierre selon Louis Blanc: Le prophète christique de la Révolution française," *Annales historiques de la Révolution française* 331 (2003): 105.

13. Henri Lacordaire, *Discours sur la vocation de la nation française: Prononcé à Notre-Dame de Paris, le 14 février 1841, pour l'inauguration de l'ordre des frères prêcheurs en France* (1841).

14. On Hegel and the problem of secularization in the European tradition, see Jean-Claude Monod, *La Querelle de la sécularisation: Théologie politique et philosophie de l'histoire d'Hegel à Blumenberg* (Paris: Vrin, 2002).

15. On social atomization in the first half of the nineteenth century as a sociological and political problem, see Frédéric Brahami, *La Raison du Peuple: Un héritage de la Révolution française, 1789–1848* (Paris: Belles Lettres, 2016). "La Restauration des Bourbons en 1814 apparut comme le triomphe du catholicisme. Il redevint la religion de l'État. . . . Les gallicans

intransigeants condamnaient sans merci tout ce qui venait de la Révolution; ils n'avaient accepté ni le Concordat de 1801, signé par un gouvernement usurpateur, ni le coup d'État de Pie VII exigeant la démission des évêques." George Weil, *Histoire du catholicisme libérale en France, 1828–1908* (Paris: Alcan, 1909).

16. For one example of how democracy responded to the impasses of liberalism and conservatism in the first half of the nineteenth century, see Jérôme Grondeux, *Socialisme, la fin d'une histoire?* (Paris: Payot, 2012); and Brahami, *La raison du peuple*.

17. Henri de Saint-Simon, *Œuvres choisies de C.-H. de Saint-Simon: Précédées d'un essai sur sa doctrine*, vol. 1 (Brussels: Flatau, 1839), 41.

18. "L'influence de l'œuvre de Bonald ne doit pas être mésestimée, ainsi que celle de Joseph de Maistre que toute cette génération avait lu." Sylvain Milbach, "1832–1835, moment mennaisien: L'esprit croyant des années 1830," *Revue de l'histoire des religions* 235, no. 3 (2018): 451–84.

19. Antoine Picon, "La religion saint-simonienne," *Revue des sciences philosophiques et théologiques* 87, no. 1 (2003), 23.

20. Saint-Simon, *Le nouveau christianisme* (Paris: Bossange, 1825), 86.

21. Saint-Simon, *Le nouveau christianisme*, 87.

22. Saint-Simon, *Le nouveau christianisme*, 91.

23. Saint-Simon, *Le nouveau christianisme*, 2.

24. Saint-Simon, *Le nouveau christianisme*, 15.

25. Saint-Simon, *Le nouveau christianisme*, 37.

26. Saint-Simon, *Le nouveau christianisme*, 37–38.

27. Saint-Simon, *Le nouveau christianisme*, 8.

28. Saint-Simon, *Le nouveau christianisme*, 12.

29. Saint-Simon, *Le nouveau christianisme*, 44–45.

30. Edgar Quinet, *Du génie des religions* (Paris: Charpentier, 1842), v. Among the many thinkers to whom Quinet is referring is Montesquieu, who argued that religious belief is a consequence of a political system. "Lorsqu'une religion naît et se forme dans un État, elle suit ordinairement le plan du gouvernement ou elle est établie; car les hommes qui la reçoivent et ceux qui la font recevoir, n'ont guère d'autres idées de police que celles de l'État dans lequel ils sont nés. Quand la religion chrétienne souffrit, il y a deux siècles, ce malheureux partage qui la divisa en catholique et en protestante, les peuples du nord embrassèrent la protestante, et ceux du midi gardèrent la catholique." Montesquieu, *Spirit of the Laws*, book 21, chapter 5: "That the Catholic religion is better suited to a monarchy, and the Protestant religion is better adapted to a republic."

31. *L'avenir*, October 22, 1830.

32. Chevé provides a paradigmatic trajectory toward a religiously infused vision of democratic socialism during this period. His works included *Programme démocratique; ou, Résumé d'une organisation complète de la Démocratie radicale* (Paris: Rouanet, 1840); *Catholicisme et démocratie ou le règne du christ* (1842); *Le dernier mot du socialisme, par un catholique* (Paris: 1848); and *Catéchisme socialiste* (Paris: Bureau de La Voix du Peuple, 1850).

33. Gustave Flaubert, *L'Éducation sentimentale* (Paris: Louis Conard, 1910), 323–24.

34. Tocqueville, *De la démocratie en Amérique*, vol. 1 (Paris: Éditions Gallimard, 1992), 114.

35. Antoine, *L'impensé de la démocratie*; Alan S. Kahan, *Tocqueville, Democracy and Religion: Checks and Balances for Democratic Souls* (Oxford, UK: Oxford University Press, 2015).

36. Louis de Carné, *Des Intérêts nouveaux en Europe depuis la Révolution de 1830* (Paris: Bonnaire, 1838), 64–65.

37. Honoré de Balzac, *Sur Catherine de Médicis* (Paris: Gallimard, 1980), 172–73. Italics in original.

38. Henri Lacordaire, *Conférences de Notre-Dame de Paris, 1844–1845*, vol. 2 (Paris: Poussièlgue, 1872), 185–86.

39. On the importance of Louis Rousseau's conception of social science for the creation of a social Catholicism, see Jean Touchard, *Aux origines du catholicisme social: Louis Rousseau, 1787–1856* (Paris: Armand Colin, 1968).

40. Louis Rousseau, *Croisade du XIXe siècle* (Paris, Debecourt, 1841).

41. Rousseau, *Croisade du XIXe siècle*, 15.

42. Rousseau, *Croisade du XIXe siècle*, 102.

43. Buchez, *Introduction à la science de l'histoire*, vol. 1 (Paris: Guillaumin, 1842 [1st ed. 1833), 1.

44. Buchez, *Introduction à la science de l'histoire*, vol. 1, p. 2.

45. François-André Isambert, *Buchez ou l'âge théologique de la sociologie* (Paris: Cujas, 1967).

46. Philippe-Joseph-Benjamin Buchez, *Essai d'un traité complet de philosophie du point de vue du catholicisme et du progrès*, vol. 1 (Paris: Eveillard, 1838), v–vi.

47. Buchez, *Essai d'un traité complet*, viii–ix.

48. Buchez, *Essai d'un traité complet*, x–xi.

49. "Du buchezisme à la première démocratie chrétienne, en 1848, la filiation est aisée à suivre. Plus généralement, l'hostilité au monde libéral, l'idée d'organisation, la conviction que l'association sera la cellule fondamentale de la société." Jean-Marie Mayeur, "Le catholicisme social en France," *Le Mouvement social* 77 (October–December, 1971): 113–21.

50. Pierre Leroux, *De l'humanité, de son principe et de son avenir où se trouve exposée la vraie définition de la religion, et où l'on explique le sens, la suite et l'enchaînement du mosaisme et du christianisme* (Paris: Perrotin, 1845), xii.

51. Pierre Leroux, *Du christianisme et de son origine démocratique* (Paris: Boussac, 1848), 16.

52. Leroux, *Du christianisme*, 19.

53. "Pour aborder les philosophies politiques qui ont muri en France vers le milieu du XIX siècle, la notion de 'citoyenneté' n'est pas vraiment propice, en raison de ses connotations juridiques ou formelles; en revanche, le monde, l'espace mondial et l'humanité ont, dans ce climat de pensée, toute leur place, ce qui n'est pas sans conséquence." Laurent Fedi, "La démocratie religieuse de Pierre Leroux, ou les Esséniens du monde," *Le Télémaque* 19, no. 1 (2001): 47–56.

54. Pierre Leroux, *De l'égalité* (Paris: Boussac, 1858), 32.

55. Leroux, *Du christianisme*, iii.

56. Leroux, *Du christianisme*, 35–36.

57. Leroux, *Du christianisme*, 48.

58. Leroux, *Du christianisme*.

59. "Il existe trois Lamennais qui se succèdent: le premier, de 1817 à 1828, figure en tête des auteurs traditionalistes; le deuxième, de 1828 à 1834, est le fondateur du catholicisme libéral; le troisième, après les condamnations de 1832 et 1834, plus difficile à classer, est démocrate, socialisant et chrétien à sa manière." Sylvain Milbach, "Lamennais: 'Une vie qui sera donc à refaire plus d'une fois encore. Parcours posthumes," *Le Mouvement social*, no. 246 (2014): 75–96, esp. 76.

60. P. Hoffmann, "Lamennais lecteur de Rousseau: La question de la vérité," *Revue d'histoire littéraire de la France* 86, no. 5 (1986): 831–55.

61. Lamennais, *De la religion considérée dans ses rapports avec l'ordre politique et civil* (Paris, 1826), 33–34.

62. Lamennais, *De la religion considérée*, 33–34.
63. Lamennais, *De la religion considérée*, 35–36.
64. Lamennais, *Des progrès de la Révolution et de la guerre contre l'église* (Paris: Belin, 1829).
65. Lamennais, *Questions politiques et philosophiques*, vol. 1 (Paris: Pagnerre, 1840), 59.
66. Lamennais, *Le livre du peuple* (Paris: Pagnere, 1839), 56.
67. "L'apôtre éprouvé de la démocratie," *Le siècle*, May 14, 1848.
68. Lamennais, *Le livre du peuple*. For the quotation, Charles Boutard, *Lamennais: Sa vie et ses doctrines*, vol. 3, *L'éducation de la démocratie, 1834–1854* (Paris: Perrin, 1913), 208–9.
69. Lamennais, *Le livre du peuple*, ix.
70. Lamennais, "De la souveraineté et du pouvoir," in *L'Almanach démocratique de la France* (1841), 13.
71. "Lamennais's concept of social reason was, Lacordaire said, the missing final page of Rousseau's Social Contract; it Catholicized Jean-Jacques' intuition that the people were just and right." Carol E. Harrison, *Romantic Catholics: France's Postrevolutionary Generation in Search of a Modern Faith* (Ithaca, NY: Cornell University Press, 2014).
72. "Nous nous sommes efforces, au contraire, de montrer qu'il y avait dans la pensée de Lamennais une unité, et que cette unité était la sociologie; parce que son rêve intellectuel et sentimental fut le rêve d'un sociologue." Claude Carcopino, *Les doctrines sociales de Lamennais* (Paris: PUF, 1942), 68.
73. Lamennais, "De la souveraineté et du pouvoir," in *L'Almanach démocratique* (1841), 15.
74. *L'ère nouvelle*, Deecember 22, 1848.
75. Jérôme Grondeux, "Réflexions sur un rêve ancien: Les religions de l'avenir," *Romantisme*, no. 4 (2013): 33–43.
76. Marcel Gauchet, "Democracy: From One Crisis to Another," *Social Imaginaries* 1, vol. 1 (2015): 163–87, esp. 168–69.
77. Chateaubriand, *Mémoires d'outre tombe*, vol. 2 (Paris: Gallimard, 1951), 312.
78. Lamennais, *Du passé et de l'avenir du peuple* (Paris: Pagnerre, 1841), 9.
79. Lamennais, *Paroles d'un croyant* (Paris: Renduel, 1834), 7.
80. "Quand on se penche sur les travaux du Lamennais démocrate, on voit à quel point il opère une relecture du christianisme qui le fait pencher du côté de l'immanence." Jérôme Grondeux, "Réflexions sur un rêve ancien: Les religions de l'avenir," *Romantisme*, no. 4 (2013): 33–43.
81. Lamennais, *Du passé et de l'avenir*, 8.
82. Lamennais, *Du passé et de l'avenir*, 9.
83. Lamennais, *Du passé et de l'avenir*, 141.
84. Saint-Simon, *Nouveau christianisme*, 4–5.
85. *Le Correspondant: Journal religieux, politique, philosophique et littéraire*, vol. 1 (March 10, 1829–February 25, 1830), 19.
86. Bernard-Raymond Fabré-Palaprat, *Lévitikon ou Exposé des principes fondamentaux de la doctrine des chrétiens-catholiques-primitifs* (Paris: Librairie des Chrétiens-primitifs, 1831), 5.
87. *Lévitikon*, 288.
88. Hortense Allart, *La femme et la démocratie de nos temps* (Paris: Delaunay, 1836), 88.
89. Leroux, *Du christianisme*, 12.
90. Leroux, *Du christianisme*, 18–19.
91. Frédéric Ozanam, *Les Dangers de Rome et ses espérances* (Paris, 1848), 24.
92. "The papacy, Ozanam confidently claimed, would turn toward democracy, and French Catholics should be prepared to follow." Harrison, *Romantic Catholics*, 224.

93. Philippe Buchez and Vital Roux, *Histoire parlementaire de la Révolution française*, vol. 1 (Paris: Paulin, 1834), 1.

94. Buchez and Roux, *Histoire parlementaire*, vol. 1, p. 2.

95. Buchez and Roux, *Histoire parlementaire*, vol. 1, p. 4.

96. Henri Feugueray, *L'Association ouvrière industrielle et agricole* (Paris: Havard, 1851), 202.

97. *Dictionnaire politique: Encyclopédie du langage et de la science politiques, rédigé par une réunion de députées, de publicistes et de journalistes* (Paris: Duclerc et Pagnerre, 1842).

98. *Dictionnaire politique*, 782.

99. *Dictionnaire politique*, 283.

100. *Dictionnaire politique*, 285.

101. *Dictionnaire politique*, 466.

102. *Dictionnaire politique*, 466–67.

103. *Dictionnaire politique*, 686.

104. *Dictionnaire politique*, 912.

105. *Conférences de Notre-Dame de Paris, 1844–1845*, 237.

106. Lamennais, "De la souveraineté et du pouvoir," 15.

107. Lamennais, "De la souveraineté et du pouvoir," 85.

108. Lamennais, "De la souveraineté et du pouvoir," 85.

109. L'abbé Henri Maret, "Réponse à M. de Montalembert," *L'ère nouvelle*, October 28, 1848.

110. "Du monde moral, la démocratie tend a passer dans les faits d'un état social," Claude Bressolette, *L'abbé Maret: Le combat d'un théologien pour une démocratie chrétienne 1830–1851* (Paris: Beauchesne, 1977).

111. François-Vincent Raspail, "Lettre sur la religion," *Almanach démocratique* (Paris: 1846), 23.

112. Raspail, "Lettre sur la religion," 28.

113. Raspail, "Lettre sur la religion," 28.

114. *L'Européen*, March 17–May 12, 1832, p. 143.

115. Isambert, *Buchez ou l'âge théologique*, 153.

116. *L'Européen*, March 17–May 12, 1832, p. 147.

117. *L'Européen*, March 17–May 12, 1832.

118. P. J. B. Buchez, *Traité de politique et de science sociale* (Paris: Amyot, 1866), cxiii.

119. Buchez, *Traité de politique*, 46.

120. Buchez, *Traité de politique*, 47.

121. Buchez, *Traité de politique*, 47.

122. Buchez, *Traité de politique*, 94.

123. He offered, in the words of Michel Bourdeau, a "radicale désassociation de Dieu et religion." "Auguste Comte et la Religion Positiviste," *Revue des sciences philosophiques et théologiques* 87, no. 1 (2003): 5–21.

124. Auguste Comte, *Catéchisme positiviste ou sommaire exposition de la religion universelle* (Paris: 1852), v.

125. Comte, *Catéchisme positiviste*, ix–x.

126. Comte, *Catéchisme positiviste*, xviii.

127. Comte, *Catéchisme positiviste*, 3.

128. Bruno Karsenti, *Politique de l'esprit: Auguste Comte et la naissance de la science sociale* (Paris: Hermann, 2006).

129. Jules Michelet, *Bible de l'humanité* (Paris: Chamerot, 1864), 481.

Chapter Eight

1. Tocqueville, editorial notes to chapter 7, "Influence of Democracy on Salaries," *Democracy in America*, 2 vols., ed. Eduardo Nolla, trans. James T. Schleifer (Indianapolis: Liberty Fund, 2012).

2. Duncan Bell, *Reordering the World: Essays on Liberalism and Empire* (Princeton, NJ: Princeton University Press, 2016); Jens-Uwe Guettel, *German Expansionism, Imperial Liberalism, and the United States, 1776–1945* (Cambridge, UK: Cambridge University Press, 2012); Domenico Lusardo, *Contre-histoire du libéralisme* (Paris: La Découverte, 2014); Uday Singh Mehta, *Liberalism and Empire: A Study in Nineteenth-Century British Liberal Thought* (Chicago: University of Chicago Press, 1999); Jennifer Pitts, *A Turn to Empire: The Rise of Imperial Liberalism in Britain and France* (Princeton, NJ: Princeton University Press, 2005).

3. Alexis de Tocqueville, *Writings on Empire and Slavery*, ed. Jennifer Pitts (Baltimore: Johns Hopkins University Press, 2001); Melvin Richter, "Tocqueville on Algeria," *Review of Politics* 25 (1963), 362–98; Tzvetan Todorov, *De la colonie en Algérie* (Éditions Complexe, 1988); Margaret Kohn, "Empire's Law: Alexis de Tocqueville on Colonialism and the State of Exception," *Canadian Journal of Political Science / Revue canadienne de science politique* 41, no. 2 (2008): 255–78.

4. Charles Cassou, *Le biographie universel: Galérie politique. Alexis de Tocqueville*, vol. 15 (Paris, 1842), 13–14.

5. As Arthur Ghins has convincingly argued, the conscious elaboration of a "French liberalism" didn't appear as a major concern until the Second Empire. Arthur Ghins, "What Is French Liberalism?" *Political Studies* 72, no. 2 (2024): 551–69.

6. One recent exception is in Eva Atanassow, *Tocqueville's Dilemmas and Ours: Sovereignty, Nationalism, Globalization* (Princeton, NJ: Princeton University Press, 2022); and Eva Atanassow, "Colonization and Democracy: Tocqueville Reconsidered," *American Political Science Review* 111, no. 1 (2017): 83–96.

7. For a brief discussion of Tocqueville's probable familiarity with Bonald, see Lucien Jaume, *Tocqueville* (Paris: Fayard, 2008).

8. Bonald writes in the introduction to book 1 of his *Théorie du pouvoir politique et religieux dans la société civile démontré par le raisonnement et par l'histoire*, vol. 2: "J'ai défini la société civile, la réunion de la société politique & de la société religieuse; j'ai traité de la société politique, & je vais traiter de la société religieuse." The book was first published in 1796, and was then re-edited during the July Monarchy in 1843.

9. The initial outline written upon his return from the United States: "Political society (relations between the federal and particular governments and the citizen of the Union and citizen of each state), civil society (relations of the citizens with each other), religious society (relations between God and the members of society, and of the religious sects with each other)." Tocqueville, *Democracy in America*, ed. Nolla. vol. 1, lxxxi.

10. Guizot writes: "La société civile a commencé pareillement en Europe, en partie du moins, par des bandes de barbares; société parfaitement libre, où chacun restait parce qu'il le voulait, sans lois ni pouvoirs institués." *Cours d'histoire moderne: Histoire Générale de la civilisation en Europe* (1828), 35.

11. The economist Charles Ganilh, in his work *Du pouvoir et de l'opposition dans la société civile* (Paris: 1824), used the term in a similar way as a transhistorical social category, which was not itself a product of history but rather a category within which historical change took place. He wrote, for example: "C'est donc encore une erreur évidente de croire que la Société civile ne peut pas exister sans un pouvoir social. Les faits repoussent cette théorie, et l'on sait que les faits donnent la véritable mesure de la vérité, ou de la fausseté des théories" (126).

12. Tocqueville, *Democracy in America*, ed. Nolla, vol. 2, 691.

13. Richard Swedberg, *Tocqueville's Political Economy* (Princeton, NJ: Princeton University Press, 2009). Though Swedberg highlights Tocqueville's relationship to Say (and to Smith through him), he does not mention Tocqueville's relationship to their economic conceptions of civil society.

14. Say writes, "Il est constant, par exemple, que nulle société civile ne pourrait subsister sans l'accumulation des capitaux, qui sont les fruits du travail et les instruments de l'industrie." Jean-Baptiste Say, *Cours complet d'économie politique pratique*, 3rd ed. (Brussels: Dumont, 1836), 661.

15. Say, *Cours complet*, 559.

16. Say, *Cours complet*, 559.

17. A. Sandelin, *Répertoire général d'économie politique ancienne et moderne*, vol. 2 (La Haye, Netherlands: Noordendorp, 1846), 284.

18. Sandelin, *Répertoire général*, vol. 2, 1212.

19. Sandelin, *Répertoire général*, vol. 2, 8.

20. Sandelin, *Répertoire général*, vol. 2, 885.

21. Sandelin, *Répertoire général*, vol. 2, 1120.

22. Cheryl Welch, *De Tocqueville* (New York: Oxford University Press, 2001), 22.

23. Tocqueville, *Democracy in America*, ed. Nolla, vol. 2, 1105.

24. Tocqueville, *Democracy in America*, ed. Nolla, vol. 2, 771.

25. Tocqueville, *Democracy in America*, ed. Nolla, vol. 2, 779.

26. Tocqueville, *Democracy in America*, ed. Nolla, vol. 2, 934.

27. Tocqueville, *Democracy in America*, ed. Nolla, vol. 2, 979.

28. Helmut O. Pappe, "Sismondi, Constant and Tocqueville" (unpublished manuscript, 2002), https://hdl.handle.net/10779/uos.23352902.v1. Guizot, who was one of the most important influences on Tocqueville and his historical conception of civil society, was also deeply influenced by Sismondi. As Pappe notes, "Guizot wrote to Sismondi on October 24, 1827: 'No one, I am sure, reads you as much as I do, neither with more serious attention nor with more pleasure and profit; before you, the development, or rather the progressive formation, of the French nation and its civilisation had not even been suspected'" (13–14).

29. Sismondi, *Nouveaux principes d'économie politique ou de la richesse dans ses rapports avec la population* (Paris: 1819), 53.

30. Sismondi, *Nouveaux principes*, 336.

31. Sismondi, *Nouveaux principes*, 885.

32. Sismondi, *Nouveaux principes*, 883n.

33. Sismondi, *Nouveaux principes*, 780.

34. Sismondi, *Nouveaux principes*, 771.

35. Tocqueville, *Democracy in America*, ed. Nolla, vol. 2, 771.

36. Tocqueville, *Democracy in America*, ed. Nolla, vol. 2, 983.

37. Tocqueville, *Democracy in America*, ed. Nolla, vol. 2, 985.

38. For the classic example, see Robert Putnam's *Making Democracy Work: Civic Traditions in Modern Italy* (with Robert Leonardi and Rafaella Y. Nonetti, Princeton: Princeton University Press, 1993) and *Bowling Alone: The Collapse and Revival of American Community* (New York: Simon and Schuster, 2000). For an extended multi-dimensional critical dialogue with this work, see Bob Edwards, Michael W. Foley and Mario Diani, "Civil Society and Social Capital, A Primer" in *Beyond Tocqueville, Civil Society and the Social Capital Debate* (Hanover, NH: Tufts University Press, 2001).

39. Tocqueville, *Democracy in America*, ed. Nolla, vol. 2, 1201.

40. Tocqueville, *Democracy in America*, ed. Nolla, vol. 2, 1202.

41. Tocqueville, *Democracy in America*, ed. Nolla, vol. 2, 1202–3.

42. On this point, see Pierre Manent, ch. 2, "Democracy and Aristocracy," in *Tocqueville and the Nature of Democracy*, John Waggoner, trans. (Lanham, MD: Rowman and Littlefield, 1996).

43. Tocqueville, *Democracy in America*, ed. Nolla, vol. 2, 904.

44. Tocqueville, *Democracy in America*, ed. Nolla, vol. 2, 1265.

45. Tocqueville, *Democracy in America*, ed. Nolla, vol. 2, 1265.

46. Tocqueville, *Democracy in America*, ed. Nolla, vol. 2, 1196.

47. This is the subject of chapter 1, "Inequality: Alexis de Tocqueville and the Democratic Foundations of a Modern Administrative Power," in Sawyer, *Demos Assembled*, 22–51.

48. Sismondi, *Nouveaux principes*, 11.

49. Alexis de Tocqueville, *Mémoire sur le paupérisme*, in *Mémoire présenté à la Société académique cherbourgeoise et publié en 1835 par celle-ci dans les Mémoires de la Société académique de Cherbourg* (1835); pp. 293–344 in *Tocqueville Œuvres*, vol. 1 (Paris: Gallimard, 1991), 1180.

50. Tocqueville, "*Mémoire sur le paupérisme*," 1184.

51. Many have used the term, but I am borrowing the term "spatial fix" specifically from David Harvey, "The Spatial Fix: Hegel, Von Thunen and Marx," in *Spaces of Capital: Towards a Critical Geography* (New York: Routledge, 2001). Harvey does not include Tocqueville in the cast of characters who used space to solve the antinomies of capital.

52. Tocqueville, *Democracy in America*, ed. Nolla, vol. 1, 650n.

53. Tocqueville, *Democracy in America*, ed. Nolla, vol. 1, 651.

54. Tocqueville, *Democracy in America*, ed. Nolla, vol. 1, 652.

55. Tocqueville, *Democracy in America*, ed. Nolla, vol. 1, 60.

56. Tocqueville, *Democracy in America*, ed. Nolla, vol. 1, 62.

57. Tocqueville, *Democracy in America*, ed. Nolla, vol. 1, 63.

58. Tocqueville, *Democracy in America*, ed. Nolla, vol. 1, 64.

59. Tocqueville, *Democracy in America*, ed. Nolla, vol. 1, 64.

60. Tocqueville, *Democracy in America*, ed. Nolla, vol. 1, 65.

61. Tocqueville, *Democracy in America*, ed. Nolla, vol. 1, 67.

62. J.-C.-L. Simonde de Sismondi, *De l'expédition contre l'Alger* (Paris: 1830), 13.

63. Sismondi, *Nouveaux principes*, 77–78.

64. Sismondi, *Nouveaux principes*, 77–78.

65. Sismondi, *Nouveaux principes*, 77–78.

66. Sismondi, *Nouveaux principes*, 81.

67. Richard Swedberg's *Tocqueville's Political Economy* (Princeton, NJ: Princeton University Press, 2018) offers a groundbreaking take on Tocqueville's political economy, but it is striking that it makes almost no mention of Tocqueville's writing on Algeria, considering how much

political economic questions saturate those writings. For a thorough treatment of the political economy behind the French conquest of Algeria, see David Todd, *A Velvet Empire: French Informal Imperialism in the Nineteenth Century* (Princeton, NJ: Princeton University Press, 2021).

68. Alexis de Tocqueville, "Notes de voyage en Algérie de 1841," in *Tocqueville Œuvres*, vol. 1 (Paris: Gallimard, 1991), 664.

69. Alexis de Tocqueville, "Voyage en Algérie, novembre-décembre 1846," in *Tocqueville Œuvres*, vol. 1 (Paris: Gallimard, 1991), 768.

70. Alexis de Tocqueville, "Travail sur l'Algérie, octobre 1841," in *Tocqueville Œuvres*, vol. 1 (Paris: Gallimard, 1991), 735.

71. Tocqueville, "Travail sur l'Algérie, octobre 1841," 735–36.

72. Tocqueville, "Travail sur l'Algérie, octobre 1841," 727.

73. Tocqueville, "Travail sur l'Algérie, octobre 1841," 728.

74. Tocqueville, "Notes de voyage en Algérie de 1841," 665–66.

75. Tocqueville, "Voyage en Algérie 1846," 772.

76. Tocqueville, "Voyage en Algérie 1846," 777.

77. Tocqueville, "Voyage en Algérie 1846," 777.

78. Tocqueville, "Fragment D, 14 décembre [18]46 Bône," in *Tocqueville Œuvres*, vol. 1 (Paris: Gallimard, 1991), 781.

79. Tocqueville, "Fragment B, 2 décembre [18]46," in *Tocqueville Œuvres*, vol. 1 (Paris: Gallimard, 1991), 773.

80. Tocqueville, "Notes de voyage en Algérie de 1841," 667.

81. Tocqueville, "Notes de voyage en Algérie de 1841," 680.

82. Tocqueville, "Travail sur l'Algérie," 731.

83. Tocqueville, "Travail sur l'Algérie, octobre 1841," 731.

84. Tocqueville, "Notes du voyage en Algérie de 1841," 668.

85. Tocqueville, "Travail sur l'Algérie," 731–32.

86. "État social et politique de la France avant et depuis 1789" (1836), in *Tocqueville Œuvres*, vol. 3 (Paris: Gallimard, 2004), 3–42; "La centralization administrative et le système representatif" (1844), in *Tocqueville Œuvres*, vol. 1 (Paris: Gallimard, 1991), 1115–20.

87. Tocqueville, "Notes du voyage en Algérie 1841," 679.

88. Tocqueville, "Travail sur l'Algérie, octobre 1841," 733.

89. Tocqueville, "Travail sur l'Algérie, octobre 1841," 735.

90. Tocqueville, "Rapport fait par M. de Tocqueville sur le projet de lois relatif aux crédits extraordinaires demandés pour l'Algérie," in *Tocqueville Œuvres*, vol. 1 (Paris: Gallimard, 1991), 826.

91. Tocqueville, "Rapport fait par M. de Tocqueville sur le projet," 835–36.

92. Tocqueville, "Rapport fait par M. de Tocqueville sur le projet," 837.

93. Tocqueville, "Travail sur l'Algérie, octobre 1841," 731–32.

94. Tocqueville, "Travail sur l'Algérie, octobre 1841," 732.

95. Tocqueville, "Travail sur l'Algérie, octobre 1841," 735.

96. Tocqueville, "Travail sur l'Algérie, octobre 1841," 739.

97. Tocqueville, "Travail sur l'Algérie, octobre 1841," 744–45.

98. Tocqueville, "Travail sur l'Algérie, octobre 1841," 744–45.

99. Tocqueville, "Travail sur l'Algérie, octobre 1841," 735.

100. Tocqueville, "Travail sur l'Algérie, octobre 1841," 747.

101. Tocqueville, "Travail sur l'Algérie, octobre 1841," 731–32.

102. Tocqueville, "Travail sur l'Algérie, octobre 1841," 754.

103. Tocqueville, "Travail sur l'Algérie, octobre 1841," 754–55.
104. Tocqueville, "Notes du voyage en Algérie de 1841," 669–70.
105. Tocqueville, "Notes du voyage en Algérie de 1841," 669–70.

Conclusion

1. David Meyer and Sydney Tarrow have suggested that we have entered a "social movement society" in which protest has shifted from a sporadic, marginal aspect of political life to becoming "institutionalized." *The Social Movement Society: Contentious Politics for a New Century* (Oxford, UK: Rowman & Littlefield, 1998). On the normalization of protest literature, see also, for example, Endre Borbáth and Theresa Gessler, "Different Worlds of Contention? Protest in Northwestern, Southern and Eastern Europe," *European Journal of Political Research* 58, no. 1 (November 2020): 910–35; Hans-Dieter Klingemann and Dieter Fuchs, *Citizens and the State* (Oxford, UK: Oxford University Press, 1995); R. Dalton, R., A. Van Sickle, and A. and S. Weldon, "The Individual-Institutional Nexus of Protest Behavior," *British Journal of Political Science* 40, no. 01 (2010): 51–73. On the pessimism that has accompanied this normalization of protest, see for example, D. E. Campbell and C. Wolbrecht, "The Resistance as Role Model: Disillusionment and Protest among American Adolescents after 2016," *Political Behavior* 42 (2020): 1143–68.

2. "Les démocraties contemporaines sont issues d'une forme de gouvernement que ses fondateurs opposaient à la démocratie." Bernard Manin, *Principes du gouvernement représentatif* (Paris, 1995), 11.

3. Massimiliano Tomba, *Insurgent Universality: An Alternative Legacy of Modernity* (New York: Oxford University Press, 2019).

4. Krishan Kumar, "Civil Society: An Inquiry into the Usefulness of a Historical Term," *British Journal of Sociology* 44, no. 3 (199): 375–95.

5. Michael Walzer, "A Better Vision: The Idea of Civil Society," in *The Civil Society Reader*, ed. Virginia Hodgkinson and Michael W. Foley (Hanover, NH: Tufts University Press, 2003). Originally published in *Dissent* (Spring 1991): 296–304.

6. Sheri Berman, "Civil Society and the Collapse of the Weimar Republic," *World Politics* 49, no. 3 (1997): 401–29.

7. Simone Chambers and Jeffrey Kopstein, "Bad Civil Society," *Political Theory* 29, no. 6 (2001): 837–65.

8. William Novak, "The American Law of Association: The Legal-Political Construction of Civil Society," *Studies in American Political Development* 15 (Fall 2001): 163–88.

9. George Sand, *Mauprat*, vol. 1 (Paris: Gallimard, 2019), 652.

10. As Rousseau argued in the opening to his chapter "Mixed Government": "Strictly speaking, there's no such thing as a simple or unmixed government."

11. John Rawls, *A Theory of Justice* (Cambridge, MA: Belknap, 1971), 11.

12. Jeremy Waldron, "John Locke: Social Contract versus Political Anthropology," *Review of Politics* 51, no. 1 (Winter 1989): 2–28.

13. Papy Louis, "Le problème de la restauration des Landes de Gascogne," *Cahiers d'outre-mer* 3, no. 11 (July–September 1950): 231–79.

14. Stephen W. Sawyer, "Locating Paris: The Parisian Municipality in Revolutionary France, 1789–1852." PhD dissertation, University of Chicago, 2008.

15. Florence Bourillon, "La loi du 13 avril 1850 ou lorsque la Seconde République invente le logement insalubre," *Revue d'histoire du XIXe siècle* 20/21, no. 1 (2000): 117–34.

16. Monique Kieffer, "La Législation Prud'homale de 1806 à 1907," *Le mouvement social*, no. 141 (1987): 9–23.

17. Dougui Nourredine, "Les origines de la libération des sociétés de capitaux à responsabilité limitée, 1856–1863," *Revue d'histoire moderne et contemporaine* 28, no. 2 (April–June 1981): 268–92.

18. Jean Maurain, *La politique ecclésiastique du Second Empire de 1852 à avril 1869* (Paris: Alcan, 1930).

19. This third moment is the subject of Stephen W. Sawyer, *Demos Assembled: Democracy and the International Origins of the Modern State, 1840–1880* (Chicago: University of Chicago Press, 2018).

Index

Abensour, Miguel, *La démocratie contre l'État*, 258n95
Ackerknecht, Erwin, 103–4, 128–29
administrative decentralization, and laws of 1837 and 1838, 85. *See also* decentralization; Paris city administration
administrative democracy. *See* Paris city administration
administrative regulation: contract between constitution and administration, 24–25; and democracy, 18, 21–31; importance of French law to US law, 254n11; and prevention of bureaucratic despotism, 18, 254n11; transformation of, 19–21, 240. *See also* commercial enterprise regulation; forest regulation; public health administration; regulatory police power; workplace regulation
Agulhon, Maurice, *The Republican Experiment*, 268n74
Aide-toi, le ciel t'aidera, 77
Algeria, colonization of, 212, 244. *See also* Tocqueville, Alexis de, writings on Algeria
Allart, Hortense: on improvement of health and hospitals, 110; *La femme et la démocratie de nos temps*, 7, 12, 33, 201; on role of women in governing democratic society, 7, 12; on Rousseau's social contract, 33
Alletz, Edouard, *The New Democracy*: and old-regime structures, 160, 162; and principles of governing commerce, 160
Alletz, P.-Julien, *Dictionary of Modern Police*, 53
Annales: Histoire, Sciences Sociales, 253n57
Annales forestières (*Forest Annals*): and German forestry, 54; "Reforesting the Mountains," 44; support for forest regulation, 60–61
arable land, and deforestation, 42

Arago, François: address to local assembly, 90–91; and *Comité central de l'opposition de la Seine*, 88, 90; dedication to democratic cause, 90; on deforestation and climate change, 47–48; as municipal councillor of Paris, 88, 268n72; as president of General Council, 90, 91, 92
aristocratic liberalism, 251n34
Aristotle, and best form of government, 4, 5, 6
association: associative ideal and social science, 174–78; defined by Laborde, 176; joint-stock companies as type of, 174, 175–76; during July Monarchy, 175; limitations of in early America, 239; principle of (*l'esprit d'association*), 175–78; as socially bound, 178–83; Tocqueville on insufficiency of, 221–22; worker associations, 150–51
Atlantic revolutions, 2
Aubé, Guillaume, 90
Aulard, Alphonse, *Histoire politique de la Révolution française*, 249n3

Backouche, Isabelle, *La trace du fleuve*, 269n114
Baldwin, Peter, 103
Balzac, Honoré de: on contracts based on individual will, 31, 259n100; dedication of 1840 edition of *Gobseck* to Barchou de Penhoën, 22; on democratization of society, 6; *Le Père Goriot*, 31, 32; *Sur Catherine de Médicis*, 184, 193
Barrault, Émile, 129
Barrot, Odilon, 6
Barthe, Félix, on government authorization of large businesses, 171–72
Baudrillart, Jacques-Joseph, 55, 263n77
Beaumont, Gustave de, 218
Beckmann, J., 263n71
Berès, Émile, 143

Berg, Günther von, 54, 134
Berger, Jean Jacques, as mayor of 2nd arrondissement, 92–93
Berman, Sheri, 239
Besson, Louis, 90, 91
Bigot, Félix-Julien-Jean, 133
biological old regime, 40
Blanc, Louis, 23, 30, 129; "Alliance intellectuelle," 27; on credit, 161–62; for democratic socialist republic, 183; on democratization of society, 6; on governance, 8; Hegelianism, 8; on industrial association, 150–51, 182–83; on inequalities generated by capitalism, 161–62; *L'État et la commune*, 79; *Organisation du travail*, 6, 150, 151, 153, 182; on political centralization and administrative decentralization, 79–80; on role of Prud'hommes in establishing minimum wage, 151–52; and role of state in social justice, 24; on state as bank, 183
Blanqui, Jérome-Adolphe: on deforestation, 64; *History of Political Economy*, 180; report to Académie des sciences morales et politiques, 49, 60, 64
Bodin, Jean, on division of power, 4–5
Boeuf, M. F., 17
Bonald, Louis de: and social unity, 188; theory of political and religious power, 215, 287n8
Bordeaux Bridge Company, 169, 170, 280n40
Bourbon Restoration: and deforestation, 43; and democracy as mode of social organization, 2, 3; and re-regulation of forests, 57 (*see also* forest regulation)
Bourguignon, François, 164
Bourillon, Florence, 243
Braudel, Fernand, 39
Breckman, Warren, 23
Brock, Heinrich Christian von, 263n71
Buchez, Philippe, 129, 284n49; *A Complete Treatise of Philosophy from the Point of View of Catholicism and Progress*, 194; on egalitarian ideals of Revolution, 203; *Histoire parlementaire de la Révolution française* (with Roux), 202–3; *Introduction to the Study of Medical Science*, 117; on morality in political and administrative practice, 208–9; *Précis élémentaire d'hygiène* (with Trélat), 117; as student of Saint-Simon, 190, 193; and theological age of sociology, 194
Bulletin des lois, 169
Buttoud, Gérard, 59

Cabet, Étienne, 6, 23
Cambacérès, Jean-Jacques-Régis de, 164–65
cameral sciences, built on *Polizeiwissenschaft* tradition of German states, 54–55
capitalist enterprise, regulation of. *See* commercial enterprise regulation

Cappeau, Louis, 57
Carné, Louis de, 193
Catholicism: Chateaubriand's history of in democratic terms, 199; and individual as social being, 193; Lacordaire and, 187; Saint-Simon and, 189, 190; Tocqueville and, 186, 192. *See also* democratic social science, nonsecular foundations of
Central Committee of the Opposition of the Seine (*Comité central de l'opposition de la Seine*): banquet campaigns of, 89, 92, 268n75; organization of, 89, 268nn74–75; transformation of Parisian municipal authority, 88–89, 92
Chabrol, Gaspard de, 74–75, 76
Chalvet, Martine, 52
Chambers, Simone, 239
Chantereine, M. Avoine de, 57–58
Chaptal, Jean-Antoine, 138
Chateaubriand, François-René de: and democracy in France, 1, 5; *Génie du christianisme*, 199; *Mémoires d'outre tombe*, 199; history of Catholicism in democratic terms, 199; on practice of democracy, 14
Chevalier, Michel, "La Démocratie—La Banque," 159
Chevé, Charles-François: *Catholicisme et démocratie ou le règne du Christ*, 192; religiously infused vision of democratic socialism, 283n32
civil society: and capitalism, 216, 218; critiques of, 239–40; and development of modern democracy, 9–11, 239–40; in French politics, 9–10, 255n44; Hegel on, 20–21, 29; Jacobin rejection of, 10; as one dimension of social activity, 215; Tocqueville and, 214–15, 216–17; in twentieth-century, 239
climate change, and deforestation, 40, 44–50, 60, 63
Colbert, Jean-Baptiste, regulatory programs under Louis XIV, 180; commercial, 156, 163; forest, 50, 51–52, 56; public health, 103
Cold War, and civil society paradigm, 10
Cole, Joshua, 97
Coleman, William, *Death Is a Social Disease*, 270n6
colonial empire: and democratic society, 213; and liberalism, 212. *See also* Sismondi, J.-C.-L. Simonde de; Tocqueville, Alexis de, writings on Algeria
Comité central de la réforme, 88
Comité central de l'opposition de la Seine. *See* Central Committee of the Opposition of the Seine (*Comité central de l'opposition de la Seine*)
Commercial Code of 1807: and government authorization and oversight of joint-stock companies, 164, 165–66, 168–69, 180; and juridical controls on commercial activity, 156, 163–64. *See also* joint-stock companies (*sociétés anonymes*)

commercial enterprise regulation: administrative oversight of large businesses, 167–74; *Bulletin des lois*, 169; Commercial Code of 1807, 156, 163–64, 165, 166, 168–69, 180; Conseil d'état, 169; and corporations as agencies of government, 157; and limited silent partnerships, 180, 182; and "new aristocracy," 158–63; in new associative ideal, 174–78; and obligation, 178–83; and public interest, 157–58, 163–67, 174–78. *See also* joint-stock companies (*sociétés anonymes*)
Compagnie du Pont de Bordeaux, 169, 170, 280n40
Company of Three Bridges, 101
Comte, Auguste: invention of sociology, 209; and "religion of humanity," 209, 286n123; and Saint-Simonians, 190, 209; sociological approach to religion, 209–10; sociological critique of Rousseau's social contract, 34
Comte, Charles, 36
Conseil de salubrité (Public Health Council), 106–10, 113, 119–20, 129
Considerant, Victor, 129; and democratic movement, 23, 36–37; "A Few Considerations on Traffic in Paris and a Note on That of the 10th Arrondissement," 98; "On the Administrative Unity of the Department of the Seine," 94
constitutional monarchies: politically conservative, 1; and postrevolutionary liberals, 2–3. *See also* Bourbon Restoration; democracy, in first half of nineteenth century; July Monarchy
Cooper, James Fennimore, *The American Democrat*, 158
Coquelin, Charles, 183
Corvol, Andrée, 41
Cottereau, Alain, 139, 147–48, 277n58
Cousin, Victor, 22

d'Alembert, Jean le Rond, 134
d'Argenson, Marquis: definition of democracy in Rousseau's *Social Contract*, 77; *Jusqu'où la démocratie peut être admise dans le gouvernement monarchique*, 77; for monarchical sovereign and democratic government, 5
Darimon, Alfred, 22
d'Aunay, Hector, 83, 85
decentralization: and democratic administration, 78–79, 266n31; difficulty of establishing, 267n32; and German unification, 27; Rosanvallon interpretation of, 266n31
Declaration of the Rights of Man and Citizen, 132, 139
Decree of Allarde, 132, 133
deforestation: and climate change, 44–48; commissions, 49; and landed estates, sale of, 39, 41; phases of, 41; and public interest, 42–44, 50, 60–61; and relationship between humans and forests, 48; and wood's ubiquity, 42. *See also* forest regulation; forests
de Gaulle, Charles, 280n35
De Greef, Guillaume, *Introduction à la sociologie*, 34–35
Delangle, Claude-Alphonse, *Commentaire sur les sociétés commerciales*, 173, 174–75
Delaporte, J. B., *Commentaires sur le code de commerce*, 165–66
Delasiauve, Louis, 129
Demier, Francis, 141
democracy, in first half of nineteenth century, 1–4, 14, 238; and aristocratic privilege, 59, 71, 240; best form of government to serve, 7–9; civil society versus demos as cornerstone of, 9–11, 239–40; as mode of social organization and governance, 4–9, 14–15, 22, 23; overlooked by historians, 2, 4; popular decision making, public oversight, and social conception of individual rights in, 184; and possibility of organizing society of equals through self-government, 239; relationship with local administrative power, 77; and state/society relations, 8–9; as struggle between antimodern reaction and new republicanism, 2; and suffrage, deemphasis of, 238–39. *See also* democratic social science, nonsecular foundations of
democratic administration: as "decentralization," 78–79, 266n31; from eighteenth century through Revolution and Restoration, 4–5, 6–7, 18, 77–78; and Hegel and Rousseau, 18–19. *See also* administrative regulation; commercial enterprise regulation; forest regulation; Paris city administration; public health administration; workplace regulation
Democratic Almanach of France, The, 197
democratic almanacs: legal realism in, 153; and lives of workers and workplace regulations, 145; on practices of medicine, sanitation, and public hygiene, 111–16
democratic social science, nonsecular foundations of: historicizing, 199–205; and political practice, 205–11; and regulatory administrative action, 191–92, 206–10; religious readings of French Revolution, 202–5; and sociologization of the sacred, 185–91; universal religion, 187–90, 191–99. *See also* Catholicism; Protestant Reformation
democratic society: versus "civil society," 11; democratizing social contract, 35, 240–41; through mixed social constitution, 242; redefining regulatory power, administration, and government, 22; and role of aristocracy, 251n34. *See also* Tocqueville, Alexis de
démoc-socs, 8, 27
demos: and modern administrative state, 240; and public authority and collective obligation, 184;

demos (*cont.*)
    revolution, 1, 13, 23, 243, 244; as self-governing society of equals, 8–9, 13, 240; in work by Hugo and Marx, 12, 13, 29, 30, 240
Denis, Vincent, 51
Denys, Catherine, 51
Deroin, Jeanne, 6
Descartes, René, 186
Deutsch-Französische Jahrbücher (German-French Annals), 27, 28
Dewey, John, *Liberalism and Social Action*, 16
Dicey, A. V., 157
Dictionnaire analytique d'économie politique, and government oversight of capitalist sector, 176–77
Dictionnaire Politique, 204
Diderot, Denis, 134
Dubber, Markus, 51
Dufaure, Jules Armand Stanislas, 45
Dugied, Pierre-Henri: on environmental effects of deforestation, 43–44, 60; on relationship between private and public power, 48
Dupin, André: on deforestation, 64–65; on forest rights of communes, 65–67
Dupoty, Michel Auguste, 129
Durkheim, Émile: on Hobbes's and Rousseau's social contract theory, 35, 259n124; sociological conception of social contract, 35

East India Company, 164
Echo de la fabrique, 146, 148, 149
economic liberalism, 136
education of children, role of society in, 20
encyclicals by Gregory XVI, 199
Encyclopédie (Diderot and d'Alembert), 134
Encyclopedists, 105
Engels, Friedrich, 23
environment: biological old regime, 39–40; deforestation's effects on, 42–45; Fourier on environmental destruction and climate change, 47; political-ecological revolution, 39, 40
European public law, distinction between *potestas* (political right) and *potentia* (capacity to rule), 17, 253n8

Fabre, Jean-Antoine, *Essai sur la théorie des torrens et des rivières*, 42, 43
Fabré-Palaprat, Bernard-Raymond, on democratic nature of early Church, 201
Favrel, as opposition candidate, 94, 96, 101–2
Feugueray, Henri-Robert, and democratization of Catholicism, 198, 203
Feuillant, Étienne-Antoine, on importance of guilds, 136
Fitzsimmons, Michael, *From Artisan to Worker*, 138, 275n12

Flaubert, Gustave, *L'Éducation sentimentale*, 8, 22–23, 25, 130–31, 142, 143, 192
Fleury, Cardinal, 105
forest regulation: and "aristocratic" and "democratic" understandings of private forest rights, 59, 264n95; and balance of private and public interests, 57, 67–69; under Bourbon regime, 53–54, 56; codified by Colbert, 50, 51–52, 56, 263n60; and division between legislative and administrative powers, 56–57; Dupin on forest rights of communes, 65–67; and German cameral sciences, 54–55; laws of 1790 and 1791, 52; and livelihood of poorest rural populations, 61–64; under Louis XV and Louis XVIII, and politicization of rights of private individuals, 51; Napoleon's 1803 law, 53; opposition to, 61–63, 71; redefining public power and public interest, 57–59, 71; and relation of administrative practice to law, 58; revised forest code of 1827, 40, 55–58, 66; War of the Demoiselles, 61–62, 68
forests: and age of "arboreal necessity," 44; debates over, 38–39; as essential for daily life of peasants, 42, 61; as important natural resource for energy, agriculture, industry, and economic growth, 41–42, 261n13; and "jardinage," 61. *See also* deforestation; forest regulation
forest science: first school of forestry (school of Nancy), 55; German cameralist tradition, 54–55; Lorentz and Parade as founders of French forestry, 55
Fortunet, Françoise, 131
Foucart, Émile-Victor: on government authorization and oversight of large businesses, 171; on responsibilities of police, 17
Fouillée, Alfred, *La science sociale contemporaine*, 35–36
Fourier, Charles, on environmental destruction and climate change, 47
Franco-German exchange, and development of democratic thought, 27–28, 30
Frank, Johan Peter, and medical police, 103, 105
Franque, M. A., 148
Freedmen, Charles, 280n33
Frémery, A., on particular and general interest, 178
French Revolution of 1789, 2, 14; Blanc's history of, 187; and Declaration of the Rights of Man and Citizen, 132, 139; and Decree of Allarde, 132, 133; and deregulation of forests, 57, 60; impact on commercial activity, 165; and Le Chapelier Law, 132–33; religious readings of, 202–5; representative government generated by suffrage not considered democratic during, 238; and sale of landed estates, 39, 41; and social transformation, 11
French Revolution of 1830, 8–9, 22, 80, 86, 87
French Revolution of 1848, 102
French welfare state, foundations of, 280n35

Fuster, Joseph, *Des changements dans le climat de la France*, 48

Gaillard, Jeanne, 97–98
Ganilh, Charles, and civil society, 288n11
Ganneron, Auguste, 81, 90
Gay, Désirée, 6
Gazette municipale de la ville de Paris et du département de la Seine, 85
General Council of the Seine: accountability and transparency in elections, 95–97; Arago as president of, 90–91, 92; elections, 89–90; shift in choice of councillors, 93–97
Gérald, Sfez, 258n95
German philosophy, and French revolutionary egalitarianism, 23
Germany, unification of, and administrative decentralization, 27
Ghins, Arthur, 287n5
Gille, Bertrand, 169
Gorski, Philip, on "disciplinary revolution" in Protestant Reformation, 185
Gregory XVI, encyclicals *Mirari vos* and *Singulari nos*, 199
Grün, Karl, 23
guild system: end of, 132–33; "liberal" rejection of return to, 136–37, 138, 140; proposals to reestablish under Napoleon, 135–36, 138, 275n12. *See also* workplace regulation
Guillotin, Joseph-Ignace, 106
Guionnet, Christine, 93, 268n81
Guizot, François: on civil society, 215, 287n10; on danger of privileged hierarchy, 161, 162; on dual capacity of modern governance, 17; on governing democratic society, 7; *History of Civilization in France*, 215; on predominance of democracy, 5–6; on public rights, 161; Sismondi's influence on, 288n28; on studying society before building government, 36
Guizot, Jean-Jacques, 168

Hagerman, Jonas-Philip, 75
Handlin, Mary Flug, 157
Handlin, Oscar, 157
Hartig, Georg-Ludwig, early forestry text, 55, 263n77
Harvey, David, 10
Hauréau, Barthélemy, 204–5
Haussmann, Georges-Eugène, 97, 102, 243
Havasy, Christopher S., "Radical Administrative Law," 254n11
Hayek, Friedrich, *The Constitution of Liberty*, 254n10
health regulation. *See* public health administration
Hegel, G. W. F.: on civil society and government, distinction between, 29; on corporations as associations, 177–78; democratization of ideas on regulatory state, 19, 30; on French Revolution, and concept of police, 255n22, 255nn26–27, 255n29; idealism, 24, 26; interpretation of in "democratic" terms, 8; between liberalism and socialism, 21, 255n31; on local popular participation in unified Germany, 256n35; *Phenomenology of Spirit*, 255n27; *Philosophy of Right*, 19, 22, 32, 177; "Police and Corporations," 19–21, 31; popularity with readers of *Revue du progrès*, 281n72; "republican" elements within thought, 21, 255n32; and role of capitalism in imperial expansion, 20; on Rousseau's *Social Contract*, 32; on sovereign individual, 25; on transition from "civil society" to "state," 20–21
"Hegelian moment," in France, 19, 22–23
Hegelian school, 4, 8, 27–28
Heine, Heinrich, "On the Democratic Principle," 23
Herwegh, Georg, 23
Hess, Moses, 23
Higby, Chester, 131
Histoire parlementaire de la Révolution française (Buchez and Roux), 202–3
Hôtel de Ville: role in expansion of Parisian administrative power, 86, 91; role in French Revolution, 72
Hue de Miromensil, Armand Thomas, 163
Hugo, Victor: assessment of Prud'hommes, 131–32, 155; and demos as politically constituted self-governing society of equals, 12, 13, 240; *Les Misérables*, 12, 32, 71, 103, 238

imperial possession, political economy of, 227–32. *See also* Sismondi, J.-C.-L. Simonde de; Tocqueville, Alexis de, writings on Algeria
Industrial Democracy (Sydney Webb and Beatrice Webb), 131
Iogna-Pratt, Dominique, 282n3
ironworks, and deforestation, 42, 62
Isambert, François-André, study of Buchez, 208

Jackson, Andrew, and role of banks in United States, 158
joint-stock companies (*sociétés anonymes*): as basic form of commercial activity, 164, 165; Bordeaux Bridge Company, 169, 170, 280n40; government authorization and oversight of, 168–70, 171–73, 280n43; growth of, 167–68, 280n33; involvement in public interest and public utility, 157, 166–67, 169–70, 171; and monopolies, 164–65; under old regime, 164; regulation of, as distinct from that of small businesses, 166, 167; as social enterprises, 174, 178–80; as type of association, 174, 175–76; in United States, 281n76
Jones, Gareth Stedman, 19
Jonnès, Alexandre Moreau: on deforestation, 46–47; on "public economy," 48–49

Jorland, Gérard, 106
Journal des débats, 81, 87, 88
July Monarchy, 2; and deforestation, 43; and democracy as mode of social organization, 2, 3; and distance between national government and people of France, 90–93; and nonsecularism, 191–92; and Parisian municipal elections, 87; on political versus administrative centralization, 79; and principle of association (*l'esprit d'association*), 175; urban planning proposals, 97–98
Jung, Johann Heinrich, 263n71
Junot, General Jean Andoche, 73–74

Kant, Immanuel, 25–26, 276n19
Kaplan, Steven, 51, 133–34
Karsenti, Bruno, 36
Kervegan, Jean-François, 20
Kloppenberg, James T., "Thinking Historically," 253n57
Kobe, Zdravko, "The Interface of the Universal," 255n22, 255n27
Kopstein, Jeffrey, 239
Kumar, Krishan, 239

La Berge, Ann Elizabeth Fowler, *Mission and Method*, 104, 116, 270n7, 273n88
Laborde, Alexandre de: on joint-stock companies as type of association, 175–76; *Paris Municipe*, 83–85
Laboulaye, Édouard, 59
Lacordaire, Henri: on Catholicism, and democratic society, 186, 206; on Lamennais, 285n71; and man as social being, 193
La démocratie pacifique, 94
Ladurie, Emmanuel Le Roy, and meteorological crises leading to grain crisis, 46
"Lafarge affair" of 1840, 124, 273n88
Laffitte, Jacques: and *comité central de la réforme*, 88; as municipal councillor and opposition member throughout July Monarchy, 268n72; and new residential construction in Paris, 75
laissez-faire: in joint-stock companies, 174; and Revolution, 138–39, 150; Sismondi's critique of, 19, 21; supposed high point of, 142, 146; Tocqueville's critique of, 219
Lamartine, Alphonse de, 23
Lamennais (Félicité de La Mennais), 23, 129, 285n80; on administrative regulation in democratic state, 206–7; *Book of the People*, 197; on Catholicism, 196–97; concept of social reason, 285n71; and historical interpretation as foundation for new society, 200; reinterpretation of sovereignty in democratic age, 197–98; repudiation of traditionalist ideals of Roman Church, 199

Lardy, Charles, environmental devastation of Swiss cantons by climate change, 44–45
La revue des deux mondes, "The Contemporary Crisis of German Philosophy," 22
La revue indépendante, and relationship between French and German philosophy, 7
L'avenir, "Our Duty in the Moment," 192
Law, John, 164
Le Brun, L. S. D., treatise on management of epidemics and other health crises, 105
Le Chapelier Law, 132–33
Lechevalier, Jules, 129
Le constitutionnel, 86, 95
Ledru-Rollin, Alexandre: on balance of particular and general interest, 26; critique of legal realism, 153–54; and democracy as social practice, 26, 30; and democratization of society, 6; Hegelianism, 8, 25, 31; and Hegel's critique of sovereign individual, 25–26, 27; *Jurisprudence française*, 153–54; on Prud'hommes, 154; and social justice, 154
Lefebvre-Teillard, Anne, 280n33
Lefort, Claude, 10
legal realism, 153–54
Lemaire, Jean-Baptiste, "Mémoire sur la police de Paris," 134
Lemercier, Claire, 90, 131–32, 144, 266n15, 278n78
Le national: "Elections of the General Council," 89; and first Parisian municipal elections, 86, 268n60; new municipal platform for opposition candidates, 100; and voters as delegates of nonvoting working classes, 99
Lepetit, Bernard, *Les formes de l'expérience*, 253n57
Lerminier, Eugène, 22
Leroux, Pierre, 23, 129; on democratic structure and message of early Church, 201–2; and idea of socialism, 194; and nonsecular approach to the social, 194–95, 284n53
Le siècle, 93, 98
Le Trosne, Guillaume-François, *De l'ordre social*, 40
Levacher-Duplessis, Antoine, 135
Levy-Leboyer, Maurice, 164
liberalism: aristocratic, 251n34; and balance between governmental powers and constitutional organization of state, 137; contradictions and weaknesses of, 212; and danger of administrative state, 254n10; democratization of in Third Republic, 2, 3; economic, 136; and Second Empire, 287n5
Libération, "Tell me? What is Civil Society?," 9–10
limited silent partnerships, and fraud, 180, 182
Lindenfeld, David, on interest in natural rights following the Revolution, 276n19

INDEX

Lorentz, Bernard, 55
Loughlin, Martin: *Foundations of Public Law*, 253n8; on police powers and governance, 51; on Protestant Reformation, 185, 186; on *Rechstaat* versus *Polizeistaat*, 18
Louis XIV, 65–67
Louis-Napoleon, 102, 128. *See also* Napoleon III
Louis-Philippe, 183, 194
Lupton, Deborah, *The Imperative of Health*, 274n108
Luther, Martin, 186–87, 189, 190, 202

Macarel, Louis Antoine, 143–44
Maistre, Joseph de, 188
Maleville, Jacques de, 133
Manin, Bernard, 238
Mann, Michael, 79
Mannoni, Stefano, *Une et indivisible*, 267n32
Marat, Jean-Paul, 118
Maret, Henri, on religion in democratic society, 207, 286n110
Martelet, Pierre, 96, 99, 101
Martignac, Vicomte de, 55–56, 57
Marx, Karl: articles in *Rheinische Zeitung*, 69; critique of Hegel's constitutional monarchism, 28–30; *Critique of Hegel's "Philosophy of Right*," 13, 258n92; and democratic movement, 23; democratic theory, 28–30; on demos as self-governing society of equals, 13, 29, 30, 258n92; economic materialism, 24; on forest regulation, and relationship between state and peasants, 69–70, 189; Hegelianism, 8, 31; and imperialism, 20; on placing human need above abstract law, 70; and proletariat, 20; on theft of wood, 38
medical police, 103
Merruau, Charles, *Memoirs of the Hôtel de Ville during the Second Republic*, 97
Metzger, Gillian E., "1930s Redux," 254n11
Meyer, David, *The Social Movement Society* (with Tarrow), 291n11
Michelet, Jules: *Bible de l'humanité*, 211; on forest legislation, 57
Milliot, Vincent, *L'admirable police*, 51, 275n10
Minard, Philippe, 51, 133
Mirabeau, Comte de, 33
mixed social constitution, 241, 242, 243, 291n10
Moggach, Douglas, "Hegelianism, Republicanism, and Modernity," 254n19
Molinier, J. V., 169, 280n43
Mollot, François-Étienne, 147, 148, 151, 152
Montalembert, Charles de, 207
Montesquieu, Baron de, 105, 283n30
Montlosier, François Dominique de Reynaud, *De l'origine, de la nature et des progrès*, 200–201
Montyon Prize (Académie française), 143

Mosers, W. Gottfried von, 263n71
Mouchon, Émile, 48

Napoleon III, 2, 9; and demos revolution, 243, 244; despotism of, 243–44; and patriarchal Catholicism, 244; and Prud'hommes, 243–44; reconstruction of Paris, 102, 243; and reforestation, 243; and universal suffrage, 238, 243
Napoleon Bonaparte: and Commercial Code of 1807, 156; control of municipal administration of Paris, 71, 73–74, 78; demise of, 212; one hundred days, 43; and private use of forests, 53; Prud'hommes councils, creation of, 142; and regulatory development, 107, 133; and regulatory legislation, 142; Tocqueville's view of, 235; and war, 54, 107, 139; workplace regulatory power under, 135
Napoli, Paolo, on police powers and governance, 51, 276n19
natural law, 128, 203, 276n19
Neumann, Franz: on democratic nature of joint-stock companies, 157, 165; *The Rule of Law*, 156
Niboyet, Eugénie, 6
Nineteen Citizens Accused of Plotting to Replace the Royal Government with a Republic, 111, 272n35
nonsecularism. *See* democratic social science, nonsecular foundations of
Novak, William J.: on associative life in early America, 239; "Possibilidades de uma História Pragmática do Político" (with Sawyer), 253n57; on role of administration in democratic governance, 254n13

octroi, 73, 94, 100–101
Orfila, Mathieu, 273n88
Orleanists, and administrative elections, 81–82
Ott, A.: on Hegel, 22; *Treatise on Politics and Society*, 208
Ozanam, Frédéric: on papacy, 285n92; and "*Passons aux Barbares*," 202

Pagnerre, Louis-Antoine: on accountability of local administrators, 96; *Dictionnaire politique*, 204
Palmer, Robert R., on democracy in eighteenth century, 2, 4, 249n3
Pansey, Henrion de, 53, 140
Papayanis, Nicholas, 98
Pappe, Helmut O., "Sismondi, Constant and Tocqueville," 218, 288n28
Parade, Adolphe, 55
Paris city administration: Central Committee of the Opposition of the Seine, 88–89, 92, 268nn74–75; and central government, 72–77; and conception of democracy, 77–78; and corporations, 74, 75–76; decentralization of, 76–80; democratization

Paris city administration (*cont.*)
of through popular revolt, 86–102; duties of, 82–84; and elections, 72, 80–88, 267n43, 268n66, 268n81; as execution of legislation, 78–79; and finance, 74–76; General Council of the Seine, 74, 89–97 (*see also* General Council of the Seine); interests of, 74, 97–102; octroi tax and toll bridges, 94, 100–101, 269n113; old-regime, as labyrinthine, 71, 72; and old-regime conceptions of municipal power, 74–75; piecemeal approach to, 98–99, 100; relationship between elected officials and population, 95; and suffrage, 81, 86–87, 268n60; and transformation of municipal mandate, 93–97; and twelve arrondissements, 72–73; and water system, 101

Paris Commune of 1794, 72, 81, 82

Passy, Hyppolite, 64

Penhoën, Barchou de, *Histoire de la philosophie allemande depuis Leibnitz jusqu'à Hegel*, 22

Pfeiffer, Johann Friedrich von, 263n71

police regulation. *See* regulatory police power

political economy, and civil society, 216, 218

Ponchelet, D., 264n95

Portalis, Joseph, 65, 133

"Possibilidades de uma História Pragmática do Político" (Sawyer and Novak), 253n57

postrevolutionary liberals: and democracy as social organization, 5–6; and fight for expanded suffrage, women's rights, abolition of slavery, and condition of working class, 3; on individualism and new modes of liberty, 2

potestas (political right) versus *potentia* (capacity to rule), 17, 253n8

Pouthas, Charles, 83

pragmatic history of the political: accounts of, 253n57; and historical experience, 14; methodological influences, 253n57

Précis élémentaire d'hygiène (Buchez and Trélat), 117

Prévost, Louis, 22

Pritchard, Sara B., 40

Protestant Reformation: and "disciplinary revolution," 185; and individualism, 185–86, 187, 189, 194; limited success of, 202; and medieval forms of social and political hierarchy, 186–87; and scientific materialism, 189; and self-government, 187

Proudhon, Pierre-Joseph, 23, 129; as disciple of Hegel, 33, 259n113; revision of contract theory, 33–34

Prud'hommes councils: antidespotism of, 147–48, 149; creation of, 142–49; elections for, 131, 146; and interpretation of regulations, 148, 152–53; legislation on, 142, 276n35; and mediation of social relations, 145, 146; as models of equitable regulation, 131, 149, 152, 155; origins of, in exceptional courts and corporations, 144; policies based on local practices, 153, 278n73; publication of decisions, and "Code de Prud'hommes," 148; representation of both workers and management, 148; and social welfare, 148–49; undermined by Napoleon III, 243–44

public city. *See* Paris city administration

public health administration: Academy of Medicine, 107; and *Annales de l'hygiène publique et la médécine légale*, 107–8; authoritarian or statist approach to, 104, 270n7; centralized, and epidemics, 105–11; Colbert's regulatory program under Louis XIV, 103; Comité de salubrité de la Constituante, 105–6; Conseil de salubrité, 106–10, 113, 119–20, 129; Conseil supérieur de santé, 107, 129; and critiques of poverty, 105; and democratic almanacs, 111–16; and democratization of public health, 110–16; implementation of new public health and hygiene measures, 129; and industrialization and urbanization, 109; law on insalubrious housing, 129, 243; liberal approach to, 104, 105, 117, 270n6, 274n108; "medical police," 103; and public health movement, 106–11; in public interest, 109–10; and reform, 105–11; "relief and health agency," 106; reports on regulatory investigations, 108–10; social contract for, 116–29; as social science and politics, coupling of, 104, 105, 106, 107; transformation of, 103. *See also* Raspail, François-Vincent

Quinet, Edgar: *Du génie des religions*, 191, 283n30; on political systems and socio-religious orders, 191

Raeff, Mark, 54

Rambuteau, Count of, 87, 88

Raspail, François-Vincent: addressing workers, 123; on autonomous bureaucracy, 120, 125–26; as candidate for president of Second Republic, 128; as central figure of democratic movement, 118; on efficient democratic administration, 120–21, 124–25, 127–28; *Essai de chimie organique*, 117; Hegelianism, 8; on humanitarian administration, 125; and "Lafarge affair" of 1840, 124, 273n88; *Le réformateur*, 117–18, 125; "Letter on Religion," 207; and Marat, 118; medical-administrative model of democratic revolution in public health, 128; on medical practice and firsthand experience, 118–19, 122–23; *Nouveau système de chimie organique*, 117; and policies of Second Republic, 128; popularity in France, 273n75; popularization of medical knowledge, 118–19, 121–23, 273nn74–75; on postrevolutionary religion, and science, 207; on prisons, 8, 119–20; on purpose of revolutionary activity, 125–26; on relationship between doctors and state, 119, 121; on relationship between medical practitioners and patients, 122; and social con-

INDEX

tract, 120–21; treating working-class patients, 123; trial for illegal practice of medicine, 123–24; on universal suffrage, 126–27
Rauch, François-Antoine: on deforestation, 46; as founding father of modern ecology, 46, 261n27
Rawls, John, 240
Reddy, William, 278n73
règlements d'atelier (workshop regulations), 142
Regnaud de Saint-Jean-d'Angély, 140–41
Regnault, Elias, *Histoire du gouvernement provisoire*, 268n75
regulatory police power: and attempts at liberalization, 51; as central feature of early modern governance, 51; democratic, 154–55; as democratic problem, 16; dual imperative of, 133–34; and scale and extent of public provision, 134–35, 275n10; transformation of before and during Revolution, 51, 133–34. *See also* administrative regulation
Reinhard, Marcel, 249n3
Revolution of 1789. *See* French Revolution of 1789
Revue de Paris, and influence of Hegel, 22
Revue du progrès social: and Hegel, 22, 281n72; "Science sociale," 175, 178
Revue générale de l'architecture et des travaux publics, 98
Revue indépendante, "L'École de Hegel à Paris," 27–28
Robespierre, Maximilien, 33, 187
Rorty, Richard, 11
Rosanvallon, Pierre, 268n73; on civil society in modern France, 10; on "histoire conceptuelle du politique," 253n57; interpretation of "decentralization," 266n31
Rosen, Charles, on critiques of poverty in old-regime public health policy, 105, 270n9
Rosenkranz, Karl, biography of Hegel, 22
Rossi, Pellegrino, *Cours d'économie politique*, 2, 3, 5
Rougier de La Bergerie, Jean-Baptiste, *Mémoires et observations sur les abus des défrichements et la destruction des bois et forêts*, 42–43
Rousseau, Jean-Jacques: definition of democracy, 5, 78, 251n21; *Letters from the Mountain*, 77–78; on mixed constitution of government, 241, 291n10; on popular sovereignty versus popular government, 5; *Social Contract*, 31, 37, 77, 78, 241, 251n21
Rousseau, Louis, *The Nineteenth-Century Crusade*, 193
Roux, Vital: and commercial code, 163, 165; on egalitarian ideals of Revolution, 203; *Histoire parlementaire de la Révolution française* (with Buchez), 202–3
Royal Academy of Brussels, essay contest on deforestation and climate change, 46
Royal Society of Medicine, 105

Royer, Jean-Pierre, *Histoire de la justice en France*, 132
Royer-Collard, Pierre-Paul: on democratization of society, 1, 5, 6; on ills of administrative centralization, 79; and self-administration of democratic society, 78, 80
Ruge, Arnold: and democratic movement, 23; *Deutsch-Französische Jahrbücher* (German-French Annals), 27, 28; *The Origins of the Franco-German Couple*, 27; preface to German edition of Blanc's *Histoire de dix ans*, 27; "Toward an Entente between the Germans and the French," 27

Sahlins, Peter, 61–62, 68
Saint Pierre, l'Abbé de, 105
Saint-Simon, Henri de: avoidance of language of "democracy," 190–91; on Catholicism's historical concern for the poor, 200; influence on invention of sociology, 190; *Le nouveau christianisme*, 188–89, 200; *Lettres d'un habitant de Genève à ses contemporains*, 188; "New Christianity," 189–90; nonsecular approach to the social, 190
Salverte, Eusèbe, 81, 82
Sand, George: on changing society, 36; on democratization of society, 6, 23, 240; *Indiana*, 32, 38; *Mauprat*, 32
Savary, Jacques, 163
Sawyer, Stephen W., *Demos Assembled*: on consolidation of democracy, 3; and *Demos Rising*, 3–4; about new moment in history of democracy, 244, 292n19; on political liberty and self-government, 3; on social and political modes of democracy, 3
Say, Horace: on duty of voters, 99; *Études sur l'administration de la ville de Paris et du département de la Seine*, 101
Say, Jean-Baptiste: on accumulation of capital and civil society, 216, 288n14; *Cours complet d'économie politique pratique*, 216, 218; opposition to return of guilds, 136–37
"Science sociale," *Revue du progrès social*, 175
Scottish Enlightenment, 216
Second Republic, 2, 6, 12, 102; implementation of new public health and hygiene measures, 129; law on insalubrious housing, 129; and local elections in Paris, 102
Seine, toll bridges, 101, 269nn113–14
Simon, Jules, 34
Sismondi, J.-C.-L. Simonde de: on Algerian conquest and French working class, 227–29; on balancing individual interest and social obligation, 219; on constitutional and administrative roles of government, 16–17; influence on Guizot, 288n28; influence on Hegel, 19, 218;

Sismondi, J.-C.-L. Simonde de (*cont.*)
influence on Tocqueville, 223; on laissez-faire economic policy, 19, 21; on modern industrialization, problems of, 228–29; *Nouveaux principes d'économie politique*, 16, 19, 218–19; on regulation grounded in liberty and equality, 19, 138; on Adam Smith, 218–19, 223, 228

Smith, Adam, 33, 193, 216; and democratic condition driving private interests, 217; Sismondi's critique of, 19, 20, 218–19, 223, 228

social contract, democratization of, 14, 19, 31–37; effects of, 36–37; and expansion of administrative power, 18, 254n13; and mixed social constitution, 243; and public health regulation, 116–29; through redefining relationship between political right and administrative action, 17; and Rousseauian theory, 32–35, 37; and socially situated relations between individuals, 35; and sociology, founding of, 34–36; structural role of history and sociology in, 35, 241–42

social contract theory, and utilitarianism, 31, 258n98

social leveling, 11, 18, 162, 186, 217, 227

Social Movement Society, The (Meyer and Tarrow), 291n1

social sciences: and action toward collective good, 185; birth of, 34–36; "pragmatic turn," 253n57; and universal, egalitarian, and solidaristic revision of Catholicism, 193

"social scientists," first, 24, 210

sociétés anonymes. See joint-stock companies (*sociétés anonymes*)

sociology, founding of, 34–36

Spector, Céline, 36

Stahl, Johann Friedrich, 263n71

Steger, Friedrich, 2, 3, 5

Stein, Lorenz von: on constitution and administration, relationship between, 24–25; and French socialism, 24, 257n56; Hegelianism, 8, 31; on social democracy, 25, 257n66; "social history" of state, 24; and transformation of society through administrative action, 31

suffrage: and antidemocratic political systems, 238; impact of on democratic revolution, 238–39, 243; Parisian limitation on, 81, 86–87, 268n60

Surell, Alexandre: *Étude sur les torrents des Hautes-Alpes*, 45, 60; and state action on deforestation, 49

Swedberg, Richard, *Tocqueville's Political Economy*, 288n13, 289n67

Tallien, Jean-Lambert, 46

Tarrow, Sydney, *The Social Movement Society* (with Meyer), 291n1

Terror, the, 18, 204, 242, 276n25

Thiers, Adolphe: *De la propriété*, 181; on demand for wood, 42; on democratization of society, 6, 7; on government intervention in economy, 180–82; refusal to sell forest lands, 43

Third Republic, 2, 3

Tisserand, Éric, 261n13

Tocqueville, Alexis de: on administrative power and inequality, relationship between, 220–23; on American frontier, 224–27; on Catholicism, 186, 192–93; on civil and democratic society, distinction between, 214–15, 216–17; on commercial practices, industrial development, and democratic society, 159; *Democracy in America*, 1, 12, 23, 32–33, 186, 192–93, 213–14, 216, 224–27, 232, 287n9; on democratization of administrative power, 222–23; on democratization of society, 5, 6, 12; on despotism and association, 221–22; on equality driving private interests, 217–18; on "equality of condition," 1, 5, 11; "État social et politique de la France avant et depuis 1789," 232; on form of government, 7, 12; "La centralisation administrative et le système représentatif," 232–33; *Mémoires sur le paupérisme*, 223, 224, 231; and "new aristocracy," 159–60, 162; *The Old Regime and the French Revolution*, 1, 12, 18, 232; on political versus administrative centralization, 79; on Protestant Reformation, 185–86; on public power as constitutive of democratic society, 217; revision of Rousseau's social contract, 33; Sismondi's influence on, 223; on social aid, 223; "spatial fix" for inequality, 223–27, 289n51; on structural drives within democratic society that produce isolation, polarization, and inequality, 219–20, 289n38

Tocqueville, Alexis de, writings on Algeria: on Africa as not having social body, 234; on boundary problem of empire, 232–37; on colonial conquest as building administrative power at home, 213–14; and contradictions of liberalism, 212; on economic development in periphery, 230–32; on governance of conquered subjects, 237; on limits of democratic administration in imperial context, 237; on management of colonial societies, 213, 229–30, 232–34; on periphery's importance for alleviating inequalities in metropole, 230–32, 236–37; on transition from military to civil government, 234–36

Todd, David, *A Velvet Empire*, 289n67

Trélat, Ulysse: call for popular uprising, 111; on failure of health system, 116; on improvement of public hygiene, health, and sanitation, 110–11; on medical profession, 116–17; and *Nineteen Citizens Accused of Plotting to Replace the Royal Government with a Republic*, 111, 272n35; *Précis élémentaire d'hygiène* (with Buchez), 117

Tribe, Keith, 275n19
Tristan, Flora, 23; on best form of government for democratic society, 7; on health problems of working poor, 111
Tronchet, François-Denis, 133
Troplong, Raymond-Théodore, 178–80
Trunk, Johann Jakob, 263n71
Tuck, Richard, 4
Tudesq, André-Jean, 95

Vacherot, Étienne, *De la démocratie* (On Democracy), 156, 278n1; "The Economic Conditions of Democracy," 162; on judicial systems, 154–55; on Prud'hommes, 155
Vicq d'Azyr, Félix, 105
Villermé, Louis-René, 97
Vincens, Emile: on government authorization of large businesses, 172; on joint-stock companies, 168; on "spirit of association," 175
Virchow, Rudolf, 103, 104
Vivien, Alexandre, 81, 119
Voice of Women, 7–8
Voltaire, 186
Von Thadden, Rudolf, 81
Vovelle, Michelle, 52

Waldron, Jeremy, "anthropological" contractualism, 241–42
Walzer, Michael, 239
War of the Demoiselles, 61–62

Waterloo, Battle of, 18
Weale, Albert, 254n14, 258nn97–98
Webb, Sydney and Beatrice, *Industrial Democracy*, 131
Weiner, Dora B., "François-Vincent Raspail," 124, 273n75
Welch, Cheryl, 217
Whitman, Walt, 184
William, Joseph, *Histoire de la philosophie allemande depuis Kant jusqu'à Hegel*, 22
Willis, Caroline, 131
Wolowski, Louis, on capitalist enterprise, 173–74
worker's passport (*livret ouvrier*), 142
workplace regulation: debates on, 139–41, 154; Decree of Allarde, 132, 133; and democratic almanacs, 145; and democratic regulation of labor, 149–55; and democratic revolution, 131; and deregulation, impact on markets, 139–41, 276n25; employer's right to establish workshop regulations, 142, 276n35; in factories, 143; and freedom to work, 141; and guild system, 132–33; Le Chapelier Law, 132–33; and "liberal" rejection of return to guild system, 136–37, 138, 140; under Napoleon, 135–36, 138, 275n12; nondespotic and nonarbitrary, 133, 137–39; by police, 142; and Prud'hommes councils, 131, 142–49; worker's passport, 142. *See also* Prud'hommes councils; regulatory police power

Zeller, Thomas, 40

www.ingramcontent.com/pod-product-compliance
Lightning Source LLC
Chambersburg PA
CBHW022037290426
44109CB00014B/893